D0504855

WITHDRAWN
FROM
BROMLEY LIBRARIES

WRITINGS ON BRITISH HISTORY
1967–68

Writings on British History, 1901–1933 (5 vols. in 7. Jonathan Cape for the Royal Historical Society, 1968–70)

I Auxiliary Sciences and General Works
II The Middle Ages, 450–1485
III The Tudor and Stuart Periods, 1485–1714
IV The Eighteenth Century, 1714–1815, 2 pts.
V 1815–1914, 2 pts.

Complementary to the above volumes and not repeating entries in them is *A Guide to the Historical and Archaeological Publications of Societies in England and Wales, 1901–1933*, compiled for the Institute of Historical Research by E. L. C. Mullins (The Athlone Press, 1968)

Writings on British History, 1934–45, compiled by A. T. Milne (8 vols. Jonathan Cape for the Royal Historical Society, 1937–60)

Writings on British History, 1946–48, compiled by D. J. Munro (Institute of Historical Research, 1973)

Writings on British History, 1949–51, edited by D. J. Munro (Institute of Historical Research, 1975)

Writings on British History, 1952–54, edited by J. M. Sims (Institute of Historical Research, 1975)

Writings on British History, 1955–57, edited by J. M. Sims and P. M. Jacobs (Institute of Historical Research, 1977)

Writings on British History, 1958–59, edited by H. J. Creaton (Institute of Historical Research, 1977)

Writings on British History, 1960–61, edited by C. H. E. Philpin and H. J. Creaton (Institute of Historical Research, 1978)

Writings on British History, 1962–64, edited by H. J. Creaton (Institute of Historical Research, 1979)

Writings on British History, 1965–66, edited by H. J. Creaton (Institute of Historical Research, 1981)

Writings on British History, 1967–68, edited by H. J. Creaton (Institute of Historical Research, 1982)

WRITINGS ON
BRITISH HISTORY
1967-1968

A Bibliography of books and articles on the history of Great Britain from about 450 A.D. to 1939, published during the years 1967–68 inclusive with an Appendix containing a select list of publications in these years on British history since 1939

Edited by
HEATHER J. CREATON

UNIVERSITY OF LONDON
INSTITUTE OF HISTORICAL RESEARCH
1982

First published, 1982

ISBN 0–901179–69–8
ISSN 0084–2753

Printed in Great Britain
by New Western Printing Limited, Bristol

CONTENTS

PART I. GENERAL WORKS

PART II. PERIOD HISTORIES

INTRODUCTION

This volume of *Writings on British History* follows in scope, arrangement and method of compilation the preceding volume which covered publications of the years 1965 to 1966.

SCOPE OF THE BIBLIOGRAPHY. The aim of *Writings on British History, 1967–68* is to provide a full list of books and articles on British history published during 1967–68, together with a few items omitted from earlier volumes. All periods from the Anglo-Saxon invasion of Britain to the year 1939 are included, with a 'Select list of books published in the years 1967–68 on British history since 1939' as an appendix. Writings on the Norman, Angevin and Plantagenet domains in France are noted in the bibliography when they concern English history, but the local history of French fiefs is omitted. Similarly, the later expansion of England overseas is included, but the domestic history of Commonwealth countries is noted only when Britain was directly concerned. Both the local and national histories of Scotland and Wales are included. Some aspects of the history of science, literature and the arts which are adequately covered in other bibliographies are excluded here. The selection of material for the twentieth century section is more rigorous than in the rest of the bibliography and the Appendix is necessarily highly selective.

A list of bibliographies which include publications relating to British history not included in *Writings on British History* is given in the introduction to the volume for 1946–48 and earlier volumes. Items in Russian are not included, but they are listed in the bibliographical section of *Problemy Britanskoy Istorii/Studies on British History* (Moscow: Nauka). Japanese articles and monographs on British history may be traced in *Zasshi Kiji Sakuin* and *Zennihon Shuppanbutsu Somokuroku* (Tokyo: National Diet Library).

ARRANGEMENT. Items are arranged by subject within the divisions of the bibliography. Similar material within a section is grouped and these groups are arranged in the order considered most useful. The order within groupings is chronological unless some more appropriate order is suggested by the material. The arrangement of the Scottish and Welsh sections closely follows the general scheme of the bibliography. The classification is the same as in previous volumes, with modifications in the use of subdivisions according to the nature and quantity of material in each section.

Publications containing material relevant to more than one period or section have been noted only once, in the section where their greatest weight lies, and therefore general and related sections should not be overlooked. The index contains a large number of subject entries.

SEARCHING OF BOOKS AND PERIODICALS. Entries relating to British books have been gathered principally from the *British National Bibliography, 1967–68*. Only a few of the books have been personally examined. School text books, brief guides to churches and country houses and pamphlets of ten pages or less have generally been excluded unless of evident importance. As in previous volumes reliance has been placed on reviews and other bibliographical lists for works published abroad.

Approximately 400 periodicals were searched systematically. A list of those from which material was taken is printed below. A number of articles in other periodicals which were not seen have been included where the references were thought reliable. Articles of four pages or less have not been included unless thought to be historically important. The date given in round brackets is the year of actual publication and in most cases the year for which the transactions or other publications of a society were issued is also given. The principle followed when using abbreviations for the titles of periodicals has been to make each easily recognizable without the necessity of turning to an elaborate key. Definite and indefinite articles and prepositions have been omitted, except where required for clarity. A list of the principal abbreviations will be found on p. xiii.

ACKNOWLEDGEMENTS. The Institute of Historical Research gratefully acknowledges the assistance given by other libraries in the preparation of this bibliography, and has especially to thank the British Library and the University of London Library.

As usual much of the collection has been done by the Library staff of the Institute of Historical Research who have assisted the editor throughout. Mr. Clyve Jones, Mr. Robert Lyons, Mrs. Valerie McCormick, Dr. Keith Manley, Mr. Donald Munro and Miss Rosemary Taylor searched periodicals in the Institute and in the University Library.

June, 1982 H.J.C.

PRINCIPAL ABBREVIATIONS USED

N.B.—In titles of periodicals prepositions and definite articles are omitted except where required for clarity, e.g., *Soc. Antiq. Newcastle Proc.* = *Proceedings of the Society of Antiquaries of Newcastle-upon-Tyne.*

Acad.	Academia, Académie, Academy
Agric.	Agricultural
Akad.	Akademia, Akademie
Amer.	America(n)
Ann.	Annuaire, Annual, Annuel, etc.
Antiq.	Antiquarian, Antiquaries, Antiquities, etc.
Archaeol.	Archaeological, Archaeology, etc.
Archéol.	Archéologie, Archéologique
Archit.	Architect(s), Architectural
Assoc.	Associated, Association
B.B.C.	British Broadcasting Corporation
Beitr.	*Beiträge*
Bib.	Bibliothèque
Bibliog.	Bibliographical, Bibliographie, Bibliography, etc.
Bijd.	*Bijdragen*
Biog.	Biographical
Bl.	Blessed
Bol.	*Boletim, Boletin*
Boll.	*Bolletino*
Brit.	Britain, British
Bull.	*Bulletin, Bulletino*
C.C.	County Council
C.N.R.S.	Centre Nationale de la Recherche Scientifique
C.O.I.	Central Office of Information
C.R.O.	County Record Office
C.U.P.	Cambridge University Press
Cent.	Centuries, Century
Chatto	Chatto and Windus
Chron.	Chronicle(s)
Coll.	Collective, Collection(s), Collected
Comm.	Commission, Committee
Comp.	Compiled by, Compiler
Contd.	Continued
Dept.	Department
Dépt.	Département
Dist.	District
E.H.R.	*English Historical Review*
ELH	*ELH. A Magazine of English Literary History*
Eccles.	Ecclesiastical
Econ. or Écon.	Economic(s), Économie, Economy, etc.
Ed(s).	Edited by, Editor(s)
Edn. or Édn(s).	Edition, Édition(s), etc.
Educ.	Education(al)
Engl.	England, Englische, English
F.C.	Field Club
Filos.	Filosofía
Geneal. or Généal.	Genealogical, Généalogique, etc.
Geog. or Géog.	Geographical, Géographie, Geography, etc.
Gesch.	Geschichte, Geschiedenis
Geschichtswiss.	Geschichtswissenschaft

Govt.	Government
H.M.S.O.	Her Majesty's Stationery Office
Hist.	Histoire, Historical, Historique, Historische, History, etc.
Hodder	Hodder & Stoughton
Hollis	Hollis & Carter
I.O.M.	Isle of Man
I.O.W.	Isle of Wight
Inst.	Institut, Institute, Institution, etc.
Internat.	International(e)
Introd.	Introduction
Ist.	Istituto
Jahrb.	*Jahrbuch*
Jour.	*Journal*
K.	Kaiserlich, Königlich, Koninklijk
L.S.E.	London School of Economics
Lang.	*Language*
Lib.	Librairie, Libraries, Library
Lit.	Literärische, Literary, etc.
Litt.	Littéraire, Littérature
Mag.	*Magazine*
Milit.	Militaire, Military, etc.
Misc.	*Miscellanea, Miscellany*, etc.
Mitteil.	*Mitteilungen*
Mod.	Modern(e)
Murray	John Murray
N. & Q.	*Notes and Queries*
N.Z.	New Zealand
Nat.	National, Natural
Numis.	Numismatic, Numismatical, Numismatique, etc.
O.U.P.	Oxford University Press
Occas.	Occasional
P.	Press, Presses
PMLA	*PMLA. Publication of the Modern Language Association of America*
P.R.O.	Public Record Office, London
P.U.F.	Presses Universitaires de France
Palaeog.	Palaeography
Philol.	Philological, Philologie, Philology, etc.
Philos.	Philosophical, Philosophie, Philosophy, etc.
Polit.	Political, Politics, Politik, Politique
Print.	Printing
Proc.	*Proceedings*
Pub.	Public
Pubb.	Pubblicazioni
Pubd.	Published
Pubg.	Publishing
Pubn(s).	Publication(s)
Quart.	*Quarterly*
R.H.S.	Royal Historical Society
R.I.B.A.	Royal Institute of British Architects
Rec.	Record(s)
Rept.	*Report*
Rev.	*Review, Revista, Revue*
rev.	revised (by)
Rev. Hist.	*Revue Historique*
Riv.	*Rivista*
Routledge	Routledge & Kegan Paul
Roy.	Royal
S.C.M.	Student Christian Movement

S.E.V.P.E.N.	Service de Vente de Publications de l'Éducation Nationale
S.P.C.K.	Society for the Propagation of Christian Knowledge
Scot.	Scotland, Scottish
Scribner	Charles Scribner's Sons
Secker	Secker & Warburg
Sect.	Section
Soc.	Sociedad, Societat, Société, Society
Sociol.	Sociological, Sociology
Stor.	Storia, Storico, etc.
Suppl.	Supplement
Theol.	Theological, Theologische, Theology, etc.
Tijds.	*Tijdschrift*
Trans.	*Transactions*
transcr.	transcriber, transcribed (by)
transl.	translator, translated (by)
U.D.C.	Urban District Council
U.P.	University Press
Univ.	Universität, Université, University, etc.
V.	Verlag
W.E.A.	Workers' Educational Association
Weidenfeld	Weidenfeld & Nicolson
Zeit.	*Zeitschrift*

LIST OF PERIODICALS

Articles are included from the following serials which were searched systematically. A number of other journals were searched but yielded nothing (mainly holdings of the Institute of Historical Research). The bibliography includes references to articles seen in some periodicals not in this list which were not systematically searched.

Aberdeen University Review
Aevum
Agricultural History
Agricultural History Review
Amateur Historian
Ambix
American Historical Review
American Journal of Legal History
American Neptune
American Philosophical Society Proceedings
American Philosophical Society Transactions
Ancient Monuments Society Transactions
Anglesey Antiquarian Society and Field Club Transactions
Annales
Annales du Midi
Annals of Science
Antiquaries Journal
Antiquity
Apollo
Archaeologia
Archaeologia Aeliana
Archaeologia Cambrensis
Archaeologia Cantiana
Archaeological Journal
Architectural History
Architectural Review
Archives
Archives Internationales d'Histoire des Sciences
Archivum Franciscanum Historicum
Archivum Historicum Societatis Iesu
Arms and Armour Society Journal
Army Quarterly
Ars Quatuor Coronatorum
Art Bulletin
Australian Journal of Politics and History

Baptist Quarterly
Barbados Museum Journal
Bathafarn
Bengal Past and Present
Berkshire Archaeological Journal
Bermuda Historical Quarterly
Berwickshire Naturalists' Club History
Bibliographical Society of America Papers
Birmingham Archaeological Society Transactions
Board of Celtic Studies Bulletin
Bodleian Library Record
Bradford Antiquary
Bristol and Gloucestershire Archaeological Society Transactions
British Academy Proceedings
British Archaeological Association Journal
British Journal of Educational Studies
British Journal of the History of Science
British Journal of Sociology
British Museum Quarterly
British Numismatic Journal
Brycheiniog
Bulletin of the History of Medicine
Burlington Magazine
Business Archives
Business History
Business History Review

Caernarvonshire Historical Society Transactions
Cahiers de Civilisation Médiévale
Cake and Cockhorse
Cambridge Antiquarian Society Proceedings
Cambridge Bibliographical Society Transactions
Cambridge Law Journal
Canadian Historical Association Report
Canadian Historical Review
Catholic Historical Review
Ceredigion
Cheshire Round
Chester Archaeological Society Journal
Church History
Church Quarterly Review
Classica et Medievalia
Clergy Review
Comparative Studies in Society and History
Congregational Historical Society Transactions
Connoisseur
Cornish Archaeology
Cumberland and Westmorland Antiquarian and Archaeological Society Transactions
Cylchgrawn Cymdeithas Hanes y Methodistiaid Calfinaidd

Denbighshire Historical Society Transactions
Derbyshire Archaeological Journal
Devon and Cornwall Notes and Queries

Devonshire Association Report and Transactions
Dorset Natural History and Archaeological Society Proceedings
Downside Review
Dublin Review
Dumfriesshire and Galloway Natural History and Antiquarian Society Transactions
Durham and Northumberland Architectural and Archaeological Society Transactions
Durham Research Review
Durham University Journal

East London Papers
East Lothian Antiquarian Society Transactions
East Midland Geographer
Economic History Review
Economic Journal
Economica
Educational Review
Efrydiau Athronyddol
Eighteenth Century Studies
English Historical Review
English Miscellany
Essex Archaeological Society Transactions
Explorations in Entrepreneurial History

Flintshire Historical Society Publications
Folk Life
Folklore
Franciscan Studies
Friends' Historical Society Journal
Friends' Quarterly
Frühmittelalterliche Studien
Furniture History

Genealogical Quarterly
Genealogists' Magazine
Geographical Journal
Geography
Guildhall Miscellany

Halifax Antiquarian Society Transactions
Hampshire Field Club Proceedings
Harvard Library Bulletin
Hawick Archaeological Society Transactions
Hermathena
Hispanic American Historical Review
Historian
Historic Society of Lancashire and Cheshire Transactions
Historical Journal
Historical Magazine of the Protestant Episcopal Church
Historical Society of the Church in Wales Journal
Historical Studies
Historical Studies of Australia and New Zealand
Historische Zeitschrift
Historisches Jahrbuch
History
History and Theory
History of Education Quarterly
History of Medicine
History of Science
History Today
Honourable Society of Cymmrodorion Transactions
Huguenot Society of London Proceedings
Hunter Archaeological Society Transactions
Huntington Library Quarterly

Imago Mundi
Indian Archives
Industrial Archaeology
Innes Review
Institute of British Geographers Transactions
Institute of Historical Research Bulletin
International Affairs
International Review of Social History
Irish Ecclesiastical Record
Irish Historical Studies
Irish Sword
Isis
Isle of Man Natural History and Antiquarian Society Proceedings

Jamaican Historical Review
Jewish Historical Society of England Transactions
John Rylands Library Bulletin
Journal of Asian Studies
Journal of British Studies
Journal of Ecclesiastical History
Journal of Economic History
Journal of Indian History
Journal of Modern History
Journal of Negro History
Journal of Political Economy
Journal of Presbyterian History
Journal of Religious History
Journal of Southern History
Journal of the History of Ideas
Journal of the History of Medicine and Allied Sciences
Journal of the Royal Artillery
Journal of World History
Juridical Review

Lancashire and Cheshire Antiquarian Society Transactions
Law Quarterly Review
Leatherhead and District Local History Society Proceedings

Leeds Philosophical and Literary Society Proceedings, Literary and Historical Section
Leicestershire Archaeological Society Transactions
Library
Library History
Lichfield Archaeological and Historical Society Transactions
Lincolnshire History and Archaeology
Llên Cymru
Local Historian
Local Population Studies
London and Middlesex Archaeological Society Transactions
London and Middlesex Historian
London Quarterly and Holborn Review

Manchester Literary and Philosophical Society Memoirs and Proceedings
Manchester School of Economics and Social Studies
Manx Museum Journal
Mariner's Mirror
Mediaeval Studies
Medical History
Medieval and Renaissance Studies
Medieval Archaeology
Medievalia et Humanistica
Merioneth Historical and Record Society Journal
Military Affairs
Montgomeryshire Collections
Monumental Brass Society Transactions
Morgannwg
Music and Letters

National Library of Wales Journal
National Register of Archives West Riding Northern Section Bulletin
New York Public Library Bulletin
Newcomen Society Transactions
Norfolk Archaeology
North Staffordshire Journal of Field Studies
Northamptonshire Past and Present
Northern History
Notes and Queries
Nottingham Mediaeval Studies
Nova Scotia Historical Society Collections
Numismatic Chronicle

Old Edinburgh Club Book
Osiris
Oxoniensia

Pacific Historical Review
Paedagogica Historica
Parliamentary Affairs
Past and Present
Polar Record
Political Science Quarterly
Political Studies
Population Studies
Postal History
Post-Medieval Archaeology
Public Administration

Quaker History
Quarterly Review of Historical Studies

Radnorshire Society Transactions
Records of Buckinghamshire
Recusant History
Renaissance and Modern Studies
Renaissance Quarterly
Revue Belge de Philologie et d'Histoire
Revue d'Histoire de la 2e Guerre Mondiale
Revue d'Histoire Diplomatique
Revue d'Histoire Ecclésiastique
Revue d'Histoire Economique et Sociale
Revue d'Histoire Moderne et Contemporaine
Revue du Nord
Revue Historique
Royal Agricultural Society Journal
Royal Asiatic Society Journal
Royal Asiatic Society, Malaysian Branch Journal
Royal Australian Historical Society Journal
Royal College of Surgeons of England Annals
Royal Cornwall Polytechnic Society Annual Report
Royal Historical Society Transactions
Royal Institute of British Architects Journal
Royal Institution of Cornwall Journal
Royal Institution of Great Britain Proceedings
Royal Irish Academy Proceedings, Section C
Royal Musical Association Proceedings
Royal Society of Antiquaries of Ireland Journal
Royal Society of London Notes and Records
Royal United Service Institution Journal
Ryedale Historian

Saga Book
Scandinavian Economic History Review
School of Oriental and African Studies Bulletin
Scottish Church History Society Records
Scottish Gaelic Studies
Scottish Genealogist
Scottish Geographical Magazine
Scottish Historical Review
Scottish Journal of Political Economy
Scottish Journal of Theology
Shropshire Archaeological Society Transactions
Slavonic and East European Review
Société Guernesiaise Report and Transactions
Société Jersiaise Bulletin Annuel

Society for Army Historical Research Journal
Society of Antiquaries of Scotland Proceedings
Society of Archivists Journal
Sociological Review
Somerset Archaeological and Natural History Society Proceedings
South African Library Quarterly Bulletin
South Atlantic Quarterly
Speculum
Stewarts
Studi Medievali
Studies in Medieval and Renaissance History
Studies in the History and Philosophy of Science
Studies in the Renaissance
Suffolk Review
Surrey Archaeological Collections
Sussex Archaeological Collections
Sussex Notes and Queries

Textile History
Theology
Thoroton Society Transactions
Three Banks Review
Tijdschrift voor Geschiedenis
Traditio
Traethodydd
Trafodion Cymdeithas Hanes Bedyddwyr Cymru

Ulster Folklife
Unitarian Historical Society Transactions
University of Birmingham Historical Journal
University of Edinburgh Journal
University of Leeds Review
University of Toronto Quarterly
Urban History Newsletter
Urban Studies

Victoria and Albert Museum Bulletin
Victorian Studies

Walpole Society Annual Volume
Warburg and Courtauld Institutes Journal
Warwickshire History
Welsh Historical Review
Wesley Historical Society Proceedings
William and Mary Quarterly
Wiltshire Archaeological and Natural History Magazine
Woolhope Naturalists' Field Club Transactions
Worcestershire Archaeological Society Transactions
Worcestershire Recusant

Yorkshire Archaeological Journal
Yorkshire Bulletin of Economic and Social Research

PART ONE: GENERAL WORKS

AUXILIARY SCIENCES

DICTIONARIES

1. COTTLE, BASIL. The Penguin dictionary of surnames. Harmondsworth, Middx.: Penguin, 1967. 334 pp.

2. ZUPKO, RONALD EDWARD. A dictionary of English weights and measures from Anglo-Saxon times to the 19th century. Madison, Wis., London: Wisconsin U.P., 1968. xvi, 224 pp.

3. FISHER, JOHN LIONEL. A medieval farming glossary of Latin and English words taken mainly from Essex records. Nat. Council of Social Service, for Standing Conference for Local Hist., 1968. 41 pp.

4. WARE, DORA. A short dictionary of British architects. Allen & Unwin, 1967. 312 pp., illus.

5. WILSON, ARNOLD. A dictionary of British marine painters. Leigh-on-Sea, Essex: F. Lewis, 1967. 90 pp., illus.

6. PAVIÈRE, SYDNEY HERBERT. A dictionary of Victorian landscape painters. Leigh-on-Sea, Essex: F. Lewis, 1968. 143 pp., illus.

PALAEOGRAPHY AND DIPLOMATIC

7. BISHOP, T. A. M. An early example of Insular-Caroline. *Cambridge Bibliog. Soc. Trans.*, IV no. 5 (1968) 396–400.

8. WHITELOCK, DOROTHY. The will of Aethelgifu: a 10th century Anglo-Saxon manuscript. O.U.P., for Roxburghe Club, 1968. 92 pp., illus.

9. MOORE, R. I. The reconstruction of the cartulary of Fontevrault. *Inst. Hist. Research Bull.*, XLI (1968) 86–95.

10. BROOKE, CHRISTOPHER NUGENT LAWRENCE. Approaches to medieval forgery. *Soc. Archivists Jour.*, III no. 8 (1968) 377–86.

11. MAJOR, KATHLEEN. The teaching and study of diplomatic in England. *Archives*, VIII (1967–8) 114–18.

12. CHAPLAIS, PIERRE. Some early Anglo-Saxon diplomas on single sheets: originals or copies? *Soc. Archivists Jour.*, III no. 7 (1968) 315–36.

13. BARNES, PATRICIA M., *and* HECTOR, LEONARD CHARLES (*comps.*). Guide to seals in the Public Record Office. 2nd edn. (Public Record Office Handbooks, 1). H.M.S.O., 1968. xii, 66 pp., illus. [Previous edn. 1954.]

HERALDRY

14. WAGNER, *Sir* ANTHONY. Heralds of England: a history of the office and College of Arms. H.M.S.O., 1967. xvii, 609 pp., illus.

15. FRANKLYN, JULIAN. Shield and crest: an account of the art and science of heraldry. 3rd edn. MacGibbon & Kee, 1967. xvii, 521 pp., illus. [Previous edn. 1961.]

16. SUMMERS, PETER GILBERT. How to read a coat of arms. Nat. Council of Social Service, for Standing Conference for Local Hist., 1968. 24pp., illus.

17. PETCHEY, WILLIAM JOHN. A short account of the armorial bearings of the sovereigns of England. Rev. edn. Nat. Council of Social Service, for Standing Conference for Local Hist., 1967. 28 pp. [Previous edn. 1962.]

18. THOMPSON, B. L. Royal Arms in the churches of the diocese of Carlisle. *Cumberland & Westmorland Antiq. & Archaeol. Soc. Trans.*, LXVII (1967) 152–67.

19. Rolls of arms, Henry III. (Harleian Soc. Pubns., 113–14). Oxford: O.U.P., for the Society, 1967. xvi, 281 pp., illus. [Simultaneously pubd. by Soc. Antiquaries.]

20. Notes from an armory of 1842. *Geneal. Quart.*, XXXIII no. 3 (1967) 104–40, no. 4 (1967) 152–87, XXXIV no. 1 (1967) 8–42, no. 2 (1967) 56–92, no. 3 (1968) 104–39, no. 4 (1968) 152–83, XXXV no. 1 (1968) 8–41, no. 2 (1968) 55–90. [Continuing.]

21. WALKER, VIOLET W. Thoroton's illustrations of coats of arms. *Thoroton Soc. Trans.* for 1967, LXXI (1968) 55–8.

22. TESTER, M. Funeral hatchments in Kent. *Archaeologia Cantiana* for 1966, LXXXI (1967) 79–94.

COINAGE AND NUMISMATICS

23. GRIERSON, PHILIP. The volume of Anglo-Saxon coinage. *Econ. Hist. Rev.*, 2nd ser. XX (1967) 153–60.

24. LYON, STEWART. Historical problems of Anglo-Saxon coinage. Pts. 1–2. *Brit. Numis. Jour.*, XXXVI (1967) 215–21, XXXVII (1968) 216–38.

25. METCALF, DAVID MICHAEL, *and* WALKER, D. R. The 'wolf' sceattas. *Brit. Numis. Jour.*, XXXVI (1967) 11–28.

26. BLUNT, CHRISTOPHER EVELYN, *and* DOLLEY, REGINALD HUGH MICHAEL. A gold coin of the time of Offa. *Numis. Chronicle*, 7th ser. VIII (1968) 151–60.

27. DOLLEY, R. H. M. O. E. *Christðegn*: an unsuspected instance of early Middle Irish influence on English name-giving. *Brit. Numis. Jour.*, XXXVI (1967) 40–5.

28. SMART, VERONICA J. Moneyers of the late Anglo-Saxon coinage, 973-1016. *Kungl. Vitterhets Hist. och Antikvitets Akad. Handlingar, Antik. Serien*, XIX (1968) 191–276.

29. STEWART, IAN H. The St. Martin coins of Lincoln. *Brit. Numis. Jour.*, XXXVI (1967) 46–54.

30. DOLLEY, REGINALD HUGH MICHAEL. Some Hiberno-Norse coins of Dublin recently discovered on the Baltic island of Gotland. *Roy. Soc. Antiq. Ireland Jour.*, XCVIII (1968) 57–62.

31. DOLLEY, R. H. M., *and* O'SULLIVAN, WILLIAM. 'The chronology of the first Anglo-Irish coinage.' *In* North Munster Studies, *ed.* E. Rynne (Limerick: Thomond Archaeol. Soc., 1967) pp. 437–78.

32. BLUNT, CHRISTOPHER EVELYN, *and others*. On some hoards of the time of Stephen. *Brit. Numis. Jour.*, XXXVII (1968) 35–42.

33. NORTH, JEFFREY JAMES. The coinages of Edward I and II. Spink, 1968. 39 pp., illus.

34. DOLLEY, REGINALD HUGH MICHAEL. The Irish mints of Edward I in the light of the coin-hoards from Ireland and Great Britain. *Roy. Irish Acad. Proc. Section C*, LXVI (1966) 235–97.

35. REDDAWAY, THOMAS FIDDIAN. The king's mint and exchange in London, 1343–1543. *E.H.R.*, LXXXII (1967) 1–23.

36. BLUNT, CHRISTOPHER EVELYN. Unrecorded heavy nobles of Henry IV and some remarks on that issue. *Brit. Numis. Jour.*, XXXVI (1967) 106–13.

37. STEWART, IAN H., *and* MURRAY, JOAN E. L. Unpublished Scottish coins. 4, Early James III. *Numis. Chronicle*, 7th ser. VII (1967) 147–61.

38. CHALLIS, C. E. Tower II, 1545–52. *Brit. Numis. Jour.*, XXXVII (1968) 93–7. [Tower mint.]

39. MURRAY, J. K. R. The Scottish coinage of 1553. *Brit. Numis. Jour.*, XXXVII (1968) 98–109.

40. DOLLEY, REGINALD HUGH MICHAEL. The identity of the 'Dominick grote'. *Numis. Chronicle*, 7th ser. VII (1967) 163–6. [16th cent. Irish coin.]

41. DOLLEY, R. H. M. Elizabethan Bungal (1): a contribution to Anglo-Irish lexicography. *Brit. Numis. Jour.*, XXXVI (1967) 118–21.

42. STEWART, IAN H. Some Scottish ceremonial coins. *Soc. Antiq. Scotland Proc.* for 1964–6, XCVIII (1967) 254–75.

43. MURRAY, J. K. R. A further note on the forty shilling piece of James VI of Scotland. *Numis. Chronicle*, 7th ser. VIII (1968) 161–7.

43a. MURRAY, J. K. R. Some notes on the small silver money of James I and VI. *Numis. Chronicle*, 7th ser. VIII (1968) 169–72.

44. TAYLOR, ROBERT F. The St. Annes hoard and other Civil War coin hoards in Lancashire. *Hist. Soc. Lancs. & Cheshire Trans.* for 1966, CXVIII (1967) 39–50.

45. COOPER, F. R. Silver crowns of the Tower mint of Charles I. *Brit. Numis. Jour.*, XXXVII (1968) 110–37.

46. SEABY, HERBERT ALLEN, *and* RAYNER, P. ALAN. The English silver coinage from 1649. 3rd rev. edn. Seaby, 1968. 201 pp., illus. [Previous edn. 1957, as *British imperial coinage*.]

47. SCHNEIDER, HERBERT. The hammered gold coins of Charles II. *Brit. Numis. Jour.*, XXXVI (1967) 122–68.

48. STEVENSON, D. The Irish emergency coinages of James II, 1689–91. *Brit. Numis. Jour.*, XXXVI (1967) 169–75.

49. BERRY, GEORGE. New light on the 17th century token issuers of Chepping Wycombe. *Records of Bucks.*, XVIII pt. 2 (1967) 150–63.

50. BELL, ROBERT CHARLES. Specious tokens and those struck for general circulation, 1784–1804. Newcastle-upon-Tyne: Corbitt & Hunter Ltd., 1968. xvii, 258 pp., illus.

51. POLLARD, J. G. Matthew Boulton and J. P. Droz. *Numis. Chronicle*, 7th ser. VIII (1968) 241–65.

52. SMYTH, *Sir* JOHN. The story of the George Cross. Barker, 1968. 208 pp., illus.

COSTUME, UNIFORMS, ARMS AND ARMOUR

53. COOKE, PATRICIA GERRARD. English costume: its history and its design. Liverpool: Gallery P., 1968. 127 pp., illus.

54. YARWOOD, DOREEN. Outline of English costume. Batsford, 1967. 48 pp., illus.

55. YARWOOD, D. English costume: from the 2nd century B.C. to 1967. 3rd edn. Batsford, 1967. xviii, 302 pp., illus. [Previous edn. 1961.]

56. CUNNINGTON, PHILLIS, *and* LUCAS, CATHERINE. Occupational costume in England: from the 11th century to 1914. Black, 1967. 427 pp., illus.

57. CUNNINGTON, CECIL WILLETT, *and* CUNNINGTON, PHILLIS. Handbook of English costume in the 17th century. 2nd edn. Faber, 1967. 222 pp., illus. [Previous edn. 1963.]

58. BRADFIELD, NANCY. Costume in detail: women's dress, 1730–1930. Harrap, 1968. ix, 383 pp., illus.

59. ARNOLD, JANET. Patterns of fashion: Englishwomen's dresses and their construction, *c.* 1860–1940. Wace, 1967. 88 pp., illus.

60. COSTUME SOCIETY. La Belle Époque: costume, 1890–1914: proceedings of the 1st annual conference of the Society, 1967. Victoria & Albert Museum, for the Society, 1968. 65 pp., illus.

61. LAWSON, CECIL CONSTANT PHILIP. A history of the uniforms of the British army. Vol. 5. Kaye & Ward, with Norman Military Pubns., 1967. viii, 184 pp., illus.

62. BARNES, ROBERT MONEY. The British Army of 1914: its history, uniforms and contemporary continental armies. Seeley, 1968. 296 pp. illus.

63. SMITHERMAN, PHILIP HENRY. Uniforms of the yeomanry regiments, 1783–1911. Evelyn, 1967. 71 pp., illus.

64. CARMAN, W. Y. The dress of Erle's regiment in 1704 and 1709. *Soc. Army Hist. Research Jour.*, XLVI (1968) 202–5.

65. MOLLO, JOHN. Uniforms and equipment of the Light Brigade. Historical Research Unit, 1968. iii, 61 pp., illus.

66. COX, B. W. The sergeants' arm badge of the 1st King's Dragoon Guards. *Soc. Army Hist. Research Jour.*, XLVI (1968) 43–8.

67. COX, B. W. The arm badges of the 14th (King's) Hussars, the 14th/20th King's Hussars, and the 20th Hussars. *Soc. Army Hist. Research Jour.*, XLV (1967) 97–101.

68. EVISON, VERA I. A sword from the Thames at Wallingford Bridge. *Archaeol. Jour.* for 1967, CXXIV (1968) 160–89.

69. EVISON, V. I. The Dover ring-sword and other sword-rings and heads. *Archaeologia*, CI (1967) 63–118.

70. FEATHERSTONE, DONALD FREDERICK. The bowmen of England: the story of the English longbow. Jarrolds, 1967. 200 pp., illus.

71. TYLDEN, GEOFFREY (*comp.*). The principal small arms carried by British regular infantry. *Soc. Army Hist. Research Jour.*, XLV (1967) 242–7.

72. CAREY, ARTHUR MERWYN. English, Irish and Scottish firearms makers . . . from the middle of the 16th century to the end of the 19th century. 2nd British edn. Edgware, Middx.: Arms & Armour P., 1967. xv, 121 pp., illus. [Previous British edn. Edinburgh: W. & R. Chambers, 1955.]

73. BLAIR, CLAUDE. The origin of Mons Meg. *Arms & Armour Soc. Jour.*, V no. 12 (1967) 425–52. [Gun preserved at Edinburgh Castle.]

74. GLENDENNING, IAN. British pistols and guns, 1640–1840. 2nd edn. Arms & Armour P., 1967. viii, 195 pp., illus. [Previous edn. Cassell, 1951.]

75. HAYWARD, JOHN FORREST. The Huguenot gun-makers of London. *Arms & Armour Soc. Jour.*, VI no. 4 (1968) 117–43.

76. BAKER, H. A. The tribulations of gun founding in the 1780s. *Arms & Armour Soc. Jour.*, V no. 9 (1967) 368–83. [Royal Artillery at Woolwich.]

77. LENMAN, BRUCE. The weapons of war in 18th century India. *Soc. Army Hist. Research Jour.*, XLVI (1968) 33–43.

78. NEAL, WILLIAM KEITH, *and* BACK, DAVID HENRY LEMPRIERE. The Mantons: gunmakers. Jenkins, 1967. xv, 300 pp., illus.

79. JAMES, LAWRENCE. The cost and distribution of armour in the 14th century. *Monumental Brass Soc. Trans.*, X pt. 4 (1967) 226–31.

ICONOGRAPHY

80. TURNER, G. L'E. A portrait of James Short, F.R.S., attributable to Benjamin Wilson, F.R.S. *Roy. Soc. Notes & Records*, XXII (1967) 105–12.

81. ANNAND, A. M. Charles, 5th duke of Richmond and his charger 'Busaco'. *Soc. Army Hist. Research Jour.*, XLVI (1968) 213–16. [Paintings, *c.* 1825–9.]

82. CARMAN, W. Y. The Worcestershire Yeomanry and Richard Dighton. *Soc. Army Hist. Research Jour.*, XLV (1967) 63–6. [Painting, *c.* 1832.]

BRASSES, MONUMENTS ETC.

83. CORBOULD, PAUL. The monumental brasses of Devon. *Devon Assoc. Repts. & Trans.*, C (1968) 29–43.

84. EVANS, H. F. OWEN. Palimpsest brasses at Ossington, Notts. *Monumental Brass Soc. Trans.*, X pt. 4 (1967) 303–10.

85. MCQUEEN, P. I. The Maltravers fret. *Monumental Brass Soc. Trans.*, X pt. 4 (1967) 244–8.

86. LINSCOTT, ELIZABETH. The art of the tomb. *History Today*, XVIII (1968) 382–9.

87. HEALEY, KENNETH. English churchyard memorials. *Roy. Soc. Arts Jour.*, CXV (1966–7) 260–74.

88. DOUCH, ROBERT. Monuments and memorials in Southampton. (Southampton Papers, 6). Southampton: Southampton Record Offices, 1968. 48 pp., illus.

89. DI FOLCO, JOHN. Kirkyards in the Laich of Moray: an illustrated survey. *Soc. Antiq. Scotland Proc.* for 1966–7, XCIX (1968) 211–54. [Inventory of monuments.]

HISTORICAL GEOGRAPHY

90. HARLEY, JOHN BRIAN. Maps for the local historian: a guide to British sources. Pts. 1–5. *Amateur Historian*, VII (1967) 196–208, 223–31, 265–74, *Local Historian*, VIII (1968) 61–71, 86–97.

91. LOBEL, MARY D. The value of early maps as evidence for the topography of English towns. *Imago Mundi*, XXII (1968) 50–61.

92. HARVEY, PAUL DEAN ADSHEAD. A 13th century plan from Waltham Abbey, Essex. *Imago Mundi*, XXII (1968) 10–12.

93. STONE, JEFFREY C. An evaluation of the 'Nidisdaile' manuscript map by Timothy Pont. *Scot. Geog. Mag.*, LXXXIV (1968) 160–71.

94. STONE, J. C. The early printed maps of Dumfriesshire and Galloway. *Dumfries. & Galloway Nat. Hist. & Antiq. Soc. Trans.*, XLIV (1967) 182–95.

95. MOIR, D. G., *and* SKELTON, RALEIGH ASHLIN. New light on the first atlas of Scotland. *Scot. Geog. Mag.*, LXXXIV (1968) 149–59. [*Atlas Novus* vol. V (1654).]

96. FAIRHURST, HORACE. An old estate plan of Auchindrain, mid-Argyll. *Scot. Studies*, XII (1968) 183–7.

97. BLACK, J. The Blathwayt Atlas: maps used by British colonial administrators in the time of Charles II. *Imago Mundi*, XXII (1968) 20–9.

98. HARLEY, JOHN BRIAN. Ogilby and Collins: Cheshire by road and sea. *Cheshire Round*, I no. 7 (1967) 210–25.

99. HARLEY, J. B. Cheshire maps, 1787–1831. *Cheshire Round*, I no. 9 (1968) 290–305.

100. HARLEY, J. B. Maps of early Georgian Cheshire. *Cheshire Round*, I no. 8 (1967) 256–69.

101. BAPTIST, MARY. Eighteenth century maps and estate plans of Bromley, Beckenham and Penge. *Archaeologia Cantiana* for 1966, LXXXI (1967) 31–8.

102. PRAGNELL, HUBERT JOHN. The London panoramas of Robert Barker and Thomas Girtin, *c.* 1800. (London Topographical Soc. Pubns., 109). The Society, 1968. 29 pp., illus.

103. RITCHIE, GEORGE STEPHEN. The Admiralty chart: British naval hydrography in the 19th century. Hollis, 1967. xii, 388 pp., illus.

104. WALLIS, HELEN. Thematische Elemente auf frühen englischen Globen, 1592–1900. *Globusfreund*, XV-XVI (1967) 75–85.

BIBLIOGRAPHIES AND INDEXES

105. GUILDHALL LIBRARY. A list of books printed in the British Isles and of English books printed abroad before 1701 in Guildhall Library. Pt. 2, L-Z. Corporation of London, 1967. 83–222 pp.

106. KITE, V. J. (*comp.*). Printed books 1476–1640 in Bath Municipal Libraries: a catalogue. Bath, Som.: Bath Municipal Libs., 1968. 93 pp.

107. ROYAL HISTORICAL SOCIETY. Writings on British history, 1901–33. Cape, 1968. 3 vols.

108. MULLINS, EDWARD LINDSAY CARSON (*comp.*). A guide to the historical and archaeological publications of societies in England and Wales, 1901–33. Athlone P., 1968. xiii, 850 pp.

109. MILNE, ALEXANDER TAYLOR. A centenary guide to the publications of the Royal Historical Society, 1868–1968, and of the former Camden Society, 1838–97. (R. H. S. Guides and Handbooks, 9). Royal Historical Soc., 1968. xi, 249 pp.

110. KELLAWAY, WILLIAM (*comp.*). Bibliography of historical works issued in the United Kingdom, 1961–5. London Univ. Inst. Hist. Research, 1967. xv, 298 pp.

111. HAVIGHURST, ALFRED F. Paperbacks on British history. *Jour. Brit. Studies*, VI no. 2 (1967) 124–65.

112. WILSON, DAVID M. (*comp.*). Medieval Britain in 1965 . . . 1966. 1, Pre-conquest. *Medieval Archaeol.* for 1966, X (1967) 168–76, for 1967, XI (1968) 262–72.

113. HURST, D. GILLIAN (*comp.*). Medieval Britain in 1965 . . . 1966. 2, Post-conquest. *Medieval Archaeol.* for 1966, X (1967) 177–219, for 1967, XI (1968) 272–319.

114. ROACH, JOHN PETER CHARLES (*ed.*). A bibliography of modern history. C. U. P., 1968. xxiv, 388 pp.

115. ANDERSSON, BO. Engelsk partihistoria, 1603-60: några aspekter. *Hist. Tidskrift* [Sweden] (1968) 302–42.

116. LIBRARY ASSOCIATION. COUNTY LIBRARIES GROUP. Readers' guide to books on Hanoverian Britain. 2nd. edn. Library Assoc. County Libraries Group, 1968. 40 pp. [Previous edn. 1952.]

117. La bataille de l'Atlantique: bibliographie. *Rev. d'Hist. de la 2e Guerre Mondiale*, XVIII no. 69 (1968) 113–26.

118. LAMBERT, SHEILA (*ed.*). List of House of Commons sessional papers, 1701–50. (List & Index Soc. Special ser., 1). Swift, 1968. xviii, 155 ff.

119. BLAND, DESMOND SPARLING (*comp.*). A bibliography of the Inns of Court and Chancery. (Selden Soc. Supplementary ser., 3). Selden Soc., 1965. ix, 75 pp.

120. JEWELL, ANDREW (*comp.*). Crafts, trades and industries: a book list for local historians. Nat. Council of Social Service, for Standing Conference for Local Hist., 1968. 24 pp.

121. TATE, WILLIAM EDWARD. Public house bibliography. *Local Historian*, VIII (1968) 126–30.

122. HARRISON, BRIAN. Drink and sobriety in England, 1815–72: a critical bibliography. *Internat. Rev. Soc. Hist.*, XII (1967) 204–76.

123. HERBERT, ARTHUR SUMNER. Historical catalogue of printed editions of the English Bible, 1525–1961. Rev. edn. British & Foreign Bible Soc., 1968. xxxi, 549 pp. [Previous edn. by T. H. Darlow and H. F. Moule, 1903.]

124. KER, NEIL RIPLEY. Notes on some books in the library of L' Église Protestante, Soho Square, London. *Huguenot Soc. London Proc.*, XXI no. 2 (1967) 143–7.

125. ST. MARY'S SEMINARY, OSCOTT. Recusant books at St. Mary's, Oscott. New Oscott, Warwicks.: the Seminary, 1967. 2 pts.

126. CORDEAUX, EDWARD HAROLD, *and* MERRY, D. H. A bibliography of printed works relating to the University of Oxford. Oxford: Clarendon P., 1968. xxvii, 809 pp.

127. MYRES, JOHN NOWELL LINTON. Recent discoveries in the Bodleian Library. *Archaeologia*, CI (1967) 151–68.

128. SZRETER, R. The history of education in non-education periodicals, 1937–67: a bibliography. *Brit. Jour. Educ. Studies*, XVI (1968) 318–28.

129. GREAVES, MONICA ALICE. Education in British India, 1698–1947: a bibliography and guide to sources of information in London. London Univ. Inst. Educ., 1967. xx, 182 pp.

130. FORD, WYN K. Music in England before 1800: a select bibliography. Library Assoc., 1967. xiv, 128 pp.

131. FORRESTER, FELICITÉE SHEILA. Ballet in England: a bibliography and survey, *c.* 1700–1966. (Library Assoc. Bibliogs., 9). Library Assoc., 1968. 224 pp.

132. MCQUEEN, P. I. Towards a bibliography of monumental brasses. *Monumental Brass Soc. Trans.*, X pt. 4 (1967) 249–53.

133. RIDER, KENNETH JOHN. The history of science and technology: a select bibliography for students. Library Assoc., 1967. 60 pp.

134. LIVERPOOL MEDICAL INSTITUTION. Catalogue of the books in the Liverpool Medical Institution library to the end of the 19th century. Liverpool: the Institution, 1968. 569 pp.

135. THOMPSON, ALICE MARY CHARLOTTE (*ed.*). A bibliography of nursing literature, 1859–1960, with an historical introduction. Library Assoc., for Royal College of Nursing, 1968. xx, 132 pp.

136. HODGSON, HENRY WIGSTON (*comp.*). A bibliography of the history and topography of Cumberland and Westmorland. (Joint Archives Committee for Cumberland, Westmorland and Carlisle Record Office Pubns., 1). Carlisle: the Committee, 1968. 301 pp.

137. MANDERS, F. W. D. (*comp.*). Historic Gateshead: a select bibliography. Gateshead, Durham: Gateshead Pub. Libs., 1967. 33 pp.

138. FORREST, G. Southampton's history: a guide to the printed resources. Southampton: Southampton Pub. Libs., 1968. 20 pp.

139. TUPLING, GEORGE HENRY (*comp.*). Lancashire directories, 1684–1957, *rev.* S. Horrocks. (Lancashire Bibliog. pt. 1). Manchester: Central Lib., 1968. x, 78 pp.

140. GAINSBOROUGH PUBLIC LIBRARIES. Village history: notes on some sources for the study of Lindsey villages. Gainsborough, Lincs.: Pub. Lib., 1967. 15 pp.

141. DREWERY, ROBERT FORRESTER (*comp.*). A select list of books on Hull and district. Hull, Yorks.: City Libs., 1968. vi, 32 pp.

142. MITCHELL, WILLIAM SMITH (*comp.*). Catalogue of the incunabula in Aberdeen University Library. (University of Aberdeen Studies, 150). Edinburgh, London: Oliver & Boyd, for the Univ., 1968. xi, 107 pp., illus.

143. FORSYTH, W. Urban history in Scotland: an introductory bibliography with notes on sources. *Urban Hist. Newsletter*, no. 8 (1967) 7–14.

144. BYRNE, FRANCIS J. Ireland before the Norman invasion. *Irish Hist. Rev.*, XVI (1968) 1–14.

145. STEVENSON, NORAGH. Belfast before 1820: a bibliography of printed material. Belfast: Belfast Lib., 1968. 64 pp.

146. *Beckford.* GEMMETT, ROBERT J. William Beckford: bibliographical addenda. *Bull. Bibliog.*, XXV (1967) 62–4.

147. *Browne.* KEYNES, *Sir* GEOFFREY. A bibliography of Sir Thomas Browne Kt. M.D. 2nd edn. rev. Oxford: Clarendon P., 1968. xv, 293 pp., illus. [Previous edn. C.U.P., 1924.]

148. *Browning.* BARNES, WARNER. A bibliography of Elizabeth Barrett Browning. Austin, Tex.: Humanities Research Center, 1967. 179 pp.

149. *Chalmers.* FERRIER, FRANCIS. William Chalmers, 1596–1678: étude bibliographique. Paris: P.U.F., 1968. 196 pp.

150. *Craig.* FLETCHER, IFAN KYRLE, *and* ROOD, ARNOLD. Edward Gordon Craig: a bibliography. Soc. for Theatre Research, 1967. 117 pp.

151. *Evelyn.* KEYNES, *Sir* GEOFFREY. John Evelyn: a study in bibliophily with a bibliography of his writings. Oxford, London: Clarendon P., 1968. xix, 313 pp., illus. [Previous edn. C.U.P., 1937.]

152. *Godwin.* PALACIO, JEAN DE. État présent des études Godwiniennes. *Études Anglaises*, XX (1967) 149–59.

153. *Lawrence.* EDWARDS, LUCY IRENE (*comp.*). D. H. Lawrence: a finding list: holdings in the city, county and university libraries of Nottingham. Nottingham: Notts. County Lib., 1968. ix, 125 pp.

154. *Locke.* HERDE, PETER. Neue Forschungen über John Locke. *Hist. Jahrbuch*, LXXXVII (1967) 103–11.

155. *Ockham.* REILLY, JAMES P. Ockham bibliography, 1950–67. *Franciscan Studies*, XXVIII (1968) 197–214.

156. *Owen.* WHITE, WILLIAM. Wilfred Owen: a bibliography. Kent, Ohio: Kent State U.P., 1967. 41 pp.

157. *Wells.* H. G. WELLS SOCIETY. H. G. Wells: a comprehensive bibliography. 2nd edn. rev. The Society, 1968. vi, 69 pp. [Previous edn. 1966.]

CUMULATIVE INDEXES TO SERIALS

158. WILLIAMS, ALBERT HUGHES. A contribution to an index: *The Arminian*, *The Methodist* and *The Wesleyan Methodist Magazines*, 1778–1878. *Bathafarn*, XXIII (1968) 32–42.

159. WILLIAMS-JONES, KEITH (*comp.*). Index to the *Transactions*, vols. 1–24, 1939–63. *Caernarvons. Hist. Soc. Trans.*, XXVIII pt. 2 (1967) 5–160.

ARCHIVES AND COLLECTIONS

GENERAL

160. DELL, RICHARD F. Some differences between Scottish and English archives. *Soc. Archivists Jour.*, III no. 8 (1968) 386–97.

161. GORTON, L. J. Arrangement and cataloguing of modern historical papers in the British Museum. *Archives*, VIII (1967–8) 2–7.

162. EDE, J. R. The Public Record Office and its users. *Archives*, VIII (1967–8) 185–92.

163. PUBLIC RECORD OFFICE. Calendar of inquisitions miscellaneous (Chancery) preserved in the P.R.O. Vol. 7, 1399–1422. H.M.S.O., 1968. vii, 501 pp.

164. LATHAM, R. E. (*ed.*). Calendar of Memoranda Rolls (Exchequer) preserved in the P.R.O.: Michaelmas 1326–Michaelmas 1327. H.M.S.O., 1968. xlii, 523 pp.

165. CABINET OFFICE. War cabinet minutes, Dec. 1916–March 1918. (List & Index Soc. Pubns., 40). Swift, 1969. 229ff.

166. MUNBY, LIONEL MAXWELL (*ed.*). Short guides to records. 15, Commissioners of Sewers, by A.E.B. Owen. 16, Land tax assessments, by H. G. Hunt. 17, Parliamentary surveys, by S. C. Newton. 18, Turnpikes, by B. F. Duckham. 19, Fire insurance policy registers, by J. H. Thomas. *History*, LII (1967) 35–8, 283–6, LIII (1968) 51–4, 217–20, 381–4.

167. BARLOW, D. The records of the Forfeited Estates Commission. (P.R.O. Handbooks, 12). H.M.S.O., 1968. v, 147 pp.

168. RIGG, ARTHUR GEORGE. A Glastonbury miscellany of the 15th century: a descriptive index of Trinity college, Cambridge, Ms. 0.9.38. O.U.P., 1968, vii, 161 pp.

169. BROOKE, JOHN. The Prime Ministers' papers, 1801–1902: a survey of the privately preserved papers of those statesmen who held the office of Prime Minister during the 19th century. H.M.S.O., 1968. 79 pp.

170. DAVIS, ARTHUR KYLE, *Jnr.* Matthew Arnold's letters, a descriptive checklist. Charlottesville, Va.: Virginia Univ. Bibliog. Soc., 1968. 429 pp.

171. STEER, FRANCIS WILLIAM (*ed.*). Arundel Castle archives. Chichester, Sussex: West Sussex C.C, 1968. vi, 258 pp.

172. HEMLOW, JOYCE. Preparing a catalogue of the Burney family correspondence, 1749–1878. *New York Public Lib. Bull.*, LXXI (1967) 486–95.

173. GILL, PATRICIA (*ed.*). The Cobden and Unwin papers: a catalogue. Chichester, Sussex: West Sussex C.R.O., 1967. v, 50 pp.

174. HASSELL, WILLIAM OWEN. The English illuminated manuscripts of Chief Justice Coke. *Connoisseur*, CLXVIII (1968) 24–30.

175. HANCOCK, N. J. (*ed.*). Handlist of Hardinge papers at the University Library, Cambridge. Cambridge: the Library, 1968. xiii, 107 pp.

176. HUDLESTON, CHRISTOPHE ROY (*comp.*). List of the Howard family documents now deposited in the Department of Palaeography and Diplomatic, Durham. Durham: Univ. Dept. of Palaeog., 1967. 143ff.

177. DURHAM UNIVERSITY. DEPT. OF PALAEOGRAPHY AND DIPLOMATIC. Howard family documents: list of miscellaneous papers relating to Cumberland. Durham: the Dept., 1968. 125 ff.

178. FLEEMAN, J. D. (*ed.*). A preliminary handlist of documents and manuscripts of Samuel Johnson. (Oxford Bibliog. Soc. Occas. Pubns., 2). Oxford: the Society, 1967. 51 pp.

179. FRASER, I. H. C. The manuscripts in the library of the University of Keele. *N. Staffs. Jour. Field Studies*, VII (1967) 58–62.

180. OSBORNE, NOEL H. (*ed.*). The Lytton manuscripts: a catalogue. Chichester: W. Sussex C.C., 1967. ix, 79 pp.

181. BILL, EDWARD GEOFFREY WATSON. Catalogue of the papers of Roundell Palmer, 1812–95, 1st earl of Selborne. Lambeth Palace Lib., 1967. 56 pp.

182. STEER, FRANCIS WILLIAM, *and* OSBORNE, NOEL H. (*eds.*). The Petworth House archives: a catalogue. Vol. 1. Chichester, Sussex: West Sussex C.C., 1968. xvi, 207 pp.

183. GIUSEPPI, M. S., *and* OWEN, G. D. (*eds.*). Calendar of the manuscripts of the marquess of Salisbury. Pt. 20, 1608. H.M.S.O., 1968. xxiv, 434 pp.

184. SAWYER, PETER HAYES. Anglo-Saxon charters: an annotated list and bibliography. (Royal Historical Soc. Guides and Handbooks, 8). The Society, 1968. xiii, 538 pp.

185. OWEN, DOROTHY M. A catalogue of Lambeth Ms. 889 to 901: charters in Lambeth Palace Library. The Library, 1968. 213 pp.

186. MEEKINGS, C. A. F., *and* SHEARMAN, PHILIP (*eds.*). Fitznell's cartulary: a calendar of Bodleian Library Ms. Rawlinson B 430. (Surrey Record Soc. Pubns., 26). Guildford, Surrey: the Society, 1968. clxvii, 156 pp., illus. [Estates in Epsom and Ewell.]

ECONOMIC, RELIGIOUS AND CULTURAL

187. LEESON, FRANCIS. A guide to the records of the British state tontines and life annuities of the 17th and 18th centuries. (Pinhorns Handbooks, 3). Isle of Wight: Pinhorns, 1968. ix, 20 pp.

188. DURHAM UNIVERSITY. DEPT. OF PALAEOGRAPHY AND DIPLOMATIC. List of documents relating to the manor of Chester Deanery. Durham: the Dept., 1967. 48 pp.

189. GREG, *Sir* WALTER WILSON (*ed.*). A companion to Arber: being a calendar of documents in Edward Arber's 'Transcript of the registers of the Company of Stationers of London, 1554–1640'. Oxford: Clarendon P., 1967. ix, 451 pp.

190. WILLIS, ARTHUR JAMES (*comp.*). A calendar of Southampton apprenticeship registers, 1609–1740, *ed.* A.L. Merson. (Southampton Records ser., 12). Southampton: Southampton U.P., 1968. lxxxiii, 135 pp.

191. WILSON, R. G. Records for a study of the Leeds woollen merchants, 1700–1830. *Archives*, VIII (1967–8) 8–15.

192. GOLLANCZ, MARGUERITE. The records of Merstham limeworks. *Surrey Archaeol. Coll.*, LXIV (1967) 142–7.

193. PURVIS, JOHN STANLEY. The archives of York. *Studies in Church Hist.*, IV (1967) 1–14.

194. HOUSTON, JANE. Catalogue of ecclesiastical records of the Commonwealth, 1643–60, in Lambeth Palace Library. Farnborough, Hants.: Gregg, 1968. vii, 338 pp.

195. STEER, FRANCIS WILLIAM, *and* KIRBY, ISABEL M. (*comps.*). A catalogue of the records of the dean and chapter, vicars choral, St. Mary's Hospital, colleges and schools. Chichester, Sussex: W. Sussex C.C., 1967. xviii, 102 pp.

196. OWEN, DOROTHY M. Bringing home the records: the recovery of the Ely chapter muniments at the Restoration. *Archives*, VIII (1967–8) 123–9.

197. KIRBY, ISABEL M. (*comp.*). A catalogue of the records of the bishop and archdeacons. (Records of the Diocese of Gloucester, 1). Gloucester: Gloucester City Corporation, 1968. xxiv, 208 pp.

198. KIRBY, I. M. (*comp.*). Diocese of Gloucester: a catalogue of the records of the dean and chapter, including the former St. Peter's abbey. (Records of the Diocese of Gloucester, 2). Gloucester: City Corporation, 1967. xv, 200 pp.

199. MANNING, ELFRIDA (*transl.*). A book of the several customes of all the lord bishop of Winton's lands . . . Farnham, Surrey: Farnham Museum Soc., 1967. 15 pp. [Cover title: *A customary of the manor of Farnham*, 1617.]

200. The Old Brotherhood of the English secular clergy: catalogue of the archives. Catholic Record Soc., 1968. 64 pp.

201. KNIGHTBRIDGE, A. A. H. Inventories of church goods (Documents in the P.R.O., 4). *Amateur Historian*, VII (1967) 219–22.

202. ROBINSON, E. J. The records of the Church Commissioners. *Soc. Archivists Jour.*, III no. 7 (1968) 347–56.

203. PETTI, ANTHONY G. Recusant documents from the Ellesmere manuscripts. (Catholic Record Soc. Pubns., Records ser., 60). The Society, 1968. xvi, 368 pp.

204. SMITH, JANET. The local records of Nonconformity. *Local Historian*, VIII (1968) 131–4.

205. ORCHARD, STEPHEN, *and* WELCH, CHARLES EDWIN. Archives at Cheshunt College, Cambridge. *Congregational Hist. Soc. Trans.*, XX (1967) 202–4.

206. WELCH, C. E. Nonconformist trust deeds. *Soc. Archivists Jour.*, III no. 8 (1968) 397–403.

207. HAMM, CHARLES. A catalogue of anonymous English music in 15th century continental manuscripts. *Musica Disciplina*, XXII (1968) 47–76.

LOCAL

208. CHARMAN, D. Local authority records: a comment. *Scot. Hist. Rev.*, XLVII (1968) 1–9.

209. BOND, SHELAGH (*ed.*). The first hall book of the borough of New Windsor, 1653–1725. (Windsor Borough Hist. Records Pubns., 1). Windsor, Berks.: Royal Borough of New Windsor, 1968. xliv, 193 pp.

210. PIERCE, E. (*comp.*). The Weardale chest: list of documents relating to the Forest of Weardale and Stanhope Park, deposited in the Department of Palaeography and Diplomatic, Durham. Durham: Univ. Dept. of Palaeog., 1967. 46 ff.

211. ELRINGTON, CHRISTOPHER ROBIN. Records of the Cordwainers Society of Tewkesbury, 1562–1941. *Bristol & Glos. Archaeol. Soc. Trans.* for 1966, LXXXV (1967) 164–74.

212. WILLIS, ARTHUR JAMES (*comp.*). Winchester settlement papers, 1667–1842, from the records of several Winchester parishes. Folkestone, Kent: the compiler, 1967. 124 pp.

213. WILLIS, A. J. (*comp.*). Winchester guardianships after 1700: from diocesan records. Folkestone, Kent: the compiler, 1967. 88 pp.

214. WILLIS, A. J. (*comp.*). Exhibit books, terriers and episcopatus redivivus from records of the [Winchester] Diocesan Registry. (Hampshire Miscellany, 4). Folkestone, Kent: the compiler, 1967. 201–84 pp.

215. LEICESTER. Records of the borough of Leicester. Vol. 6, Chamberlains' accounts, 1688–1835, *ed.* G. A. Chinnery. Leicester: Leicester U.P., 1967. xii, 581 pp.

216. GUILDHALL LIBRARY. London rate assessments and inhabitants lists in Guildhall Library and the Corporation of London Records Office. 2nd. edn. rev. Corporation of London Lib. Committee, 1968. 63 pp. [Previous edn. 1961.]

217. STEER, FRANCIS WILLIAM (*ed.*). A catalogue of Sussex maps, vol. 2. (Sussex Record Soc. Pubns., 66). Chichester: W. Sussex C.C., 1968. vi, 228 pp.

WALES, SCOTLAND, IRELAND AND THE EMPIRE

218. PARRY, BRYN R. The Caernarvonshire Record Office. *Local Historian*, VIII (1968) 22–7.

219. HOWELLS, BRIAN ELWYN. A calendar of letters relating to North Wales, 1533–*c.* 1700: from the Llanfair-Brynodol, Gloddaeth, Crosse of Shaw Hill and Rhual collections in the National Library of Wales. Cardiff: Wales U.P., 1967. x, 287 pp.

220. CHARLES, BERTIE GEORGE (*ed.*). Calendar of the records of the borough of Haverfordwest, 1539–1660. (Univ. Wales Board of Celtic Studies Hist. and Law ser., 24). Cardiff: Wales U.P., 1967. viii, 274 pp.

221. GRUFFYDD, R. GERAINT. Humphrey Llwyd of Denbigh: some documents and a catalogue. *Denbighs. Hist. Soc. Trans.*, XVII (1968) 54–107.

222. DELL, RICHARD F. Some fragments of medieval mss. in Glasgow City Archives. *Innes Rev.*, XVIII (1967) 112–17.

223. SCOTLAND. PRIVY COUNCIL. The register of the Privy Council of Scotland. 3rd ser. Vol. 15, A.D. 1690, *ed.* E. W. M. Balfour-Melville. Edinburgh: H.M.S.O., 1968. xxiii, 850 pp.

224. SCOTTISH RECORD OFFICE. Index to particular register of sasines for sheriffdoms of Inverness, Ross, Cromarty and Sutherland preserved in H.M. General Register House. Vol. 2, 1606–1721. Edinburgh: H.M.S.O., 1967. 148 pp.

225. SCOTTISH RECORD OFFICE. Index to particular register of sasines for sheriffdoms of Ross, Cromarty and Sutherland. Vol. 3, 1721–80. Edinburgh: H.M.S.O., 1968. 127 pp.

226. BARBOUR, G. R. The Melville papers in the Scottish Record Office. *Indian Archives*, XVII (1967–8) 19–25.

227. ADAMS, IAN H. Large-scale manuscript plans in Scotland. *Soc. Archivists Jour.*, III no. 6 (1967) 286–90.

228. AINSWORTH, JOHN. Survey of documents in private keeping. 3rd ser. *Analecta Hibernica*, XXV (1967) 1–273.

229. QUINN, DAVID BEERS (*ed.*). Calendar of the Irish Council book, 1 Mar. 1581 to 1 Jul. 1586, made by John P. Prendergast, 1867–9. *Analecta Hibernica*, XXIV (1967) 91–180.

230. GOODBODY, OLIVE C. Guide to Irish Quaker records, 1654–1860, with contributions on Northern Ireland records by B. G. Hutton. Dublin: Stationery Office, for Irish Mss. Commission, 1967. 237 pp.

231. GORTON, L. J. Collection of papers relating to India in the British Museum. *Indian Archives*, XVII (1967–8) 26–30.

232. SETHI, R. R. (*ed.*). Fort William-India House correspondence and other contemporary papers relating thereto (Public ser.). Vol. 3. 1760–3. Delhi: Nat. Archives of India, 1968. xlvii, 618 pp.

233. SMITH, BRIAN STANLEY. Catalogue of the Ducarel papers relating to India in the Gloucestershire Records Office, England. *Indian Archives*, XVII (1967–8) 38–49.

234. PONG, DAVID. The Kwangtung provincial archives at the Public Record Office of London: a progress report. *Jour. Asian Studies*, XXVIII (1968) 139–43.

HISTORIOGRAPHY, STUDY AND TEACHING

HISTORIOGRAPHY

235. KEIR, D. L. Old ways and new in history. *Irish Hist. Studies*, XV (1966–7) 214–27.

236. WOODWARD, *Sir* ERNEST LLEWELLYN. 'The rise of the professional historian in England'. *In* Studies in international history, *ed.* K. Bourne *and* D. C. Watt (Hamden, Conn.: Archon Books, 1967) pp. 16–34.

237. SANDERSON, J. B. The historian and the 'masters' of political thought. *Polit. Studies*, XVI (1968) 43–54.

238. GEORGE, C. H. Puritanism as history and historiography. *Past & Present*, no. 41 (1968) 77–104.

239. PIGGOTT, STUART. Celts, Saxons and the early antiquaries. (O'Donnell Lectures, 1966). Edinburgh: Edinburgh U.P., 1967. 25 pp.

240. BRIGGS, ASA. Saxons, Normans and Victorians. Historical Assoc., 1966. 26 pp.

241. MILNE, ALEXANDER TAYLOR. The Victorian historian. *Colorado Quart.*, XV no. 4 (1967) 301–17.

242. HIBBERD, PAUL. The Rochdale tradition in co-operative history: is it justified? *Annals of Pub. & Co-operative Econ.*, XXXIX (1968) 531–57.

243. RUBINSTEIN, STANLEY. Historians of London: an account of the many surveys, histories, perambulations, maps and engravings made about the city. Owen, 1968. 239 pp., illus.

244. MOYSE-BARTLETT, MOYSE. Military historiography, 1850–60. *Soc. Army Hist. Research Jour.*, XLV (1967) 199–213.

245. HEREN, LOUIS. Remarks on the historian's contribution to Anglo-American misunderstanding. *Amer. Oxonian*, LIV (1967) 249–52.

246. WARD, JOHN M. The historiography of the British Commonwealth. *Hist. Studies Australia & N.Z.*, XII (1967) 556–70.

HISTORIANS

247. *Bede.* WALLACE-HADRILL, JOHN MICHAEL. Gregory of Tours and Bede: their views on the personal qualities of kings. *Frühmittelalterliche Studien*, II (1968) 31–44.

248. *Carlyle.* LAVALLEY, ALBERT J. Carlyle and the idea of the modern. New Haven, Conn., London: Yale U.P., 1968. xi, 351 pp.

249. *Carlyle.* MITFORD, NANCY. Tam and Fritz: Carlyle and Frederick the Great. *History Today*, XVIII (1968) 3–13.

250. *Churchill.* ASHLEY, MAURICE. Churchill as historian. Secker, 1968. vii, 246 pp.

251. *Collingwood.* MINK, LOUIS O. Collingwood's dialectic of history. *History & Theory*, VII (1968) 3–37.

252. *Collingwood.* CULLERÉ, JAIME. La idea de proceso histórico en Collingwood. *Rev. Univ. Nacional de Córdoba* (Argentina), VII nos. 4–5 (1967) 567–79.

253. *Deprez.* MAHAUT, M. C. Eugène Deprez, la Guyenne et la Guerre de Cent Ans. *Annales du Midi*, LXXX (1968) 215–20. [Deprez's *Préliminaires de la Guerre de Cent Ans* (1902).]

254. *Gardiner.* FAHEY, DAVID M. Gardiner and Usher in perspective. *Jour. Hist. Studies*, I (1967–8) 137–50.

255. *Gardiner.* FAHEY, D. M. Gardiner as dramatist: a commentary. *Jour. Hist. Studies*, I (1967–8) 351–4.

256. *Gibbon.* TREVOR-ROPER, HUGH REDWALD. Gibbon: greatest of historians. *Jour. Hist. Studies*, I (1967–8) 109–16.

257. *Gibbon.* SCHEIBE, FRIEDRICH CARL. Christentum und Kulturverfall im Geschichtsbild Edward Gibbons. *Archiv für Kulturgesch.*, L (1968) 240–75.

258. *Gibbon.* SMITH, BEVERLEY E. Gibbon and Mohammedanism. *Studies in Eng.*, IX (1968) 11–22.

259. *Gibbon.* MASON, H. A. Gibbon's irony. *Cambridge Quart.*, IV (1968) 309–17.

260. *Gilbert.* DIXON, F. E. Sir John T. Gilbert, 1829–98. *Dublin Hist. Rec.*, XXII (1968) 272–87.

261. *Hallam.* CLARK, PETER. Henry Hallam reconsidered. *Quart. Rev.*, CCCV (1967) 410–19.

262. *Lingard.* JONES, EDWIN. John Lingard

and the Simancas archives. *Hist. Jour.*, X (1967) 57–76.

263. *Macaulay*. HILL, BRIDGET, *and* HILL, CHRISTOPHER. Catherine Macaulay and the 17th century. *Welsh Hist. Rev.*, III (1966–7) 381–402.

264. *Macaulay*. WEBER, RONALD. Singer and seer: Macaulay on the historian as poet. *Eng. Lang. & Lit. Papers*, III (1967) 210–19.

265. *Macaulay*. HARTLEY, LODWICK. A late Augustan circus: Macaulay on Johnson, Boswell and Walpole. *South Atlantic Quart.*, LXVII (1968) 513–26.

266. *Marx*. COLLINS, KINS. Marx on the English agricultural revolution: theory and evidence. *History & Theory*, VI (1967) 351–81.

267. *Massingberd*. BAKER, W. J. F. C. Massingberd: historian in a Lincolnshire parish. *Lincs. Hist. & Archaeol.*, no. 3 (1968) 3–10.

268. *Namier*. BERLIN, *Sir* ISAIAH. L. B. Namier: a personal impression. *Jour. Hist. Studies*, I (1967–8) 117–36.

269. *Newman*. MACDOUGALL, HUGH A. Newman: historian or apologist? *Canadian Hist. Assoc. Rept.* (1968) 152–63.

270. *Oppenheim*. MINCHINTON, WALTER E. Michael Oppenheim, 1853–1927: a memoir. *Mariner's Mirror*, LIV (1968) 85–93.

271. *Skene*. ANDERSON, JAMES. William Forbes Skene: Celtic Scotland *v*. Caledonia. *Scot. Hist. Rev.*, XLVI (1967) 140–50.

272. *Stenton*. SLADE, C. F. Sir Frank Stenton, 1880–1967. *Berks. Archaeol. Jour.*, LXIII (1967–8) 1–4.

273. *Stubbs*. BRENTANO, ROBERT. The sound of Stubbs. *Jour. Brit. Studies*, VI no. 2 (1967) 1–14.

274. *Tawney*. FAHEY, DAVID M. R. H. Tawney and the sense of community. *Centennial Rev.*, XII (1968) 455–65.

275. *Temple*. MCCONNELL, THEODORE A. William Temple's philosophy of history. *Hist. Mag. Protestant Episcopal Church*, XXXVII (1968) 87–104.

276. *Toynbee*. HENNINGSEN, MANFRED. Menschheit und Geschichte: Untersuchungen zu Arnold Joseph Toynbees *A study of history*. Munich: List, 1967. 159 pp.

277. *Toynbee*. BOER, W. DEN. Toynbee's wraak. *Tijds. voor Geschiedenis*, LXXX (1967) 145–57. ['Toynbee's revenge'.]

278. *Trevelyan*. MONSAGRATI, GIUSEPPE. George Macaulay Trevelyan, storico del Risorgimento. *Rassegna Stor. del Risorgimento*, LIV (1967) 511–24.

STUDY AND TEACHING

279. LONDON UNIVERSITY. INSTITUTE OF HISTORICAL RESEARCH. Historical research for university degrees in the United Kingdom. Theses completed 1966, and Theses in progress, 1967. The Institute, 1967. 2 vols.

280. HARCUP, SARA E. (*comp.*). Historical, archaeological and kindred societies in the British Isles: a list. Rev. edn. Inst. Hist. Research, 1968. 57 pp. [Previous edn. 1965.]

281. BUCHANAN, R. A. The National Record of Industrial Monuments. *Industrial Archaeol.*, IV (1967) 358–65.

282. DYMOND, DAVID PERCY. Archaeology for the historian. (Helps for Students of History, 7). Historical Assoc., 1967. 27 pp.

283. LOMAX, DEREK W. Los estudios medievales en Inglaterra. *Anuario de Estudios Medievales*, no. 4 (1967) 519–35.

284. O'NEILL, THOMAS PATRICK. British parliamentary papers: a monograph on Blue Books. Dublin: Irish U.P., 1968. 32 pp.

285. BUTTERFIELD, HERBERT. Narrative history and the spade-work behind it. *History*, LIII (1968) 165–80.

286. HURSTFIELD, JOEL. Political corruption in modern England: the historian's problem. *History*, LII (1967) 16–34.

287. EMMISON, FREDERICK GEORGE. How to read local archives, 1550–1700. Historical Assoc., 1967. 21 pp.

288. DIBBEN, ALAN ARTHUR. Title deeds, 13th–19th centuries. (Helps for Students of History, 72). Historical Assoc., 1968. 30 pp.

289. IREDALE, DAVID. How can I trace the history of my house? *Amateur Historian*, VII (1967) 182–9.

290. THOMAS, J. H. Paper-making and local history: a guide to sources. *Local Historian*, VIII (1968) 42–6.

291. EVANS, BRIAN M. Sources for the study of the history of Welsh agriculture. *Amateur Historian*, VII (1967) 154–60.

292. RICHARDS, PETER S. Writing a railway history. *Local Historian*, VIII (1968) 10–15.

1770–1870'. *In* Proc. 3rd International Conference of Economic History, Munich, 1965 (Paris, Hague: Mouton & Co., 1968) pp. 335–65.

380. DEANE, PHYLLIS MARY. New estimates of gross national product for the United Kingdom, 1830–1914. *Rev. Income & Wealth*, XIV (1968) 95–112.

381. SAYERS, RICHARD SIDNEY. A history of economic change in England, 1880–1939. O.U.P., 1967. vii, 179 pp.

382. SOLTOW, LEE. Long-run changes in British income inequality. *Econ. Hist. Rev.*, 2nd. ser. XXI (1968) 17–29.

383. HILL, CHRISTOPHER. 'Pottage for freeborn Englishmen: attitudes to wage labour in the 16th and 17th centuries'. *In* Socialism, capitalism and economic growth, *ed.* C. H. Feinstein (C.U.P., 1967) pp. 338–50.

384. WILES, RICHARD C. The theory of wages in later English mercantilism. *Econ. Hist. Rev.*, 2nd ser. XXI (1968) 113–26.

385. COATS, ALFRED W. Sociological aspects of British economic thought (*c.* 1880–1930). *Jour. Polit. Econ.*, LXXV (1967) 706–29.

Finance

386. RABB, THEODORE K. Enterprise and empire: merchant and gentry investment in the expansion of England, 1575–1630. Cambridge, Mass.: Harvard U.P.; London: O.U.P., 1968. xiii, 420 pp.

387. DICKSON, PETER GEORGE MUIR. The financial revolution in England: a study in the development of public credit, 1688–1756. London: Macmillan; New York: St. Martin's P., 1967. xxi, 580 pp., illus.

388. CHECKLAND, S. G. Banking history and economic development: seven systems. *Scot. Jour. Polit. Econ.*, XV (1968) 144–66.

389. CAMERON, RONDO. 'Banking in the early stages of industrialization: England, 1750–1844'. *In* Banking in the early stages of industrialization (New York, London, Toronto: O.U.P., 1967) pp. 15–59.

390. CHANDLER, GEORGE. Four centuries of banking, Vol. 2, The northern constituent banks. Batsford, 1968. 608 pp., illus. [Martins Bank Ltd.]

391. SIMON, MATTHEW. The enterprise and industrial composition of new British portfolio foreign investment, 1865–1914. *Jour. Development Studies*, III no. 3 (1967) 280–92.

392. STONE, IRVING. British long-term investment in Latin America, 1865–1913. *Business Hist. Rev.*, XLII (1968) 311–39.

393. SAYERS, RICHARD SIDNEY. Gilletts in the London money market, 1867–1967. Oxford: Clarendon P., 1968. x, 204 pp., illus.

Industry

394. MARSHALL, JOHN DUNCAN, *and* DAVIES-SHIEL, M. Industrial archaeology in the Lake counties and Furness. *Northern Hist.*, II (1967) 112–33.

395. WALROND, LIONEL F. J. Industrial archaeology in the Stroud area. *Bristol & Glos. Archaeol. Soc. Trans.* for 1967, LXXXVI (1968) 173–82.

396. BROADBRIDGE, S. R. Industrial archaeology in the parish of Penkridge. *N. Staffs. Jour. Field Studies*, VII (1967) 44–57.

397. JONES, F. M. Liverpool dock buildings as historical evidence. *Hist. Soc. Lancs. & Cheshire Trans.* for 1966, CXVIII (1967) 87–103.

398. ROWLANDS, MARIE B. Industry and social change in Staffordshire, 1660–1760: a study of the probate and other records of tradesmen. *Lichfield Archaeol. & Hist. Soc. Trans.*, IX (1968) 37–58.

399. REES, WILLIAM. Industry before the Industrial Revolution, incorporating a study of the chartered companies of the Society of Mines Royal and of Mineral and Battery Works. Cardiff: Wales U.P., 1968. 2 vols.

400. ARNOT, ROBERT PAGE. 'Probleme der Geschichte der Britischen Bergarbeiterbewegung'. *In* Beiträge zur Geschichte des Bergbaus und Hüttenwesens, vol. 4 (Leipzig: Deutscher V. für Grundstoffindustrie, 1967) pp. 107–18.

401. HUDSON, GRAHAM S. Garforth collieries and the Aberford railway. *Nat. Reg. Archives, W. Riding N. Section Bull.*, X (1967) 16–34.

402. HARRIS, ALAN. The Ingleton coalfield. *Industrial Archaeol.*, V (1968) 313–26.

403. ANDERSON, D. Blundell's collieries: technical developments, 1776–1966. *Hist. Soc. Lancs & Cheshire Trans.* for 1967, CXIX (1968) 113–79.

404. KIRKHAM, NELLIE. Derbyshire lead mining through the centuries. Truro, Cornwall: Barton, 1968. 132 pp.

405. FORD, TREVOR D., *and* RIEUWERTS, J. H. (*eds.*). Lead mining in the Peak District.

Bakewell, Derbys.: Peak Park Planning Board, 1968. iv, 123 pp., illus.

406. BROOK, F. Fallowfield lead and witherite mines. *Industrial Archaeol.*, IV (1967) 311–22.

407. BARTON, DENYS BRADFORD. Essays in Cornish mining history. Vol. 1. Truro, Cornwall: the author, 1968. 198 pp., illus.

408. BARTON, D. B. A history of tin mining and smelting in Cornwall. Truro: Barton, 1967. 302 pp., illus.

409. BARTON, D. B. A history of copper mining in Cornwall and Devon. 2nd edn. Truro, Cornwall: the author, 1968. 102 pp., illus. [Previous edn. 1961.]

410. HAMILTON, HENRY. The English brass and copper industries to 1800. 2nd edn. Cass, 1967. xxxvii, 338 pp. [Previous edn. Longmans, 1926.]

411. ROWSE, ALFRED LESLIE. The Cornish china-clay industry. *History Today*, XVII (1967) 483–6.

412. KENT, J. M. The Delabole slate quarry. *Roy. Inst. Cornwall Jour.*, n.s. V (1968) 317–23.

413. GRAVETT, K. W. E., *and* WOOD, ERIC S. Merstham limeworks. *Surrey Archaeol. Coll.*, LXIV (1967) 124–41.

414. RAYBOULD, T. J. The development and organization of Lord Dudley's mineral estates, 1774–1845. *Econ. Hist. Rev.*, 2nd ser. XXI (1968) 529–44.

415. RAYBOULD, T. J. Systems of management and administration on the Dudley estates, 1774–1833. *Business Hist.*, X (1968) 1–11.

416. GALE, WALTER KEITH VERNON. The British iron and steel industry: a technical history. Newton Abbot, Devon: David & Charles, 1967. 198 pp., illus.

417. TYLECOTE, RONALD F. Le développement des techniques sidérurgiques en Grande-Bretagne. *Rev. Hist. Sidérurgie*, VII (1966) 87–112.

418. SMITH, RICHARD S. Sir Francis Willoughby's ironworks, 1570–1610. *Renaissance & Mod. Studies*, XI (1967) 90–140.

419. BIRCH, ALAN. The economic history of the British iron and steel industry, 1784–1879. Cass, 1967. xv, 398 pp.

420. GALE, WALTER KEITH VERNON. The rolling of iron. *Newcomen Soc. Trans.* for 1964–5, XXXVII (1967) 35–46.

421. COCHRANE, LOUISE. Linch and its iron resources. *Sussex Archaeol. Coll.*, CV (1967) 37–48.

422. COCKS, E. J., *and* WALTERS, B. A history of the zinc smelting industry in Britain. Harrap, 1968. x, 224 pp., illus.

423. HARRIS, JOHN RAYMOND. Origins of the St. Helens glass industry. *Northern Hist.*, III (1968) 105–17.

424. KENYON, GEORGE HUGH. The glass industry of the Weald. Leicester: Leicester U.P., 1967. xxii, 231 pp., illus.

425. PERCIVAL, ARTHUR. The Faversham gunpowder industry and its development. (Faversham Soc. Papers, 4). Faversham, Kent: the Society, 1967. iv, 32 pp.

426. PERCIVAL, A. The Faversham gunpowder industry. *Industrial Archaeol.*, V (1968) 1–42, 120–34.

427. WELCH, CHARLES EDWIN (*ed.*). Plymouth building accounts of the 16th and 17th centuries. (Devon & Cornwall Record Soc. Pubns., n.s. 12). Exeter: the Society, 1967. xvii, 117 pp.

428. SAUL, SAMUEL BERRICK. The market and development of mechanical engineering industries in Britain, 1860–1914. *Econ. Hist. Rev.*, 2nd ser. XX (1967) 111–30.

429. SAUL, S. B. The machine tool industry in Britain to 1914. *Business Hist.*, X (1968) 22–43.

430. CHENEY, CHRISTOPHER ROBERT. Cheney & Sons: two centuries of printing in Banbury. *Cake & Cockhorse*, III (1967) 167–75.

431. NUTTALL, D. A history of printing in Chester. *Chester Archaeol. Soc. Jour.*, LIV (1967) 37–95.

432. HOUSEMAN, LORNA. The house that Thomas built: the story of De La Rue. Chatto, 1968. xv, 207 pp., illus.

433. TANN, JENNIFER. Gloucestershire woollen mills: industrial archaeology. Newton Abbot, Devon: David & Charles, 1967. 254 pp., illus.

434. GOODCHILD, JOHN. The Ossett Mill Company. *Textile Hist.*, I no. 1 (1968) 46–61.

435. BAINES, *Sir* EDWARD. History of the cotton manufacture in Great Britain. 2nd edn. New York: Augustus M. Kelley; London: Cass, 1966. 544 pp., illus. [Previous edn. Fisher, Fisher & Jackson, 1835.]

436. SHAPIRO, SEYMOUR. Capital and the cotton industry in the Industrial Revolution.

Ithaca, N.Y.: Cornell U.P., 1967. xiii, 293 pp.

437. WELLS, FREDERICK ARTHUR. Hollins and Viyella: a study in business history. Newton Abbot, Devon: David & Charles, 1968. 264 pp., illus.

438. TYSON, WILLIAM. Rope: a history of the hard fibre cordage industry in the United Kingdom. Wheatland Journals, for Hard Fibre Cordage Institute, 1967. xiii, 165 pp.

439. STERN, WALTER M. Control *v.* freedom in leather production from the early 17th to the early 19th century. *Guildhall Misc.*, II no. 10 (1968) 438–58.

440. WOODWARD, D. M. The Chester leather industry, 1558–1625. *Hist. Soc. Lancs. & Cheshire Trans.* for 1967, CXIX (1968) 65–111.

441. WATTS, H. D. Agricultural industries: the decline of the small business. *Business Hist.*, IX (1967) 118–25.

442. NIELSEN, V. C. Cheese-making and cheese chambers in Gloucestershire. *Industrial Archaeol.*, V (1968) 162–70.

443. MASON, KATE. Yorkshire cheese-making. *Folk Life*, VI (1968) 7–17.

444. THACKER, D. M. DUGGAN. Country cider. *Folk Life*, VI (1968) 104–12.

445. ROPER, JOHN STEPHEN. Early north Worcestershire scythesmiths and scythe-grinders: a study based on wills and probate inventories, 1541–1647. Dudley, Worcs.: the author, 1967. 20 ff.

446. LOCKETT, TERENCE ANTHONY. The pottery industry and the local historian. *Local Historian*, VIII (1968) 54–60, 78–85.

447. SMITH, BARBARA M. D. The Galtons of Birmingham: Quaker gun-merchants and bankers, 1702–1831. *Business Hist.*, IX (1967) 132–50.

448. DREW, JOHN H. The horn comb industry of Kenilworth. *Birmingham Archaeol. Soc. Trans.* for 1965, LXXXII (1967) 21–7.

449. WATTS, D. G. Water-power and the Industrial Revolution. *Cumberland & Westmorland Antiq. & Archaeol. Soc. Trans.*, LXVII (1967) 199–205.

450. NORRIS, HAROLD. The water-powered corn mills of Cheshire. *Lancs. & Cheshire Antiq. Soc. Trans.* for 1965–6, LXXV–LXXVI (1968) 33–71.

451. SPAIN, R. J. The Len watermills. *Archaeologia Cantiana* for 1967, LXXXII (1968) 32–104.

452. PATMORE, F. W., *and others*. Hoveringham watermill. *Thoroton Soc. Trans.* for 1966, LXX (1967) 71–80.

453. CARTER, JOHN. Watermills in north Oxfordshire: some notes on a recent survey. *Cake & Cockhorse*, III (1968) 215–22.

454. WAILES, REX. Suffolk watermills. *Newcomen Soc. Trans.* for 1964–5, XXXVII (1967) 99–116.

455. DOUCH, HENRY LESLIE. Windmills in Cornwall and Devon. *Devon & Cornwall N. & Q.*, XXXI (1968) 56–9.

456. MINCHINTON, WALTER E. Windmills in Devon. *Devon & Cornwall N. & Q.*, XXXI (1968) 78–82.

457. MAJOR, J. KENNETH. An inventory of windmills in Northumberland and Durham. *Industrial Archaeol.*, IV (1967) 331–9.

458. FARRIES, KENNETH GEORGE, *and* MASON, MARTIN THOMAS. The windmills of Surrey and inner London. Skilton, 1967. 276 pp., illus.

Trade and commerce

459. ALFORD, BERNARD WILLIAM ERNEST, *and* BARKER, THEODORE CARDWELL. A history of the Carpenters' Company. Allen & Unwin, 1968. 271 pp., illus.

460. MAYER, EDWARD. The Curriers and the City of London: a history of the Worshipful Company of Curriers. The Company, 1968. xi, 212 pp., illus.

461. OXLEY, JAMES EDWIN. The Fletchers and Longbowstringmakers of London. Worshipful Co. of Fletchers, 1968. 160 pp., illus.

462. MICHAELIS, RONALD F. (*comp.*). A short history of the Worshipful Company of Pewterers of London, and a catalogue of pewter in its possession. The Company, 1968. 103 pp., illus.

463. STEER, FRANCIS WILLIAM. Scriveners' Company Common Paper, 1357–1628, with a continuation to 1678. (London Record Soc. Pubns., 4). The Society, 1968. xxviii, 157 pp.

464. FOX, ADAM (*comp.*). A brief description of the Worshipful Company of Skinners. Rev. edn. The Company, 1968. 72 pp. [Previous edn. 1956.]

465. YOUINGS, JOYCE. Tuckers Hall, Exeter: the history of a provincial city company through five centuries. Exeter, Devon: University, Incorporation of Weavers, Fullers and Shearmen, 1968. xiv, 258 pp., illus.

466. HEY, DAVID G. Fresh light on the south Yorkshire saltways. *Hunter Archaeol. Soc. Trans.*, IX pt. 3 (1967) 151–7.

467. SIGSWORTH, ERIC MILTON. The brewing trade during the Industrial Revolution: the call of Yorkshire. (Borthwick Papers, 31). York: St. Anthony's P., 1967. 36 pp.

468. COXHEAD, J. R. W. Honiton inns and taverns. *Devon & Cornwall N. & Q.*, XXXI (1968) 14–19, 34–41.

469. SWIFT, ERIC. Inns and inn signs of Leicestershire and Rutland. *Leics. Archaeol. Soc. Trans.* for 1965–6, XLI (1967) 57–64.

470. CHURCH, ROY ANTHONY. Kenricks in hardware: a family business, 1791–1966. Newton Abbot, Devon: David & Charles, 1968. 340 pp., illus.

471. BATEY, CHARLES. The Oxford partners: some notes on the administration of the University Press, 1780–1881. *Printing Hist. Soc. Jour.*, III (1967) 51–65.

472. ISAAC, PETER CHARLES GERALD, *and* WATSON, W. M. The history of the book trade in the north: a review of a research project. *Printing Hist. Soc. Jour.*, IV (1968) 87–98.

473. FORRY, J. B. 'The Virginia Company, 1606–1924'. *In* The formative era of American enterprise, *ed.* R. W. Hidy *and* P. E. Cawein (Boston, Mass.: D. C. Heath, 1967) pp. 1–36.

474. BAKSHI, S. R. Early trade and expansion of the East India Company. *Modern Rev.*, CXXI (1967) 286–93.

475. MĄCZAK, ANTONI. The Sound toll accounts and the balance of English trade with the Baltic zone, 1565–1646. *Studia Hist. Oecon.*, III (1968) 93–114.

476. CULLEN, L. M. Anglo-Irish trade, 1660–1800. Manchester: Manchester U.P., 1968. viii, 252 pp.

477. PAYNE, P. L. The emergence of the large-scale company in Great Britain, 1870–1914. *Econ. Hist. Rev.*, 2nd ser. XX (1967) 519–42.

478. DON, YEHUDA. Comparability of international trade statistics: Great Britain and Austria-Hungary before World War I. *Econ. Hist. Rev.*, 2nd ser. XXI (1968) 78–92.

479. WRIGHT, WINTHROP R. Foreign-owned railways in Argentina: a case study of economic nationalism. *Business Hist. Rev.*, XLI (1967) 62–93.

Labour and industrial relations

480. THOMPSON, EDWARD PALMER. The making of the English working class. New edn. Harmondsworth, Middx.: Penguin, 1968. 958 pp. [Previous edn. Gollancz, 1963.]

481. THOMPSON, E. P. Time, work-discipline, and industrial capitalism. *Past & Present*, no. 38 (1967) 56–97.

482. SMELSER, NEIL J. Sociological history: the Industrial Revolution and the British working class family. *Jour. Social Hist.*, I (1967) 17–35.

483. BRIGGS, ASA, *and* SAVILLE, JOHN (*eds.*). Essays in labour history in memory of G. D. H. Cole. Rev. edn. London: Macmillan; New York: St. Martin's P., 1967. vii, 364 pp. [Previous edn. 1960. Contains: 'The language of class in early 19th century England' by A. Briggs, pp. 43–73; '19th century co-operation: from community building to shopkeeping' by S. Pollard, pp. 74–112; 'Custom, wages and work-load in 19th century industry' by E. J. Hobsbawm, pp. 113–39; 'The *Bee-Hive* newspaper: its origin and early struggles' by S. Coltham, pp. 174–204; 'Prof. Beesly and the working-class movement' by R. Harrison, pp. 205–41; 'The English branches of the First International' by H. Collins, pp. 242–75; 'Homage to Tom Maguire' by E. P. Thompson, pp. 276–316; 'Trade unions and free labour: the background to the Taff Vale decision' by J. Saville, pp. 317–50.]

484. HOBSBAWM, ERIC JOHN. Trade union history. *Econ. Hist. Rev.*, 2nd ser. XX (1967) 358–64.

485. BÜNGER, SIEGFRIED. Die Rolle der liberalen Bourgeoisie bei der Herausbildung des Trade-Unionismus in Grossbritannien. *Zeit. für Geschichtswiss.*, XV (1967) 1193–1206.

486. GALTIER, BERNARD. 1868–1968: les cent ans du T.U.C. *Les Langues Modernes*, VI (1968) 749–57.

487. WILLIAMS, JAMES ECCLES. L'esprit militant chez les mineurs britanniques, 1890–1914. *Mouvement Social*, LXV (1968) 81–91.

488. CANNON, I. C. The roots of organisation among journeymen printers. *Printing Hist. Soc. Jour.*, IV (1968) 99–107.

Social history

489. ARNOLD, RALPH. A social history of England 55 B.C. to A.D. 1215. London: Constable; Toronto: Longmans Canada, 1967. xvi, 423 pp., illus.

490. BRYANT, *Sir* ARTHUR. Protestant island. Collins, 1967. 359 pp.

491. HARWOOD, H. W. As things were: a social study of Upper Calder Valley. *Halifax Antiq. Soc. Trans.* (1968) 15–26.

492. KERR, BARBARA. Bound to the soil: a social history of Dorset, 1750–1918. Baker, 1968. xix, 287 pp., illus.

493. RAMELSON, MARIAN. The petticoat rebellion: a century of struggle for women's rights. Lawrence & Wishart, 1967. 208 pp., illus.

494. CUDDEFORD, GLADYS MCGILVRAY. Women and society from Victorian times to the present day. H. Hamilton, 1967. 120 pp., illus.

495. ARNSTEIN, WALTER L. Votes for Women: myths and reality. *History Today*, XVIII (1968) 531–9.

496. HENDERSON, WILLIAM OTTO. J. C. Fischers Besuche in London zwischen 1794 und 1851. *Tradition*, XII (1967) 349–64, 416–26.

497. WOODROOFE, KATHLEEN. The making of the welfare state in England: a summary of its origin and development. *Jour. Social Hist.*, I (1968) 303–24.

498. MARSHALL, JOHN DUNCAN. The Old Poor Law, 1795–1834. (Studies in Economic History). Macmillan, 1968. 50 pp.

499. HANHAM, HAROLD JOHN. The suppression of the charities in Ashburton. *Devon Assoc. Repts. & Trans.*, XCIX (1967) 111–37.

500. MORGAN, FREDERICK CHARLES. Hereford poor and prisons in olden days. *Woolhope Naturalists' F.C. Trans.* for 1966, XXXVIII (1967) 220–35.

501. NEATE, ALAN ROBERT. The St. Marylebone Workhouse and Institution, 1730–1965. (St. Marylebone Soc. Pubns., 9). The Society, 1967. 43 pp., illus.

502. STEANE, J. M. The poor in Rothwell, 1750–1840. *Northants. Past & Present*, IV no. 3 (1968) 143–8.

503. BRETT, GERARD. Dinner is served: a history of dining in England, 1400–1900. Hart-Davis, 1968. 144 pp., illus.

504. TREASE, GEOFFREY. The Grand Tour. Heinemann, 1967. xi, 251 pp., illus.

505. MURDOCH, CATHERINE. Some Yorkshire innocents abroad. *Nat. Reg. Archives, W. Riding N. Section Bull.*, X (1967) 35–49.

506. HERN, ANTHONY. The seaside holiday: the history of the English seaside resort. Cresset P., 1967. xiii, 209 pp.

Population

507. LASLETT, PETER. Le brassage de la population en France et en Angleterre aux 17e et 18e siècles: comparaison préliminaire de villages français et anglais. *Annales de Démographie Historique* (1968) 99–109.

508. BOYLE, K. The Irish immigrant in Britain. *Northern Ireland Legal Quart.*, XIX (1968) 418–45.

Agrarian and manorial history

509. COOPER, J. P. The social distribution of land and men in England, 1436–1700. *Econ. Hist. Rev.*, 2nd ser. XX (1967) 419–40.

510. THOMPSON, FRANCIS MICHAEL LONGSTRETH. 'The social distribution of landed property in England since the 16th century'. *In* Proc. 3rd International Conference of Economic History, Munich, 1965 (Paris, Hague: Mouton & Co., 1968) pp. 471–86.

511. FINBERG, HERBERT PATRICK REGINALD (*ed.*). The agrarian history of England and Wales. Vol. 4, 1500–1640, *ed.* J. Thirsk. C.U.P., 1967. xi, 919 pp.

512. PETTIT, PHILIP ARTHUR JOHN. The royal forests of Northamptonshire: a study in their economy, 1558–1714. (Northants. Record Soc. Pubns., 23). Gateshead, Northumb.: Northumberland P., for the Society, 1968. xvi, 236 pp., illus.

513. HOSKINS, WILLIAM GEORGE. Harvest fluctuations and English economic history, 1620–1759. *Agric. Hist. Rev.*, XVI (1968) 15–31.

514. JONES, ERIC LIONEL (*comp.*). Agriculture and economic growth in England, 1650–1815. London: Methuen; New York: Barnes & Noble, 1967. xi, 195 pp.

515. CLAY, CHRISTOPHER. Marriage, inheritance, and the rise of large estates in England, 1660–1815. *Econ. Hist. Rev.*, 2nd ser. XXI (1968) 503–18.

516. SUTHERLAND, DOUGLAS. The landowners. Blond, 1968. x, 180 pp., illus. [1700–1968.]

517. JONES, ERIC LIONEL. The development of English agriculture, 1815–73. (Studies in Economic History). Macmillan, 1968. 40 pp.

518. HOBSBAWM, ERIC JOHN. Les soulèvements de la campagne anglaise, 1795–1850. *Annales*, XXIII (1968) 9–30.

519. RICHES, NAOMI. The Agricultural Revolution in Norfolk. 2nd edn. Cass, 1967. x, 194 pp., illus. [Previous edn. North Carolina U.P., 1937.]

520. BROWNSDON, T. E. An historical note on Manx agriculture. *Isle of Man Nat. Hist. & Antiq. Soc. Proc.*, n.s. VII no. 1 (1967) 5–12.

521. TATE, WILLIAM EDWARD. The English village community and the enclosure movements. Gollancz, 1967. 231 pp., illus.

522. MINGAY, GORDON EDMUND. Enclosure and the small farmer in the age of the Industrial Revolution. (Studies in Economic History). Macmillan, 1968. 47 pp.

523. YELLING, J. A. Common land and enclosure in east Worcestershire, 1540–1870. *Inst. Brit. Geographers' Trans.*, XLV (1968) 157–68.

524. GRIGG, DAVID B. The changing agricultural geography of England: a comment on the sources available for the reconstruction of the agricultural geography of England, 1770–1850. *Inst. Brit. Geographers' Trans.*, XLI (1967) 73–96.

525. BECKWITH, IAN S. The remodelling of a common-field system. *Agric. Hist. Rev.*, XV (1967) 108–12.

526. POCOCK, ERNEST A. The first fields in an Oxfordshire parish. *Agric. Hist. Rev.*, XVI (1968) 85–100. [Clanfield.]

527. WHITTINGTON, GRAEME. Towards a terminology for strip lynchets. *Agric. Hist. Rev.*, XV (1967) 103–7.

528. ARMSTRONG, A. W. Ridge and furrow in the Guisborough area. *Cleveland & Teesside Local Hist. Soc. Bull.*, III (1968) 15–21.

529. WHITEHEAD, JANE. The management and land-use of water meadows in the Frome valley, Dorset. *Dorset Nat. Hist. & Archaeol. Soc. Proc.*, LXXXIX (1968) 257–81.

530. COOKE, G. W. Advice on using fertilisers, 1861–1967. *Roy. Agric. Soc. Jour.*, CXXVIII (1967) 107–24.

531. BELLIS, D. B. Pig farming in the United Kingdom: its development and future trends. *Roy. Agric. Soc. Jour.*, CXXIX (1968) 24-42.

532. COATES, BRYAN E. Parklands in transition: medieval deer-park to modern landscape park. *Hunter Archaeol. Soc. Trans.*, IX pt. 3 (1967) 132–50.

533. FOWKES, D. V. Nottinghamshire parks in the 18th and 19th centuries. *Thoroton Soc. Trans.* for 1967, LXXI (1968) 72–89.

534. CHENEVIX TRENCH, CHARLES POCKLINGTON. The poacher and the squire: a history of poaching and game preservation in England. Longmans, 1967. 248 pp., illus.

535. HARDY, EVELYN. Life on a Suffolk manor in the 16th and 17th centuries. *Suffolk Rev.*, III (1968) 225–37. [Groton.]

536. COLEMAN, DELPHINE J. Orcop: aspects of manorial life. *Woolhope Naturalists' F.C. Trans.*, XXXIX (1968) 354–61.

537. KING, J. S. The manor of Horton in Bradford-Dale. *Bradford Antiquary*, n.s. pt. XLIII (1967) 210–14.

Transport and communications

538. JOYCE, JAMES. The story of passenger transport in Britain. Allan, 1967. 208 pp., illus.

539. PHILLIPS, RICHARD. Fashions in horseflesh. *Folk Life*, V (1967) 58–64.

540. CROFTS, JOHN ERNEST VICTOR. Pack-horse, waggon and post: land carriage and communications under the Tudors and Stuarts. London: Routledge; Toronto: Toronto U.P., 1967. xi, 147 pp., illus.

541. MARGETSON, STELLA. Journey by stages: some account of the people who travelled by stage-coach and mail in the years between 1660 and 1840. Cassell, 1967. 230 pp., illus.

542. DUCKHAM, BARON FREDERICK. The transport revolution, 1750–1830. (Aids for Teachers, 14). Historical Assoc., 1967. 16 pp.

543. COPELAND, JOHN. Roads and their traffic, 1750–1850. Newton Abbot, Devon: David & Charles, 1968. 205 pp., illus.

544. URWIN, ALAN CHARLES BELL. The Hampton-Staines turnpike, 1773–1859. (Borough of Twickenham Local Hist. Soc. Papers, 11). Twickenham, Middx.: the Society, 1968. 18 pp.

545. PRIESTLEY, JOSEPH. Historical account of the navigable rivers, canals and

railways throughout Great Britain. 2nd edn. Cass, 1967. 895 pp., illus. [Previous edn. London, Longman; Wakefield, Yorks.: Nichols, 1831.]

546. GLADWIN, DAVID DANIEL, *and* WHITE, J. M. English canals. Pt. 2, Engineers and engineering. Lingfield, Surrey: Oakwood P., 1968. 80 pp., illus.

547. ROBINSON, H. Cheshire river navigations with special reference to the river Dee. *Chester Archaeol. Soc. Jour.*, LV (1968) 63–87.

548. CLEW, KENNETH R. The Kennet and Avon canal. Newton Abbot, Devon: David & Charles, 1968. 206 pp., illus.

549. WELCH, CHARLES EDWIN. Cann Quarry canal and railway. *Devon Assoc. Repts. & Trans.*, C (1968) 111–23.

550. TOMLINSON, V. I. The Manchester, Bolton and Bury Canal Navigation and Railway Company, 1790–1845. *Lancs. & Cheshire Antiq. Soc. Trans.* for 1965–6, LXXV–LXXVI (1968) 231–99.

551. BECKWITH, IAN S. The river trade of Gainsborough, 1500–1850. *Lincs. Hist. & Archaeol.*, no. 2 (1967) 3–20.

552. DUCKHAM, BARON FREDERICK. The Fitzwilliams and the navigation of the Yorkshire Derwent. *Northern Hist.*, II (1967) 45–61.

553. SIMMONS, JACK. The railways of Britain: an historical introduction. 2nd edn. Macmillan, 1968. xii, 276 pp., illus. [Previous edn. Routledge, 1961.]

554. BAGWELL, PHILIP SIDNEY. The Railway Clearing House in the British economy, 1842–1922. Allen & Unwin, 1968. 320 pp., illus.

555. NOCK, OSWALD STEVENS. North Western: a saga of the premier line of Great Britain, 1846–1922. Shepperton, Middx.: Allan, 1968. xii, 312 pp., illus.

556. GOODMAN, WILLIAM LOUIS. British plane-makers from 1700. Bell, 1968. 135 pp., illus.

557. MACKAY, JAMES ALEXANDER. Great Britain: the story of Great Britain and her stamps. Philatelic Publishers, 1967. 158 pp., illus.

558. BIRCH, J. ALFRED. The North Sea mails: postal relations between Britain, Scandinavia and northern Europe, 1660–1910. *Postal Hist.*, no. 156 (1968) 66–70.

559. DIBDEN, W. G. STITT. The India Mail officer. *Postal Hist.*, no. 148 (1967) 29–32, no. 149 (1967) 39–41.

Miscellaneous

560. JENKINS, J. GERAINT. Post-medieval archaeology and folk-life studies. *Post-Medieval Archaeol.*, II (1968) 1–9.

561. JONES, ERIC LIONEL. The reduction of fire damage in southern England, 1650–1850. *Post-Medieval Archaeol.*, II (1968) 140–9.

562. CURRER-BRIGGS, NOEL. Contemporary observations on security from the Chubb collectanea, 1818–1968. Chubb & Sons Lock & Safe Co., 1968. 57 pp., illus.

563. BERGERON, DAVID M. The emblematic nature of English civic pageantry. *Renaissance Drama*, n.s. I (1968) 167–89.

564. DICKINSON, PHILIP G.M. Earth-cut, church and topiary mazes. *Records of Hunts.*, I pt. 3 (1967) 33–9.

565. WOOLNER, DIANA. New light on the white horse. *Folklore*, LXXVIII (1967) 90–111.

566. FINDLER, GERALD. Folklore of the Lake counties. Clapham-via-Lancaster, Yorks.: Dalesman, 1968. 80 pp., illus.

567. ETTLINGER, ELLEN. Folklore in Buckinghamshire churches. *Folklore*, LXXVIII (1967) 275–92.

568. SMITH, ALAN. The image of Cromwell in folklore and tradition. *Folklore*, LXXIX (1968) 17–39.

569. FOOTTIT, C. R. S. English royal freemasons. *Ars Quatuor Coronatorum*, LXXXI (1968) 348–54.

570. FRERE, A. S. The organization and administration of Grand Lodge. *Ars Quatuor Coronatorum*, LXXX (1967) 305–10.

RELIGIOUS HISTORY

General and Anglicanism

571. MOORMAN, JOHN RICHARD HUMPIDGE. A history of the Church in England. 2nd edn. Black, 1967. xx, 460 pp. [Previous edn. 1953.]

572. LEROY, ALFRED. Le grand schisme d'Angleterre, 1533–1660. Paris: Spes, 1967. 241 pp.

573. RUSSELL, CONRAD S. R. Arguments for religious unity in England, 1530–1650. *Jour. Eccles. Hist.*, XVIII (1967) 201–26.

574. HART, ARTHUR TINDAL. Clergy and society, 1600–1800. (Church History Outlines). S.P.C.K., 1968. vii, 120 pp.

575. NICHOLLS, DAVID (*comp.*). Church and state in Britain since 1820. London: Routledge; New York: Humanities P., 1967. x, 252 pp.

576. SMITH, WARREN SYLVESTER. The London heretics, 1870–1914. Constable, 1967. xvii, 319 pp., illus.

577. BUDD, SUSAN. The loss of faith: reasons for unbelief among members of the secular movement in England, 1850–1950. *Past & Present*, no. 36 (1967) 106–25.

578. JASPER, RONALD C. D. The *Church Quarterly Review*, 1875–1968. *Church Quart.*, I no. 2 (1968) 136–40.

579. LE NEVE, JOHN. Fasti Ecclesiae Anglicanae, 1300–1541. Rev. edn. Vol. 12, Introduction, errata and index, *comp.* J. M. Horn. Athlone P., for Inst. Hist. Research, 1967. 202 pp.

580. Fasti parochiales. Vol. 3, Deanery of Pickering, *ed.* N. A. H. Lawrence. (Yorks. Archaeol. Soc. Record ser., 129). Leeds: the Society, 1968. xii, 138 pp.

581. MOIR, ARTHUR LOWNDES. The deans of Hereford cathedral church. Hereford: the author, 1968. 66 pp., illus.

582. FOULKES, R. FORTESCUE. Rectors of St. Mary and Holy Trinity, Buckland Filleigh. *Devon & Cornwall N. & Q.*, XXX (1967) 228–34, 249–52, 262–70.

583. HEMBRY, PHYLLIS MAY. The bishops of Bath and Wells, 1540–1640: social and economic problems. Athlone P., 1967. xi, 287 pp.

584. ANDERSON, MARJORIE. Some early churchwardens' accounts of Lichfield St. Michael's. *Lichfield Archaeol. & Hist. Soc. Trans.* for 1965–6, VII (1967) 11–20. [1555–1732.]

585. LAWRENCE, N. A. H. 'Foreign' exchanges in the East Riding. *Yorks Archaeol. Jour.*, XLII (1967) 56–60.

586. MILLIKEN, ERNEST KENNETH. English monasticism yesterday and today. Harrap, 1967. 123 pp., illus.

587. WILSON, P. A. The cult of St. Martin in the British Isles, with particular reference to Canterbury and Candida Casa. *Innes Rev.*, XIX (1968) 129–43.

588. STACPOOLE, ALBERIC. The public face of Aelred, 1167–1967. *Downside Rev.*, LXXXV (1967) 183–99, 318–25.

589. CHAPPELL, PAUL. Music and worship in the Anglican church, 597–1967. (Studies in Christian Worship, 10). Faith P., 1968. 143pp., illus.

590. PHILLIPS, CHARLES HENRY. The singing Church: an outline history of the music sung by choir and people. New edn., *rev.* A. Hutchings. Faber, 1968. 288 pp., illus. [Previous edn. 1945.]

591. KAYE, ELAINE. The history of the King's Weigh House church. Allen & Unwin, 1968. 176 pp., illus.

592. RIX, MICHAEL M. Industrial archaeology and the Church. *Industrial Archaeol.*, IV (1967) 44–50.

593. VERETÉ, MAYIR. Ray'on shivat Yisrael ba-maẖshava ha-Protestantit be-Angliya ba-shanim, 1790–1840. *Zion*, XXXIII (1968) 145–79. ['The idea of the restoration of the Jews in English Protestant thought'. English summary.]

Roman Catholicism

594. GWYNN, DENIS R. Great Britain: England and Wales. (Hist. of Irish Catholicism, vol. 6, fasc. 1). Dublin: Gill, 1968. 54 pp.

595. HODGSON, AILEEN M. The chapel and mission of Grafton Manor, 1218–1874. *Worcs. Recusant*, no. 8 (1966) 24–32.

596. AVELING, HUGH. Some aspects of Yorkshire Catholic recusant history, 1558–1791. *Studies in Church Hist.*, IV (1967) 98–121.

597. WILLIAMS, JOHN ANTHONY. Catholic recusancy in Wiltshire, 1660–1791. (Catholic Record Soc. Pubns., Monograph ser., 1). The Society, 1968. 407 pp.

598. ROWLANDS, MARIE B. The Staffordshire clergy, 1688–1803. *Recusant Hist.*, IX (1967–8) 219–41.

599. BOSSY, JOHN. Four Catholic congregations in rural Northumberland, 1750–1850. *Recusant Hist.*, IX (1967–8) 88–119.

600. HICKEY, JOHN. Urban Catholics: urban Catholicism in England and Wales from 1829 to the present day. G. Chapman, 1967. 188 pp.

601. FLAYELLE, JEAN. Un anniversaire: le Collège des Anglais, 1568–1968. *Amis Douai*, 5 ser. IV (1968) 46–9.

602. FLEISCHMANN, M. Hundert Jahre Mill Hill. *Zeit. Missionwissenschaft und Religionswissenschaft*, LI (1967) 1–12.

Protestant Nonconformity

603. MULLETT, CHARLES F. Religious nonconformity: a central theme in modern English history. *Hist. Mag. Protestant Episcopal Church*, XXXVII (1968) 215–43.

604. EMERSON, EVERETT HARVEY. English Puritanism from John Hooper to John Milton. Durham, N.C.: Duke U.P., 1968. xii, 313 pp.

605. TOON, PETER. The emergence of hyper-Calvinism in English Nonconformity, 1689–1765. Olive Tree, 1967. 176 pp.

606. NUTTALL, GEOFFREY F. Calvinism in Free Church history. *Baptist Quart.*, XXII no. 8 (1968) 418–28.

607. BOLAM, CHARLES GORDON, *and others*. The English Presbyterians: from Elizabethan Puritanism to modern Unitarianism. Allen & Unwin, 1968. 297 pp.

608. TAYLOR, JOHN H. Ordination among us. *Congregational Hist. Soc. Trans.*, XX (1968) 210–22.

609. SYDENHAM, G. Glimpses of Congregational church life in Suffolk during the 18th and 19th centuries. *Suffolk Rev.*, III (1968) 207–11.

610. NUTTALL, GEOFFREY F. The beginnings of Old Meeting, Bedworth. *Congregational Hist. Soc. Trans.*, XX (1968) 255–64.

611. POTTS, ELI DANIEL. British Baptist missionaries in India, 1793–1837: the history of Serampore and its missions. Cambridge: C.U.P., 1967. 276 pp.

612. LAIRD, M. A. The Serampore missionaries as educationists, 1794–1824. *Baptist Quart.*, XXII no. 6 (1968) 320–5.

613. CURRIE, ROBERT. A micro-theory of Methodist growth. *Wesley Hist. Soc. Proc.*, XXXVI (1967–8) 65–73.

614. GRUNDY, DONALD M. A history of the Original Methodists. *Wesley Hist. Soc. Proc.*, XXXVI (1967–8) 22–7, 49–58, 80–5, 115–18, 143–8, 181–6. [Contd. from vol. XXXV.]

615. SHAW, THOMAS. A history of Cornish Methodism. Truro, Cornwall: Barton, 1967. 145 pp., illus.

616. BECKERLEGGE, OLIVER AVEYARD (*comp.*). United Methodist ministers and their circuits, 1797–1932. Epworth P., 1968. 268 pp.

617. MORROW, THOMAS MANSER. Early Methodist women. Epworth P., 1967. 119 pp.

618. THOMSON, DAVID PATRICK. Lady Glenorchy and her churches: the story of 200 years. Crieff, Perths.: The Research Unit, 1967. 80 pp., illus.

619. BECKWITH, FRANK. A lost Leeds chapel: 'Albion'. *Univ. Leeds Rev.*, X (1966–7) 255–65.

620. SELLECK, A. D. A Quaker history. Pt. 2, Meeting-houses and burial grounds. *Devon Assoc. Repts. & Trans.*, XCIX (1967) 213–61.

621. BEAMISH, LUCIA. The silent century: Quaker ministry from 1750 to 1850. *Friends' Quart.*, XV no. 9 (1967) 386–96.

622. EDWARDS, GEORGE W. Quakers south of the bridge. *Friends' Quart.*, XV no. 11 (1967) 512–23. [Southwark Monthly Meeting.]

623. DIAMOND, HOWARD. A backward glance over a hundred years. *Friends' Quart.*, XV no. 9 (1967) 396–406. [History of the *Friends' Quarterly Examiner*.]

CULTURAL HISTORY

General

624. FRANTZ, R. W. The English traveller and the movement of ideas, 1660–1732. Lincoln, Nebr.: Nebraska U.P., 1967. 176 pp.

625. PARKS, GEORGE B. The decline and fall of the English Renaissance admiration of Italy. *Huntington Lib. Quart.*, XXXI (1967–8) 341–57.

626. LYNCH, BARBARA D., *and* LYNCH, THOMAS F. The beginnings of a scientific approach to prehistoric archaeology in 17th and 18th century Britain. *Southwestern Jour. Anthropology*, XXIV (1968) 33–65.

627. HARGREAVES-MAWDSLEY, W. N. The English Della Cruscans and their time, 1783–1828. The Hague: Nijhoff, 1967. 322 pp.

628. MACINTYRE, ALASDAIR CHALMERS. Secularization and moral change. (Newcastle-upon-Tyne University Riddell Memorial Lecture, 1964). O.U.P., 1967. 76 pp. [1800–1966.]

629. DORSON, RICHARD MERCER. The British folklorists: a history. Routledge, 1968. x, 518 pp. illus.

630. KER, NEIL RIPLEY. Cathedral libraries. *Library Hist.*, I (1967) 38–45.

631. BLAKISTON, J. M. G. Unfamiliar libraries, XI: Winchester College. *Book Collector*, XVI (1967) 297–304.

632. NOALL, CYRIL. The Penzance Library, 1818–1968. Penzance, Cornwall: the Library, 1968. 32 pp.

633. MORLEY, JOHN. Newark Book Society, 1777–1872. *Library Hist.*, I (1968) 77–86.

634. KELLY, THOMAS. Norwich, pioneer of public libraries. *Norfolk Archaeol.*, XXXIV pt. 2 (1967) 215–22.

635. FERRY, E. F. Two east Suffolk public libraries. *Suffolk Rev.*, III (1968) 202–6. [Shotley and Cratfield.]

636. LEEDS LIBRARY. The Leeds Library, 1768–1968. Leeds: the Library, 1968. 126 pp., illus.

Education

637. DULCK, JEAN. L'enseignement en Grande-Bretagne. Paris: A. Colin, 1968. 255 pp.

638. MURPHY, JAMES. Religion, the state and education in England. *Hist. Educ. Quart.*, VIII (1968) 3–34.

639. KASPER, HILDEGARD. Freiheit und Planung im englischen Schulwesen der Gegenwart: Analyse der offiziellen Reports und ihre Stellung innerhalb der englischen Pädagogik. Brunswick: Westermann, 1968. 176 pp.

640. TOY, HENRY SPENCER. A history of education at Launceston. Marazion, Cornwall: Wordens of Cornwall, 1967. 408 pp.

641. FLETCHER, JOHN M. The teaching of arts at Oxford, 1400–1520. *Paedagogica Historica*, VII (1967) 417–54.

642. FLETCHER, A. J. The expansion of education in Berkshire and Oxfordshire, 1500–1870. *Brit. Jour. Educ. Studies*, XV (1967) 51–9.

643. SIMON, BRIAN (*ed.*). Education in Leicester, 1540–1940: a regional study. Leicester: Leicester U.P., 1968. xvi, 270 pp., illus.

644. SANDERSON, MICHAEL. Social change and elementary education in industrial Lancashire, 1780–1840. *Northern Hist.*, III (1968) 131–54.

645. SANDERSON, M. Education and the factory in industrial Lancashire, 1780–1840. *Econ. Hist. Rev.*, 2nd ser. XX (1967) 266–79.

646. WARDLE, DAVID. Education in Nottingham in the age of apprenticeship, 1500–1800. *Thoroton Soc. Trans.* for 1967, LXXI (1968) 36–54.

647. SELLECK, RICHARD JOSEPH WHEELER. The new education, 1870–1914. Pitman, 1968. xv, 374 pp.

648. SELLECK, R. J. W. The scientific educationalist, 1870–1914. *Brit. Jour. Educ. Studies*, XV (1967) 148–65.

649. TOMLINSON, LEILA. Oxford University and the training of teachers: the early years (1892–1921). *Brit. Jour. Educ. Studies*, XVI (1968) 292–307.

650. MCINTOSH, PETER CHISHOLM. Physical education in England since 1800. Rev. edn. Bell, 1968. 320 pp., illus. [Previous edn. 1952.]

651. GRAY, *Sir* JOHN. Jesus College Grammar School. *Cambridge Antiq. Soc. Proc.*, LX (1967) 97–105.

652. LLOYD, E. S. The history of Huntington school. *Woolhope Naturalists' F.C. Trans.* for 1966, XXXVIII (1967) 211–19.

653. TONKIN, MURIEL. Onneslo's charity school, Aymestrey, 1516–1965. *Woolhope Naturalists' F.C. Trans.*, XXXIX (1967) 93–103.

654. CROSBY, BRIAN. The Song School at Durham. *Durham Univ. Rev.*, XXIX no. 2 (1968) 63–72.

Literature, drama and music

655. BAUGH, ALBERT CROLL (*ed.*). A literary history of England. 2nd edn. Routledge, 1967. xv, 1796 pp. [Previous edn. 1950.]

656. PATTERSON, LYMAN RAY. Copyright and author's rights: a look at history. *Harvard Lib. Bull.*, XV (1967) 370–84.

657. BÉRANGER, JEAN. Les hommes de lettres et la politique en Angleterre de la révolution de 1688 à la mort de Georges Ier. Vol. 1. Bordeaux: Univ. Faculté des Lettres, 1968. 659 pp.

658. MCHUGH, ROGER, *and* EDWARDS, PHILIP. Jonathan Swift, 1667–1967: a Dublin tercentenary tribute. Dublin: Dolmen P., 1967. 231 pp., illus.

659. BIGNAMI, MARIALUISA. Le origini del giornalismo inglese. Bari: Adriatica (Tipo Sud), 1968. 351 pp.

660. NEUBURG, VICTOR EDWARD. The penny histories: a study of chapbooks for young readers over two centuries. O.U.P., 1968. 227 pp., illus.

661. STRAWSON, WILLIAM. The *London Quarterly and Holborn Review*, 1853–1968. *Church Quart.*, I no. 1 (1968) 41–52.

662. LESTER, JOHN A., *Jnr*. Journey through despair, 1880–1914: transformations in British literary culture. Princeton, N. J.: Princeton U.P., 1968. xxiii, 211 pp.

663. MANDER, RAYMOND, *and* MITCHENSON, JOE. The lost theatres of London. Hart-Davis, 1968. 576 pp., illus.

664. TROUBRIDGE, ST. VINCENT. The benefit system in the British theatre. Soc. Theatre Research, 1967. 172 pp.

665. YOUNG, PERCY MARSHALL. A history of British music. Benn, 1967. xi, 641 pp., illus.

666. WOODFILL, WALTER L. 'Patronage and music in England.' *In* Aspects of the Renaissance, *ed.* A. R. Lewis (Austin, Tex., London: Texas U.P., 1967) pp. 59–68.

667. LE HURAY, PETER. Music and the Reformation in England, 1549–1660. Jenkins, 1967. ix, 454 pp., illus.

668. WILSON, MICHAEL. The English chamber organ: history and development, 1650–1850. Cassirer, 1968. xix, 148 pp., illus.

669. ROSENTHAL, HAROLD. Opera at Covent Garden: a short history. Gollancz, 1967. 192 pp., illus.

Architecture

670. YARWOOD, DOREEN. The architecture of England: from prehistoric times to the present day. 2nd edn. Batsford, 1967. xvi, 680 pp., illus. [Previous edn. 1963.]

671. DANIELS, JEFFERY. Architecture in England. Weidenfeld, 1968. 128 pp., illus.

672. ALLSOPP, BRUCE (*ed.*). Historic architecture of Newcastle-upon-Tyne. Newcastle-upon-Tyne: Oriel P., 1967. 96 pp., illus.

673. STOLL, ROBERT THOMAS. Architecture and sculpture in early Britain: Celtic, Saxon, Norman. *Transl.* from German by J. M. Brownjohn. Thames & Hudson, 1967. 356 pp., illus. [Originally pubd. as *Britannia Romanica*. Vienna: A. Schroll, 1966.]

674. PEVSNER, *Sir* NIKOLAUS. Bedfordshire and the county of Huntingdon and Peterborough. (Buildings of England ser.). Harmondsworth, Middx.: Penguin, 1968. 414 pp., illus.

675. PEVSNER, *Sir* NIKOLAUS. Cumberland and Westmorland. (Buildings of England ser.). Harmondsworth, Middx.: Penguin, 1967. 339 pp., illus.

676. PEVSNER, *Sir* NIKOLAUS, *and* LLOYD, DAVID W. Hampshire and the Isle of Wight. (Buildings of England ser.). Harmondsworth, Middx.: Penguin, 1967. 832 pp., illus.

677. PEVSNER, *Sir* NIKOLAUS. Yorkshire: the West Riding. 2nd edn., *rev.* E. Radcliffe. (Buildings of England ser.). Harmondsworth, Middx.: Penguin, 1968. 652 pp., illus. [Previous edn. 1959.]

678. PEVSNER, *Sir* NIKOLAUS. Worcestershire. (Buildings of England ser.). Harmondsworth, Middx.: Penguin, 1968. 376 pp., illus.

679. LLOYD, DAVID W. Dorchester buildings. *Dorset Nat. Hist. & Archaeol. Soc. Proc.*, LXXXIX (1968) 181–217.

680. STEANE, J. M. Building materials used in Northampton and the area around. *Northants. Past & Present*, IV no. 2 (1967) 71–82.

681. CHERRY, B. Recent work on Romanesque art and architecture in the British Isles. *Anuario de Estudios Medievales* (1967) 467–87.

682. ARCHER, MILDRED. Indian architecture and the British, 1780–1830. Feltham, Middx.: Country Life Books, 1968. 64 pp., illus.

683. MARSTON, F. Cruck frames of Derbyshire, an interim report. *Derbys. Archaeol. Jour.* for 1967, LXXXVII (1968) 117–22.

684. BENNETT, JOHN DAVID. Leicestershire architects, 1700–1850. Leicester Museums, 1968. 68 pp., illus.

685. ADDLESHAW, G. W. O. Architects, sculptors, painters, craftsmen, 1660–1960, whose work is to be seen in York minster. *Archit. Hist.*, X (1967) 89–119.

686. CLIFTON-TAYLOR, ALEC. The cathedrals of England. Thames & Hudson, 1967. 288 pp., illus.

687. BETJEMAN, JOHN (*ed.*). Collins pocket guide to English parish churches. Rev. edn. Collins, 1968. 2 vols. [Previous edn. in one vol., 1958.]

688. SLADER, JOHN MALCOLM. The churches of Devon. Newton Abbot, Devon: David & Charles, 1968. 160 pp., illus.

689. BARNES, GORDON. Stepney churches: an historical account. Faith P., for Ecclesiological Soc., 1967. 123 pp., illus.

690. DOVE, WILLIAM W. The Temple Church and its restoration. *London &*

Middlesex Archaeol. Soc. Trans., XXI pt. 3 (1967) 164–71.

691. BRIGGS, G. W. D. Monolithic tracery in the churches of Northumberland. *Durham & Northumberland Archit. & Archaeol. Soc. Trans.*, n.s. I (1968) 73–83.

692. FISHER, M. J. C. The churches of the north Staffordshire moorlands. *N. Staffs. Jour. Field Studies*, VIII (1968) 54–69.

693. MCDOWALL, R. W. The church of St. George, Crowhurst, Surrey. *Surrey Archaeol. Coll.*, LXIV (1967) 148–53.

694. RENN, DEREK FRANK. The early church at Great Bookham. *Leatherhead & District Local Hist. Soc. Proc.*, III no. 1 (1967) 19–24.

695. PERCY, KAY. The church of St. Peter, Limpsfield, Surrey. *Surrey Archaeol. Coll.*, LXIV (1967) 154–9.

696. MCDOWALL, R. W. The church of St. John the Baptist, Puttenham. *Surrey Archaeol. Coll.*, LXV (1968) 105–10.

697. LEWIN, SYLVIA. The church of St. Nicholas, Pyrford. *Surrey Archaeol. Coll.*, LXV (1968) 111–15.

698. DENMAN, JOHN LEOPOLD. A short survey of the structural development of Sussex churches on behalf of the Sussex Historic Churches Trust. Chichester: the Trust, 1967. 63 pp., illus.

699. BRETTON, ROWLAND. Halifax parish church. *Halifax Antiq. Soc. Trans.* (1967) 73–91.

700. WELCH, CHARLES EDWIN. Dissenters' meeting houses in Plymouth, 1852–1939. *Devon Assoc. Repts. & Trans.*, XCIX (1967) 181–212.

701. MEADE, DOROTHY M. The hospital of St. Giles at Kepier, near Durham, 1112–1545. *Durham & Northumberland Archit. & Archaeol. Soc. Trans.*, n.s. I (1968) 45–57.

702. DAVISON, BRIAN K. The origins of the castle in England. *Archaeol. Jour.* for 1967, CXXIV (1968) 202–11.

703. SWAIN, ERIC R. Starkey Castle, Wouldham. *Archaeologia Cantiana* for 1966, LXXXI (1967) 118–25.

704. WATERER, JOHN W. Dunster Castle, Som., and its painted leather hangings. *Connoisseur*, CLXIV (1967) 142–7.

705. COLVIN, HOWARD MONTAGU. Royal buildings. Feltham, Middx.: Country Life Books, 1968. 64 pp., illus.

706. HEDLEY, OLWEN. Windsor Castle. Hale, 1967. 240 pp., illus.

707. HARRIS, JOHN, *and others.* Buckingham Palace. Nelson, 1968. 320 pp., illus.

708. HUDSON, DEREK. Kensington Palace. P. Davies, 1968. xvii, 141 pp., illus.

709. FORGE, JAMES WILLIAM LINDUS. Oatlands Palace. 3rd rev. edn. (Walton and Weybridge Hist. Soc. Papers, 1). Walton-on-Thames, Surrey: the Society, 1968. 24 pp., illus. [Previous edn. 1966.]

710. Athelhampton and its collections. *Connoisseur*, CLXVIII (1968) 1–7.

711. LEES-MILNE, JAMES. Sudeley Castle, Glos. *Connoisseur*, CLXIV (1967) 72–7.

712. POWELL, J. H. Highcliffe Castle, near Christchurch, Hampshire. *Ancient Monuments Soc. Trans.* for 1967–8, n.s. XV (1968) 83–94.

713. MUSGRAVE, CLIFFORD. Twyford House, Hants. *Connoisseur*, CLXVI (1967) 207–12.

714. BATES, LEONARD MAURICE. Somerset House: 400 years of history. Muller, 1967. x, 230 pp. illus.

715. HUDSON, DEREK. Holland House in Kensington. P. Davies, 1967. xviii, 142 pp., illus.

716. SAMBROOK, J. J. Honingham Hall, Norfolk. *Norfolk Archaeol.*, XXXIV pt. 3 (1968) 303–13.

717. WARD, JOHN TREVOR. The saving of a Yorkshire estate: George Lane-Fox and Bramham Park. *Yorks. Archaeol. Jour.*, XLII (1967) 63–71.

718. COOK, OLIVE. The English house through seven centuries. Nelson, 1968. 320 pp., illus.

719. CHESHER, VERONICA MARY, *and* CHESHER, F. J. The Cornishman's house: an introduction to the history of traditional domestic architecture in Cornwall. Truro, Cornwall: Barton, 1968. 142 pp., illus.

720. SMITH, JOHN THOMAS, *and* YATES, E. M. On the dating of English houses from external evidence. *Field Studies*, II (1968) 537–77.

721. BERESFORD, GUY. Northend Farm House, Long Crendon. *Records of Bucks.*, XVIII pt. 2 (1967) 125–35.

722. JENKINS, J. MARSHALL. Old House Museum, Bakewell. *Derbys. Archaeol. Jour.* for 1967, LXXXVII (1968) 130–48.

723. COPELAND, G. W. Devonshire church houses. Pt. 7. *Devon Assoc. Repts. & Trans.*, XCIX (1967) 263–8.

724. ALCOCK, N. W. Devon farmhouses. Pt. 1. *Devon Assoc. Repts. & Trans.*, C (1968) 13–28.

725. DUTTON, RALPH. Hinton Ampner: a Hampshire manor. Batsford, 1968. 136 pp., illus.

726. TONKIN, J. W. An introduction to the houses of Herefordshire. *Woolhope Naturalists' F.C. Trans.*, XXXIX (1968) 186–97.

727. PARKIN, E. W. Vanishing houses of Kent. 6, The old cottage at Upper Hardres. *Archaeologia Cantiana* for 1966, LXXXI (1967) 53–61.

728. PARKIN, E. W. Vanishing houses of Kent. 7, Harringe Court, Sellindge. *Archaeologia Cantiana* for 1967, LXXXII (1968) 257–62.

729. HULL, FELIX. The Spittlehouse of Key Street. *Archaeologia Cantiana* for 1966, LXXXII (1967) 179–83.

730. COLMAN, SYLVIA. Two small medieval houses: Walnut Tree cottage, Wattisfield and Friars Hall, Rattlesden, the effects of modernisation. *Suffolk Inst. Archaeol. Proc.* for 1967, XXXI (1968) 64–71.

731. SMALLWOOD, FRANK T. The story of Terrace House, Battersea (Old Battersea House). *Surrey Archaeol. Coll.*, LXIV (1967) 91–112.

732. BARTLETT, ROBINA. Elmfield House, Teddington. (Twickenham Local Hist. Soc. Papers, 9). Twickenham, Middx.: the Society, 1967. 30 pp., illus.

733. STEER, FRANCIS WILLIAM. The John Edes House, West Street, Chichester. (Chichester Papers, 52). Chichester, Sussex: West Sussex C.C., 1968. 15 pp., illus.

734. TONKIN, J. W. The White House, Aston Munslow. *Shropshire Archaeol. Soc. Trans.* for 1966, LVIII pt. 2 (1968) 140–52.

735. WEST, STANLEY E. Griff manor house (Sudeley Castle), Warwickshire. *Brit. Archaeol. Assoc. Jour.*, 3rd ser. XXXI (1968) 76–101.

736. LEATHERBARROW, J. S. Some Worcestershire parsonages. *Worcs. Archaeol. Soc. Trans.* for 1964, n.s. XLI (1967) 36–54.

737. WEBSTER, C. D. Clare Hall, Halifax. *Halifax Antiq. Soc. Trans.* (1967) 123–37.

738. BRETTON, ROWLAND. Heath Hall, Skircoat. *Halifax Antiq. Soc. Trans.* (1968) 1–14.

739. LOMAS, JONATHAN. The old doors and doorways of Barnstaple. *Devon Assoc. Repts. & Trans.*, XCIX (1967) 37–48.

740. DOLBY, M. J. The Whitwell tithe barn. *Derbys. Archaeol. Jour.* for 1966, LXXXVI (1967) 106–11.

741. ROWAN, ALISTAIR. Garden buildings. Feltham, Middx.: Country Life Books, 1968. 64 pp., illus. [1620–1860.]

742. CAIGER, JOHN E. L. The Vale Mascal bath house. *Archaeologia Cantiana* for 1967, LXXXII (1968) 227–34.

743. WILD, J. Halifax railway station. *Halifax Antiq. Soc. Trans.* (1967) 27–35.

Arts and crafts

744. HUTCHINSON, SIDNEY CHARLES. The history of the Royal Academy, 1768–1968. Chapman & Hall, 1968. 268 pp., illus.

745. CLIFTON-TAYLOR, ALEC. Two hundred years of the Royal Academy. *Connoisseur*, CLXVIII (1968) 229–32.

746. SCHRIJVER, ELKA. Dutch prints of Anglo-Dutch history. *History Today*, XVIII (1968) 622–8.

747. GLOAG, JOHN EDWARDS. Georgian grace: a social history of design from 1660 to 1830. New edn. Spring Books, 1967. xix, 426 pp., illus. [Previous edn. Black, 1956.]

748. GEORGE, MARY DOROTHY. Hogarth to Cruikshank: social change in graphic satire. Penguin P., 1967. 224 pp., illus.

749. MARKS, ARTHUR S. David Wilkie's 'Letter of Introduction'. *Burlington Mag.*, CX (1968) 125–33.

750. NEGUS, *Sir* VICTOR EWINGS. Artistic possessions at the Royal College of Surgeons of England. Edinburgh, London: E. & S. Livingstone, 1967. xii, 212 pp.

751. ROGERS, JOHN CHARLES. English furniture. Rev. edn. by M. Jourdain. Feltham, Middx.: Spring Books, 1968. 244 pp. [Previous edn. 1950.]

752. WOLSEY, SAMUEL WILFRED, *and* LUFF, R. W. P. Furniture in England: the age of the joiner. Barker, 1968. 105 pp., illus. [1550–1660.]

753. COLERIDGE, ANTHONY. English furniture and cabinet makers at Hatfield House, *c.* 1600–1823. *Burlington Mag.*, CIX (1967) 63–8, 201–9.

754. GILBERT, CHRISTOPHER. The Temple

Newsam furniture bills. *Furniture Hist.*, III (1967) 16–28. [1663–1774.]

755. CROMPTON, SIDNEY (*ed.*). English glass. Ward Lock, 1967. 255 pp., illus.

756. HUGHES, THERLE, *and* HUGHES, BERNARD. English painted enamels. New edn. Spring Books, 1967. 156 pp., illus. [Previous edn. Country Life, 1951.]

757. LEVINE, GEORGE. Norwich goldsmiths' marks. *Norfolk Archaeol.*, XXXIV pt. 3 (1968) 293–302.

758. RIDGWAY, MAURICE HILL. Chester goldsmiths from early times to 1726. Altrincham, Cheshire: Sherratt, 1968. xvi, 198 pp., illus. [Reprinted from *Chester and N. Wales Archit., Archaeol. and Hist. Soc. Jour.*, 1968.]

759. CRIPPS, WILFRED JOSEPH. Old English plate: ecclesiastical. decorative and domestic: its makers and marks. New edn. Spring Books, 1967. xxvi, 540 pp., illus. [Previous edn. John Murray, 1926.]

760. GILCHRIST, JAMES. Anglican church plate. Connoisseur, M. Joseph, 1967. 120 pp., illus.

761. PEPLOW, WILLIAM AUGUSTUS, *and* PEPLOW, W. R. H. Church plate of the archdeaconry of Worcester and the cathedral church. Stourbridge, Worcs.: Mark & Moody Ltd., 1967. 124 pp. illus.

762. DAVEY, LESLIE STUART. The civic insignia and plate of the Corporation of Lewes. Lewes, Sussex: Lewes Corporation, 1967. 32 pp., illus.

763. OMAN, CHARLES. The civic plate and insignia of the city of York. *Connoisseur*, CLXVI (1967) 71–3, 138–43.

764. LAWRANCE, DAVID. English silver from the 16th century to the 19th century. Melbourne, London: O.U.P., 1968. 31 pp., illus.

765. OMAN, CHARLES. English domestic silver. 7th edn. Black, 1968. xii, 240 pp., illus. [Previous edn. 1965.]

766. HALLS, HENRY. 'Essex' copper plate: copper fire plates issued by the Essex and Suffolk Insurance Co. Ltd. between 1802–29. Guardian Royal Exchange Group, 1968. 37 pp.

767. GOAMAN, MURIEL. English clocks. The Connoisseur, 1967. 119 pp., illus.

768. BELLCHAMBERS, JACK KENNETH. Somerset clockmakers. (Antiquarian Horological Soc. Monographs, 4). The Society, 1968. 79 pp., illus. [To 1894.]

769. GOODISON, NICHOLAS. Clocks in the collection of Lord Harris at Belmont Park, Kent. *Connoisseur*, CLXVIII (1968) 72–81, 149–57.

770. KENDRICK, ALBERT FRANK. English needlework. 2nd. edn., *rev.* P. Wardle. Black, 1967. xvi, 212 pp., illus. [Previous edn. 1933.]

771. ATKINSON, D. R. Further notes on Sussex clay tobacco pipes and pipe makers. *Sussex N. & Q.*, XVI no.9 (1967) 312–17, XVII no. 1 (1968) 11–14.

SCIENCE AND MEDICINE

772. MARTIN, D. C. Former homes of the Royal Society. *Roy. Soc. Notes & Records*, XXII (1967) 12–19.

773. CARDWELL, DONALD STEPHEN LOWELL. Some factors in the early development of the concepts of power, work and energy. *Brit. Jour. Hist. Science*, III (1967) 209–24.

774. DEBUS, ALLEN G. Fire analysis and the elements in the 16th and 17th centuries. *Annals of Science*, XXIII (1967) 127–47.

775. DEBUS, A. G. Palissy, Plat and English agricultural chemistry in the 16th and 17th centuries. *Archives Internat. d'Hist. des Sciences*, XXI (1968) 67–88.

776. NOVY, LUBOS. L'école algébrique anglaise. *Rev. Synthèse*, LXXXIX (1968) 211–22.

777. RONAN, COLIN ALISTAIR. Their Majesties' astronomers: a survey of astronomy in Britain between the two Elizabeths. Bodley Head, 1967. xi, 240 pp., illus.

778. ALLAN, MEA. The Hookers of Kew, 1785–1911. Joseph, 1967. 273 pp., illus.

779. MINNEY, RUBEIGH JAMES. The two pillars of Charing Cross: the story of a famous hospital. Cassell, 1967. xiv, 235 pp., illus.

780. ANNING, STEPHEN TOWERS. The General Infirmary at Leeds, 1767–1967. *Univ. Leeds Rev.*, X (1966–7) 349–57.

781. HURRELL, GEORGE. The history of Newcastle General Hospital. Newcastle-upon-Tyne: Hospital Management Committee, 1967. x, 118 pp.

782. SALISBURY GENERAL HOSPITAL. Salisbury 200: the bi-centenary of Salisbury Infirmary, 1766–1966. Salisbury, Wilts.: Salisbury General Hospital, 1967. 162 pp., illus.

783. MCCONAGHEY, R. M. S. The evolution of the cottage hospital. *Medical Hist.*, XI (1967) 128–40.

784. SHAW, A. BATTY. The oldest medical societies in Great Britain. *Medical Hist.*, XII (1968) 232–44.

785. COPEMAN, WILLIAM SYDNEY CHARLES. The Worshipful Society of Apothecaries of London: a history, 1617–1967. Oxford, London: Pergamon, 1967. 112 pp., illus.

786. GRIFFIN, NICHOLAS. Epidemics in Loughborough, 1539–1640. *Leics. Archaeol. Soc. Trans.* for 1967–8, XLIII (1968) 24–34.

787. MACNALTY, *Sir* ARTHUR SALUSBURY. The prevention of small pox: from Edward Jenner to Monckton Copeman. *Medical Hist.*, XII (1968) 1–18.

788. BRITISH MEDICAL JOURNAL. Porphyria: a royal malady: articles published in or commissioned by the *British Medical Journal*. British Medical Association, 1968. vii, 68 pp., illus.

789. STEWART, GRACE G. A history of the medicinal use of tobacco, 1492–1860. *Medical Hist.*, XI (1967) 228–68.

790. HOELDTKE, ROBERT. The history of associationisms and British medical psychology. *Medical Hist.*, XI (1967) 46–65.

791. HARVEY, WARREN. Some dental and social conditions of 1696–1852 connected with St. Bride's church, Fleet Street, London. *Medical Hist.*, XII (1968) 62–75.

792. WELLS, CALVIN. Dental pathology from a Norwich, Norfolk, burial ground. *Jour. Hist. Medicine & Allied Sciences*, XXIII (1968) 372–9.

MILITARY HISTORY

793. YOUNG, PETER. The British army. Kimber, 1967. 286 pp., illus.

794. COUSINS, GEOFFREY. The defenders: a history of the British volunteer. Muller, 1968. 224 pp., illus.

795. HARGREAVES, REGINALD. 'Poor profligate wretch'. *Quart. Rev.*, CCCV (1967) 318–29. [The soldier.]

796. HARGREAVES, R. The bloodybacks: the British serviceman in North America and the Caribbean, 1655–1783. Hart-Davis, 1968. 368 pp.

797. DREW, *Sir* ROBERT (*comp.*). Commissioned officers in the medical services of the British Army, 1660–1960. (Wellcome Hist. Medical Lib. Monograph ser., 14). The Library, 1968. 2 vols. [Vol. 1 originally pubd. Aberdeen U.P. 1917, here reprinted.]

798. FRENCH BLAKE, ROBERT LIFFORD VALENTINE. The 17th-21st Lancers. Hamilton, 1968. 173 pp., illus.

799. HASWELL, JOCK. The Queen's Royal Regiment (West Surrey; the 2nd Regiment of Foot). Hamilton, 1967. 153 pp., illus.

800. FOSS, MICHAEL. The Royal Fusiliers (the 7th Regiment of Foot). Hamilton, 1967. 154 pp.

801. CAREW, TIM. The Royal Norfolk Regiment (the 9th Regiment of Foot). Hamilton, 1967. 157 pp., illus.

802. POPHAM, HUGH. The Somerset Light Infantry (Prince Albert's; 13th Regiment of Foot). Hamilton, 1968. 151 pp., illus.

803. POWELL, GEOFFREY. The Green Howards (the 19th Regiment of Foot). Hamilton, 1968. 144 pp., illus.

804. ADAMS, JACK. The South Wales Borderers (the 24th Regiment of Foot). Hamilton, 1968. 157 pp., illus.

805. WYKES, ALAN. The Royal Hampshire Regiment (37th-67th Regiments of Foot). Hamilton, 1968. 128 pp., illus.

806. HOWARD, PHILIP. The Black Watch (Royal Highland Regiment; 42nd Regiment of Foot). Hamilton, 1968. 141 pp., illus.

807. MYATT, FREDERICK. The Royal Berkshire Regiment (49th-66th Regiments of Foot). Hamilton, 1968. 136 pp., illus.

808. WOOD, HERBERT FAIRLIE. The King's Royal Rifle Corps (the 60th Regiment of Foot). Hamilton, 1967. 149 pp., illus.

809. CREIGHTON-WILLIAMSON, DONALD. The York and Lancaster Regiment (65th and 84th Regiments of Foot). Leo Cooper Ltd., 1968. 135 pp., illus.

810. SINCLAIR-STEVENSON, CHRISTOPHER. The Gordon Highlanders. Hamilton, 1968. 133 pp., illus.

811. SAUNDERS, A. D. Hampshire coastal defence since the introduction of artillery with a description of Fort Wallington. *Archaeol. Jour.* for 1966, CXXIII (1967) 136–71.

812. CURPHEY, R. A. The coastal batteries. *Manx Museum Jour.*, VII no. 83 (1967) 50–7, VII no. 84 (1968) 89–92.

813. KING, *Sir* EDWIN. The Knights of St. John in the British realm: being the official history of the Most Venerable Order of the Hospital of St. John of Jerusalem. 3rd edn., *rev.* Sir Harry Luke. The Order, 1968. xxiii, 307 pp., illus. [Previous edn. as *Knights of St. John in the British Empire* (1934).]

NAVAL AND MARITIME HISTORY

814. GARDINER, LESLIE. The British Admiralty. Edinburgh, London: Blackwood, 1968. 418 pp., illus.

815. ARCHIBALD, EDWARD HUNTER HOLMES. The wooden fighting ship in the Royal Navy, A.D. 897–1860. Blandford P., 1968. 174 pp., illus.

816. LLOYD, CHRISTOPHER. The British seaman, 1200–1860: a social survey. Collins, 1968. 319 pp., illus.

817. LLOYD, C. The press gang and the law. *History Today*, XVII (1967) 683–90.

818. HAMMAR, MAGNUS. Ett hundra år brittisk maritim strategi, 1867–1967. *Aktuellt och Historisk* (1968) 23–64. ['One hundred years of British naval strategy'.]

819. LIPSCOMB, FRANK WOODGATE. Heritage of sea power: the story of Portsmouth. Hutchinson, 1967. 256 pp., illus.

820. NORTH, DOUGLASS C. Sources of productivity change in ocean shipping, 1660–1850. *Jour. Polit. Econ.*, LXXVI (1968) 953–70.

821. FISHER, HAROLD EDWARD STEPHEN (*ed.*). The South West and the sea: papers of a seminar on the maritime history of the South West of England. (Exeter Papers in Economic Hist., 1). Exeter, Devon: the University, 1968. 73 pp. [Contains: 'The South West and the Atlantic trades, 1660–1770' by H. E. S. Fisher, pp. 7–14; 'British shipping and British North American shipbuilding in the early 19th century, with special reference to Prince Edward Island' by R. S. Craig, pp. 21–37; 'Shipping of the port of Dartmouth in the 19th century' by J. E. Horsley, pp. 45–55; 'Custom House registers of the West Country' by G. Farr, pp. 57–71.]

822. OPPENHEIM, MICHAEL. The maritime history of Devon. Exeter, Devon: the University, 1968. xxv, 175 pp., illus.

823. STOREY, ARTHUR. Trinity House of Kingston-upon-Hull. Hull, Yorks.: Trinity House, 1967. 146 pp., illus.

824. NOALL, CYRIL. Cornish lights and shipwrecks. Truro, Cornwall: Barton, 1968. 170 pp., illus.

825. DE BOER, GEORGE. A history of the Spurn lighthouses. (East Yorks. Local Hist. ser., 24). York: the Society, 1968. 72 pp., illus.

826. PERKS, RICHARD HUGH. A history of Faversham sailing barges. Billericay, Essex: Soc. for Spritsail Barge Research, 1967. 30 pp. illus.

827. SALISBURY, WILLIAM. Early tonnage measurement in England. Pt. 4, Rules used by shipwrights and merchants. Pt. 5, Colliers, deadweight and displacement tonnage. *Mariner's Mirror*, LIII (1967) 251–64, LIV (1968) 69–76.

828. SALAMAN, R. A. Tools of the shipwright, 1650–1925. *Folk Life*, V (1967) 19–51.

829. HOLE, CHRISTINA. Superstitions and beliefs of the sea. *Folklore*, LXXVIII (1967) 184–9.

FOREIGN RELATIONS

830. WOODWARD, *Sir* ERNEST LLEWELLYN. British foreign policy in retrospect. *Internat. Jour.*, XXIII (1968) 507–19.

831. NALIVAJKO, F. Les pourparlers d' alliance entre la France et l'Angleterre. *Annuaire d'Études Françaises* (1966) 107–122.

832. SCHMITT, BERNADOTTE EVERLY. England and Germany, 1740–1914. New York: Fertig, 1967. viii, 524 pp.

833. GIFFORD, PROSSER, *and others* (*eds.*). Britain and Germany in Africa: imperial rivalry and colonial rule. New Haven, Conn., London: Yale U.P., 1968. xvii, 825 pp. [Contains: 'Great Britain and German expansion in Africa, 1884–1919' by W. R. Louis, pp. 3–46; 'The Brussels Conference of 1889–90: the place of the slave trade in the policies of Great Britain and Germany' by S. Miers, pp. 83–118; 'Origins of the Nile struggle: Anglo-German negotiations and the Mackinnon Agreement of 1890' by R. O. Collins, pp. 119–52; 'Anglo-German rivalry and the Algeciras Conference' by S. L. Mayer, pp. 215–44; 'Anglo-German rivalry in Belgian and Portuguese Africa?' by J. Willequet, pp. 245–74; 'The British government and the disposition of the German colonies in Africa, 1914–18' by G. Smith, pp. 275–300; 'The hard death of imperialism: German and British colonial attitudes, 1919–39' by W. W. Schmokel, pp. 301–36; 'British and German imperial rivalry: a conclusion' by J. Stengers, pp. 337–50; 'The spread of Christianity: British and German missions in Africa' by K. S. Latourette, pp. 393–416; 'The British in the Cameroons, 1919–39' by D. E. Gardiner, pp. 513–56; 'The official mind of indirect rule: British policy in Tanganyika, 1916–39' by R. A. Austen, pp. 577–606; 'Resistance and rebellion in British Nyasaland and German East Africa, 1888–1915: a tentative comparison' by R. I. Rotberg, pp. 667–90; 'British and German colonial rule: a synthesis and summary' by J. D. Fage, pp. 691–708.]

834. PAUL, HANS. Britische Reiseberichte über unsere Heimat aus dem 17.–19. Jahrhundert. *Burgenländ. Heimatbl.*, XXIX (1967) 107–16.

835. BROMLEY, J. S., *and* KOSSMANN, E. H. (*eds.*). Britain and the Netherlands in Europe and Asia: papers delivered to the third Anglo-Dutch Historical Conference, 1966. Macmillan, 1968. 264 pp. [Contains: 'English attitudes to Europe in the 17th century' by J. R. Jones, pp. 37–55; 'Early English trade and settlement in Asia, 1602–90' by D. K. Bassett, pp. 83–109; 'Britain as a European power from her Glorious Revolution to the French revolutionary war' by A. C. Carter, pp. 110–37; 'England and Europe, 1815–1914' by A. Davies, pp. 160–73; 'Britain as an imperial power in S. E. Asia in the 19th century' by J. S. Bastin, pp. 174–90; 'The British retreat from empire' by A. J. Hanna, pp. 234–56.]

836. POLIŠENSKÝ, JOSEF VINCENT. Britain and Czechoslovakia: a study in contacts. Prague: Orbis, 1966. 96 pp.

837. NICHOLS, PETER. Piedmont and the English. Evelyn, 1967. xi, 136 pp., illus.

838. CRINÒ, ANNA MARIA. Italiani in Inghilterra dal trecento ai nostri giorni. *Archivio Storico Italiano*, CXXVI (1968) 363–71

839. STEENSGAARD, NIELS. Consuls and nations in the Levant from 1570 to 1650. *Scandinavian Econ. Hist. Rev.*, XV (1967) 13–55.

840. MAJUMDAR, KANCHANMOY. British attitude to Nepal's relations with Tibet and China. *Bengal Past & Present*, LXXXVI (1967) 169–84.

841. CHANG, I-TUNG. The earliest contacts between China and England. *Chinese Studies in Hist. & Philos.*, I (1968) 53–88.

842. PLATT, DESMOND CHRISTOPHER ST. MARTIN. British diplomacy in Latin America since the emancipation. *Inter-American Econ. Affairs*, XXI no. 3 (1967) 21–42.

843. LYNCH, JOHN. 'La política británica e Hispanoamérica'. *In* 4o Congreso Internacional de Historia de América, Buenos Aires, 1966, vol. 6. (Buenos Aires: Acad. Nacional de la Hist., 1967) pp. 427–60.

ENGLISH LOCAL HISTORY AND TOPOGRAPHY

GENERAL

844. FINBERG, HERBERT PATRICK REGINALD, *and* SKIPP, VICTOR HENRY THOMAS. Local history: objective and pursuit. Newton Abbot, Devon: David & Charles, 1967. ix, 132 pp.

845. HOSKINS, WILLIAM GEORGE. Fieldwork in local history. Faber, 1967. 192 pp., illus.

846. BIDDLE, MARTIN. Archaeology and the history of British towns. *Antiquity*, XLII (1968) 109–16.

847. BRILL, EDITH. Old Cotswold. Newton Abbot, Devon: David & Charles, 1968. 192 pp., illus.

848. MUNBY, LIONEL MAXWELL (*ed.*). East Anglian studies. Cambridge: Heffer, 1968. xiii, 207 pp., illus. [Contains: 'The Suffolk landscape' by D. P. Dymond, pp. 17–47; 'Clopton: the life-cycle of a Cambridgeshire village' by J. A. Alexander, pp. 48–70; 'Smaller post-medieval houses in eastern England' by P. Eden, pp. 71–93; 'Landbeach in 1549: Ket's Rebellion in miniature' by J. R. Ravensdale, pp. 94–116; 'Politics and religion in Hertfordshire, 1660–1740' by L. M. Munby; 'Colchester in the 18th century' by A. F. J. Brown, pp. 146–73.]

849. ALDERSON, FREDERICK. View North: a long look at northern England. Newton Abbot, Devon: David & Charles, 1968. 285 pp., illus.

850. RAISTRICK, ARTHUR. The Pennine dales. Eyre & Spottiswoode, 1968. 236 pp., illus.

851. CAMERON, KENNETH. '*Eccles* in English place-names'. *In* Christianity in Britain, 300–700, *ed.* M. W. Barley *and* R. P. C. Hanson (Leicester: Leicester U.P., 1968) pp. 87–92.

852. DODGSON, JOHN MCNEAL. The significance of the distribution of the English place-name in *-ingas*, *-nga-* in south east England. *Medieval Archaeol.* for 1966, X (1967) 1–29.

853. DODGSON, J. M. Various forms of Old English *-ing* in English place-names. *Beitr. zur Namenforschung*, II (1967) 325–96, III (1968) 141–89.

854. DODGSON, J. M. The *-ing* in English place-names like Birmingham and Altringham. *Beitr. zur Namenforschung*, II (1967) 221–45.

855. GELLING, MARGARET. English place-names derived from the compound *Wīchām*. *Medieval Archaeol.* for 1967, XI (1968) 87–104.

856. RAMSEY, A. R. J. The history of technology in place names. *Amateur Historian*, VII (1967) 146–9, 192–5, 250–2, *Local Historian*, VIII (1968) 16–21.

ENGLISH COUNTIES

Berkshire

857. HOWSE, JASMINE SUSAN. Denchworth through the centuries. Faringdon, Berks.: the author, 1967. 103 pp., illus.

858. SHORLAND, EILEEN (*comp.*). The parish of Warfield and Easthampstead which includes the Old Bracknell. Bracknell, Berks.: the compiler, 1967. 106 pp., illus.

Buckinghamshire

859. JENKINS, JOHN GILBERT. Chequers: a history of the Prime Minister's Buckinghamshire home. Oxford, London: Pergamon, 1967. xiii, 171 pp., illus.

Cheshire

860. TURNER, A. G. C. Some Celtic traces in Cheshire and the Pennines. *Board of Celtic Studies Bull.*, XXII pt. 2 (1967) 111–19.

861. DODGSON, JOHN MCNEAL. Place-names and street-names at Chester. *Chester Archaeol. Soc. Jour.*, LV (1968) 29–61.

862. DODGSON, J. M. The English arrival in Cheshire. *Hist. Soc. Lancs. & Cheshire Trans.* for 1967, CXIX (1968) 1–37.

863. SYLVESTER, DOROTHY. Parish and township in Cheshire and north east Wales. *Chester Archaeol. Soc. Jour.*, LIV (1967) 23–35.

Cornwall

864. THOMAS, CHARLES. Further coast and cliff-names of Gwithian and the north cliffs. *Roy. Inst. Cornwall Jour.*, n.s. V (1967) 291–6.

865. TANGYE, MICHAEL. Portreath: some chapters in its history. Redruth, Cornwall: Olson, 1968. 40 pp.

Devon

866. GOAMAN, MURIEL. Old Bideford and district. Bideford, Devon: E. M. & A. G. Cox, 1968. 96 pp., illus.

867. SLEE, A. H. Braunton marshes. *Devon Assoc. Repts. & Trans.*, C (1968) 101–10.

868. SOMERS COCKS, JOHN VERNON. The boundary of the forest of Dartmoor on the north eastern side. *Devon & Cornwall N. & Q.*, XXX (1967) 214–19, 284–7.

869. WALKER, HILDA H. Occombe in the parish of Marldon, south Devon: an historical survey. *Devon Assoc. Repts. & Trans.*, C (1968) 143–60.

870. WALKER, H. H. The Causeway near Torre abbey in south Devon. *Devon Assoc. Repts. & Trans.*, C (1968) 125–42.

Dorset

871. KERR, BARBARA. Dorset fields and their names. *Dorset Nat. Hist. & Archaeol. Soc. Proc.*, LXXXIX (1968) 233–56.

872. TAYLOR, C. C. Lost Dorset place-names. *Dorset Nat. Hist. & Archaeol. Soc. Proc.*, LXXXVIII (1967) 207–15.

873. BROCKLEBANK, JOAN. Affpuddle in the county of Dorset, A.D. 987–1953. Bournemouth: Horace G. Cummin Ltd., 1968. 126 pp., illus.

874. WARREN, P. J. K. The story of Holt church and Holt Forest, Wimborne. *Dorset Nat. Hist. & Archaeol. Soc. Proc.*, LXXXVIII (1967) 188–202.

875. SHORT, BERNARD CHARLES. The Isle of Purbeck. Poole, Dorset: J. Looker Ltd., 1967. vii, 109 pp., illus.

Durham

876. SUNDERLAND, NORMAN. A history of Darlington. Darlington, Durham: Darlington Hist. Soc., 1967. 115 pp., illus.

877. BENNETT, CHRISTOPHER. Washington local history. Washington, Durham: the author, 1967. 38 pp., illus.

Gloucestershire

878. ELRINGTON, CHRISTOPHER ROBIN (*ed.*). The Victoria history of the county of Gloucester. Vol. 8. O.U.P., for Inst. Hist. Research, 1968. xxiii, 311 pp., illus.

879. SMITH, BRIAN STANLEY (*ed.*). Gloucestershire historical studies: essays on local historical records by the University Extra Mural class at Gloucester. Bristol Univ., 1968. 43 ff.

880. MACINNES, CHARLES MALCOLM. A gateway of empire. Rev. edn. Newton Abbot, Devon: David & Charles, 1968. 456 pp., illus. [Bristol to 1929. Previous edn. Bristol: Arrowsmith, 1939.]

Hampshire

881. SEYMOUR, WILLIAM. The New Forest from Norman times. *History Today*, XVIII (1968) 614–21.

882. SPRAKE, RAYMOND FREDERICK. Shalfleet, Isle of Wight: some notes on a country parish. Yarmouth, I.O.W.: the author, 1967. 87 pp., illus.

Herefordshire

883. TONKIN, J. W. Early street-names of Hereford. *Woolhope Naturalists' F.C. Trans.* for 1966, XXXVIII (1967) 236–50.

Kent

884. FILMER, REGINALD MEAD. A chronicle of Kent, 1250–1760. Clear Copies, 1967. 206 pp.

885. CHURCH, RICHARD. Portrait of Canterbury. Rev. edn. Hutchinson, 1968. 224 pp., illus. [Previous edn. 1953.]

886. DANE, HERBERT (*comp.*). The story of a thousand years: a chronology of Faversham's history. (Faversham Papers, 5). Faversham, Kent: Faversham Soc., 1968. vii, 62 pp.

887. BUCKINGHAM, CHRISTOPHER. Lydden: a parish history. Dover, Kent: Thomas Becket Books, 1967. 98 pp., illus.

888. PENN, W. S. History of the Springhead pleasure gardens and watercress plantation (*c.* 1805–1936). *Archaeologia Cantiana* for 1966, LXXXI (1967) 62–78.

Lancashire

889. BAGLEY, JOHN JOSEPH. A history of Lancashire. 4th edn. Beaconsfield, Bucks.: Darwen Finlayson, 1967. 72 pp., illus. [Previous edn. 1964.]

890. BARNES, FRED. Barrow and district. 2nd edn. Barrow-in-Furness, Lancs.: the Corporation, 1968. 136 pp., illus. [Previous edn. 1951.]

891. JOHNSTON, FRANCIS RAYMOND. Eccles: the growth of a Lancashire town. Eccles, Lancs.: Eccles & District Hist. Soc., 1967. viii, 147 pp.

892. THOMSON, WILFRID HARRY. History of Manchester to 1852. Altrincham, Cheshire: Sherratt, 1968. xvii, 443 pp., illus.

London and Middlesex

893. LIPMAN, VIVIAN DAVID. The rise of Jewish suburbia. *Jewish Hist. Soc. Eng. Trans.* for 1962–7, XXI (1968) 78–103.

894. LEECH, KENNETH. The role of immigration in recent east London history. *East London Papers*, X (1967) 3–18.

895. HACKNEY PUBLIC LIBRARIES. A short history of the London Borough of Hackney. The Libraries, 1967. 16 pp., illus.

896. BENTWICH, HELEN CAROLINE. The Vale of Health on Hampstead Heath, 1777–1967. High Hill P., 1968. 96 pp., illus.

897. SAUNDERS, ANN. Marylebone Park. *London & Middlesex Archaeol. Soc. Trans.*, XXI pt. 3 (1967) 178–88.

898. LEFF, VERA, *and* BLUNDEN, GEOFFREY HALSTEAD. The story of Tower Hamlets. Research Writers (Pubns.), 1967. 160 pp., illus.

899. BALDWIN, K. G. A place called Feltham. Hounslow, Middx.: Hounslow & District Hist. Soc., 1967. 41 pp.

900. CLARK, NANCY. Hadley Wood: its background and development. Ward Lock, 1968. 128 pp., illus.

901. DAVIS, KENNETH RUTHERFORD (*ed.*). The story of Potters Bar and South Mimms. Potters Bar, Herts.: Potters Bar U.D.C., 1967. 144 pp., illus.

Northumberland

902. GRAHAM, FRANK. Bamburgh and the Farne Islands. 2nd edn. Newcastle-upon-Tyne: H. Hill & Son, 1967. 45 pp., illus. [Previous edn. 1962.]

Nottinghamshire

903. HEATH, JOHN EDWIN PERCIVAL. A brief history of Long Eaton and Sawley from 1750–1914. Long Eaton, Notts.: Long Eaton U.D.C., 1967. 138 pp., illus.

904. THOMIS, MALCOLM IAN. Old Nottingham. Newton Abbot, Devon: David & Charles, 1968. 200 pp., illus.

Oxfordshire

905. HARVEY, PAUL DEAN ADSHEAD. Where were Banbury's crosses? *Cake & Cockhorse*, III (1967) 183–91.

906. HARVEY, P. D. A. Where was Banbury Cross? *Oxoniensia* for 1966, XXXI (1968) 82–106.

907. FEARON, J. H. Some notes on Bodicote. *Cake & Cockhorse*, III (1967) 131–45.

908. FISHER, ARTHUR STANLEY THEODORE. The history of Broadwell, Oxfordshire. Burford, Oxon.: the author, 1968. iii, 122 pp., illus.

Shropshire

909. GAYDON, A. T. (*ed.*). The Victoria history of Shropshire. Vol. 8. O.U.P., for Inst. Hist. Research, 1968. xx, 356 pp., illus.

910. MOTT, REGINALD ARTHUR. Coalbrookdale story: facts and fantasies. *Shropshire Archaeol. Soc. Trans.* for 1966, LVIII pt. 2 (1968) 153–66.

911. LLOYD, LLEWELYN CYRIL (*ed.*). Borough of Much Wenlock, 1468–1968. Much Wenlock, Salop: Borough Council, 1968. 53 pp.

Somerset

912. KELTING, E. L. The rivers and sea walls of Somerset. *Somerset Archaeol. & Nat. Hist. Soc. Proc.*, CXII (1968) 12–20.

913. LITTLE, BRYAN. Bath portrait: the story of Bath, its life and its buildings. 2nd edn. Bristol: Burleigh P., 1968. x, 132 pp., illus. [Previous edn. 1961.]

914. SQUIBBS, PHILIP JAMES. A Bridgwater diary, 1800–1967. Bridgwater, Som.: the author, 1968. 214 pp., illus.

915. BRISTOL UNIVERSITY. DEPT. OF EXTRA-MURAL STUDIES. Wrington village records: studies of the history of a Somerset village. Bristol: the Dept., 1967. 119 pp., illus.

Staffordshire

916. GREENSLADE, MICHAEL WASHINGTON, *and* JENKINS, JOHN GILBERT (*eds.*). The Victoria history of the county of Stafford. Vol. 2, with index to vols. 1 and 2. O.U.P., for Inst. Hist. Research, 1967. xxiv, 416 pp., illus.

Suffolk

917. MUNDAY, J. T. Eriswell: the layout of a fen-edge village. *Suffolk Rev.*, III (1968) 196–201.

918. JOBSON, ALLAN. The Felixstowe story. Hale, 1968. 192 pp., illus.

919. IVIMEY, ALAN (*ed.*). Westleton from the 1830s to the 1960s: survey of a Suffolk village. Saxmundham, Suffolk: W.E.A. (Westleton Branch), 1968. 106 pp., illus.

Surrey

920. EVANS, J. A. The woodlands of the Great Bookham area, 1790–1840. *Leatherhead & District Local Hist. Soc. Proc.*, III no. 1 (1967) 27–32.

921. BENGER, F. B. Leatherhead common meadow. *Leatherhead & District Local Hist. Soc. Proc.*, III no. 2 (1968) 51–5.

922. SMITH, G. H. A history of the church and advowson of St. Mary and St. Nicholas, Leatherhead. Pts. 7–9. *Leatherhead & District Local Hist. Soc. Proc.*, III no. 1 (1967) 33–41, III no. 2 (1968) 70–4. [Contd. from vol. II.]

923. TITFORD, C. F. The Great Park of Nonsuch. *Surrey Archaeol. Coll.*, LXIV (1967) 71–90.

924. CLEW, KENNETH R. Tadworth: an illustrated history. Tadworth, Surrey: R. J. Chappell Ltd., 1968. 34 pp.

Sussex

925. HOLMES, JOHN. The Chichester dykes. *Sussex Archaeol. Coll.*, CVI (1968) 63–72.

926. WOOD, P. D. The topography of East Grinstead borough. *Sussex Archaeol. Coll.*, CVI (1968) 49–62.

927. REEVES, HARRY LESLIE. Findon: a downland village. Findon, Sussex: Sheepdown Pubns., 1968. 72 pp., illus.

Warwickshire

928. PAYNE, ARCHIBALD. Portrait of a parish. Kineton, Warwicks.: Roundwood, 1968. xv, 180 pp., illus. [Long Itchington.]

Wiltshire

929. TAYLOR, C. C. Whiteparish: a study of the development of a forest-edge parish. *Wilts. Archaeol. & Nat. Hist. Mag.*, LXII (1967) 79–102.

Yorkshire

930. TATE, WILLIAM EDWARD, *and* SINGLETON, FREDERICK BERNARD. A history of Yorkshire. 3rd edn. Beaconsfield, Bucks.: Darwen Finlayson, 1967. 72 pp., illus. [Previous edn. 1965.]

931. LEWIN, JOHN, *and* PARTON, ALAN G. Building materials and glebe terriers: the case of the East Riding. *Local Historian*, VIII (1968) 47–53.

932. COWLING, GEOFFREY CHARLES. The history of Easingwold and the Forest of Galtres. Huddersfield, Yorks.: Advertiser P., 1968. 207 pp., illus.

933. BROOK, ROY. The story of Huddersfield. MacGibbon & Kee, 1968. xxi, 394 pp., illus.

934. WADDINGTON-FEATHER, JOHN. Leeds: the heart of Yorkshire. Leeds: B. Jackson, 1967. 172 pp., illus.

935. BERESFORD, MAURICE WARWICK, *and* JONES, GLANVILLE R. J. (*eds.*). Leeds and its region. Leeds: British Assoc. Advancement of Science (Leeds Local Executive Committee), 1967. xviii, 298 pp., illus. [Contains: 'The evidence of place-names' by R. L. Thomson, pp. 101–8; 'To the building of Kirkstall abbey' by G. R. J. Jones, pp. 119–30; 'From the foundation of the borough to the eve of the Industrial Revolution' by G. C. F. Forster, pp. 131–45; 'The Industrial Revolution' by E. M. Sigsworth, pp. 146–55; 'Later phases of industrialisation, to 1918' by J. Buckman, pp. 156–66; 'Passenger transport developments' by G. C. Dickinson, pp. 167–74; 'Urban renewal, 1918–66' by F. J. Fowler, pp. 175–85; 'Prosperity Street and others: an essay in visible urban history' by M. W. Beresford, pp. 186–97; 'Early medical education in Leeds' by S. T. Anning, pp. 240–4.]

936. MOORSOM, NORMAN. The birth and growth of modern Middlesbrough. Middlesbrough, Yorks.: the author, 1967. 108 pp., illus.

937. LILLIE, WILLIAM. The history of Middlesbrough: an illustration of the evolution of English industry. Middlesbrough, Yorks.: Central Lib., 1968. xiv, 492 pp., illus.

938. TANN, JENNIFER. A survey of Thirsk, Yorkshire. *Industrial Archaeol.*, IV (1967) 232–47.

939. FAWCETT, R. H. The story of Wilsden. Pt. 3. *Bradford Antiquary*, n.s. pt. XLIII (1967) 187–209.

ISLE OF MAN

940. BREGAZZI, J. C. Douglas: past, present and future. *Isle of Man Nat. Hist. & Antiq. Soc. Proc.*, n.s. VII no. 1 (1967) 26–34.

941. KILLIP, I. M. Place-names in the parish of Rushen. *Manx Museum Jour.*, VII no. 84 (1968) 92–6.

CHANNEL ISLANDS

942. QUENTEL, PAUL, *and* GUINET, LOUIS. Les noms de Jersey et de Guernesey. *Rev. Internat. d'Onomastique*, XX (1968) 299–308.

943. SHARP, ERIC W. The evolution of St. Peter Port harbour. *Soc. Guernesiaise Rept. & Trans.* for 1967, XVIII (1968) 225–55.

WALES AND MONMOUTHSHIRE

944. FRASER, DAVID. The defenders. Cardiff: Wales U.P., 1967. xiv, 253 pp., illus. [Simultaneously pubd. as Yr amddiffynwyr, *transl.* B. L. Jones.]

945. JENKINS, DAFYDD. A lawyer looks at Welsh land law. *Hon. Soc. Cymmrodorion Trans.* (1967) 220–48.

946. LLOYD, HOWELL ARNOLD. The gentry of south west Wales, 1540–1640. Cardiff: Wales U.P., 1968. 256 pp.

947. JENKINS, J. GERAINT. Rural industry in Anglesey. *Anglesey Antiq. Soc. & F.C. Trans.* (1967) 41–65.

948. JENKINS, J. G. Rural industry in Cardiganshire. *Ceredigion*, VI no. 1 (1968) 90–127.

949. WATTS, D. G. Changes in location of the South Wales iron and steel industry, 1860–1930. *Geography*, LIII (1968) 294–307.

950. EVANS, MICHAEL C. S. The pioneers of the Carmarthenshire iron industry. *Carmarthens. Hist.*, IV (1967) 22–40.

951. DAVIES, JOHN. The Dowlais lease, 1748–1900. *Morgannwg*, XII (1968) 37–66.

952. REES, MORGAN. Copper mining in North Wales. *Archaeologia Cambrensis*, CXVII (1968) 172–97.

953. DAVIES, ALUN EIRUG. Paper-mills and paper-makers in Wales, 1700–1900. *Nat. Lib. Wales Jour.*, XV (1967–8) 1–30.

954. DAVIES, A. E. Some aspects of the operation of the Old Poor Law in Cardiganshire, 1750–1834. *Ceredigion*, VI no. 1 (1968) 1–44.

955. HOWELLS, BRIAN ELWYN. The distribution of customary acres in South Wales. *Nat. Lib. Wales Jour.*, XV (1967–8) 226–33.

956. HOWELL, DAVID W. The economy of the landed estates of Pembrokeshire *c.* 1680–1830. *Welsh Hist. Rev.*, III (1966–7) 265–86.

957. THOMAS, COLIN. Merioneth estates, 1790–1858: a study in agrarian geography. *Merioneth Hist. & Rec. Soc. Jour.*, V no. 3 (1967) 220–38.

958. DREW, JOHN H. The Welsh Road and the drovers. *Birmingham Archaeol. Soc. Trans.* for 1965, LXXXII (1967) 38–43.

959. MILLER, RONALD. Shiels in the Brecon Beacons. *Folk Life*, V (1967) 107–10.

960. JONES, FRANCIS. The lordship and manors of Dewsland. *Hist. Soc. Church in Wales Jour.*, XVII (1967) 9–39, XVIII (1968) 23–35.

961. JONES, T. THORNLEY. Districts of the ancient Welsh llannau. *Hist. Soc. Church in Wales Jour.*, XVIII (1968) 7–12.

962. DAVIES, PERCIVAL VAUGHAN (*comp.*). The College of Christ of Brecknock: some documents and notes to illustrate the history of the College, 1538–1811. Brecon: Brecknock County Museum, 1968. 46 pp.

963. RICHARDS, GWYNFRYN. Llanllyfni: an unusual dedication. *Caernarvons. Hist. Soc. Trans.*, XXVIII pt. 1 (1967) 5–12.

964. LEWIS, E. T. Agweddau ar y berthynas rhwyng Cymdeithaseg a ffyniant y Bedyddwyr yng Nghymru. *Trafodion Cymdeithas Hanes Bedyddwyr Cymru* (1967) 5–23. ['Attitudes to schism and the Association among Welsh Baptists.']

965. JONES, FRANCIS. Portraits and pictures in old Carmarthenshire houses. *Carmarthens. Hist.*, V (1968) 43–66.

966. TALBOT, ERIC J. Welsh ceramics: a documentary and archaeological survey. *Post-Medieval Archaeol.*, II (1968) 119–39.

967. CLEAVER, EMRYS. Musicians of Wales: an account of the lives and work of the major musicians of Wales in the 19th century and into the 20th, *transl.* E. L. Jones. Ruthin, Denbighs.: John Jones, 1968. 108 pp., illus. [Originally pubd. Llandybie, Carm.: Llyfrau'r Dryw, 1964, as *Gŵyr y Gân.*]

968. THOMAS, J. LLOYD. Eisteddfod talaith a chadair Powys. *Montgomerys. Coll.* for 1965–6, LIX (1968) 60–81. ['The Powis provincial chair eisteddfod'.]

969. HUGHES, IEUAN T., *and* JENKINS, J. RAYMOND. The church of St. Tysul, Llandysul. *Ceredigion*, V no. 4 (1967) 424–31.

970. JONES, E. P. Cartrefi entwogion Sir Frycheiniog. *Brycheiniog*, XIII (1968–9) 107–53. ['Famous homes in Brecons.']

971. JONES, STANLEY R., *and* SMITH, JOHN THOMAS. The houses of Breconshire. Pt. 4, the Cricklowell district. *Brycheiniog*, XII (1966–7) 1–91.

972. JONES, FRANCIS. Welsh interiors. 2, Abermarlais. *Archaeologia Cambrensis*, CXVI (1967) 165–91.

973. JONES, F. Taliaris. *Archaeologia Cambrensis*, CXVII (1968) 157–71.

974. BAKER-JONES, D. L. Edwinsford: a country house and its families. *Carmarthens. Hist.*, V (1968) 17–42. [Williams and Drummond families.]

975. BROOKSBY, H. The houses of Radnorshire. *Radnors. Soc. Trans.*, XXXVIII (1968) 8–25.

976. PHILLIPS, W. S. Lower House and Cottage Farm: a study of two timber framed houses in the parish of Evenjobb. *Radnors. Soc. Trans.*, XXXVII (1967) 44–65.

977. SMITH, PETER. A short architectural note on Ystradfaelog, the Bryn and Lower Gwestydd. *Montgomerys. Coll.*, for 1965–6, LIX (1968) 102–11.

978. EVANS, W. A. Three Denbighshire scientists. *Denbighs. Hist. Soc. Trans.*, XVII (1968) 183–90. [Thomas Henry (1734–1816); Robert Griffiths (1805–83); Isaac Roberts (1829–1904).]

979. PRICE, G. VERNON. The hill forts of Marford and Wrexham. *Denbighs. Hist. Soc. Trans.*, XVI (1967) 10–22.

980. PARFITT, GEOFFREY ARCHER (*ed.*). Radnorshire volunteers: a regimental history of Radnorshire, 1539–1968. Hay-on-Wye, Radnors.: Radnors. Territorial & Auxiliary Forces Assoc., 1968. 142 pp., illus.

LOCAL HISTORY

981. RICHARDS, MELVILLE. Welsh *sarn* 'road, causeway' in place-names. *Études Celtiques*, XI (1967) 383–408.

982. PIERCE, GWYNEDD OWEN. The place-names of Dinas Powys Hundred. Cardiff: Wales U.P., for Board of Celtic Studies, 1968. xxxvi, 359 pp.

983. HUGHES, DAVID LLOYD, *and* WILLIAMS, DOROTHY M. Holyhead: the story of a port. Holyhead, Anglesey: the authors, 1967. 221 pp., illus.

984. DODD, ARTHUR HERBERT. A history of Caernarvonshire, 1284–1900. Caernarvon: Caernarvons. Hist. Soc., 1968. 438 pp., illus.

985. BOWEN, E. G. Carmarthen: an urban study. *Archaeologia Cambrensis*, CXVII (1968) 1–17.

986. WILLIAMS, ELLIS WYNNE. Abergele: the story of a parish. Abergele, Denbighs.: the author, 1968. 208 pp., illus.

987. HUGHES, TREVOR. Ruthin: a town with a past. Ruthin, Denbighs.: the author, 1967. 137 pp., illus.

988. HAYES, PETER A. Some cottages in the Hawarden district. *Flints. Hist. Soc. Pubns.*, XXIII (1967–8) 54–73.

989. HIGGINS, LEONARD SUTTON. Newton Nottage and Porthcawl from prehistoric times to 1950. 2nd edn. Llandysul, Cardigs.: Gomerian P., 1968. xv, 171 pp., illus. [Previous edn. 1968.]

990. DAVIES, JOHN HENRY. History of Pontardawe and district. Llandybie, Carm.: C. Davies, 1967. 297 pp., illus.

991. AWBERY, STAN. St. Donat's and the Stradlings. Barry, Glam.: the author, 1967. 80 pp., illus.

992. MERIONETH HISTORICAL AND RECORD SOCIETY. History of Merioneth. Vol. 1, From the earliest times to the age of the native princes, by E. G. Bowen *and* C. A. Gresham. Dolgelly, Merioneth: the Society, 1967. xv, 298 pp., illus.

993. SYLVESTER, DOROTHY. Glasbury, Norton, and the problem of the nucleated village in Radnorshire. *Radnors. Soc. Trans.*, XXXVII (1967) 17–26.

SCOTLAND

994. DONALDSON, GORDON. Scottish kings. Batsford, 1967. 224 pp., illus.

995. MCNEILL, PETER G. B. The Scottish regency. *Juridical Rev.*, n.s. XII (1967) 127–48.

996. FELLOWES-GORDON, IAN. Famous Scottish lives. Odhams, 1967. 352 pp., illus.

997. CRAWFORD, IAIN A. The divide between medieval and post-medieval in Scotland. *Post-Medieval Archaeol.*, I (1967) 84–9.

998. KERMACK, WILLIAM RAMSAY. The Scottish borders, with Galloway, to 1603. Edinburgh, London: Johnston & Bacon, 1967. 112 pp., illus.

999. FERGUSON, WILLIAM. Scotland, 1689 to the present. (Edinburgh History of Scotland, 4). Edinburgh, London: Oliver & Boyd, 1968. ix, 464 pp.

1000. KELLAS, JAMES GRANT. Modern Scotland: the nation since 1870. Pall Mall P., 1968. vii, 284 pp.

1001. CARSWELL, R. D. The origins of the legal profession in Scotland. *Amer. Jour. Legal Hist.*, XI (1967) 41–56.

1002. DORWARD, GEORGE. History of the local police, pt. 2. *Hawick Archaeol. Soc. Trans.* (1967) 3–24, (1968) 3–18.

1003. CAMERON, RONDO. 'Banking in the early stages of industrialization: Scotland, 1750–1845'. *In* Banking in the early stages of industrialization (New York, London, Toronto: O.U.P., 1967) pp. 60–99.

1004. MACMILLAN, DAVID STIRLING. Scotland and Australia, 1788–1850: emigration, commerce and investment. Oxford: Clarendon P., 1967. xviii, 434 pp., illus.

1005. DONNACHIE, IAN L., *and* STEWART, NORMA K. Scottish windmills: an outline and inventory. *Soc. Antiq. Scot. Proc.* for 1964–6, XCVIII (1967) 276–99.

1006. BECKLES, N. I. Textiles and port growth in Dundee. *Scot. Geog. Mag.*, LXXXIV (1968) 90–8.

1007. THOMS, DAVID BOATH. The guildry of Brechin. Brechin, Angus: Guildry of Brechin, 1968. 122 pp.

1008. REID, JAMES MCARTHUR. A history of the Merchants' House of Glasgow. Glasgow: T. L. Grahame Reid, 1967. 87 pp., illus.

1009. MARWICK, WILLIAM HUTTON. A short history of labour in Scotland. Edinburgh, London: Chambers, 1967. 119 pp., illus.

1010. TUCKETT, ANGELA. The Scottish carter: the history of the Scottish Horse and Motormen's Association. Allen & Unwin, 1967. 448 pp., illus.

1011. TURNOCK, DAVID. Depopulation in north east Scotland with reference to the countryside. *Scot. Geog. Mag.*, LXXXIV (1968) 256–68.

1012. COULL, JAMES R. A comparison of demographic trends in the Faroe and Shetland Islands. *Inst. Brit. Geographers' Trans.*, XLI (1967) 159–66.

1013. STORRIE, MARGARET C. Landholdings and population in Arran from the late 18th century. *Scot. Studies*, XI (1967) 49–74.

1014. ROBERTSON, ISOBEL M. L. Changing form and function of settlement in south west Argyll, 1841–1961. *Scot. Geog. Mag.*, LXXXIII (1967) 29–45.

1015. HOOD, JAMES. A short history of transport and agriculture in Berwickshire. *Berwicks. Naturalists' Club Hist.* for 1967, XXXVI pt. 3 (1968) 189–99.

1016. FENTON, ALEXANDER. Plough and spade in Dumfries and Galloway. *Dumfries. & Galloway Nat. Hist. & Antiq. Soc. Trans.*, XLV (1968) 147–83.

1017. MILLER, RONALD. Land use by summer shielings. *Scot. Studies*, XI (1967) 193–219.

1018. RYDER, M. L. The evolution of Scottish breeds of sheep. *Scot. Studies*, XII (1968) 127–67.

1019. RYDER, M. L. The history of sheep in Scotland. *Bradford Textile Soc. Jour.* (1967–8) 33–48.

1020. ANDERSON, MARK LOUDEN. A history of Scottish forestry, *ed.* C. J. Taylor. Nelson, 1967. 2 vols.

1021. COULL, JAMES R. Salmon-fishing in the north east of Scotland before 1800. *Aberdeen Univ. Rev.*, XLII (1967–8) 31–8.

1022. ADAMS, IAN H. The land surveyor and his influence on the Scottish rural landscape. *Scot. Geog. Mag.*, LXXXIV (1968) 248–55.

1023. ANDERSON, ALEX D. The development of the road system in the stewartry of Kirkcudbright, 1590–1890. *Dumfries. & Galloway Nat. Hist. & Antiq. Soc. Trans.*, XLIV (1967) 205–22, XLV (1968) 211–27.

1024. DRAFFEN, GEORGE. Scottish Masonic usage and custom. *Ars Quatuor Coronatorum*, LXXX (1967) 314–18.

1025. SHAW, DUNCAN (*ed.*). Reformation and revolution: essays presented to the Very Rev. Hugh Watt, D.D., D.Litt. Edinburgh: St. Andrew P., 1967. 322 pp. [Contains: 'Of the troubles begun at Frankfurt, A.D. 1554' by M. A. Simpson, pp. 17–33; 'Reassessments of the reformers' by I. Henderson, pp. 34–41; 'John Willock' by D. Shaw, pp. 42–69; 'Worship in the kirk: Knox, Westminster and the 1940 Book' by A. C. Cheyne, pp. 70–81; 'Baptism in Scotland after the Reformation' by A. I. Dunlop, pp. 82–99; 'John Craig, minister of Aberdeen and King's chaplain' by T. A. Kerr, pp. 100–23; 'A constant platt achieved: provision for the ministry, 1600–38' by W. R. Foster, pp. 124–40; 'Some Scottish bishops and ministers in the Irish Church, 1605–35' by J. M. Barkley, pp. 141–59; 'The Five Articles of Perth' by I. B. Cowan, pp. 160–77; 'The entry of sects into Scotland' by W. I. Hoy, pp. 178–211; 'The doctrine of the Church in the later covenanting period' by I. B. Doyle, pp. 212–36; 'The Church Union attempt at the General Assembly of 1692' by T. Maxwell, pp. 237–57; 'The theological climate in early 18th century Scotland' by S. Mechie, pp. 258–72; 'Thomas Ayton's *The original constitution of the Christian Church*' by T. F. Torrance, pp. 273–97.]

1026. HANDLEY, JAMES E. Great Britain: Scotland. (Hist. of Irish Catholicism, vol. 6, fasc. 1). Dublin: Gill, 1968. 28 pp.

1027. MACWILLIAM, ALEXANDER S. Catholic Dundee, 1787 to 1836. *Innes Rev.*, XVIII (1967) 75–87.

1028. MARWICK, WILLIAM H. Studies in Scottish Quakerism. *Scot. Church Hist. Soc. Records*, XVI pt. 2 (1967) 89–98.

1029. FINLAYSON, C. P., *and* SIMPSON, S. M. The Library of the University of Edinburgh: the early period, 1580–1710. *Library Hist.*, I (1967) 2–23.

1030. BONE, THOMAS RENFREW. Studies in the history of Scottish education, 1872–1939. (Scottish Council for Research in Education Pubns., 54). Univ. London P., 1967. 317 pp.

1031. CRUICKSHANK, MARJORIE. Education in the Highlands and Islands of Scotland: an historical retrospect. *Paedagogica Historica*, VII (1967) 361–77.

1032. SHANKS, ALASTAIR. Strichen School. *Aberdeen Univ. Rev.*, XLII (1967–8) 48–53.

1033. WHYTE, DONALD. Schoolmasters of Abercorn parish, 1646–1872. *Scot. Geneal.*, XV (1968) 7–13.

1034. TOBIN, TERENCE. The beginnings of drama in Scotland. *Theatre Survey*, VIII no. 1 (1967) 1–16.

1035. FLETT, J. F., *and* FLETT, T. M. The Scottish country dance: its origins and development. *Scot. Studies*, XI (1967) 1–11, 124–47.

1036. WEST, THOMAS WILSON. A history of architecture in Scotland. Univ. London P., 1967. 208 pp., illus.

1037. GOMME, ANDOR, *and* WALKER, DAVID M. Architecture of Glasgow. Lund Humphries, 1968. 320 pp., illus. [To 1914.]

1038. HORN, DAVID BAYNE. The building of the Old Quad, 1767–1841. *Univ. Edinburgh Jour.*, XXIII no. 4 (1968) 309–21.

1039. STONES, EDWARD LIONEL GREGORY, *and* HAY, GEORGE. Notes on Glasgow cathedral. *Innes Rev.*, XVIII (1967) 88–98.

1040. PATTULLO, NAN. Castles, houses and gardens of Scotland. Edinburgh, London: Blackwood, 1967. 160 pp., illus.

1041. FORMAN, SHEILA. Scottish country houses and castles. Glasgow, London: Collins, 1967. 176 pp., illus.

1042. DRUMMOND, A. ISOBEL R. The domestic architecture of a Fife river port prior to 1810: Kincardine-on-Forth. *Soc. Antiq. Scot. Proc.* for 1964–6, XCVIII (1967) 300–11.

1043. FENTON, ALEXANDER. Das Bauernhaus auf Orkney und Shetland. *Deutsches Jahrb. für Volkskunde*, XIII (1967) 50–68.

1044. WHITTINGTON, GRAEME. The imprint of former occupations and the improver movement on house types in Fife. *Folk Life*, V (1967) 52–7.

1045. STEPHEN, WALTER M. Toll-houses of the greater Fife area. *Industrial Archaeol.*, IV (1967) 248–54.

1046. LAMONT, WILLIAM DAWSON. Ancient and medieval sculptured stones of Islay. Edinburgh, London: Oliver & Boyd, 1968. xvi, 60 pp., illus.

1047. EELES, FRANCIS CAROLUS, *and* CLOUSTON, RANALD W. M. The church and other bells of the stewartry of Kirkudbright. *Soc. Antiq. Scot. Proc.* for 1966–7, XCIX (1968) 191–210.

1048. GUTHRIE, DOUGLAS. The Aesculapian Club of Edinburgh. *Univ. Edinburgh Jour.*, XXIII no. 3 (1968) 245–50.

LOCAL HISTORY

1049. SKINNER, BASIL CHISHOLM. Local history in Scotland: a comment on its status and some recent writings. *Scot. Hist. Rev.*, XLVII (1968) 160–7.

1050. NICOLAISEN, W. F. H. Scottish place-names. 28, Old English *wic.* 29, Scandinavian personal names in the place-names of south east Scotland. 30, *Fintry. Scot. Studies*, XI (1967) 75–84, 223–36, XII (1968) 178–82.

1051. WHITTINGTON, GRAEME, *and* SOULSBY, J. A. A preliminary report on an investigation into *pit* place-names. *Scot. Geog. Mag.*, LXXXIV (1968) 117–25.

1052. WYNESS, FENTON. Royal valley: the story of the Aberdeenshire Dee. Aberdeen: Alex. P. Reid & Son, 1968. 390 pp., illus.

1053. JONES, S. J. (*ed.*). Dundee and district. Dundee, Angus: British Assoc. for Advancement of Science, 1968. xvi, 391 pp., illus. [Contains: 'Prehistoric, Roman and Pictish settlement' by D. B. Taylor, pp. 127–43; 'Place-names' by W. H. F. Nicolaisen, pp. 144–52; 'Historical development of the Tayside region in the Middle Ages' by R. G. Cant, pp. 153-61; 'The industrial history of the Dundee region from the 18th to the early 20th century' by B. P. Lenman and E. E. Gauldie, pp. 162–73; 'Rural settlements' by W. H. K. Turner, pp. 226–36; 'Population' by H. R. Jones, pp. 237–56; 'Historical geography of Dundee' by S. J. Jones, pp. 259–78; 'The architecture of Dundee' by D. M. Walker, pp. 284–300; 'Politics in Dundee' by D. G. Southgate, pp. 347–51; 'Notes on the first visit of the British Association to Dundee and the early history of University College, Dundee' by A. D. Walsh, pp. 371–81.]

1054. TURNER, W. H. K. The growth of Dundee. *Scot. Geog. Mag.*, LXXXIV (1968) 76–89.

1055. FRASER, DUNCAN. Montrose before 1700. Montrose, Angus: Standard P., 1967. 179 pp., illus.

1056. LAMONT, WILLIAM DAWSON. The early history of Islay, 500–1726. Glasgow: the author, 1967. 89 pp.

1057. WALTON, R. H. Hedgeley Moor battlefield and cross. *Berwicks. Naturalists' Club Hist.* for 1966, XXXVII pt. 2 (1967) 108–12.

1058. STORRIE, MARGARET C. Balliekine, Arran: survivor of two revolutions. *Folk Life*, V (1967) 92–9.

1059. SIMPSON, R. ROY (*ed.*). Historical Cumbernauld. Cumbernauld, Dunbartons.: Cumbernauld Hist. Soc., 1968. 57 pp., illus.

1060. PREVOST, WILLIAM AUGUSTIN JOHN. Dumcrieff and its owners. *Dumfries. & Galloway Nat. Hist. & Antiq. Soc. Trans.*, XLV (1968) 200–11.

1061. GRAHAM, ANGUS. The old harbours of Dunbar. *Soc. Antiq. Scot. Proc.* for 1966–7, XCIX (1968) 173–90.

1062. PORTEOUS, ROBERT. Grangemouth's ancient heritage. Grangemouth, E. Stirling: the author, 1967. 137 pp.

IRELAND

Note: Writings on Irish domestic or local history are not included unless they have a direct bearing on English history.

1063. MOODY, T. W., *and* MARTIN, F. X. (*eds.*). The course of Irish history. Cork: Mercier P., 1967. 404 pp., illus.

1064. HALLSETH, BENEDICTE TULINIUS. Irlandafsnittet i konungs skuggsía. *Maal og Minne* (1967) 50–63.

1065. GUINNESS, DESMOND. Portrait of Dublin. Batsford, 1967. 96 pp., illus. [1680–1855.]

1066. LYSAGHT, CHARLES EDWARD. The Irish peers and the House of Lords. *N.I. Legal Quart.*, XVIII (1967) 277–301.

1067. HAND, GEOFFREY JOSEPH PHILIP. The constitutional position of the Irish military establishment from the Restoration to the Union: an introductory note. *Irish Jurist*, n.s. III (1968) 330–5.

1068. MCCAFFREY, LAWRENCE J. The Irish question, 1800–1922. Lexington, Ky.: Kentucky U.P., 1968. x, 202 pp.

1069. MCCARTNEY, DONAL. 'From Parnell to Pearse'. *In* The course of Irish history, *ed.* T. W. Moody *and* F. X. Martin (Cork: Mercier P., 1967) pp. 294–312.

1070. YALE, D. E. C. A historical note on the jurisdiction of the Admiralty in Ireland. *Irish Jurist*, n.s. III (1968) 146–61.

1071. LUCAS, A. T. Cloth finishing in Ireland. *Folk Life*, VI (1968) 18–67.

1072. LEE, JOSEPH. Marriage and population in pre-famine Ireland. *Econ. Hist. Rev.*, 2nd ser. XXI (1968) 283–95.

1073. CULLEN, L. M. Irish history without the potato. *Past & Present*, no. 40 (1968) 72–83. [Population growth.]

1074. LUCAS, A. T. 'The plundering and burning of churches in Ireland, 7th to 16th century'. *In* North Munster Studies, *ed.* E. Rynne (Limerick: Thomond Archaeol. Soc., 1967) pp. 172–229.

1075. BURKE-SAVAGE, ROLAND. The growth of devotion to the Sacred Heart in Ireland. *Irish Eccles. Record*, 5th ser. CX (1968) 185–208.

1076. HAMELL, PATRICK J. (*comp.*). Maynooth students and ordinations, 1795–1895: index. *Irish Eccles. Record*, 5th ser. CVIII (1967) 353–71, CIX (1968) 28–40, 122–34, 196–203, 256–64, 335–40, 407–16, CX (1968) 84–99, 173–82, 277–88, 381–6. [Continuing.]

1077. BARKLEY, JOHN M. The Presbyterian church in Ireland. Pt. 2. *Jour. Presbyterian Hist.*, XLV (1967) 33–48.

1078. HUGHES, ATHRO T. JONES. Yr iaith Wyddeleg. *Y Traethodydd*, CXXII (1967) 173–85. ['The Irish language'.]

1079. MUNTER, ROBERT LAVERNE. The history of the Irish newspaper, 1685–1760. C.U.P., 1967. xiii, 217 pp., illus.

1080. BRETT, CHARLES EDWARD BAINBRIDGE. Buildings of Belfast, 1700–1914. Weidenfeld, 1967. xii, 72 pp., illus.

1081. AALEN, F. H. A. Furnishings of traditional houses in the Wicklow Hills. *Ulster Folklife*, XIII (1967) 61–7.

1082. KELHAM, BRIAN B. The Royal College of Science for Ireland, 1867–1926. *Studies*, LVI (1967) 297–309.

1083. WIDDESS, JOHN DAVID HENRY. The Royal College of Surgeons in Ireland and its medical school, 1784–1966. 2nd edn. Edinburgh, London: E. & S. Livingstone, 1967. 152 pp., illus. [Previous edn. pubd. 1949, as *Account of the schools of surgery, Royal College of Surgeons*.]

BRITISH EMPIRE AND COMMONWEALTH

Note: The domestic history of Commonwealth countries is not included unless it has a direct bearing on British history.

1084. RICHARDSON, PATRICK. Empire and slavery. Longmans, 1968. x, 158 pp.

1085. ANSTEY, ROGER T. Capitalism and slavery: a critique. *Econ. Hist. Rev.*, 2nd ser. XXI (1968) 307–20.

1086. THOMAS, ROBERT PAUL. The sugar colonies of the Old Empire: profit or loss for Great Britain? *Econ. Hist. Rev.*, 2nd ser. XXI (1968) 30–45.

1087. BOLTON, GEOFFREY CURGENVEN. The idea of a colonial gentry. *Hist. Studies Australia & N.Z.*, XIII (1968) 307–28.

1088. STEELE, IAN KENNETH. Politics of colonial policy: the Board of Trade in colonial administration, 1696–1720. Oxford: Clarendon P., 1968. xvi, 217 pp.

1089. REESE, TREVOR R. The history of the Royal Commonwealth Society, 1868–1968. O.U.P., 1968. xii, 280 pp., illus.

1090. JUDD, DENIS. Balfour and the British Empire: a study in imperial evolution, 1874–1932. Macmillan, 1968. 392 pp., illus.

1091. KENDLE, JOHN EDWARD. The Colonial and Imperial Conferences, 1887–1911: a study in imperial organisation. (Imperial Studies, 28). Longmans, for Roy. Commonwealth Soc., 1967. xi, 264 pp.

1092. SAVELLE, MAX. The origins of American diplomacy: the international history of Anglo-America, 1492–1763. New York: Macmillan, 1967. xiii, 624 pp.

1093. BARROW, THOMAS CHURCHILL. Trade and empire: the British customs service in colonial America, 1660–1775. Cambridge, Mass.: Harvard U.P.; London: O.U.P., 1967. xii, 336 pp.

1094. SUTHERLAND, STELLA H. Colonial statistics. *Explorations in Entreneurial Hist.*, 2nd ser. V (1967) 58–107. [American.]

1095. WALTON, GARY M. Sources of productivity change in American colonial shipping, 1675–1775. *Econ. Hist. Rev.*, 2nd ser. XX (1967) 67–78.

1096. WALTON, G. M. A measure of productivity change in American colonial shipping. *Econ. Hist. Rev.*, 2nd ser. XXI (1968) 268–82.

1097. COWAN, HELEN I. British immigration before Confederation. (Hist. booklet, 22). Ottawa: Canadian Historical Assoc., 1968. 24 pp.

1098. KITZAN, LAWRENCE. The London Missionary Society in Upper Canada. *Ontario Hist.*, LIX (1967) 39–45.

1099. METFORD, J. C. J. Falklands or Malvinas? The background to the dispute. *International Affairs*, XLIV (1968) 463–81.

1100. LLEONART Y ANSELEM, ALBERTO J. Del Gibraltar inglés: su inconsistencia legal e histórica. Madrid: Punta Europa, 1968. 296 pp.

1101. PORTER, R. English chief factors on the Gold Coast, 1632–1753. *African Hist. Studies*, I (1968) 199–209.

1102. PERRATON, H. D. British attitudes towards East and West Africa, 1880–1914. *Race*, VIII (1967) 223–46.

1103. DULY, LESLIE CLEMENT. British land policy at the Cape, 1795–1844: a study of administrative procedures in the Empire. Durham, N. C.: Duke U.P., 1968. xix, 226 pp.

1104. HUTCHINS, FRANCIS G. The illusion of permanence: British imperialism in India. Princeton, N.J.: Princeton U.P., 1967. 217 pp.

1105. HARNETTY, PETER. The British impact on India: some recent interpretations. *Pacific Affairs*, XXXIX (1966–7) 361–75.

1106. TINKER, HUGH. Power and influence in Britain and India. *Modern Asian Studies*, II (1968) 71–8.

1107. SEYMOUR, WILLIAM. The Indian states under the British Crown. *History Today*, XVII (1967) 819–27.

1108. PURI, B. N. The training of civil servants under the Company. *Jour. Indian Hist.*, XLV (1967) 749–71.

1109. MARSHALL, PETER JAMES. Problems of empire: Britain and India, 1757–1813. (Historical Problems: Studies and Documents, 3). Allen & Unwin, 1968. 239 pp.

1110. AMBIRAJAN, S. Economic ideas and economic policy in British India. *Indian Econ. Jour.*, XV (1967) 188–208.

1111. EDWARDES, MICHAEL. British India, 1772–1947: a survey of the nature and effects of alien rule. Sidgwick & Jackson, 1967. ix, 396 pp., illus.

1112. EDWARDES, M. Glorious sahibs: the romantic as empire-builder, 1799–1838. Eyre & Spottiswoode, 1968. 248 pp., illus.

1113. MUKHERJEE, AMITABHA. Reform and regeneration in Bengal, 1774–1823. Calcutta: Rabindra Bharati Univ., 1968. xx, 392 pp.

1114. HASRAT, BIKRAMA JIT. Anglo-Sikh relations, 1799–1849: a reappraisal of the rise and fall of the Sikhs. Hoshiapur: V. V. Research Inst. Book Agency, 1968. 411 pp.

1115. ELLIOTT, JAMES GORDON. The Frontier, 1839–1947: the story of the North-West Frontier of India. Cassell, 1968. xii, 306 pp., illus.

1116. SWINSON, ARTHUR. North-West Frontier: people and events, 1839–1947. Hutchinson, 1967. 354 pp., illus.

1117. SEN, A. K. 'The pattern of British enterprise in India, 1854–1914: a causal analysis'. *In* Social and economic change, *ed.* B. *and* V. B. Singh (Bombay: Allied Publ., 1967) pp. 409–29.

1118. SINCLAIR, KEITH. The British advance in Johore, 1885–1914. *Roy. Asiatic Soc. Malaysian Branch Jour.*, XL pt. 1 (1967) 93–110.

1119. THIO, EUNICE. British policy towards Johore: from advice to control. *Roy. Asiatic Soc. Malaysian Branch Jour.*, XL pt. 1 (1967) 1–41.

1120. THIO, E. Some aspects of the Federation of the Malay States, 1896–1910. *Roy. Asiatic Soc. Malaysian Branch Jour.*, XL pt. 2 (1968) 3–15.

GENEALOGY AND FAMILY HISTORY

GENERAL

1121. REANEY, PERCY HIDE. The origin of English surnames. Routledge, 1967. xix, 415 pp.

1122. PARRY, COLIN JOHN (*comp.*). Index of baronetage creations. Canterbury, Kent: Inst. Heraldic & Geneal. Studies, 1967. 177 pp.

1123. DICKINSON, H. T. The correspondence of Sir James Clavering. (Surtees Soc. Pubns., 178). Gateshead: Northumberland P., for the Society, 1967. xvi, 240 pp.

1124. DELDERFIELD, ERIC RAYMOND. West country historic houses and their families. Vol. 1. Newton Abbot, Devon: David & Charles, 1968. 160 pp., illus.

1125. HEDLEY, W. PERCY. Northumberland families. Vol. 1. Newcastle-upon-Tyne: H. Hill, for Society of Antiquaries of Newcastle-upon-Tyne, 1968. xi, 289 pp.

1126. COWIN, H. S. Genealogy in the Isle of Man. *Isle of Man Nat. Hist. & Antiq. Soc. Proc.*, n.s. VII no. 1 (1967) 13–25.

1127. BARTRUM, PETER C. Notes on the Welsh genealogical manuscripts. *Hon. Soc. Cymmrodorion Trans.* (1968) 63–98.

1128. BARTRUM, P. C. Pedigrees of the Welsh tribal patriarchs, contd. *Nat. Lib. Wales Jour.*, XV (1967–8) 157–65. [Contd. from vol. XIII pp. 93–146.]

1129. MONCREIFFE, *Sir* IAN. The Highland clans. Barrie & Rockliff, 1967. 255 pp., illus.

1130. SHEPPARD, WALTER LEE, *Jnr*. Royal bye-blows. Pt.3, Illegitimate descendants of the Scottish kings to James VI. *New England Hist. & Geneal. Reg.*, CXXII (1968) 265–74.

1131. BARRY, JOHN G. The study of family history in Ireland. Dublin: Nat. Univ. Ireland, 1967. 36 pp.

INDIVIDUAL FAMILIES

1132. BARRAUD, ENID MARY. Barraud: the story of a family. Research Pubg. Co., 1967. 190 pp., illus.

1133. *Belloc*. ARTUR, P. E. La dynastie de Hilaire Belloc: des ancêtres nantais a l'écrivain anglais. *Rev. Bas-Poitou*, LXXIX (1968) 29–56.

1134. *Bowlby*. HILL, WILLIAM J. Seven generations of the Bowlby family from Helmsley. *Ryedale Historian*, no. 3 (1967) 33–41.

1135. *Brougham*. DAVEY, C. R. Further sources for a study of the Brougham family. *Cumberland & Westmorland Antiq. & Archaeol. Soc. Trans.*, LXVII (1967) 112–24.

1136. *Brown*. VERITY, T. E., *and others*. The Browns of Burnfoot: the decline and fall of a yeoman family. *Cumberland & Westmorland Antiq. & Archaeol. Soc. Trans.*, LXVIII (1968) 169–91.

1137. *Byrom*. THOMSON, WILFRID HARRY. The Byroms of Manchester. Vol. 3. Manchester: the author, 1968. 111 pp., illus.

1138. *Carew*. HALLIDAY, FRANK. A Cornish chronicle: the Carews of Antony from Armada to Civil War. Newton Abbot, Devon: David & Charles, 1967. 171 pp.,

1139. *Chase*. NOBLE, ARTHUR HENRY. The Chase family. Heraldry Today, 1967. 113 pp.

1140. *Chevallier*. TYE, WALTER. The Chevalliers of Aspall Hall, their cider press and barley corn. *Soc. Jersiaise Bull. Annuel*, XIX pt. 4 (1968) 307–14.

1141. *Cocks*. SOMERS COCKS, JOHN VERNON. A history of the Cocks family. Pt. 4. Newton Abbot, Devon: the author, 1967. 151 pp., illus.

1142. *Cookson*. HEDLEY, W. PERCY, *and* HUDLESTON, CHRISTOPHE ROY. Cookson of Penrith, Cumberland and Newcastle-upon-Tyne. Kendal, Westmor.: R. C. Cookson, 1968. 34 pp.

1143. CRASTER, *Sir* EDMUND. The early history of the Craster family. *Berwicks. Naturalists' Club Hist.* for 1966, XXXVII pt. 2 (1967) 133–49, pt. 3 (1968) 241–9.

1144. *Crawshay*. TAYLOR, MARGARET STEWART. The Crawshays of Cyfarthfa Castle: a family history. Hale, 1967. 190 pp., illus.

1145. *Cumine*. DICKIE, J. The Cumines of Rattray. *Buchan Trans.*, XVIII (1967) 31–8.

1146. *Denham*. HEHIR, BRENDAN O. The family of Denham of Egham. *Surrey Archaeol. Coll.*, LXV (1968) 71–85.

1147. *Denton.* HUDLESTON, CHRISTOPHE ROY. Denton Holme. Pt. 1. *Cumberland & Westmorland Antiq. & Archaeol. Soc. Trans.*, LXVIII (1968) 72–116.

1148. *Dryhurst.* WILLIAM, DAFYDD WYN. Teulu'r Dryhursts ym Mon. *Anglesey Antiq. Soc. & F. C. Trans.* (1968) 20–37. ['The Dryhurst family in Anglesey'.]

1149. *Eyre.* MEREDITH, ROSAMOND. The Eyres of Hassop, and some of their connections, from the Test Act to emancipation. *Recusant Hist.*, IX (1967–8) 5–52, 267–87.

1150. *Farmer.* WEBSTER, C. D. A Farmer descent. *Halifax Antiq. Soc. Trans.* (1968) 37–43.

1151. *Foster.* BARRETT, FRANK. The Fosters of Black Dyke Mills. *Halifax Antiq. Soc. Trans.* (1967) 55–72.

1152. *Fuller.* SALT, MARY C. L. The Fullers of Brightling Park. Pt. 2. *Sussex Archaeol. Coll.*, CVI (1968) 73–88.

1153. *Gordon.* MITCHELL, G. W. Huntly and the Gordons. *Buchan Trans.*, XVIII (1967) 11–16.

1154. GORRIE, R. MACLAGAN. The siol Gorrie. *Scot. Geneal.*, XV (1968) 36–43.

1155. *Hanscombe.* HANSCOMB, CHARLES E. Common blood: an exercise in family history. Queen Anne P., 1967. 192 pp., illus.

1156. *Harward.* BRAGGE, N. W. Hayne House and the Harward family. *Devon & Cornwall N. & Q.*, XXX (1967) 270–4.

1157. *Hastings.* SMITH, J. A. CLARENCE. Hastings of Little Easton. *Essex Archaeol. Soc. Trans.*, 3rd ser. II pt. 2 (1968) 101–22.

1158. *Herbert.* LEVER, *Sir* TRESHAM. The Herberts of Wilton. Murray, 1967. xiv, 270 pp., illus.

1159. *Hog.* WHYTE, DONALD. The Hogs of Harcase and Bogend. *Scot. Geneal.*, XIV (1967) 21–4.

1160. *Houstoun.* WHYTE, DONALD. The Houstouns of Houstoun. *Scot. Geneal.*, XV (1968) 66–9, 86–92.

1161. *Knight.* INGLIS-JONES, ELISABETH. The Knights of Downton Castle. *Nat. Lib. Wales Jour.*, XV (1967–8) 237–64, 366–88.

1162. *Lacy.* WIGHTMAN, WILFRED E. The Yorkshire Lacys, 1066–1193. *Univ. Leeds Rev.*, X (1966–7) 120–32.

1163. *Lamplugh.* JABEZ-SMITH, A. R. The Lamplughs of Cockermouth and a Yorkshire inheritance. *Cumberland & Westmorland Antiq. & Archaeol. Soc. Trans.*, LXVII (1967) 80–92.

1164. LINDSAY, *Sir* DARYL. The leafy tree: my family. Melbourne: F. W. Cheshire; London: Newnes, 1967. ix, 198 pp., illus.

1165. *Longvillers.* CLAY, *Sir* CHARLES TRAVIS. The family of Longvillers. *Yorks. Archaeol. Jour.*, XLII (1967) 41–51.

1166. *MacDonald.* The MacDonalds (MacConnell) of Largie in Kintyre. *Scot. Geneal.*, XIV (1967) 76–80.

1167. *McGuinness.* MATHEWS, ANTHONY. Origin of the surname McGuinness, with a short history of the sept. Dublin: the author, 1968. 35 pp.

1168. MCLACHLAN, T. McLachlans at sea. *Scot. Geneal.*, XV (1968) 1–5.

1169. *MacQuarrie.* MUNRO, ROBERT WILLIAM. The MacQuarries of Ulva. *Scot. Geneal.*, XV (1968) 25–31.

1170. *Minet.* MATSON, COLIN. Men of Kent, 3, Minet and Fector of Dover. *Archaeologia Cantiana* for 1966, LXXXI (1967) 39–43.

1171. *Montgomerie.* FRANKLYN, CHARLES AUBREY HAMILTON. A genealogical history of the families of Montgomerie of Garboldisham, Hunter of Knap and Montgomerie of Fittleworth. Ditchling, Sussex: Ditchling P., 1967. xvi, 124 pp., illus.

1172. MURIEL, JOHN HALLAM LESLIE. A fenland family: some notes on the history of a family surnamed Muriel. Ipswich, Suffolk: East Anglian Magazine Ltd., 1968. 95 pp.

1173. *O'Flaherty.* MATHEWS, ANTHONY. Origin of the surname O'Flaherty, with a short history of the sept. Dublin: the author, 1968. 43 pp., illus.

1174. *Ogilvy.* FRASER, DUNCAN. The land of the Ogilvys. Rev. edn. Montrose, Angus: Standard P., 1967. 159 pp., illus. [Previous edn. 1964.]

1175. *O'Kelly.* MATHEWS, ANTHONY. Origin of the surname O'Kelly, with a short history of the sept. Dublin: the author, 1968. 50 pp.

1176. *Pegge.* MEREDITH, ROSAMOND. Beauchief Abbey and the Pegges. *Derbys. Archaeol. Jour.* for 1967, LXXXVII (1968) 86–116.

1177. PHILIP, PETER. The story of a Fifeshire family. *Scot. Geneal.*, XV (1968) 59–65. [Philip.]

1178. POWELL, ANTHONY DYMOKE. The Powell family of Castleton, Priory Wood, and Dorstone, Herefordshire. *Radnors. Soc. Trans.*, XXXVIII (1968) 54–60.

1179. *Pringle.* BUIST, A. A. Some notes on the Pringle family. *Berwicks. Naturalists' Club Hist.* for 1967, XXXVII pt. 3 (1968) 234–40.

1180. *Rawdon.* ARMITAGE, HELEN. The Rawdon family. *Halifax Antiq. Soc. Trans.* (1967) 37–53.

1181. RIVIERE, MICHAEL V. B. The Hugenot family of Riviere in England. *Huguenot Soc. London Proc.*, XXI no. 3 (1968) 219–40.

1182. *Rocheid.* ARMET, HELEN. The Rocheids of Inverleith, 1634–1737. *Scot. Geneal.*, XIV (1967) 10–20.

1183. *Savage.* DONE, W. E. P. Notes on the Sussex family of Savage. *Sussex Archaeol. Coll.*, CV (1967) 76–83.

1184. *Saville.* BRETTON, ROWLAND. The Saville family. *Halifax Antiq. Soc. Trans.* (1968) 45–55.

1185. *Seyntclere.* HANHAM, HAROLD JOHN. The Seyntcleres of Tidwell: the rise and fall of a Budleigh family. *Devon Assoc. Repts. & Trans.*, XCIX (1967) 139–46.

1186. *Sheldon.* MINNEY, T. BRENDAN. The Sheldons of Beoley. *Worcs. Recusant*, no. 5 (1965) 1–17.

1187. *Shelley.* STEVENS, F. BENTHAM. The exodus from Sussex of the Shelleys. *Sussex N. & Q.*, XVII no. 1 (1968) 1–9.

1188. *Somervill.* NISBETT, HAMILTON MORE. The Somervills of the Drum. *Berwicks. Naturalists' Club Hist.* for 1966, XXXVII pt. 2 (1967) 115–19.

1189. STEWART, R. M. The Stewarts of Glengalmadale: cadets of Ardsheal. *Stewarts*, XIII no. 1 (1968) 20–8.

1190. *Walmesley.* BRIGG, MARY. The Walmesleys of Dunkenhalgh: a family of Blackburn Hundred in the Elizabethan and Stuart periods. *Lancs. & Cheshire Antiq. Soc. Trans.* for 1965–6, LXXV–LXXVI (1968) 72–102.

1191. *Watson.* BREY, JANE W. T. A Quaker saga: the Watsons of Strawberryhowe, the Wildmans and other allied families from England's north counties and the Lower Bucks County in Pennsylvania. Philadelphia, Penn.: Dorrance, 1967. xxvi, 646 pp.

1192. *Washington.* HEDLEY, W. PERCY, *and* WASHINGTON, GEORGE. The Washingtons of Helton Flecket, Westmorland. *Cumberland & Westmorland Antiq. & Archaeol. Soc. Trans.*, LXVIII (1968) 42–56.

1193. YOUNG, W. E. V. Notes on the Young family of Ebbesbourne Wake. *Wilts. Archaeol. & Nat. Hist. Mag.*, LXII (1967) 110–14.

PARISH REGISTERS, MONUMENTAL INSCRIPTIONS, WILLS, ETC.

1194. TILLOTT, P. M. Transcribing parish registers. *Amateur Historian*, VII (1967) 138–45.

1195. STEEL, DONALD JOHN. National index of parish registers. Vol. 1, Sources of births, marriages and deaths before 1837. Soc. Genealogists, 1968. xxvi, 439 pp.

1196. GUILDHALL LIBRARY. Parish registers: a handlist. Pt. 3, 'Foreign registers', i.e. registers and register transcripts of Anglican communities abroad. Corporation of London Lib. Committee, 1967. 12 pp.

1197. NOBLE, ARTHUR HENRY. The parish registers of Chardstock, Devon. *Devon Assoc. Repts. & Trans.*, C (1968) 227–9.

1198. MASTERS, BETTY R., *and* RALPH, ELIZABETH (*eds.*). The church book of St. Ewen's, Bristol, 1454–1584. (Bristol and Glos. Archaeol. Soc. Records Section Pubns., 9). Bristol: the Society, 1967. xxxix, 291 pp.

1199. DICKINSON, ROBERT (*ed.*). The registers of the parish of Childwall. Pt. 1, 1557–1680. (Lancs. Parish Register Soc. Pubns., 106). Manchester: the Society, 1967. vii, 222 pp.

1200. SPENCER, WILFRED M. (*ed.*). The parochial chapelry of Colne burial register, 1790–1812. Colne, Lancs.: the editor, 1968. viii, 159 pp.

1201. LEONARD, KATHLEEN, *and* LEONARD, G. O. G. (*eds.*). The second register book of the parish of Hawkshead, 1705–97. Hawkshead, Lancs.: Hawkshead Parochial Church Council, 1968. xiii, 151 ff.

1202. DICKINSON, FLORENCE (*ed.*). The registers of St. Helen's chapel in the parish of Prescot. Pt. 1, 1713–87. (Lancs. Parish Register Soc. Pubns., 107). Manchester: the Society, 1968. viii, 246 pp.

1203. WILSHERE, JONATHAN E. O. (*ed.*). Glenfield, Leics., parish register transcripts,

1604–1837. Kirby Muxloe, Leics.: the editor, 1968. iii, 93 pp.

1204. GIBSON, JEREMY SUMNER WYCHERLEY (*ed.*). Baptism and burial register of Banbury, Oxon. Pt. 2, 1653–1723. (Banbury Hist. Soc. Pubns., 9). Banbury, Oxon.: the Society, 1968. xviii, 268 pp.

1205. RICHARDSON, HAROLD (*ed.*). The parish registers of Askham Bryan, vols. 1–6, 1695–1837, and Askham Richard, 1813–37. Leeds: Yorks. Archaeol. Soc. Parish Register Section, 1967. x, 123 pp.

1206. THWAITE, HARTLEY (*ed.*). The parish register of Wensley. Vol. 2, 1701–1837. Leeds: Yorks. Archaeol. Soc. Parish Register Section, 1967. xi, 263 pp. [Vol. 1 pubd. Wakefield, Yorks.: Yorks. Parish Register Soc., 1939.]

1207. MITCHELL, JOHN FOWLER. Registers of births, deaths and marriages. *Scot. Geneal.*, XIV (1967) 26–35. [Pre-1855, not in custody of Registrar-General for Scotland.]

1208. CARGILL, DAVID C. Some more Presbyterian meeting-house registers. *Scot. Geneal.*, XV (1968) 32–5.

1209. MACPHERSON, ALAN G. An old Highland parish register: survivals of clanship and social change in Laggan, Inverness-shire, 1775–1854. *Scot. Studies*, XI (1967) 149–92, XII (1968) 81–111.

1210. PAYNE, R. W. J. List of memorials in the parish church of St. Peter Port. *Soc. Guernesiaise Rept. & Trans.* for 1966, XVIII (1967) 87–110.

1211. MITCHELL, JOHN FOWLER. Burial ground inscriptions. *Scot. Geneal.*, XIV (1967) 59–67. [List.]

1212. MITCHELL, J. F., *and* MITCHELL, SHEILA (*comps.*). Monumental inscriptions (pre-1855) in Clackmannanshire. Scottish Geneal. Soc., 1968. 2 vols.

1213. GILCHRIST, GEORGE (*comp.*). Memorials of Applegarth and Sibbaldie parish. Vol. 1, Sibbaldie. Annan, Dumfries.: the compiler, 1967. 14 pp.

1214. GILCHRIST, G. (*comp.*). Memorials of Caerlaverock parish. Annan, Dumfries.: the compiler, 1968. 46 pp.

1215. GILCHRIST, G. (*comp.*). Memorials of Dryfesdale parish. Annan, Dumfries.: the compiler, 1967. 63 pp., illus.

1216. GILCHRIST, G. (*comp.*). Memorials of Ewes parish. Annan, Dumfries.: the compiler, 1968. 21 pp.

1217. GILCHRIST, G. (*comp.*). Memorials of Hutton and Corrie parish. Annan, Dumfries.: the compiler, 1968. 43 pp.

1218. GILCHRIST, G. (*comp.*). Memorials of Kirkmichael parish. Annan, Dumfries.: the compiler, 1968. 21 pp.

1219. GILCHRIST, G. (*comp.*). Memorials of Langholm parish. Vol. 1, Wauchope. Annan, Dumfries.: the compiler, 1968. 41 pp.

1220. GILCHRIST, G. (*comp.*). Memorials of Lochmaben parish. Annan, Dumfries.: the compiler, 1967. 68 pp., illus.

1221. GILCHRIST, G. (*comp.*). Memorials of Mouswald parish. Annan, Dumfries.: the compiler, 1967. 54 pp., illus.

1222. GILCHRIST, G. (*comp.*). Memorials of Torthorwald parish. Annan, Dumfries: the compiler, 1968. 31 pp.

1223. GILCHRIST, G. (*comp.*). Memorials of Wamphray parish. Annan, Dumfries.: the compiler, 1968. 14 pp.

1224. MITCHELL, JOHN FOWLER, *and* MITCHELL, SHEILA (*comps.*). Monumental inscriptions (pre-1855) in Kinross-shire. Scottish Geneal. Soc., 1967. v, 93 pp.

1226. SELKIRKSHIRE ANTIQUARIAN SOCIETY. Gravestone inscriptions prior to 1855. Vol. 1, Selkirk, Ashkirk and Lindean old churchyards. Vol. 2, Galashiels old cemetery, Ladhope and Bewlie cemeteries. Selkirk: the Society, 1968. 2 vols.

1227. CLARKE, RICHARD SAMUEL JESSOP (*comp.*). Gravestone inscriptions. Vol. 2, County Down: baronies of Upper and Lower Castlereagh. (Ulster-Scot Geneal. ser.). Belfast: Ulster-Scot Hist. Soc., 1968. x, 105 pp., illus.

1228. HARRISON, J. V. Five Bewcastle wills, 1587–1617. *Cumberland & Westmorland Antiq. & Archaeol. Soc. Trans.*, LXVII (1967) 93–111.

1229. DARLINGTON, IDA (*ed.*). London Consistory Court wills, 1492–1547. (London Record Soc. Pubns., 3). The Society, 1967. xxv, 206 pp.

1230. WILLIS, ARTHUR JAMES (*comp.*). Wills, administrations and inventories with the Winchester diocesan records. Folkestone, Kent: the compiler, 1968. 94 pp.

1231. SKILLINGTON, FLORENCE E. Enclosed in clay: a study in Leicester wills. *Leics. Archaeol. Soc. Trans.* for 1966–7, XLII (1968) 35–52. [16th century.]

1232. THWAITE, HARTLEY (*ed.*). Abstracts of Abbotside wills, 1552–1688. (Yorks. Archaeol. Soc. Record ser., 130). Leeds: the Society, 1968. xiv, 146 pp.

1233. COLE, ERNEST JOHN LESLIE. Radnorshire wills: archdeaconry of Brecon. Pt. 1. *Radnors. Soc. Trans.*, XXXVIII (1968) 44–50.

1234. FITCH, MARC (*ed.*). Index to administrations in the Prerogative Court of Canterbury. Vol. 5, 1609–19. British Record Soc., 1968. viii, 192 pp.

1235. ROPER, JOHN STEPHEN (*ed.*). Dudley probate inventories, 3rd ser., with abstracts of wills and notes from Dudley parish registers. Dudley, Worcs.: the editor, 1968. 38 ff.

1236. WEBB, NEVILLE. Probate records at the Borthwick Institute of Historical Research, York. *Nat. Reg. Archives, W. Riding N. Section Bull.*, X (1967) 1–15.

1237. WILLIS, ARTHUR J. (*comp.*). Canterbury marriage licences, 1751–80. Folkestone, Kent: the compiler, 1967. 372 pp.

COLLECTED BIOGRAPHY

1238. COSTIGAN, GIOVANNI. Makers of modern England: the force of individual genius in history. New York: Macmillan (N.Y.); London: Collier-Macmillan, 1967. xiii, 334 pp., illus.

1239. DUPUY, MICHELINE. Françaises, reignes d'Angleterre. Paris: Perrin, 1968. 409 pp., illus.

1240. PECKHAM, W. D. Additions and corrections to J. and J. A. Venn, *Alumni Cantabrigienses. Sussex Archaeol. Coll.*, CVI (1968) 1–39.

1241. LOCKETT, TERENCE ANTHONY. Three lives: Samuel Bamford, Alfred Darbyshire, Ellen Wilkinson. Univ. London P., 1968. 64 pp., illus.

PART TWO: PERIOD HISTORIES

PRE-CONQUEST PERIOD, *c.* A.D. 450–1066

GENERAL

1242. KIRBY, DAVID PETER. The making of early England. Batsford, 1967. 320 pp., illus.

1243. WILSON, DAVID M. Archaeological evidence for the Viking settlements and raids in England. *Frühmittelalterliche Studien*, II (1968) 291–304.

1244. JANSSON, SVEN BIRGER FREDRIK. Swedish Vikings in England: the evidence of the rune stones. (Dorothea Coke Memorial Lecture, 1965). H. K. Lewis for University College London, 1967. 20 pp., illus.

1245. CRAMP, ROSEMARY. Anglian and Viking York. (Borthwick Papers, 33). York: St. Anthony's P., 1967. 21 pp., illus.

1246. BERSU, GERHARD. The Vikings in the Isle of Man. *Manx Museum Jour.*, VII no. 84 (1968) 83–8.

1247. VON FEILITZEN, OLOF. Some Old English uncompounded personal names and bynames. *Studia Neophilologica*, XL (1968) 5–16.

POLITICAL HISTORY

1248. RUBY, A. T. The coming of the Saxons. *Leatherhead & District Local Hist. Soc. Proc.*, III no. 2 (1968) 45–8.

1249. PORTER, HENRY MAURICE. The Saxon conquest of Somerset and Devon. Bath, Som.: Brodie, 1967. 87 pp.

1250. HOLLISTER, C. WARREN. 'Military obligation in late Saxon and Norman England'. *In* Ordinamenti militari in Occidente nell' alto Medioevo (Settimane di Studio del Centro italiano di studi sull' alto Medioevo, 15. Spoleto: Panetto & Petrelli, 1968) Vol. 1, pp. 169–86.

1251. PRESTWICH, JOHN OSWALD. King Aethelhere and the battle of the Winwaed. *E. H. R.*, LXXXIII (1968) 89–95.

1252. LOYN, HENRY ROYSTON. Alfred the Great. O.U.P., 1967. 64 pp.

1253. NELSON, JANET L. The problem of King Alfred's royal anointing. *Jour. Eccles. Hist.*, XVIII (1967) 145–63.

1254. LANCASTER, JOAN CADOGAN. Godiva of Coventry. (Coventry Papers, 1). Coventry, Warwicks.: the Corporation, 1967. ix, 114 pp.

1255. KAYE, J. M. The sacrabar. *E.H.R.*, LXXXIII (1968) 744–58.

1256. WHITELOCK, DOROTHY. 'Wulfstan *cantor* and Anglo-Saxon law'. *In* Nordica et anglica, *ed.* A. H. Orrick (Paris, The Hague: Mouton, 1968) pp. 83–92.

ECONOMIC AND SOCIAL HISTORY

1257. DUFERMONT, J.-C. Les pauvres d'après les sources anglo-saxonnes, du 7e au lle siecle, *Rev. du Nord*, L (1968) 189–201.

1258. GELLING, MARGARET. The charter bounds of Æscesbyrig and Ashbury. *Berks. Archaeol. Jour.*, LXIII (1967–8) 5–13.

1259. MACQUEEN, JOHN. Saints, legends and Celtic life. *Folk Life*, V (1967) 5–18.

RELIGIOUS HISTORY

1260. BARLEY, MAURICE WILLMORE, *and* HANSON, RICHARD PATRICK CROSLAND (*eds.*). Christianity in Britain, 300–700; papers presented to the Conference on Christianity in Roman and sub-Roman Britain, 1967. Leicester: Leicester U.P., 1968. 221 pp., illus.

1261. CHANEY, WILLIAM A. The royal role in the conversion of England. *Jour. Church & State*, IX (1967) 317–31.

1262. MCALPINE, ROBERT GEORGE. Celtic Christianity: the story of the Celtic religion in the British Isles. Harrogate, Yorks.: Merrythought P., 1967. 118 pp.

1263. BIELER, LUDWIG. The Christianisation of the insular Celts. *Celtica*, VIII (1968) 112–25.

1264. BIELER, LUDWIG. 'La conversione al cristianesimo dei celti insulari e le sue repercussioni nel continente'. *In* La conversione al cristianesimo nell'Europa dell' alto Medioevo (Settimane di studio del Centro italiano di studi sull'alto Medioevo, 14. Spoleto: Panetto & Petrelli, 1967) pp. 559–80.

1265. GREENE, D. 'Some linguistic evidence relating to the British Church'. *In* Christianity in Britain, 300–700, *ed.* M. W. Barley *and* R. P. C. Hanson (Leicester: Leicester U.P., 1968) pp. 75–86.

1266. FENN, R. W. D. Early Christianity in Herefordshire. *Woolhope Naturalists' F.C. Trans.*, XXXIX (1968) 333–47.

1267. THOMAS, ANTHONY CHARLES. 'The evidence from North Britain'. *In* Christianity in Britain, 300–700, *ed.* M. W. Barley *and* R. P. C. Hanson (Leicester: Leicester U.P., 1968) pp. 93–121.

1268. BRECHTER, SUSO. 'Zur Bekehrungsgeschichte der Angelsachsen'. *In* La conversione al cristianesimo nell'Europa dell' alto Medioevo (Settimane di studio del Centro italiano di studi sull'alto Medioevo, 14. Spoleto: Panetto & Petrelli, 1967) pp. 191–215.

1269. WILSON, DAVID M. The Vikings' relationship with Christianity in Northern England. *Brit. Archaeol. Assoc. Jour.*, 3rd ser. XXX (1967) 37–46.

1270. SHAW, R. CUNLIFFE. Prolegomena to a reappraisal of early Christianity in Man relative to the Irish Sea Province. *Isle of Man Nat. Hist. & Antiq. Soc. Proc.*, n.s. VII no. 1 (1967) 49–84.

1271. LAMB, JOHN WILLIAM. The archbishopric of York: the early years. Faith P., 1967. 156 pp.

1272. MAYR-HARTING, HENRY MARIA ROBERT EGMONT. Paulinus of York. *Studies in Church Hist.*, IV (1967) 15–21.

1272a. COOPER, JANET. The dates of the bishops of Durham in the first half of the 11th century. *Durham Univ. Jour.*, XXIX no. 3 (1968) 131–7.

1273. KIRBY, DAVID PETER. The Saxon bishops of Leicester, Lindsey (*Syddensis*), and Dorchester. *Leics. Archaeol. Soc. Trans.* for 1965–6, XLI (1967) 1–8.

1274. STENTON, *Sir* FRANK MERRY. The founding of Southwell minster. *Thoroton Soc. Trans.* for 1967, LXXI (1968) 13–17.

1275. HANSON, RICHARD PATRICK CROSLAND. St. Patrick: his origins and career. Oxford: Clarendon P., 1968. 248 pp.

1276. BIELER, LUDWIG. 'St. Patrick and the British Church'. *In* Christianity in Britain, 300–700, *ed.* M. W. Barley *and* R. P. C. Hanson (Leicester: Leicester U.P., 1968) pp. 123–30.

1277. FINBERG, HERBERT PATRICK REGINALD. St. Patrick at Glastonbury. *Irish Eccles. Record*, 5th ser. CVII (1967) 345–61.

1278. CRAWFORD, JANE. St. Bertellin of Stafford. *Downside Rev.*, LXXXVI (1968) 56–67.

1279. ALBERTSON, CLINTON. Anglo-Saxon saints and heroes. New York: Fordham U.P., 1967. 347 pp.

1280. PRICE, MARY ROPER. Bede and Dunstan. (Clarendon Biographies, 21). O.U.P., 1968. 64 pp., illus.

LITERATURE, ART AND ARCHITECTURE

1281. BOLTON, WHITNEY FRENCH. A history of Anglo-Latin literature, 597–1066. Vol. 1. 597–740. Princeton, N.J.: Princeton U.P., 1967. xiv, 305 pp.

1282. OGILVY, J. D. A. Books known to the English, 597–1066. Cambridge, Mass.: Medieval Acad. America, 1967. 320 pp.

1283. WEIJENBORG, R. Deux sources grecques de la *Confession de Patrice. Rev. d'Hist. Écclesiastique*, LXII (1967) 361–78.

1284. HARRISON, KENNETH. The beginning of the year among Bede's successors. *Yorks. Archaeol. Jour.*, XLII (1968) 193–7.

1285. WHITELOCK, DOROTHY. The genuine Asser. (Stenton Lectures, 1967). Reading: the University, 1968. 21 pp.

1286. DEROLEZ, R. An epitome of the 'Anglo-Saxon Chronicle' in Lambert of St. Omer's 'Liber Floridus'. *Eng. Studies*, XLVIII (1967) 226–31.

1287. BARKER, E. E. The 'Anglo-Saxon Chronicle' used by Aethelweard. *Inst. Hist. Research Bull.*, XL (1967) 74–91.

1288. WHITBREAD, L. 'Beowulf' and archaeology: two further footnotes. *Neuphilologische Mitteil.*, LXIX (1968) 63–72.

1289. BRUCE-MITFORD, R. L. S. 'The reception by the Anglo-Saxons of Mediterranean art following their conversion from Ireland and Rome'. *In* La conversione al cristianesimo nell'Europa dell'alto Medioevo (Settimane di studio del Centro italiano di studi sull'alto Medioevo, 14. Spoleto: Panetto & Petrelli, 1967) pp. 797–825.

1290. SMITH, PETER TIMMIS. The glory of the Saxon crosses at Sandbach, Cheshire. Altrincham, Cheshire: Sherratt, 1968. 49 pp., illus.

1291. OKASHA, ELISABETH. The non-runic scripts of Anglo-Saxon inscriptions. *Cambridge Bibliog. Soc. Trans.*, IV no. 5 (1968) 321–38.

1292. WERCKMEISTER, OTTO-KARL. Irish-northumbrische Buchmalerei des 8. Jahrhunderts und monastische Spiritualität. Berlin: de Gruyter, 1967. 186 pp., illus.

1293. GUILMAIN, JACQUES. On the classicism of the 'classic' phase of Franco-Saxon manuscript illumination. *Art Bull.*, XLIX (1967) 231–5.

1294. BRISCOE, TERESA. The Anglo-Saxon S-shaped brooch in England with special reference to one from Lakenheath, Suffolk. *Cambridge Antiq. Soc. Proc.*, LXI (1968) 45–53.

1295. LUIS GARCÍA-MONTOTO, CARLOS MARÍA DE. 'La arquitectura primitiva cristiana en Inglaterra y sus relaciones con el prerrománico asturiano'. *In* Symposium sobre cultura asturiana de la Alta Edad Media (Oviedo: Ayuntamiento, 1967) pp. 51–8.

1296. GILBERT, EDWARD. The church of St. Laurence, Bradford-on-Avon. *Wilts. Archaeol. & Nat. Hist. Mag.*, LXII (1967) 38–50.

1297. TAYLOR, HAROLD MCCARTER. Belfry towers in Anglo-Saxon England. *N. Staffs. Jour. Field Studies*, VIII (1968) 9–18.

EARLY WALES

1298. DAVIES, W. H. 'The Church in Wales'. *In* Christianity in Britain, 300–700, *ed.* M. W. Barley *and* R. P. C. Hanson (Leicester: Leicester U.P., 1968) pp. 131–50.

1299. FENN, R. W. D. The character of early Christianity in Radnorshire. *Radnors. Soc. Trans.*, XXXVII (1967) 7–16, XXXVIII (1968) 26–38.

1300. WATKINS, M. P. Lann Custehinn Garthbenni. *Woolhope Naturalists' F. C. Trans.* for 1966, XXXVIII (1967) 196–203. [Near Welsh Bicknor, now in Herefs.]

EARLY SCOTLAND

1301. HENDERSON, ISABEL. The Picts. Thames & Hudson, 1967. 228 pp., illus.

1302. ANGUS-BUTTERWORTH, LIONEL MILNER. Ancient Pictish monuments in Angus and Perthshire. *Ancient Monuments Soc. Trans.* for 1966–7, n.s. XIV (1968) 39–56.

1303. GORDON, C. A. The Pictish animals observed. *Soc. Antiq. Scot. Proc.* for 1964–6, XCVIII (1967) 215–24.

1304. SMALL, ALAN. The historical geography of the Norse Viking colonisation of the Scottish Highlands. *Norsk Geog. Tidsskrift*, XXII (1968) 1–16.

1305. RADFORD, COURTENAY ARTHUR RALEGH. The early Church in Strathclyde and Galloway. *Medieval Archaeol.* for 1967, XI (1968) 105–26.

1306. BOYLE, ALEXANDER. St. Ninian: some outstanding problems. *Innes. Rev.*, XIX (1968) 57–70.

EARLY IRELAND

1307. BANNERMAN, JOHN W. 'The Dal Riata and Northern Ireland in the 6th and 7th centuries'. *In* Celtic studies, *ed.* J. Carney *and* D. Greene (Routledge, 1968) pp. 1–11.

1308. DE PAOR, LIAM. 'The age of the Viking wars'. *In* The course of Irish history, *ed.* T. W. Moody *and* F. X. Martin (Cork: Mercier P., 1967) pp. 91–106.

1309. RYAN, JOHN. 'Brian Borumha, King of Ireland'. *In* North Munster studies, *ed.* E. Rynne (Limerick: Thomond Archaeol. Soc., 1967) pp. 355–74.

1310. O'FIAICH, TOMÁS. 'The beginnings of Christianity'. *In* The course of Irish history, *ed.* T. W. Moody *and* F. X. Martin (Cork: Mercier P., 1967) pp. 61–75.

1311. SCOTT, WILLIAM HENRY. Celtic culture and the conversion of Ireland. *Internat. Rev. Missions*, LVI (1967) 193–204.

1312. KEANE, EDWARD. 'St. Patrick's journey through West Limerick.' *In* North Munster Studies, *ed.* E. Rynne (Limerick: Thomond Archaeol. Soc., 1967) pp. 169–71.

1313. O'FIAICH, TOMÁS, *and* CONNOLLY, THURLOUGH. Irish cultural influence in Europe, 6th to 12th century. Dublin: Cultural Relations Committee of Ireland, 1967. 44 pp.

1314. COCCIA, EDMONDO. La cultura irlandese precarolingia: miracolo o mito? *Studi Medievali*, 3 ser. VIII (1967) 257–420.

1315. HENRY, FRANÇOISE. Irish art during the Viking invasions, 800–1020 A.D. Methuen, 1967. xvi, 236 pp., illus.

1316. DRAAK, MAARTJE. The higher teaching of Latin grammar in Ireland during the 9th century. Amsterdam: Noord-Hollandsche U.M., 1967. 38 pp.

MEDIEVAL PERIOD, 1066–1485

GENERAL

1317. DERWENT, KENNETH. Medieval London. Macdonald & Co., 1968. 126 pp., illus.

1318. BRECHIN, DEREK. The Conqueror's London. Macdonald & Co., 1968. 125 pp., illus.

1319. ROBERTSON, DURANT WAITE. Chaucer's London. New York, Chichester: Wiley, 1968. xiii, 241 pp., illus.

1320. URRY, WILLIAM. Canterbury under the Angevin Kings. Athlone P., 1967. xvi, 514 pp.

1321. DULLEY, A. J. F. Four Kent towns at the end of the Middle Ages. *Archaeologia Cantiana* for 1966, LXXXI (1967) 95–108. [Ashford, Hythe, Milton, Sittingbourne.]

1322. VIRGOE, ROGER. The government and society of Suffolk in the later Middle Ages. *Lowestoft Archaeol. & Local Hist. Soc. Annual Rept.* (1967–8) 28–32.

1323. WILKINSON, BERTIE. Fact and fancy in 15th century English history. *Speculum*, XLII (1967) 673–92.

CONSTITUTIONAL AND POLITICAL HISTORY

1324. DOUGLAS, DAVID. Les réussites normandes, 1050–1100. *Rev. Hist.*, CCXXXVII (1967) 1–16.

1325. POESSEL, ANDRÉ-EDGAR. La conquête de l'Angleterre. Mayenne: J. Floch, 1966. 167 pp.

1326. MAUROIS, ANDRÉ (*ed.*). La conquête de l'Angleterre par les normands. Paris: A. Michel, 1968. 365 pp.

1327. LOYN, HENRY ROYSTON. The Norman Conquest. 2nd edn. Hutchinson, 1968. 212 pp. [Previous edn. 1965.]

1328. BROWN, R. ALLEN. The Norman Conquest. *Roy. Hist. Soc. Trans.*, 5th ser. XVII (1967) 109–30.

1329. GALBRAITH, VIVIAN HUNTER. 1066 and all that: Norman Conquest commemoration lecture. Leicester: Leics. Archaeol. & Hist. Soc., 1967. 7 pp.

1330. HOLLISTER, C. WARREN. 1066: the 'feudal revolution'. *Amer. Hist. Rev.*, LXXIII no. 3 (1968) 708–23.

1331. CLARKE, H. B. The Norman Conquest of the West Midlands. *Vale Evesham Hist. Soc. Research Papers*, I (1967) 17–26.

1332. COUTANCHE, ALEXANDER MONCRIEFF, *Baron Coutanche*. The consequences of the Norman Conquest of England in relation to Jersey. *Soc. Jersiaise Bull. Annuel*, XIX pt. 3 (1967) 201–11.

1333. WALKER, DAVID. William the Conqueror. (Clarendon Biographies, 22). O.U.P., 1968. 60 pp., illus.

1334. LUCKOCK, ELIZABETH. The reign of the Conqueror. Wheaton, 1968. vii, 168 pp.

1335. GRINNELL-MILNE, DUNCAN. The killing of William Rufus: an investigation in the New Forest. Newton Abbot, Devon: David & Charles, 1968. 174 pp., illus.

1336. DAVIS, RALPH HENRY CARLESS. King Stephen, 1135–54. Longmans, 1967. 156 pp., illus.

1337. CRONNE, HENRY ALFRED, *and* DAVIS, R. H. C. (*eds.*). Regesta regum Anglo-Normannorum, 1066–1154. Vol. 3, Regesta regis Stephani ac Mathildis imperatricis ac Gaufridi et Henrici ducum Normannorum, 1135–54. Clarendon P., 1968. liii, 422 pp.

1338. WINSTON, RICHARD. Thomas Becket. Constable, 1967. 422 pp.

1339. DUGGAN, ALFRED. Thomas Becket of Canterbury. 2nd edn. Faber, 1967. 228 pp., illus. [Previous edn. 1952.]

1340. EDWARDS, J. GORONWY. 'Henry II and the fight at Coleshill': some further reflections. *Welsh Hist. Rev.*, III (1966–7) 251–63.

1341. PERNOUD, RÉGINE. Eleanor of Aquitaine, *transl.* P. Wiles. Collins, 1967. 286 pp., illus. [Originally pubd. Paris: Michel, 1965 as *Aliénor d'Aquitaine*.]

1342. FICHTENAU, HEINRICH. 'Akkon, Zypern und das Lösegeld für Richard Löwenherz'. *In* Bausteine zur Geschichte Österreichs (*Archiv für Osterreichische Gesch.*, 125; Graz, Wien, Köln: Böhlau, 1966) pp. 11–32.

1343. YOUNG, CHARLES R. Hubert Walter, lord of Canterbury and lord of England. Durham, N. C.: Duke U.P., 1968. viii, 196 pp.

1344. CHEYNEY, CHRISTOPHER ROBERT. Hubert Walter. Nelson, 1967. x, 198 pp.

1345. CHENEY, C. R. The twenty-five barons of Magna Carta. *John Rylands Lib. Bull.*, L (1967–8) 280–307.

1346. BEAN, JOHN MALCOLM WILLIAM. The decline of English feudalism, 1215–1540. Manchester: Manchester U.P., 1968. xii, 335 pp.

1347. CLANCHY, M. T. Did Henry III have a policy? *History*, LIII (1968) 203–16.

1348. HEWITT, HERBERT JAMES. Cheshire under the three Edwards. Chester: Cheshire Community Council, 1967. x, 118 pp.

1349. SALZMAN, LOUIS FRANCIS. Edward I. Constable, 1968. 224 pp., illus.

1350. STONES, EDWARD LIONEL GREGORY. Edward I. (Clarendon Biographies, 19). O.U.P., 1968. 60 pp., illus.

1351. SCHNITH, KARL. Staatsordnung und Politik in England zu Anfang des 14. Jahrhunderts. *Hist. Jahrbuch*, LXXXVIII (1968) 36–53.

1352. LAMBRICK, GABRIELLE. The impeachment of the abbot of Abingdon in 1368. *E.H.R.*, LXXII (1967) 250–76.

1353. CATTO, J. I. An alleged Great Council of 1374. *E.H.R.*, LXXXII (1967) 764–71.

1354. JONES, RICHARD HUTTON. The royal policy of Richard II: absolutism in the later Middle Ages. (Studies in Medieval Hist., 10). Oxford: Blackwell, 1968. viii, 199 pp.

1355. BARRON, CAROLINE M. The tyranny of Richard II. *Inst. Hist. Research Bull.*, XLI (1968) 1–18.

1356. TUCK, J. A. Richard II and the border magnates. *Northern Hist.*, III (1968) 27–52.

1357. MATHEW, GERVASE. The court of Richard II. Murray, 1968. xi, 227 pp., illus.

1358. ROGERS, ALAN. Henry IV and the revolt of the earls, 1400. *History Today*, XVIII (1968) 277–83.

1359. ROGERS, A. The political crisis of 1401. *Nottingham Medieval Studies*, XII (1968) 85–96.

1360. HUTCHISON, HAROLD FREDERICK. Henry V: a biography. Eyre & Spottiswoode 1967. 287 pp., illus.

1361. ALLMAND, C. T. Henry V. (Gen. ser., 68). Historical Assoc., 1968. 26 pp., illus.

1362. LEFÈVRE, RAYMONDE. Le cinquième Henry: Henry V, roi d'Angleterre 1413–22. Goudargues: Salamandre, 1967. 196 pp.

1363. ROGERS, ALAN. Maintenance and the Wars of the Roses. *History Today*, XVII (1967) 198–203.

1364. GRIFFITHS, RALPH A. Local rivalries and national politics: the Percies, the Nevilles, and the duke of Exeter, 1452–55. *Speculum*, XLIII (1968) 589–632.

1365. MCKENNA, J. W. The Coronation oil of the Yorkist kings. *E.H.R.*, LXXXII (1967) 102–4.

1366. LANDER, JACK ROBERT. The treason and death of the duke of Clarence: a re-interpretation. *Canadian Jour. Hist.*, II pt. 2 (1967) 1–28.

1367. MYERS, ALEC REGINALD. Richard III and historical tradition. *History*, LIII (1968) 181–202.

1368. SPUFFORD, PETER (*comp.*). Origins of the English parliament. Longmans, 1967. xiii, 221 pp.

1369. RICHARDSON, HENRY GERALD, *and* SAYLES, GEORGE OSBORNE. The earliest known official use of the term 'parliament'. *E.H.R.*, LXXXII (1967) 747–50.

1370. TAYLOR, JOHN. The manuscript of the 'Modus Tenendi Parliamentum'. *E.H.R.*, LXXXIII (1968) 673–88.

1371. ROSKELL, JOHN SMITH. A consideration of certain aspects and problems of the English 'Modus Tenendi Parliamentum'. *John Rylands Lib. Bull.*, L (1967–8) 411–42.

1372. POWELL, J. ENOCH, *and* WALLIS, KEITH. The House of Lords in the Middle Ages: a history of the English House of Lords to 1540. Weidenfeld, 1968. xix, 671 pp., illus.

1373. GOODMAN, ANTHONY. Sir Thomas Hoo and the parliament of 1376. *Inst. Hist. Research Bull.*, XLI (1968) 139–49.

1374. ROGERS, ALAN. Parliamentary electors in Lincolnshire in the 15th century. Pt. 1. *Lincs. Hist. & Archaeol.*, no. 3 (1968) 41–79.

1375. ROSENTHAL, JOEL T. The King's 'wicked advisers' and medieval baronial rebellions. *Political Science Quart.*, LXXXII (1967) 595–618.

1376. MASSEY, HECTOR J. John of Salisbury: some aspects of his political philosophy. *Classica et Mediaevalia*, XXVIII (1967) 357–72.

1377. ROUSE, RICHARD H., *and* ROUSE,

MARY A. John of Salisbury and the doctrine of tyrannicide. *Speculum*, XLII (1967) 693–709.

ADMINISTRATIVE AND LEGAL HISTORY

1378. WALKER, BARBARA MACDONALD. King Henry I's 'Old Men'. *Jour. Brit. Studies*, VIII no. 1 (1968) 1–21.

1379. BOND, SHELAGH. The medieval constables of Windsor Castle. *E.H.R.*, LXXXII (1967) 225–49.

1380. POLLARD, GRAHAM. The medieval town clerks of Oxford. *Oxoniensia* for 1966, XXXI (1968) 43–76.

1381. MAY, TERESA. The Cobham family in the administration of England, 1200–1400. *Archaeologia Cantiana* for 1967, LXXXII (1968) 1–31.

1382. CAPP, B. S. Sir Nicholas de Dagworth: the career of a royal servant in the 14th century. *Norfolk Archaeol.*, XXXIV pt. 2 (1967) 111–18.

1383. PRONAY, NICHOLAS. The Hanaper under the Lancastrian Kings. *Leeds Philos. & Lit. Soc. Proc., Lit. & Hist. Section*, XII pt. 3 (1967) 73–86.

1384. MORRIS, COLIN. William I and the Church courts. *E.H.R.*, LXXXII (1967) 449–63.

1385. TURNER, RALPH V. The king and his courts: the role of John and Henry III in the administration of justice, 1199–1240. Ithaca, N.Y.: Cornell U.P., 1968. xiv, 310 pp.

1386. TURNER, R. V. The royal courts treat disseizin by the king: John and Henry III, 1199–1240. *Amer. Jour. Legal Hist.*, XII (1968) 1–18.

1387. TURNER, R. V. The origins of the medieval English jury: Frankish, English, or Scandinavian? *Jour. Brit. Studies*, VII no. 2 (1968) 1–10.

1388. SAYLES, GEORGE OSBORNE (*ed.*). Select cases in the Court of King's Bench. Vol. 6, Under Edward III. (Selden Soc. Pubns., 82). Quaritch, 1965. 496 pp.

1389. CAM, HELEN MAUD (*ed.*). The Eyre of London, 14 Edward II, A.D. 1321. Vol. 1. (Year Books of Edward II, 26 pt. 1). Quaritch, 1968. 107 pp.

1390. GUTERMAN, SIMEON L. 'The transition from personality to territoriality of law in feudalism'. *In* Album J. Balon (Namur: Godenne, 1968) pp. 157–67.

1391. HANUS, JEROME J. Certiorari and policy-making in English history. *Amer. Jour. Legal Hist.*, XII (1968) 63–94.

1392. CLANCHY, M. T. The franchise of return of writs. *Roy. Hist. Soc. Trans.*, 5th ser. XVII (1967) 59–82.

1393. STONES, EDWARD LIONEL GREGORY. The text of the writ 'Quod omnes tangit' in Stubbs' *Select Charters. E.H.R.*, LXXXIII (1968) 759–60.

1394. LOGAN, F. DONALD. Excommunication and the secular arm in medieval England: a study in legal procedure from the 13th to the 16th century. (Studies & Texts, 15). Toronto: Pontifical Inst. of Medieval Studies, 1968. 239 pp.

1395. PRANGNELL, DUNSTAN (*ed.*). The chronicle of William of Byholte, 1310–20: an account of the legal system known as frankpledge. Westgate-on-Sea, Kent: the editor, 1967. 25 pp.

1396. DODWELL, BARBARA. Holdings and inheritance in medieval East Anglia. *Econ. Hist. Rev.*, 2nd ser. XX (1967) 53–66.

1397. RODEN, DAVID. Inheritance customs and succession to land in the Chiltern Hills in the 13th and early 14th centuries. *Jour. Brit. Studies*, VII no. 1 (1967) 1–11.

1398. MUNDAY, J. T. Eriswell: justice in a medieval west Suffolk community. *Suffolk Rev.*, III (1968) 238–46.

1399. ROWLEY, R. T. The Clee Forest: a study in common rights. *Shropshire Archaeol. Soc. Trans.* for 1965, LVIII pt.1 (1967) 48–67.

1400. IVES, ERIC WILLIAM. The common lawyers in pre-Reformation England. *Roy. Hist. Soc. Trans.*, 5th ser. XVIII (1968) 145–73.

1401. GALBRAITH, VIVIAN HUNTER. A draft of Magna Carta (1215). *Brit. Acad. Proc.*, LIII (1967) 345–60.

1402. MURPHY, BRYAN. The lawyer as historian: Magna Carta and public rights of fishery. *Irish Jurist*, n.s. III (1968) 131–45.

1403. MEEKINGS, C. Y. F. Robert of Nottingham, justice of the bench, 1244–6. *Inst. Hist. Research Bull.*, XLI (1968) 132–8.

1404. SUTHERLAND, D. W. Peytevin *v.* La Lynde. *Law Quart. Rev.*, LXXXIII (1967) 527–46.

1405. HARTLEY, T. G. The statute 23 Henry VI c. Kt: the problem of the texts. *E.H.R.*, LXXXII (1967) 544–8.

1406. KELLY, H. A. Canonical implications of Richard III's plan to marry his niece. *Traditio*, XXIII (1967) 269–311.

1407. PUGH, RALPH BERNARD. Imprisonment in medieval England. C.U.P., 1968. xvi, 420 pp., illus.

ECONOMIC AND SOCIAL HISTORY

Finance, industry and trade

1408. BERESFORD, MAURICE WARWICK. New towns of the Middle Ages: town plantation in England, Wales and Gascony. Lutterworth P., 1967. xx, 670 pp., illus.

1409. HILTON, RODNEY HOWARD. A medieval society: the west Midlands at the end of the 13th century. Weidenfeld, 1967. x, 305 pp., illus.

1410. WATTS, D. G. A model for the early 14th century. *Econ. Hist. Rev.*, 2nd ser. XX (1967) 543–7.

1411. HARVEY, S. Royal revenue and Domesday terminology. *Econ. Hist. Rev.*, 2nd ser. XX (1967) 221–8.

1412. TOMKINSON, A. The carucage of 1220 in an Oxfordshire hundred. *Inst. Hist. Research Bull.*, XLI (1968) 212–16.

1413. FRASER, CONSTANCE M. (*ed.*). The Northumberland lay subsidy roll of 1296. (Soc. Antiquaries Newcastle-upon-Tyne Record ser., 1). Newcastle-upon-Tyne: the Society, 1968. xxvi, 230 pp.

1414. BRYANT, W. N. The financial dealings of Edward III with the county communities, 1330–60. *E.H.R.*, LXXXIII (1968) 760–71.

1415. FRYDE, EDMUND BOLESLAW. Financial resources of Edward III in the Netherlands, 1337–40. Pt. 2. *Rev. Belge de Philol. et d'Hist.*, XLV (1967) 1142–215.

1416. DAVIES, R. REES. Baronial accounts, incomes, and arrears in the later Middle Ages. *Econ. Hist. Rev.*, 2nd ser. XXI (1968) 211–29.

1417. DYER, CHRISTOPHER. A redistribution of incomes in 15th century England? *Past & Present*, no. 39 (1968) 11–33.

1418. PUGH, RALPH BERNARD. Some medieval moneylenders. *Speculum*, XLIII (1968) 274–89.

1419. KNOOP, DOUGLAS, *and* JONES, GWILYM PEREDUR. The medieval mason: an economic history of English stone building in the later Middle Ages and early modern times. 3rd edn. Manchester: Manchester U.P.; New York: Barnes & Noble, 1967. xiv, 272 pp. [Previous edn. 1949.]

1420. JOHNSON, H. THOMAS. Cathedral building and the medieval economy. *Explorations in Entrepreneurial Hist.*, 2nd ser. IV (1967) 191–210, V (1967) 108–10.

1421. HELLE, KNUT. Trade and shipping between Norway and England in the reign of Håkon Håkonsson, 1217–63. *Sjøfartshist. Årb.* (1967) 7–34.

1422. STURLER, JEAN DE. 'Debita mercatorum Brabancie': documents anglais relatifs aux articles livrés à la Garde-robe par des négociants brabançons, au paiement tardif de ces fournitures ainsi qu'aux modes de paiement (1296–1321). *Acad. Roy. Belgique, Comm. Roy. d'Hist. Bull.*, CXXXIV (1968) 285–356.

1423. CARUS-WILSON, ELEANORA MARY. Medieval merchant venturers: collected studies. 2nd edn. Methuen, 1967. xxxvi, 314 pp., illus. [Previous edn. 1954.]

1424. CARUS-WILSON, E. M. The overseas trade of Bristol in the later Middle Ages. 2nd edn. Merlin P., 1967. xii, 338 pp. [Previous edn. Bristol Record Soc., 1937.]

1425. SHORTT, HUGH. A 13th century 'steelyard' balance from Huish. *Wilts. Archaeol. & Nat. Hist. Mag.*, LXIII (1968) 66–71.

1426. BLAKE, J. B. The medieval coal trade of north east England: some 14th century evidence. *Northern Hist.*, II (1967) 1–26.

1427. IVES, ERIC WILLIAM. Andrew Dymmock and the papers of Anthony, Earl Rivers, 1482–3. *Inst. Hist. Research Bull.*, XLI (1968) 216–29. [Business interests.]

1428. DUNNING, ROBERT WILLIAM (*ed.*). The Hylle cartulary. (Somerset Record Office Pubns., 68). Yeovil, Som.: Somerset R.O., 1968. xxxi, 188 pp.

1429. PATTERSON, ROBERT B. Stephen's Shaftesbury charter: another case against William of Malmesbury. *Speculum*, XLIII (1968) 487–92.

Social history

1430. BLACKLEY, F. D., *and* HERMANSEN, G. A household book of Queen Isabella of England, 1311–12. *Canadian Hist. Assoc. Rept.* (1968) 140–51.

1431. MYERS, ALEC REGINALD. The household of Queen Elizabeth Woodville, 1466–7. *John Rylands Lib. Bull.*, L (1967–8) 207–35.

1433. HILTON, RODNEY HOWARD. Villges désertés et histoire économique: recherches françaises et anglaises. *Études Rurales*, XXXII (1968) 104–9.

1434. STANFORD, S. C. The deserted medieval village of Hampton Wafer, Herefordshire. *Woolhope Naturalists' F.C. Trans.*, XXXIX (1967) 71–92.

1435. STANFORD, S. C. A medieval settlement at Detton Hall, Shropshire. *Shropshire Archaeol. Soc. Trans.* for 1965, LVIII pt. 1 (1967) 27–47.

1436. BARKER, P. A. The deserted medieval hamlet of Braggington. *Shropshire Archaeol. Soc. Trans.* for 1966, LVIII pt. 2 (1968) 122–39.

1437. TAYLOR, C. C. Three deserted medieval settlements in Whiteparish. *Wilts. Archaeol. & Nat. Hist. Mag.*, LXIII (1968) 39–45. [Whelpley, Cowsfield Green, More.]

1438. DYER, CHRISTOPHER. The deserted medieval village of Woollashill, Worcestershire. *Worcs. Archaeol. Soc. Trans.* for 1965–7, 3rd ser. I (1968) 55–61.

1439. WALMSLEY, J. F. R. The *censarii* of Burton abbey and the Domesday population. *N. Staffs. Jour. Field Studies*, VIII (1968) 73–80.

1440. ROBERTS, B. K. A study of medieval colonization in the Forest of Arden, Warickshire. *Agric. Hist. Rev.*, XVI (1968) 101–13.

1441. GOULD, J. Food, foresters, fines and felons: a history of Cannock Forest, 1086–1300. *Lichfield Archaeol. & Hist. Soc. Trans.* for 1965–6, VII (1967) 21–39.

1442. RAFTIS, J. A. Changes in an English village after the Black Death. *Mediaeval Studies*, XXIX (1967) 158–77. [Upwood, Hunts.]

Agrarian and manorial history

1443. DARBY, HENRY CLIFFORD, *and* FINN, REX WELLDON (*eds.*). The Domesday geography of south west England. C.U.P., 1967. xiv, 469 pp.

1444. SOMERS COCKS, J. V. Dartmoor and Domesday book. *Devon & Cornwall N. & Q.*, XXX (1967) 290–3.

1445. EVERETT, SUSANNA. The Domesday geography of three Exmoor parishes. *Somerset Archaeol. & Nat. Hist. Soc. Proc.*, CXII (1968) 54–60.

1446. FINN, REX WELLDON. The eastern counties. Longmans, 1967. xv, 231 pp. [Domesday.]

1447. FINN, R. W. The teamland of the Domesday Inquest. *E.H.R.*, LXXXIII (1968) 95–101.

1448. ORWIN, CHARLES STEWART, *and* ORWIN, CHRISTABEL SUSAN. The open fields. 3rd edn. Oxford: Clarendon P., 1967. xxvi, 196 pp., illus. [Previous edn. 1954.]

1449. HART, CYRIL. The hidation of Huntingdonshire. *Cambridge Antiq. Soc. Proc.*, LXI (1968) 55–66.

1450. HUGHES, C. J. Hides, carucates and yardlands in Leicestershire: the case of Saddington. *Leics. Archaeol. Soc. Trans.* for 1967–8, XLIII (1968) 19–23.

1451. BAKER, ALAN R. H. 'Some fields and farms in medieval Kent'. *In* Genese Siedlungs-Agrarlandschaft in Europa, *ed.* H. Jäger *and others* (Wiesbaden: Steiner, 1968) pp. 1–11.

1452. HALLAM, HERBERT ENOCH. The agrarian economy of south Lincolnshire in the mid-15th century. *Nottingham Medieval Studies*, XI (1967) 86–95.

1453. DYER, CHRISTOPHER. Population and agriculture on a Warwickshire manor in the later Middle Ages. *Univ. Birmingham Hist. Jour.*, XI (1967–8) 113–27.

1454. SIDDLE, D. J. The rural economy of medieval Holderness. *Agric. Hist. Rev.*, XV (1967) 40–5.

1455. WIGHTMAN, W. R. The pattern of vegetation in the Vale of Pickering area *c.* 1300 A.D. *Inst. Brit. Geographers' Trans.*, XLV (1968) 125–42.

1456. WAITES, BRYAN. Moorland and vale-land farming in north east Yorkshire: the monastic contribution in the 13th and 14th centuries. (Borthwick Papers, 32). York: St. Anthony's P., 1967. 35 pp.

1457. WAITES, B. Aspects of 13th and 14th century arable farming on the Yorkshire Wolds. *Yorks. Archaeol. Jour.*, XLII (1968) 136–42.

1458. CANTOR, L. M. The medieval forests and chases of Staffordshire. *N. Staffs. Jour. Field Studies*, VIII (1968) 39–53.

1459. CANTOR, L. M., *and* WILSON, J. D. The medieval deer-parks of Dorset. *Dorset Nat. Hist. & Archaeol. Soc. Proc.*, LXXXVIII (1967) 176–85, LXXXIX (1968) 171–80.

1460. LINDLEY, EDWARD SEARLES. The Manor of Yate. *Bristol & Glos. Archaeol. Soc. Trans.* for 1966, LXXXV (1967) 156–63.

1461. HOSFORD, W. H. The manor of Sleaford in the 13th century. *Nottingham Medieval Studies*, XII (1968) 21–39.

1462. LLOYD, ELEANOR. The farm accounts of the manor of Hendon, 1316–1416. *London & Middlesex Archaeol. Soc. Trans.*, XXI pt. 3 (1967) 157–63.

1463. QUAIFE, JILL. Reeve's account of the manor of Burnham 14–15 Richard II, A.D. 1390–1. *Essex Archaeol. Soc. Trans.*, 3rd ser. II pt. 2 (1968) 146–58.

1464. BRENT, JUDITH A. Alciston manor in the later Middle Ages. *Sussex Archaeol. Coll.*, CVI (1968) 89–102.

1465. AULT, WARREN O. Manor, court and parish church in 15th century England: a study of village by-laws. *Speculum*, XLII (1967) 53–67.

1466. GREEN, ANGELA. The stewardship of the liberty of the eight and a half hundreds. *Suffolk Inst. Archaeol. Proc.* for 1966, XXX (1967) 255–62.

RELIGIOUS HISTORY

General

1467. TAYLOR, JOHN. The Norman Conquest and the Church in Yorkshire. *Univ. Leeds Rev.*, X (1966–7) 231–55,

1468. BETHELL, DENIS. William of Corbeil and the Canterbury-York dispute. *Jour. Eccles. Hist.*, XIX (1968) 145–59.

1469. BRENTANO, ROBERT. Two churches: England and Italy in the 13th century. Princeton, N.J.: Princeton U.P., 1968. xvi, 372 pp.

1470. CHENEY, CHRISTOPHER ROBERT. England and the Roman Curia under Innocent III. *Jour. Eccles. Hist.*, XVIII (1967) 173–86.

1471. GRAY, J. W. The Church and Magna Charta in the century after Runnymede. *Hist. Studies*, VI (1968) 23–38.

1472. LUNT, WILLIAM E. Accounts rendered by papal collectors in England, 1317–68, *ed.* E. B. Graves. (Amer. Philos. Soc. Memoirs, 70). Philadelphia, Pa.: the Society, 1968. liv, 579 pp.

1473. PALMER, J. J. N. England and the Great Western Schism, 1388–99. *E.H.R.*, LXXXIII (1968) 516–22.

1474. ASTON, MARGARET. Thomas Arundel: a study of church life in the reign of Richard II. Oxford: Clarendon P., 1967. xiv, 456 pp.

1475. HAY, DENYS. The Church of England in the later Middle Ages. *History*, LIII (1968) 34–50.

1476. BROOKE, CHRISTOPHER NUGENT LAWRENCE. Religious sentiment and church design in the later Middle Ages. *John Rylands Lib. Bull.*, L (1967–8) 13–33.

1477. PAM, DAVID OWEN. Late medieval religion in Enfield, Edmonton and Tottenham. (Edmonton Hundred Hist. Soc. Occas. Papers, n.s. 12). The Society, 1968. 18 pp., illus.

Diocesan and parochial history

1478. JACOB, ERNEST FRASER. Archbishop Henry Chichele. Nelson, 1967. ix, 133 pp.

1479. SAYERS, JANE E. A record of the archbishop of Canterbury's feudal rights. *Soc. Archivists Jour.*, III no. 5 (1967) 213–21.

1480. HILL, ROSALIND MARY THEODOSIA. The labourers in the vineyard: the visitations of Archbishop Melton in the archdeaconry of Richmond. (Borthwick Papers, 35). York: St. Anthony's P., 1968. 21 pp.

1481. CROSBY, EVERETT U. 'The organisation of the English episcopate under Henry I'. *In* Studies in medieval and renaissance history, vol. 4, *ed.* W. M. Bowsky (Lincoln, Nebr.: Nebraska U.P., 1967) pp. 1–88.

1482. EDWARDS, KATHLEEN. The English secular cathedrals in the Middle Ages: a constitutional study with special reference to the 14th century. 2nd edn. Manchester: Manchester U.P.; New York: Barnes & Noble, 1967. xx, 412 pp., illus. [Previous edn. 1949.]

1483. OFFLER, HILARY SETON (*ed.*). Durham episcopal charters, 1071–1152. (Surtees Soc. Pubns., 179). Gateshead: Northumberland P., for the Society, 1968. xvi, 192 pp.

1484. STOREY, ROBIN LINDSAY (*ed.*). The register of Thomas Langley, bishop of Durham, 1406–37. Vol. 5. (Surtees Soc. Pubns., 177). Durham: Andrews & Co. for Surtees Soc.; London: Quaritch, 1966. ix, 197 pp.

1486. DUNSTAN, GORDON REGINALD (*ed.*). The register of Edmund Lacy, bishop of Exeter, 1420–55, 'Registrum Commune'. Vol. 3. (Devon and Cornwall Record Soc. Pubns., n.s. 13). Exeter: the Society, with Canterbury and York Society, 1968. 398 pp.

1487. SCOTT, J. G. M. Casting a bell for Exeter cathedral, 1372. *Devon Assoc. Repts. & Trans.*, C (1968) 191–203.

1488. LINCOLN CATHEDRAL. The 'Registrum antiquissimum' of the cathedral church of Lincoln. Vol. 9, *ed.* K. Major. (Lincoln Record Soc. Pubns., 62). Lincoln: the Society, 1968. xxxii, 329 pp.

1489. GALBRAITH, VIVIAN HUNTER. Notes on the career of Samson, bishop of Worcester (1096–1112). *E.H.R.*, LXXXII (1967) 86–101.

1490. HAINES, ROY M. Aspects of the episcopate of John Carpenter, bishop of Worcester, 1444–76. *Jour. Eccles. Hist.*, XIX (1968) 11–40.

1491. HAINES, R. M. Bishop Carpenter's injunctions to the diocese of Worcester in 1451. *Inst. Hist. Research Bull.*, XL (1967) 203–7.

1492. DUNNING, ROBERT WILLIAM. Rural deans in England in the 15th century. *Inst. Hist. Research Bull.*, XL (1967) 207–13.

1493. BOWKER, MARGARET. The secular clergy in the diocese of Lincoln, 1495–1520. (Cambridge Studies in Medieval Life and Thought, n.s. 13). C.U.P., 1968. xii, 253 pp.

1494. LE NEVE, JOHN. Fasti ecclesiae anglicanae, 1066–1300. Rev. edn. 1, St. Paul's, London, *comp.* D. E. Greenway. Inst. Hist. Research, Athlone P., 1968. xx, 115 pp. [Originally pubd. H. Clements, 1716.]

1495. BILL, PETER ANTONY. The Warwickshire parish clergy in the later Middle Ages. (Dugdale Soc. Occas. Papers, 17). Stratford-upon-Avon, Warwicks.: the Society, 1967. 29 pp.

1496. KEMP, BRIAN R. The mother church of Thatcham. *Berks. Archaeol. Jour.*, LXIII (1967–8) 15–22.

1497. DOBSON, R. B. The foundation of perpetual chantries by the citizens of medieval York. *Studies in Church Hist.*, IV (1967) 22–38.

1498. HOCKEY, S. F. The Newport chantry. *Hants. F.C. Trans.*, XXIII (1968) 90–5. [Isle of Wight.]

Religious orders

1499. CHIBNALL, MARJORIE. Monks and pastoral work: a problem in Anglo-Norman history. *Jour. Eccles. Hist.*, XVIII (1967) 165–72.

1500. HILL, BENNETT DAVID. English Cistercian monasteries and their patrons in the 12th century. Urbana, Ill., London: Illinois U.P., 1968. xiii, 188 pp.

1501. DICKINSON, JOHN C. Les constructions des premiers chanoines réguliers en Angleterre. *Cahiers de Civilisation Médiévale*, X (1967) 179–98.

1502. HULL, PETER LAWRENCE. 'The foundation of St. Michael's Mount in Cornwall, a priory of the abbey of Mont. St. Michel'. *In* Millénaire monastique du Mont St. Michel, vol. 1, *ed.* J. Laporte (Paris: Lethielleux, 1967) pp. 703–24.

1503. MATTHEW, DONALD. 'Mont St. Michel and England'. *In* Millénaire monastique du Mont St. Michel, vol. 1, *ed.* J. Laporte (Paris: Lethielleux, 1967) pp. 677–700.

1504. HOCKEY, S. F. Otterton priory and Mont St. Michel, its mother-house. *Devon & Cornwall N. & Q.*, XXXI (1968) 1–10.

1505. SALTMAN, AVROM (*ed.*). The cartulary of Dale abbey. H.M.S.O., 1967. 423 pp.

1506. SALTMAN, A. The history of the foundation of Dale abbey or, the so-called 'Chronicle of Dale': a new edition. *Derbys. Archaeol. Jour.* for 1967, LXXXVII (1968) 18–38.

1507. MOREY, ADRIAN, *and* BROOKE, CHRISTOPHER NUGENT LAWRENCE (*eds.*). The letters and charters of Gilbert Foliot, abbot of Gloucester (1139–48), bishop of Hereford (1148–63) and London (1163–87): an edition projected by the late Z. N. Brooke. Cambridge: C.U.P., 1967. liv, 576 pp., illus.

1508. STRINGER, K. J. Some documents concerning a Berkshire family and Monk Sherborne priory, Hampshire. *Berks. Archaeol. Jour.*, LXIII (1967–8) 23–37. [Achard family.]

1509. WILLIAMS, DAVID HENRY. The white monks of Dore, 1147–1536. Chepstow, Mon.: the author, 1967. 14 pp.

1510. KEMP, BRIAN R. The monastic dean of Leominster. *E.H.R.*, LXXXIII (1968) 505–15.

1511. EMDEN, ALFRED BROTHERSTON. Donors of books to St. Augustine's abbey, Canterbury. (Oxford Bibliog. Soc. Occas. Pubns., 4). Oxford: the Society, 1968. viii, 46 pp.

1512. HARVEY, BARBARA F. Abbot Gervase de Blois and the fee-farms of Westminster Abbey. *Inst. Hist. Research Bull.*, XL (1967) 127–42.

1513. LUFFIELD PRIORY. Luffield priory charters. Pt. 1, *ed.* G. R. Elvey. (Northants. Record Soc. Pubns., 22 pt. 1). Oxford: the Society, 1968. xviii, 298 pp.

1514. SEARLE, ELEANOR. Battle abbey and exemption: the forged charters. *E.H.R.*, LXXXIII (1968) 449–80.

1515. SEARLE, E., *and* ROSS, BARBARA (*eds.*). The cellarers' rolls of Battle abbey, 1275–1513. (Sussex Record Soc. Pubns., 65). Lewes, Sussex: the Society, 1967. xxiii, 199 pp.

1516. MUMFORD, W. F. Tercians of the estates of Wenlock priory. *Shropshire Archaeol. Soc. Trans.* for 1965, LVIII pt. 1 (1967) 68–76.

1517. DARLINGTON, REGINALD RALPH (*ed.*). The cartulary of Worcester cathedral priory. (Pipe Roll Soc. Pubns., n.s. 38). The Society, 1968. lxx, 375 pp., illus.

1518. HALSOP, G. S. The creation of Brother John Sherburn as abbot of Selby. *Yorks. Archaeol. Jour.*, XLII (1967) 25–30. [1368.]

1519. DOBSON, BARRIE. The election of John Ousthorp as abbot of Selby in 1436. *Yorks. Archaeol. Jour.*, XLII (1967) 31–40.

Theology and worship

1520. DIVERRES, A. H. An Anglo-Norman life of St. Melor. *Nat. Lib. Wales Jour.*, XV (1967–8) 167–75.

1521. HALLIER, AMÉDÉE. God is friendship: the key to Aelred of Rievaulx's Christian humanism. *Amer. Benedictine Rev.*, XVIII (1967) 393–420.

1522. ROBERTS, PHYLLIS BARZILLAY. Stephanus de lingua-tonante: studies in the sermons of Stephen Langton. (Studies & Texts, 16). Toronto: Pontifical Inst. of Medieval Studies, 1968. xii, 271 pp.

1523. GIEBEN, SERVUS. Robert Grosseteste on preaching, with the edition of the sermon 'Ex rerum initiatarum' on redemption. *Collectanea Franc.*, XXXVII (1967) 100–41.

1524. CATTO, J. I. New light on Thomas Docking, O.F.M. *Medieval & Renaissance Studies*, VI (1968) 135–49.

1525. ZENK, JOSEPH P. Henry of Wile (*d.* 1329): a witness to the condemnations at Oxford. *Franciscan Studies*, XXVIII (1968) 215–48.

1526. BROOMFIELD, F. (*ed.*). Thomae de Chobham *Summa Confessorum.* (Analecta Mediaevalia Namurcensia, 25). Louvain: Nauwelaerts, 1968. lxxxviii, 719 pp.

1527. GÁL, GIDEON. Gualteri de Chatton et Guillelmi de Ockham controversia de natura conceptus universalis. *Franciscan Studies*, XXVII (1967) 191–212.

1528. BROWN, STEPHEN F. Sources for Ockham's prologue to the *Sentences*. Pt. 2. *Franciscan Studies*, XXVII (1967) 39–107.

1529. MIETHKE, JÜRGEN. Zu Wilhelm Ockhams Tod. *Archivum Franciscanum Historicum*, LXI (1968) 79–98.

1530. CROMPTON, JAMES. John Wyclif: a study in mythology. *Leics. Archaeol. Soc. Trans.* for 1966–7, XLII (1968) 6–34.

1531. DYSON, THOMAS. Wycliff reviewed. *Church Quart. Rev.*, CLXVIII (1967) 423–33.

1532. LEFF, GORDON. Wyclif and Hus: a doctrinal comparison. *John Rylands Lib. Bull.*, L (1967–8) 387–410, 443–81.

1533. FINES, JOHN. William Thorpe: an early Lollard. *History Today*, XVIII (1968) 495–503.

1534. HODGSON, PHYLLIS. Three 14th century English mystics. Longmans, for British Council, and National Book League, 1967. 47 pp. ['Cloud of unknowing'; Richard Rolle; Walter Hilton.]

1535. DOIRON, MARILYN, *and* PORETE, MARGARET. 'The mirror of simple souls': a Middle English version. *Arch. Ital. Stor. Pietà*, V (1967) 241–362.

1536. ROBBINS, ROSSELL HOPE. A middle English prayer to St. Mary Magdalen. *Traditio*, XXIV (1968) 458–64.

1537. COLLEDGE, EDMUND, *and* CHADWICK, NOEL. 'Remedies against temptations': the third English version of William Flete. *Arch. Ital. Stor. Pietà*, V (1967) 201–40.

1538. LOVATT, ROGER. The 'Imitation of Christ' in late medieval England. *Roy. Hist. Soc. Trans.*, 5th ser. XVIII (1968) 97–121.

1539. HARGREAVES, HENRY. 'The Mirror of Our Lady': Aberdeen University Library

MS. 134. *Aberdeen Univ. Rev.*, XLII (1967–8) 267–80.

1540. DEVEREUX, JAMES A. The primers and prayer book collects. *Huntington Lib. Quart.*, XXXII (1968–9) 29–44.

1541. GRAY, ANDREW. A Carthusian *Carta Visitationis* of the 15th century. *Inst. Hist. Research Bull.*, XL (1967) 91–101.

Judaism

1542. LIPMAN, VIVIAN DAVID. The anatomy of medieval Anglo-Jewry. *Jewish Hist. Soc. Eng. Trans.* for 1962–7, XXI (1968) 64–77.

1543. LIPMAN, V. D. The Jews of medieval Norwich. Jewish Hist. Soc. England, 1967. x, 355 pp., illus.

1544. RABINOWITZ, LOUIS. The London *Get* of 1287. *Jewish Hist. Soc. Eng. Trans.* for 1962–7, XXI (1968) 314–22.

CULTURAL HISTORY

Learning and education

1545. LEFF, GORDON. Paris and Oxford universities in the 13th and 14th centuries: an institutional and intellectual history. New York, London: Wiley, 1968. xi, 331 pp.

1546. SCHOECK, R. J. On rhetoric in 14th century Oxford. *Mediaeval Studies*, XXX (1968) 214–25.

1547. POLLARD, GRAHAM. The oldest statute book of the university. *Bodleian Lib. Record*, VIII no. 2 (1968) 69–91.

1548. CHENEY, MARY G. Master Geoffrey de Lucy, an early chancellor of the university of Oxford. *E.H.R.*, LXXXII (1967) 750–63.

1549. EMDEN, ALFRED BROTHERSTON. Accounts relating to an early Oxford house of scholars. *Oxoniensia* for 1966, XXXI (1968) 77–81.

1550. DALES, RICHARD C., *and* GIEBEN, SERVUS. The prooemium to Robert Grosseteste's 'Hexaemeron'. *Speculum*, XLIII (1968) 451–61.

1551. WEISHEIPL, JAMES A. Ockham and some Mertonians. *Mediaeval Studies*, XXX (1968) 163–213.

1552. PINBORG, JAN. Walter Burleigh on the meaning of propositions. *Classica et Mediaevalia* XXVIII (1967) 394–404.

1553. WEISS, ROBERTO. Uno scolaro inglese dello Studio padovano: John Tiptoft, conte di Worcester (*c.* 1427–70). *Quaderni Stor. Univ. Padova*, I (1968) 73–81.

1554. WEISS, R. Humanism in England during the 15th century. 3rd edn. Oxford: Blackwell, 1967. 206 pp. [Previous edn. 1957.]

1555. HUMPHREYS, KENNETH. Distribution of books in the English West Midlands in the later Middle Ages. *Libri*, XVII (1967) 1–12.

1556. SCATTERGOOD, V. J. Two medieval book lists. *Library*, 5th ser. XXIII (1968) 236–9.

1557. ROTHWELL, W. The teaching of French in medieval England. *Mod. Language Rev.*, LXIII (1968) 37–46.

1558. ZETTERSTEN, ARNE (*ed.*). A Middle English lapidary: Bodleian Lib. Ms. Eng. Misc. e. 558. (Acta Univ. Lundensis, 1/10). Lund: Gleerup, 1968. 50 pp.

Literature and drama

1559. WHITEHEAD, F. Norman French: the linguistic consequences of the Conquest. *Manchester Lit. & Philos. Soc. Memoirs & Proc.*, CIX (1967) 78–83.

1560. KRISTENSSON, GILLIS. A survey of Middle English dialects, 1290–1350: the six northern counties and Lincolnshire. (Lund Studies in English, 35). Lund, Gleerup, 1967. 299 pp.

1561. HEILBRONNER, WALTER L. Printing and the book in 15th century England. Charlottesville, Va.: Virginia U.P., 1967. 105 pp.

1562. ROSSI, SERGIO. Il significato di William Caxton. *English Misc.*, XVIII (1967) 33–48.

1563. FOX, DENTON. Henryson and Caxton. *Jour. Eng. & Germanic Philol.*, LXVII (1968) 586–93.

1564. WOOLF, ROSEMARY. The English religious lyric in the Middle Ages. Oxford: Clarendon P., 1968. xi, 426 pp.

1565. ZETTERSTEN, ARNE. The Middle English lyrics in the Wellcome Library. *Neuphilol. Mitteil.*, LXVIII (1967) 288–94.

1566. ENGELS, L. J. Dichters over Willem de Veroveraar: het 'Carmen de Hastingae Proelio'. Groningen: Wolters, 1967. 24 pp. ['Poems about William the Conqueror'.]

1567. BALDWIN, ANNE W. Henry II and 'The Owl and the Nightingale'. *Jour. Eng. & Germanic Philol.*, LXVI (1967) 207–29.

1568. HALLIDAY, FRANK ERNEST. Chaucer and his world. Thames & Hudson, 1968. 144 pp., illus.

1569. SERRAILLER, IAN. Chaucer and his world. Lutterworth P., 1967. 48 pp.

1570. D'ARDENNE, S. R. T. O. 'Chaucer the Englishman'. *In* Chaucer und seine Zeit, *ed.* A. Esch (Tübingen: Niemeyer, 1968) pp. 47–54.

1571. HATTON, THOMAS J. Chaucer's crusading knight: a slanted ideal. *Chaucer Rev.*, III (1968) 77–87.

1572. HANDS, RACHEL. Juliana Berners and 'The Boke of St. Albans'. *Rev. Eng. Studies*, XVIII (1967) 373–86.

1573. KINGHORN, ALEXANDER MANSON. Medieval drama. Evans Bros., 1968. 160 pp., illus.

1574. BLAND, DESMOND SPARLING. The Chester mystery plays. *Cheshire Round*, I no. 7 (1967) 232–9.

1575. BROWN, ARTHUR. 'York and its plays in the Middle Ages'. *In* Chaucer und seine Zeit, *ed.* A. Esch (Tübingen: Niemeyer, 1968) pp. 407–18.

Architecture

1576. BRAUN, HUGH. An introduction to English medieval architecture. 2nd ed. Faber, 1968. 297 pp., illus. [Previous edn. 1951.]

1577. LANFREY, GEORGES. Les voûtures primitives romanes normandes à croisées d'ogives dans la province et en Angleterre. *Bull. Comm. Antiq. Seine-Maritime*, XXVI (1968) 247–55.

1578. KUNST, HANS-JOACHIM. Der Chor von Westminster Abbey und die Kathedrale von Reims. *Zeit. für Kunstgesch.*, XXXI (1968) 122–42.

1579. SVENDGAARD, PETER. Byland abbey: the builders and their marks. *Ryedale Historian*, no. 3 (1967) 26–9.

1580. JOHNSON, MARGOT. Recent work on the refectory of Durham cathedral. *Archaeol. & Archit. Soc. Durham & Northumberland Trans.*, n.s. I (1968) 85–93.

1581. GEE, ERIC. Discoveries in the frater at Durham. *Archaeol. Jour.* for 1966, CXXIII (1967) 69–78.

1582. FAULKNER, PATRICK ARTHUR. Ely: the monastic buildings south of the cloister. *Archaeol. Jour.* for 1967, CXXIV (1968) 216–21.

1583. EVERETT, A. W., *and* HOPE, VYVYAN. The rebuilding of Exeter cathedral *c.* 1270–1360. *Devon Assoc. Repts. & Trans.*, C (1968) 179–90.

1584. HUGHES, J. Recent discoveries at St. Oswald's church, Dean. *Cumberland & Westmorland Antiq. & Archaeol. Soc. Trans.*, LXVIII (1968) 35–41.

1585. BAYLEY, THOMAS DENIS SCOTT. Grey Friars' church, Chichester: the problem of the nave. *Sussex Archaeol. Coll.*, CV (1967) 70–5.

1586. HARRISON, KENNETH. Vitruvius and acoustic jars in England during the Middle Ages. *Ancient Monuments Soc. Trans.* for 1967–8, n.s. XV (1968) 49–58.

1587. RENN, DEREK FRANK. Norman castles in Britain. Baker, 1968. xiii, 364 pp., illus.

1588. DAVISON, BRIAN K. 'Three 11th century earthworks in England: their excavation and implications'. *In* Château Gaillard: Studien zur mittelalterlichen Wehrbau- und Siedlungsforschung, 2. Kolloquium Büderich bei Düsseldorf, 1964 (Cologne, Graz: Böhlau, 1967) pp. 39–48.

1589. GARDELLES, J. L'architecture militaire anglaise et les châteaux de Gascogne, 13e–14e siècles. *Bull. Monumental*, CXXV (1967) 133–56.

1590. LONG, BRIAN. Castles of Northumberland: the medieval fortifications of the county. Newcastle-upon-Tyne: H. Hill, 1967. 186 pp., illus.

1591. KEDNEY, K. J. Suffolk castles. *Lowestoft Archaeol. & Local Hist. Soc. Annual Rept.* (1967–8) 33–6.

1592. CHARLES, FREDERICK WILLIAM BOLTON. Medieval cruck-building and its derivatives: a study of timber-framed construction based on buildings in Worcestershire. (Soc. Medieval Archaeol. Monographs, 2). The Society, 1967. xiv, 70 pp., illus.

1593. HILL, PETER J., *and* PENROSE, DAVID G. Medieval timber framed houses in east Suffolk: an essay in classification. *Suffolk Inst. Archaeol. Proc.* for 1966, XXX (1967) 263–9.

1594. CHESTER, FRANK. The late medieval house at Colquite, St. Mabyn. *Cornish Archaeol.*, VI (1967) 57–64.

1595. FAULKNER, PATRICK ARTHUR. Medieval undercrofts and town houses. *Archaeol. Jour.* for 1966, CXXIII (1967) 120–35.

1596. RIGOLD, STUART EBORALL. Fourteenth century halls in the East Weald. *Archaeologia Cantiana* for 1967, LXXXII (1968) 246–56.

1597. RIGOLD, S. E. Some major Kentish timber barns. *Archaeologia Cantiana* for 1966, LXXXI (1967) 1–30.

1598. RIGOLD, S. E. The Cherhill barn. *Wilts. Archaeol. & Nat. Hist. Mag.*, LXIII (1968) 58–65.

1599. HEWETT, CECIL A. Jettying and floor-framing in medieval Essex. *Medieval Archaeol.* for 1966, X (1967) 89–112.

1600. ADAMS, J. H. A new type of cresset stone? *Cornish Archaeol.*, VI (1967) 47–57.

Arts and crafts

1601. VARTY, KENNETH. Reynard the Fox: a study of the fox in medieval English art. Leicester: Leicester U.P., 1967. 169 pp., illus.

1602. WORMALD, FRANCIS. Some pictures of the Mass in an English 14th century manuscript. *Walpole Soc. Annual Vol.*, XLI (1968) 39–45.

1603. STROHM, PAUL. The imagery of a missing window at Great Malvern priory church. *Worcs. Archaeol. Soc. Trans.* for 1965–7, 3rd ser. I (1968) 65–8.

1604. ROUSE, CLIVE, *and* BAKER, AUDREY. Wall-paintings in Stoke Orchard church, Gloucestershire, with particular reference to the cycle of the life of St. James the Great. *Archaeol. Jour.* for 1966, CXXIII (1967) 79–119.

1605. KASKE, R. E. Some newly discovered wall-paintings at Madley, Herefordshire. *Traditio*, XXIV (1968) 464–71.

1606. ROBERTS, EILEEN. The St. William of York mural in St. Albans abbey and *opus anglicanum*. *Burlington Mag.*, CX (1968) 236–41.

1607. MARSH-EDWARDS, J. C. The medieval Easter sepulchres of England. *Irish Eccles. Record*, 5th ser. CIX (1968) 116–21.

1608. PURCELL, DONOVAN. The De Thorp tomb at Ashwellthorpe. *Norfolk Archaeol.*, XXXIV pt. 3 (1968) 253–8.

1609. CARTER, R. O. M., *and* CARTER, H. M. The foliate head in England. *Folklore*, LXXVIII (1967) 269–74.

1610. PRITCHARD, VIOLET. English medieval graffiti. Cambridge: C.U.P., 1967. xii, 196 pp., illus.

1611. EAMES, ELIZABETH SARA. Medieval tiles: a handbook. British Museum, 1968. 34 pp., illus.

1612. MILLARD, LOUISE. Some medieval pottery from north Buckinghamshire. *Records of Bucks.*, XVIII pt. 2 (1967) 109–24.

1613. RYE, C. G., *and* HURST, JOHN G. Medieval pottery from Great Yarmouth. *Norfolk Archaeol.*, XXXIV pt. 3 (1968) 279–92.

1614. BARTON, KENNETH JAMES. The medieval pottery of the city of Worcester. *Worcs. Archaeol. Soc. Trans.* for 1965–7, 3rd ser. I (1968) 29–44.

1615. DUNNING, G. C. Late medieval jugs with lettering. *Medieval Archaeol.* for 1967, XI (1968) 233–41.

1616. KING, DONALD. A relic of 'Noble Erpingham'. *Victoria & Albert Museum Bull.*, IV (1968) 59–64. [Medieval chasuble.]

1617. FEARON, J. H. Primitive sundials or mass clocks. *Cake & Cockhorse*, IV (1968) 3–10.

SCIENCE AND MEDICINE

1618. EASTWOOD, BRUCE S. Medieval empiricism: the case of Grosseteste's optics. *Speculum*, XLIII (1968) 306–21.

1619. DALES, RICHARD C. Robert Grosseteste's views on astrology. *Mediaeval Studies*, XXIX (1967) 357–63.

1620. MCVAUGH, MICHAEL. Arnald of Villanova and Bradwardine's law. *Isis*, LVIII (1967) 56–64.

1621. MOLLAND, A. G. The geometrical background to the 'Merton School'. *Brit. Jour. Hist. Science*, IV pt. 2 (1968) 108–25.

1622. LAUER, HANS HUGO. Zur Beurteilung des Arabismus in der Medizin des Mittelalterlichen England. *Sudhoffs Archiv*, LI (1967) 326–48.

1623. TATTERSALL, IAN. Multivariate analysis of some medieval British cranial series. *Man*, III (1968) 284–92.

1624. TATTERSALL, I. Dental palaeopathology of medieval Britain. *Jour. Hist. Medicine & Allied Sciences*, XXIII (1968) 380–5.

MILITARY AND MARITIME HISTORY

1625. SCHLIGHT, JOHN. Monarchs and mercenaries: a reappraisal of the importance of knight service in Norman and early Angevin England. New York: New York U.P., for Conference on British Studies at the Univ. of Bridgeport, Conn., 1968. xi, 105 pp.

1626. COX, DAVID C. Battlewell, Evesham. *Worcs. Archaeol. Soc. Trans.* for 1964, n.s. XLI (1967) 1–9. [Site of battle, 1265.]

1627. PRESTWICH, MICHAEL. Victualling estimates for English garrisons in Scotland during the early 14th century. *E.H.R.*, LXXXII (1967) 536–43.

1628. PALMER, J. J. N. The last summons of the feudal army in England (1385). *E.H.R.*, LXXXIII (1968) 771–5.

1629. DUNNING, ROBERT WILLIAM. Thomas, Lord Dacre and the West March towards Scotland, ?1435. *Inst. Hist. Research Bull.*, XLI (1968) 95–9.

1630. ADAIR, JOHN. The newsletter of Gerhard von Wesel, 17 April 1471. *Soc. Army. Hist. Research Jour.*, XLVI (1968) 65–9. [About battle of Barnet.]

1631. TIPTON, CHARLES L. 'The English Hospitallers during the Great Schism'. *In* Studies in medieval and Renaissance history, vol. 4, *ed.* W. M. Bowsky (Lincoln, Nebr.: Nebraska U.P., 1967) pp. 89–124.

1632. TIPTON, C. L. The English and Scottish Hospitallers during the Great Schism. *Annales Ordre Malte*, XXV (1967) 18–21.

1633. LAPORTE, JEAN. Les opérations navales, en Manche et Mer du Nord pendant l'année 1066. *Annales de Normandie*, XVII (1967) 3–42.

1634. FREEMAN, A. Z. A moat defensive: the coast defense scheme of 1295. *Speculum*, XLII (1967) 442–62.

1635. JONES, MICHAEL. Two Exeter ship agreements of 1303 and 1310. *Mariner's Mirror*, LIII (1967) 315–19.

1636. SHERBORNE, JAMES WILSON. The English navy: shipping and manpower, 1369–89. *Past & Present*, no. 37 (1967) 163–75.

1637. RICHMOND, C. F. English naval power in the 15th century. *History*, LII (1967) 1–15.

1638. PRYNNE, M. W. Henry V's *Grace Dieu. Mariner's Mirror*, LIV (1968) 115–28.

1639. HEATH, PETER. North Sea fishing in the 15th century: the Scarborough fleet. *Northern Hist.*, III (1968) 53–69.

1640. TOUCHARD, H. Marins bretons et marins espagnols dans les ports anglais à la fin du Moyen Age. *Cuadernos de Hist., Anexos de la Rev. Hispania*, no. 2 (1968) 81–91.

1641. QUINN, DAVID BEERS. John Day and Columbus. *Geog. Jour.*, CXXXIII (1967) 205–9.

FRANCE AND FOREIGN RELATIONS

1642. ALLMAND, C. T. Diplomacy in late medieval England. *History Today*, XVII (1967) 546–53.

1643. FOWLER, KENNETH ALAN. The age of Plantagenet and Valois: the struggle for supremacy, 1328–1498. Elek, 1967. 208 pp., illus.

1644. RENOUARD, YVES. 'Ce que l'Angleterre doit à l'Aquitaine'. *In* Études d'histoire médiévale (Paris: S.E.V.P.E.N., 1968) pp. 863–75.

1645. RENOUARD, Y. 'Les relations d'Édouard II et Clément V d'après les rôles gascons'. *In* Études d'histoire médiévale (Paris: S.E.V.P.E.N., 1968) pp. 935–57.

1646. CAPRA (*pseud.*). L'histoire monétaire de l'Aquitaine anglo-gasconne au temps du Prince Noir (1354–72). *Bull. et Mém. Soc. Archéol. Bordeaux*, LXIV (1968) 93–151.

1647. VESSEM, H. A. VAN. De Engelse partij in het Koninkrijk Frankrijk gedurende de Honderdjarige oorlog. Utrecht: Bennebrock, 1966. 242 pp.

1648. KIRBY, JOHN LAVAN. The siege of Bourg, 1406. *History Today*, XVIII (1968) 53–60.

1649. ALLMAND, C. T. The Lancastrian land settlement in Normandy, 1417–50. *Econ. Hist. Rev.*, 2nd ser. XXI (1968) 461–79.

1650. ALLMAND, C. T. The Anglo-French negotiations, 1439. *Inst. Hist. Research Bull.*, XL (1967) 1–33.

1651. MUNRO, JOHN H. The costs of Anglo-Burgundian interdependence. *Rev. Belge de Philol. et d'Hist.*, XLVI (1968) 1228–38.

1652. RENOUARD, YVES. 'Les relations de Bordeaux et de Bristol au Moyen Age'. *In* Études d'histoire médiévale (Paris: S.E.V.P.E.N., 1968) pp. 993–1008.

1653. BAUGH, ALBERT CROLL. 'The background of Chaucer's mission to Spain'. *In*

Chaucer und seine Zeit, *ed.* A.Esch (Tübingen: Niemeyer, 1968) pp. 55–69.

1654. HELLE, KNUT. Anglo-Norwegian relations in the reign of Håkon Håkonsson, 1217–63. *Medieval Scandinavia*, I (1968) 101–14.

WALES

1655. RODERICK, A. J. Marriage and politics in Wales, 1066–1282. *Welsh Hist. Rev.*, IV (1968–9) 3–20.

1656. MAUD, RALPH. David, the last Prince of Wales: the ten 'lost' months of Welsh history. *Hon. Soc. Cymmrodorion Trans.* (1968) 43–62.

1657. ROWLANDS, EURYS. Dafydd ap Gwilym. *Y Traethodydd*, CXXII (1967) 15–35.

1658. JACK, R. IAN. Records of Denbighshire lordships. 2, The lordship of Dyffryn-Clwyd in 1324. *Denbighs. Hist. Soc. Trans.*, XVII (1968) 7–53.

1659. CARR, ANTHONY D. Welshmen and the Hundred Years' War. *Welsh Hist. Rev.*, IV (1968–9) 21–46.

1660. GRIFFITHS, RALPH A. The Glyn Dŵr rebellion in North Wales through the eyes of an Englishman. *Board of Celtic Studies Bull.*, XXII pt. 2 (1967) 151–68. [Thomas Barneby, Chamberlain of North Wales.]

1661. MESSHAM, J. E. The county of Flint and the rebellion of Owen Glyndŵr in the records of the earldom of Chester. *Flints. Hist. Soc. Pubns.*, XXIII (1967–8) 1–34.

1662. DUNN, ELIZABETH. Owain Glyndŵr and Radnorshire. *Radnors. Soc. Trans.*, XXXVII (1967) 27–35.

1663. ALLMAND, C. T. A bishop of Bangor during the Glyn Dŵr revolt: Richard Young. *Hist. Soc. Church in Wales Jour.*, XVIII (1968) 47–56.

1664. SMITH, J. BEVERLEY. The last phase of the Glyndŵr rebellion. *Board of Celtic Studies Bull.*, XXII pt. 3 (1967) 250–60.

1665. DAVIES, R. REES. Owain Glyn Dŵr and the Welsh squirearchy. *Hon. Soc. Cymmrodorion Trans.* (1968) 150–69.

1666. CARR, ANTHONY D. Sir Lewis John: a medieval London Welshman. *Board of Celtic Studies Bull.*, XXII pt. 3 (1967) 260–70.

1667. TAYLOR, ALFRED JOHN. An incident at Montgomery castle on New Year's Day, 1288. *Archaeologia Cambrensis*, CXVI (1967) 159–64.

1668. USHER, GWILYM. The foundation of an Edwardian borough: the Beaumaris Charter, 1296. *Anglesey Antiq. Soc. & F.C. Trans.* (1967) 1–16.

1669. COLE, ERNEST JOHN LESLIE. An incomplete account (10/11 Edward III). *Radnors. Soc. Trans.*, XXXVIII (1968) 39–43.

1670. ROBINSON, W. R. B. An analysis of a minister's account for the borough of Swansea for 1449. *Board of Celtic Studies Bull.*, XXII pt. 2 (1967) 169–98.

1671. THOMAS, COLIN. Thirteenth century farm economies in North Wales. *Agric. Hist. Rev.*, XVI (1968) 1–14.

1672. CRAMPTON, C. B. Hafotai platforms on the north front of Carmarthen Fan. *Archaeologia Cambrensis*, CXVII (1968) 121–6.

1673. ROBINSON, W. R. B. The Church in Gower before the Reformation. *Morgannwg*, XII (1968) 5–36.

1674. RICHTER, MICHAEL. Professions of obedience and the metropolitan claim of St. Davids. *Nat. Lib. Wales Jour.*, XV (1967–8) 197–214.

1675. JONES, EVAN J. Bishop John Trevor (II) of St. Asaph. *Hist. Soc. Chuch in Wales Jour.*, XVIII (1968) 36–46.

1676. COWLEY, F. G. The Cistercian economy in Glamorgan, 1130–1349. *Morgannwg*, XI (1967) 5–26.

1677. SMITH, J. BEVERLEY. Welsh Dominicans and the crisis of 1277. *Board of Celtic Studies Bull.*, XXII pt. 4 (1968) 353–7.

1678. JONES, FRANCIS. The Grey Friars of Carmarthen. *Carmarthens. Hist.*, III (1966) 7–35.

1679. JONES, THOMAS. Historical writing in medieval Wales. *Scot. Studies*, XII (1968) 15–27.

1680. REISS, EDMUND. The Welsh versions of Geoffrey of Monmouth's *Historia. Welsh Hist. Rev.*, IV (1968–9) 97–127.

1681. BISHOP, T. A. M. The Corpus Martianus Capella. *Cambridge Bibliog. Soc. Trans.*, IV no. 4 (1967) 257–75.

1682. RICHTER, MICHAEL. A new edition of the so-called 'Vita Dauidis Secundi'. *Board of Celtic Studies Bull.*, XXII pt. 3 (1967) 245–9.

1683. WRIGHT, CECIL F. Capel Ffynnon Fair: the chapel of St. Mary's well, near Cefn, Denbighshire. *Ancient Monuments Soc. Trans.* for 1967–8, n.s. XV (1968) 59–82.

1684. HOGG, A. H. A., *and* KING, D. J. CATHCART. Masonry castles in Wales and the marches: a list. *Archaeologia Cambrensis*, CXVI (1967) 71–132.

1685. SPURGEON, C. J. The castles of Montgomeryshire. *Montgomerys. Coll.* for 1965–6, LIX (1968) 1–59.

1686. RENN, DEREK FRANK. The *donjon* at Pembroke castle. *Ancient Monuments Soc. Trans.* for 1967–8, n.s. XV (1968) 35–47.

1687. CRASTER, O. E. Skenfrith castle: when was it built? *Archaeologia Cambrensis*, CXVI (1967) 133–58.

1688. GRESHAM, COLIN ALASTAIR. Medieval stone carving in North Wales: sepulchral slabs and effigies of the 13th and 14th centuries. Cardiff: Wales U.P., for Archaeology and Art Committee of Board of Celtic Studies, 1968. xxiv, 264 pp., illus.

SCOTLAND

1689. WILLIAMS, JAMES. A medieval iron smelting site at Millhill, New Abbey. *Dumfries. & Galloway Nat. Hist. & Antiq. Soc. Trans.*, XLIV (1967) 126–32.

1690. MCROBERTS, DAVID. The Scottish Church and nationalism in the 15th century. *Innes Rev.*, XIX (1968) 3–14.

1691. THOMSON, JOHN AIDAN FRANCIS. Innocent VIII and the Scottish Church. *Innes Rev.*, XIX (1968) 23–31.

1692. DUNLOP, ANNIE I. Notes on the Church in the dioceses of Sodor and Argyll. *Scot. Church Hist. Soc. Records*, XVI pt. 3 (1968) 179–84.

1693. COWAN, IAN BORTHWICK. The parishes of medieval Scotland. (Scottish Record Soc. Pubns., 93). Edinburgh: the Soc., 1967. xv, 226 pp.

1694. COWAN, I. B. Vicarages and the cure of souls in medieval Scotland. *Scot. Church Hist. Soc. Records*, XVI pt. 2 (1967) 111–27.

1695. MCKAY, DENIS. The duties of the medieval parish clerk. *Innes Rev.*, XIX (1968) 32–9.

1696. MCKAY, D. The election of parish clerks in medieval Scotland. *Innes Rev.*, XVIII (1967) 25–35.

1697. BULLOCH, JAMES. Stobo Kirk. *Church Service Soc. Annual*, XXXVIII (1968) 27–32.

1698. DOBSON, R. B. The last English monks on Scottish soil: the severance of Coldingham priory from the monastery of Durham, 1461–78. *Scot. Hist. Rev.*, XLVI (1967) 1–25.

1699. MCROBERTS, DAVID. Dean Brown's Book of Hours. *Innes Rev.*, XIX (1968) 144–67.

1700. TODD, J. M., *and* OFFLER, HILARY SETON. A medieval chronicle from Scotland. *Scot. Hist. Rev.*, XLVII (1968) 151–9.

1701. THOMSON, DERICK S. Gaelic learned orders and literati in medieval Scotland. *Scot. Studies*, XII (1968) 57–78.

1702. TOBIN, TERENCE. The first Scottish Masters of Revels: comptrollers of popular entertainment. *Theatre Survey*, IX (1968) 65–71.

1703. SLADE, H. GORDON. Drumminor, formerly Castle Forbes: an investigation into the original building of a mid-15th century palace house. *Soc. Antiq. Scot. Proc.* for 1966–7, XCIX (1968) 148–66.

1704. LYLE, E. B. Thomas of Erceldoune: the prophet and the prophesaid. *Folklore*, LXXIX (1968) 111–21.

IRELAND

Note: Writings on Irish domestic and local history are not included unless they have a direct bearing on English history.

1705. OTWAY-RUTHVEN, ANNETTE JOCELYN. A history of medieval Ireland. Benn, 1968. xv, 454 pp.

1706. GWYNN, AUBREY. The history of medieval Ireland. *Studies*, LVII (1968) 161–73.

1707. MARTIN, F. X. 'The Anglo-Norman invasion'. *In* The course of Irish history, *ed.* T. W. Moody *and* F. X. Martin (Cork: Mercier P., 1967) pp. 123–43.

1708. O'CUIV, BRIAN. 'Ireland in the 11th and 12th centuries'. *In* The course of Irish history, *ed.* T. W. Moody *and* F. X. Martin (Cork: Mercier P., 1967) pp. 107–22.

1709. MURPHY, BRYAN. The status of the native Irish after 1331. *Irish Jurist*, n.s. II (1967) 116–28.

1710. OTWAY-RUTHVEN, ANNETTE JOCELYN. Ireland in the 1350s: Sir Thomas de

Rokeby and his successors. *Roy. Soc. Antiq. Ireland Jour.*, XCVII (1967) 47–59.

1711. COSGROVE, ART. 'The Gaelic resurgence and the Geraldine supremacy, *c.* 1400–1534'. *In* The course of Irish history, *ed.* T. W. Moody *and* F. X. Martin (Cork: Mercier P., 1967) pp. 158–73.

1712. LYDON, JAMES F. 'The medieval English colony'. *In* The course of Irish history, *ed.* T. W. Moody *and* F. X. Martin (Cork: Mercier P., 1967) pp. 144–57.

1713. HAND, GEOFFREY JOSEPH PHILIP. English law in Ireland, 1290–1324. C.U.P., 1967. xii, 280 pp.

1714. HAND, G. J. P. The common law in Ireland in the 13th and 14th centuries: two cases involving Christ Church, Dublin. *Roy. Soc. Antiq. Ireland Jour.*, XCVII (1967) 97–111.

1715. FRAME, ROBIN. The judicial powers of the medieval Irish keepers of the peace. *Irish Jurist*, n.s. II (1967) 308–26.

1716. MACNIOCAILL, GEAROID. The heir designate in early medieval Ireland. *Irish Jurist*, n.s. III (1968) 326–9.

1717. OTWAY-RUTHVEN, ANNETTE JOCELYN. The partition of the De Verdon lands in Ireland in 1332. *Roy. Irish Acad. Proc. Section C*, LXVI (1967) 401–55.

1718. GWYNN, AUBREY. The 12th century reform. (Hist. of Irish Catholicism, vol. 2, fasc. 1). Dublin: Gill, 1968. 68 pp.

1719. HAND, GEOFFREY JOSEPH PHILIP. The Church in the English lordship, 1216–1307. (Hist. of Irish Catholicism, vol. 2, fasc. 3). Dublin: Gill, 1968. 43 pp.

1720. GWYNN, AUBREY. Anglo-Irish church life: 14th and 15th centuries. (Hist. of Irish Catholicism, vol. 2, fasc. 4). Dublin: Gill, 1968. 76 pp.

1721. VAREBEKE, HUBERT JANSSENS DE. 'Benedictine bishops in medieval Ireland'. *In* North Munster Studies, *ed.* E. Rynne (Limerick: Thomond Archaeol. Soc., 1967) pp. 242–50.

1722. O'DWYER, PETER. The Carmelite order in pre-Reformation Ireland. *Irish Eccles. Record*, 5th ser. CX (1968) 350–63.

1723. O'DWYER, B. W. Gaelic monasticism and the Irish Cistercians *c.* 1228. *Irish Eccles. Record*, 5th ser. CVIII (1967) 19–28.

1724. O'DWYER, B. W. The impact of the native Irish on the Cistercians in the 13th century. *Jour. Relig. Hist.*, IV (1967) 287–316.

1725. SCHOFIELD, A. N. E. D. Ireland and the Council of Basel. *Irish. Eccles. Record*, 5th ser. CVII (1967) 374–87. [1431–49.]

1726. MACNIOCAILL, GEAROID (*ed.*). Documents relating to the suppression of the Templars in Ireland. *Analecta Hibernica*, XXIV (1967) 181–226.

1727. PAGANINI, CARLO. Presenza dei Penitenziali irlandesi nel pensiero medievale. *Stud. Doc. Hist. Iuris*, XXXIII (1967) 359–65.

1728. WATERMAN, D. M. Rectangular keeps of the 13th century at Grenan (Kilkenny) and Glanworth (Cork). *Roy. Soc. Antiq. Ireland Jour.*, XCVIII (1968) 67–73.

1729. OTWAY-RUTHVEN, ANNETTE JOCELYN. Royal service in Ireland. *Roy. Soc. Antiq. Ireland Jour.*, XCVIII (1968) 37–46.

1730. MAC IOMHAIR, DIARMUID. The battle of Fochart, 1318. *Irish Sword*, VIII (1968) 192–209.

TUDOR PERIOD, 1485–1603

CONSTITUTIONAL AND POLITICAL HISTORY

1731. LEVINE, MORTIMER. Tudor England, 1486–1603. (Bibliog. Handbooks). C.U.P., for Conference on British Studies, 1968. xii, 115 pp.

1732. COLVIN, HOWARD MONTAGU. Castles and government in Tudor England. *E.H.R.*, LXXXIII (1968) 225–34.

1733. ROBERTSON, ARTHUR GEORGE. Tudor London. Macdonald & Co., 1968. 126 pp., illus.

1734. AVERY, DAVID. The Tudor hundred of Edmonton: evidences and survivals. (Edmonton Hundred Hist. Soc. Occas. Papers, n.s. 13). The Society, 1968, 25 pp.

1735. BOLITHO, JOHN R. Tudor Tottenham. (Edmonton Hundred Hist. Soc. Occas. Papers, n.s. 11). The Society, 1967. 27 pp.

1736. HURSTFIELD, JOEL. Was there a Tudor despotism after all? *Roy. Hist. Soc. Trans.*, 5th ser. XVII (1967) 83–108.

1737. FLETCHER, ANTHONY. Tudor rebellions. (Seminar Studies in Hist.). Longmans, 1968. ix, 168 pp.

1738. SIMONS, ERIC NORMAN. Henry VII: the first Tudor king. Muller, 1968. xiv, 322 pp., illus.

1739. STOREY, ROBIN LINDSAY. The reign of Henry VII. Blandford P., 1968. xii, 243 pp., illus.

1740. LOCKYER, ROGER. Henry VII. (Seminar Studies in Hist.). Longmans, 1968. vii, 160 pp.

1741. MEAGHER, JOHN C. The first progress of Henry VII. *Renaissance Drama*, n.s.I (1968) 45–73.

1742. SCARISBRICK, JOHN JOSEPH. Henry VIII. Eyre & Spottiswoode, 1968. xiv, 561 pp., illus.

1743. ZIMMERMANN, T. C. PRICE. A note on Clement VII and the divorce of Henry VIII. *E.H.R.*, LXXXII (1967) 548–52.

1744. ELTON, GEOFFREY RUDOLPH. Sir Thomas More and the opposition to Henry VIII. *Inst. Hist. Research Bull.*, XLI (1968) 19–34.

1745. ELTON, G. R. Reform by statute: Thomas Starkey's *Dialogue* and Thomas Cromwell's policy. *Brit. Acad. Proc.*, LIV (1968) 165–88.

1746. WIATT, WILLIAM H. Sir Thomas Wyatt and Anne Boleyn. *Eng. Lang. Notes*, VI no. 2 (1968) 94–102.

1747. JORDAN, WILBUR KITCHENER. Edward VI: the young King. Vol. 1, The protectorship of the duke of Somerset. Allen & Unwin, 1968. 544 pp.

1748. VINAY, VALDO. Riformatori e lotte contadine: scritti e polemiche relative alla ribellione dei contadini nella Cornovaglia e nel Devonshire sotto Edoardo VI. *Riv. Stor. Letter. Relig.*, III (1967) 203–51.

1749. EDELEN, GEORGES (*ed.*). William Harrison: the *Description of England.* Ithaca, N.Y.: Cornell U.P., 1968. 512 pp.

1750. CRINÒ, ANNA MARIA. La *Relatione d'Inghilterra* di Guido Bentivoglio. *Studi Secenteschi*, IX (1968) 259–86.

1750a. PELLEGRINI, GIULIANO. Un fiorentino alla corte d'Inghilterra nel Cinquecento: Petruccio Ubaldini. Turin: Bottega d'Erasmo, 1968. 152 pp.

1751. WILLIAMS, NEVILLE. Elizabeth, Queen of England. Weidenfeld, 1967. xii, 388 pp., illus.

1752. HAUGAARD, WILLIAM P. The coronation of Elizabeth I. *Jour. Eccles. Hist.*, XIX (1968) 161–70.

1753. SMITH, LACEY BALDWIN. The Elizabethan world. Boston, Mass.: Houghton Mifflin, 1967. 285 pp.

1754. SMITH, ALAN GORDON RAE. The government of Elizabethan England. Edward Arnold, 1967. viii, 119 pp.

1755. BECKINGSALE, BERNARD WINSLOW. Burghley: Tudor statesman, 1520–98. London: Macmillan; New York: St. Martin's P., 1967. x, 340 pp., illus.

1756. EDWARDS, FRANCIS. The marvellous chance: Thomas Howard, fourth duke of Norfolk, and the Ridolphi plot, 1570–2. Hart-Davis, 1968. 416 pp., illus.

1757. MANNING, ROGER B. Anthony Browne, 1st Viscount Montague: the influence in county politics of an Elizabeth Catholic nobleman. *Sussex Archaeol. Coll.*, CVI (1968) 103–12.

1758. MORALES LEZCANO, VÍCTOR. La guerra contra España en la filosofía política de Sir Walter Raleigh y Francis Bacon. *Rev. de Indias*, XXVIII (1968) 125–41.

1759. WAGNER, *Sir* ANTHONY, *and* SAINTY, JOHN C. The origin of the introduction of peers into the House of Lords. *Archaeologia*, CI (1967) 119–50.

1760. MILLER, HELEN. Attendance in the House of Lords during the reign of Henry VIII. *Hist. Jour.*, X (1967) 325–51.

1761. JONES, J. E. The parliamentary representation of Berkshire and its boroughs during the reign of Elizabeth I. *Berks. Archaeol. Jour.*, LXIII (1967–8) 39–56.

1762. CRUICKSHANK, CHARLES GRIEG. The parliamentary representation of Tournai. *E.H.R.*, LXXXIII (1968) 775–6.

ADMINISTRATIVE AND LEGAL HISTORY

1763. PONKO, VINCENT, *Jnr*. The Privy Council and the spirit of Elizabethan economic management, 1558–1603. *Amer. Philos. Soc. Trans.*, n.s. LVIII pt. 4 (1968) 5–63.

1764. SMITH, ALAN GORDON RAE. The secretariats of the Cecils, *c*. 1580–1612. *E.H.R.*, LXXXIII (1968) 481–504.

1765. STONE, LAWRENCE. Office under Queen Elizabeth: the case of Lord Hunsdon and the lord chamberlainship in 1585. *Hist. Jour.*, X (1967) 279–85.

1766. LEVINE, MORTIMER. Henry VIII's use of his spiritual and temporal jurisdiction in his great causes of matrimony, legitimacy, and succession. *Hist. Jour.*, X (1967) 3–10.

1767. ELTON, GEOFFREY RUDOLPH. The law of treason in the early Reformation. *Hist. Jour.*, XI (1968) 211–36.

1768. IVES, ERIC WILLIAM. The genesis of the Statute of Uses. *E.H.R.*, LXXXII (1967) 673–97.

1769. HOGREFE, PEARL. Sir Thomas More and Doctors Commons. *Moreana*, no. 14 (1967) 15–22.

1770. JOHANSSON, BERTIL. Law and lawyers in Elizabethan England as evidenced in the plays of Ben Jonson and Thomas Middleton. (Stockholm Studies in English, 18). Stockholm: Almqvist & Wiksell, 1967. 65 pp.

1771. JONES, WILLIAM JOHN. The Elizabethan Court of Chancery. Oxford: Clarendon P., 1967. xvii, 528 pp.

1772. WELCH, CHARLES EDWIN (*ed.*). The Admiralty Court Book of Southampton, 1566–85. (Southampton Records ser., 13). Southampton: Southampton U.P., 1968. xxiv, 143 pp.

1773. SMITH, A. HASSELL. Justices at work in Elizabethan Norfolk. *Norfolk Archaeol.*, XXXIV pt. 2 (1967) 93–110.

1774. MILLER, JENNIFER, *and* ROGERS, KENNETH HERBERT. The strange death of Edward Langford. *Wilts. Archaeol. & Nat. Hist. Mag.*, LXII (1967) 103–9. [1545.]

ECONOMIC AND SOCIAL HISTORY

1775. CHALLIS, C. E. The debasement of the coinage, 1542–51. *Econ. Hist. Rev.*, 2nd ser. XX (1967) 441–66.

1776. CRINÒ, ANNA MARIA. Proposte di oneri fiscali fatte da Petruccio Ubaldini, fiorentino, alla regina Elisabetta I d'Inghilterra. *Archivio Stor. Italiano*, CXXVI (1968) 287–98.

1777. CROSS, CLAIRE. Supervising the finances of the third earl of Huntingdon, 1580–95. *Inst. Hist. Research Bull.*, XL (1967) 34–49.

1778. KEW, JOHN E. Mortgages in mid-Tudor Devonshire. *Devon Assoc. Repts. & Trans.*, XCIX (1967) 165–79.

1779. KEW, J. E. The financial exploitation of the manor of Dartington in the mid-16th century. *Devon & Cornwall N. & Q.*, XXX (1967) 209–14.

1780. CROSSLEY, DAVID W. Glassmaking in Bagot's Park, Staffordshire, in the 16th century. *Post-Medieval Archaeol.*, I (1967) 44–83.

1781. OUTHWAITE, R. B. The price of Crown Land at the turn of the 16th century. *Econ. Hist. Rev.*, 2nd ser. XX (1967) 229–40.

1782. WHOMSLEY, DENNIS. William Ramsden of Longley, gentleman, 1514–80, agent in monastic property. *Yorks. Archaeol. Jour.*, XLII (1968) 143–50.

1783. SYME, S. A. The regulation of the English book trade, 1484–1547. *Jour. Lib. Hist.*, III (1968) 32–8.

1784. OLIVER, LESLIE MAHIN. A bookseller's account book, 1545. *Harvard Lib. Bull.*, XVI (1968) 139–55.

1785. MORRIS, JOHN. Restrictive practices in the Elizabethan book trade: the Stationers' Company *v.* Thomas Thomas, 1583–8. *Cambridge Bibliog. Soc. Trans.*, IV no. 4 (1967) 276–90.

1786. ZINS, HENRYK. Anglia a Baltyk w drugiej Polowie 16 wieku: Baltycki handel kupców Angielskich z Polska w epoce Elzbietánskiej i Kompania Wschodnia. Warsaw: Zaklad Narodowy im. Ossolińskich, Wydawnictwo Polskiej Akad. Nauk, 1967. 363 pp. ['England and the Baltic Sea in the second half of the 16th cent.: the Baltic trade of the English merchants with Poland in the Elizabethan age and the Eastland Company'. English summary.]

1787. COWGILL, URSULA M. Life and death in the 16th century in the city of York. *Population Studies*, XXI (1967) 53–62. [Criticisms by L. Henry and reply by author, in vol. XXII (1968) pp. 165–70.]

1788. JAMES, J. B. Sixteenth century travellers. *History Today*, XVII (1967) 189–96.

1789. MONCKTON, HERBERT ANTHONY. English ale and beer in Shakespeare's time. *History Today*, XVII (1967) 828–34.

1790. VERNON, THELMA E. Inventory of Sir Henry Sharington: contents of Lacock House, 1575. *Wilts. Archaeol. & Nat. Hist. Mag.*, LXIII (1968) 72–82.

1791. BARRATT, D. M. A second Northumberland household book. *Bodleian Lib. Record*, VIII no. 2 (1968) 93–8.

RELIGIOUS HISTORY

General and Anglicanism

1792. DICKENS, ARTHUR GEOFFREY. The English Reformation. Rev. edn. Collins, 1967. 511 pp. [Previous edn. 1964.]

1793. DICKENS, A. G., *and* CARR, DOROTHY (*comps.*). The Reformation in England to the accession of Elizabeth I. Edward Arnold, 1967. viii, 168 pp.

1794. DICKENS, A. G. Secular and religious motivation in the Pilgrimage of Grace. *Studies in Church Hist.*, IV (1967) 39–64.

1795. DAVIES, C. S. L. The Pilgrimage of Grace reconsidered. *Past & Present*, no. 41 (1968) 54–76.

1796. OPIE, JOHN. The Anglicising of John Hooper. *Archiv. für Reformationsgesch.*, LIX (1968) 150–77.

1797. WOUDE, C. VAN DER. John Jewel: Apologeet van het Anglicanisme. *Nederlands Archief voor Kerkgesch.*, XLVIII (1967) 213–31.

1798. TYLER, PHILIP. The significance of the Ecclesiastical Commission at York. *Northern Hist.*, II (1967) 27–44.

1799. HAUGAARD, WILLIAM P. Elizabeth and the English Reformation: the struggle for a stable settlement of religion. C.U.P., 1968. xv, 392 pp.

1800. MCGRATH, PATRICK VINCENT. Papists and Puritans under Elizabeth I. Blandford P., 1967. x, 434 pp., illus.

1801. MICKLEWRIGHT, F. H. AMPHLETT. The Reformation and the local historian. *Amateur Historian*, VII (1967) 253–7.

1802. COLLINSON, PATRICK. The Elizabethan Puritan movement. Cape, 1967. 528 pp.

1803. BECKWITH, FRANK. 'Dumb dogs and caterpillars'. *Univ. Leeds Rev.*, X (1966–7) 132–42. [Puritans.]

1804. NEW, JOHN F. H. The Whitgift-Cartwright controversy. *Archiv für Reformationsgesch.*, LIX (1968) 203–12.

1805. HORST, I. B. Anabaptism and the English Reformation to 1558. Nieuwkoop: de Graaf, 1966. 164 pp.

1806. LINDER, R. D. Pierre Viret and the 16th century English Protestants. *Archiv für Reformationsgesch.*, LVIII (1967) 149–71.

1807. REID, W. STANFORD. The divisions of the Marian exiles. *Canadian Jour. Hist.*, III no. 2 (1968) 1–26.

1808. LONGHURST, JOHN E. Los primeros luteranos ingleses en España, 1539. *Bol. de Estudios Históricos sobre San Sebastián*, no. 1 (1967) 13–32.

Diocesan, parochial and monastic history

1809. DAELEY, J. I. Pluralism in the diocese of Canterbury during the administration of Matthew Parker, 1559–75. *Jour. Eccles. Hist.*, XVIII (1967) 33–49.

1810. TREVOR-ROPER, HUGH REDWALD. The bishopric of Durham and the capitalist Reformation. *Durham Research Rev.*, no. 18 (1967) 103–16.

1810a. PILL, DAVID H. Exeter diocesan courts in the early 16th century. *Devon Assoc. Repts. & Trans.*, C (1968) 43–53.

1811. BOWKER, MARGARET (*ed.*). An

episcopal court book for the diocese of Lincoln, 1514–20. (Lincoln Record Soc. Pubns., 61). Lincoln: the Society, 1967. xxxii, 161 pp.

1812. MCLAREN, COLIN A. An early 16th century act book of the diocese of London. *Soc. Archivists Jour.*, III no. 7 (1968) 336–41.

1813. LOADES, D. M. The collegiate churches of County Durham at the time of the Dissolution. *Studies in Church Hist.*, IV (1967) 65–75.

1814. TYLER, PHILIP. The status of the Elizabethan parochial clergy. *Studies in Church Hist.*, IV (1967) 76–97.

1815. CHESTERS, GEOFFREY. Beyond the cloister: the dissolution of the Cheshire monasteries. Pt. 4. *Cheshire Round*, I no. 8 (1967) 275–81.

1816. SNELL, LAWRENCE SILVESTER. The suppression of the religious foundations of Devon and Cornwall. Marazion, Cornwall: Worden, 1967. 200 pp.

1817. JACK, SYBIL MILLINER. Monastic lands in Leicestershire and their administration on the eve of the dissolution. *Leics. Archaeol. Soc. Trans.* for 1965–6, XLI (1967) 9–40.

1818. WHALLEY, GWILYM. John Paslew, last abbot of Whalley. Ilfracombe, Devon: Stockwell, 1967. 16 pp., illus.

Roman Catholicism

1819. REYNOLDS, ERNEST EDWIN. The field is won: the life and death of St. Thomas More. Burns & Oates, 1968. xv, 396 pp., illus.

1820. PINEAS, RAINER. Thomas More and Tudor polemics. Bloomington, Ind., London: Indiana U.P., 1968. xi, 262 pp.

1821. MARIUS, R. C. Thomas More and the early Church Fathers. *Traditio*, XXIV (1968) 379–407.

1822. HEADLEY, JOHN M. Thomas Murner, Thomas More, and the first expressions of More's ecclesiology. *Studies in the Renaissance*, XIV (1967) 73–92.

1823. BIETENHOLZ, PETER G. A Protestant presentation of More, 1581. *Moreana*, no. 13 (1967) 59–62.

1824. MACKLEM, MICHAEL. God have mercy: the life of John Fisher of Rochester. Ottawa: Oberon P., 1967. 277 pp.

1825. SURTZ, EDWARD. The works and days of John Fisher: an introduction to the position of St. John Fisher (1469–1535), bishop of Rochester, in the English Renaissance and the Reformation. Cambridge, Mass.: Harvard U.P.; London: O.U.P., 1967. xix, 572 pp.

1826. ROUSCHAUSSE, JEAN. Erasmus and Fisher: their correspondence, 1511–24. (De Pétrarque à Descartes, 16). Paris: J. Vrin, 1968. 108 pp.

1827. FORESTER, ANN. Bishop Tunstall's priests. *Recusant Hist.*, IX (1967–8) 175–204.

1828. CLARKE, C. W. Simon Southern's early life as a priest. *Worcs. Recusant*, no. 11 (1968) 1–8.

1829. WHATMORE, L. E. The Venerable William Pike, layman. *Recusant Hist.*, IX (1967–8) 258–63.

1830. AVERY, DAVID. Popish recusancy in the Elizabethen hundred of Edmonton. (Edmonton ser., 15). Edmonton Hundred Hist. Soc., 1968. 19 pp.

1831. HODGETTS, MICHAEL. Elizabethan recusancy in Worcestershire. Pt. 1. *Worcs. Archaeol. Soc. Trans.* for 1965–7, 3rd ser. I (1968) 69–78.

1832. HODGETTS, M. Recusant houses of Warwickshire and Worcestershire. *Worcs. Recusant*, no. 9 (1967) 8–13, no. 10 (1967) 8–13, no. 12 (1968) 12–15.

1833. HODGETTS, M. The priestholes at Hindlip Old Hall. *Worcs. Archaeol. Soc. Trans.* for 1964, n.s. XLI (1967) 10–33.

1834. BASSET, BERNARD. The English Jesuits from Campion to Martindale. Burns & Oates, 1967. xv, 477 pp., illus.

Theology and liturgy

1835. NIX, WILLIAM E. Theological presuppositions and 16th century English Bible translation. *Bibliotheca Sacra*, CXXIV (1967) 42–50, 117–24.

1836. HUME, ANTHEA. William Roye's *Brefe dialogue* (1527): an English version of a Strasburg catechism. *Harvard Theol. Rev.*, LX (1967) 307–21.

1837. MCGRADE, ARTHUR S. The public and the religious in Hooker's *Polity*. *Church Hist.*, XXXVII (1968) 409–22.

1838. RICHARDS, MICHAEL. Thomas Stapleton. *Jour. Eccles. Hist.*, XVIII (1967) 187–99.

1839. COHEN, EILEEN Z. The *Old Arcadia* in a treatise on moderation. *Rev. Belge de Philol. et d'Hist.*, XLVI (1968) 749–70.

1840. GREAVES, RICHARD L. The origins and early development of English covenant thought. *Historian*, XXXI (1968) 21–35.

1841. BOOTY, JOHN EVERITT. Preparation for the Lord's supper in Elizabethan England. *Anglican Theol. Rev.*, XLIX (1967) 131–49.

1842. SMITH, ALAN. The cultivation of music in English cathedrals in the reign of Elizabeth I. *Roy. Musical Assoc. Proc.* (1967–8) 37–49.

1843. SMITH, A. Elizabethan church music at Ludlow. *Music & Letters*, XLIX (1968) 108–21.

CULTURAL HISTORY

Learning and education

1844. LEVY, F. J. Tudor historical thought. San Marino, Calif.: Huntington Lib., 1967. xii, 305 pp.

1845. FERGUSON, ARTHUR B. Circumstances and the sense of history in Tudor England: the coming of the historical revolution. *Medieval and Renaissance Studies*, III (1968) 170–205.

1846. AVELING, HUGH, *and* PANTIN' WILLIAM ABEL (*eds.*). The letter book of Robert Joseph, monk-scholar of Evesham and Gloucester College, Oxford, 1530–3. (Oxford Hist. Soc. Pubns. n.s., 19). Oxford: Clarendon P. for the Society, 1967. lv, 300 pp.

1847. GARANDERIE, M. M. DE LA. Correspondance de Budé et More. *Moreana*, XIX–XX (1968) 41–68.

1848. MARC'HADOUR, GERMAIN. Hugh Latimer et Thomas More. *Moreana*, XVIII (1968) 29–48.

1849. MARC'HADOUR, G. Thomas More et Thomas Linacre. *Moreana*, XIII (1967) 63–9.

1850. GABRIELLI, V. G. Pico and Thomas More. *Moreana*, XV (1967) 43–58.

1851. KARPMAN, DAHLIA M. William Tyndale's response to the Hebraic tradition. *Studies in the Renaissance*, XIV (1967) 110–30.

1852. ROTT, JEAN, *and* FAERBER, ROBERT. Un Anglais à Strasbourg au milieu du 16e siècle: John Hales, Roger Ascham et Jean Sturm. *Études Anglaises*, XXI (1968) 381–94.

1853. PENNINGTON, A. E. A 16th century English Slavist. *Mod. Lang. Rev.*, LXII (1967) 680–6. [Christopher Borough.]

1854. MORGAN, PAUL. George Hartgill: an Elizabethan parson-astronomer and his library. *Annals of Science*, XXIV (1968) 295–311.

1855. GLUCKER, J. Richard Thomson to Isaac Casaubon, 1596. *Bibliothèque d'Humanisme et Renaissance*, XXX (1968) 149–53.

1856. LAWSON, JOHN. Medieval education and the Reformation. London: Routledge; New York: Humanities P., 1967. x, 115 pp., illus.

1857. GRAY, *Sir* JOHN. Thomas Alcock, Master of Jesus College, Cambridge, 1516. *Cambridge Antiq. Soc. Proc.*, LX (1967) 91–5.

1858. BENNETT, JOSEPHINE W. John Morer's will: Thomas Linacre and Prior Sellyng's Greek teaching. *Studies in the Renaissance*, XV (1968) 70–9.

1859. BOOTY, JOHN EVERITT. The expulsion of John Sanderson: trouble in an Elizabethan university. *Hist. Mag. Protestant Episcopal Church*, XXXVI (1967) 233–47. [Trinity College, Cambridge.]

Literature, drama and music

1860. BROWNLOW, F. W. 'Speke, parrot': Skelton's allegorical denunciation of Cardinal Wolsey. *Studies in Philol.*, LXV (1968) 124–39.

1861. MARC'HADOUR, GERMAIN. More's folio *Workes*, 1557: for a census and an anatomy. *Moreana*, IV no. 13 (1967) 69–78.

1862. SÜSSMUTH, HANS. Studien zur Utopia des Thomas Morus: ein Beitrag zur Geistesgeschichte des 16. Jahrhunderts. (Reformationsgeschichtliche Studien und Texte, 95). Münster-Westfalien: Aschendorff, 1967. 192 pp.

1863. CLOUGH, CECIL H. Federigo Veterani, Polydore Vergil's 'Anglica Historia' and Baldassare Castiglione's 'Epistola . . . ad Henricum Angliae regem'. *E.H.R.*, LXXXII (1967) 772–83.

1864. SLAVIN, ARTHUR J. The fugitive folio and other problems: a new edition of Edward VI's writings. *Manuscripta*, XI (1967) 94–101.

1865. SHEAVYN, PHOEBE. The literary profession in the Elizabethan age. 2nd edn. *rev.* J. W. Saunders. Manchester: Manchester U.P.; New York: Barnes & Noble,

1967. x, 248 pp. [Previous edn. Manchester: the University, 1909.]

1866. EBEL, JULIA G. A numerical survey of Elizabethan translations. *Library*, 5th ser. XXII (1967) 104–27.

1867. MORRIS, JOHN. Thomas Thomas, printer to the University of Cambridge, 1583–8. Pt. 2, Some account of his materials and bookbinding with a short-title list of his printing. *Cambridge Bibliog. Soc. Trans.*, IV no. 5 (1968) 339–62.

1868. PEPPER, ROBERT D. Francis Clement's *Petie schole* at the Vautrollier press, 1587. *Library*, 5th ser. XXII (1967) 1–12.

1869. BEVINGTON, DAVID MARTIN. Tudor drama and politics: a critical approach to topical meaning. Cambridge, Mass.: Harvard U.P.; London: O.U.P., 1968. 360 pp.

1870. ANGLO, SYDNEY. The evolution of the early Tudor disguising, pageant and mask. *Renaissance Drama*, n.s. I (1968) 3–44.

1871. HODGES, CYRIL WALTER. The Globe restored: a study of the Elizabethan theatre. 2nd edn. O.U.P., 1968. xv, 177 pp., illus. [Previous edn. 1953.]

1872. AXELRAD, JOSÉ, *and* WILLEMS, MICHELE. Shakespeare et le theâtre elizabethain. Paris: P.U.F., 1968. 128 pp.

1873. AKRIGG, GEORGE PHILIP VERE. Shakespeare and the earl of Southampton. Hamilton, 1968. xvi, 280 pp., illus.

1874. SIMON, J. E. S. Shakespeare's legal and political background. *Law Quart. Rev.*, LXXXIV (1968) 33–47.

1875. BERMAN, RONALD. Shakespeare and the law. *Shakespeare Quart.*, XVIII (1967) 141–50.

1876. HOLMES, R. Shakespeare and witchcraft. *Quart. Rev.*, CCCV (1967) 179–88.

1877. SHAW, WATKINS. William Byrd of Lincoln. *Music & Letters*, XLVIII (1967) 52–9.

1878. JEFFERY, BRIAN. The lute music of Antony Holborne. *Roy. Musical Assoc. Proc.* (1966–7) 25–31.

Architecture, arts and crafts

1879. DICKINSON, JOHN C. The buildings of the English Austin canons after the dissolution of the monasteries. *Brit. Archaeol. Assoc. Jour.*, 3rd ser. XXXI (1968) 60–75.

1880. MERCER, ERIC, *and* SUMMERS, NORMAN. The Old House, Bleasby. *Thoroton Soc. Trans.* for 1967, LXXI (1968) 18–29.

1881. STRONG, ROY COLIN. Holbein in England. *Burlington Mag.*, CIX (1967) 276–81, 698–702.

1882. STRONG, R. C. Holbein and Henry VIII. Routledge, for Paul Mellon Foundation, 1967. 75 pp., illus.

1883. WOODWARD, D. M. Robert Brerewood: an Elizabethan master craftsman. *Cheshire Round*, I no. 9 (1968) 311–16.

SCIENCE AND MEDICINE

1884. EASTON, JOY B. The early editions of Robert Recorde's *Ground of artes. Isis*, LVIII (1967) 515–32.

1885. DEBUS, ALLEN G. Renaissance chemistry and the work of Robert Fludd. *Ambix*, XIV (1967) 42–59.

1886. COHEN, BERTRAM. King Henry VIII and the Barber Surgeons. *Roy. College of Surgeons Eng. Annals*, XL (1967) 179–94.

1887. O'MALLEY, C. D. Tudor medicine and biology. *Huntington Lib. Quart.*, XXXII (1968–9) 1–27.

1888. MACLENNAN, *Sir* HECTOR. A gynaecologist looks at the Tudors. *Medical Hist.*, XI (1967) 66–74.

1889. MACDONALD, G. G. General medical practice in the time of Thomas Vicary. *Roy. College of Surgeons Eng. Annals*, XL (1967) 1–20.

1890. GALE, BARRY G. The Dissolution and the revolution in London hospital facilities. *Medical Hist.*, XI (1967) 91–6.

1891. BELLORINI, MARIA GRAZIA. Un medico italiano alla corte di Elisabetta: Giulio Borgarucci. *English Misc.*, XIX (1968) 251–71.

1892. FINNEY, GRETCHEN. Vocal exercise in the 16th century related to theories of physiology and disease. *Bull. Hist. Medicine*, XLII (1968) 422–9.

MILITARY, NAVAL AND MARITIME HISTORY

1893. CRUICKSHANK, CHARLES GRIEG. King Henry VIII's army. 1, Camp. *History Today*, XVIII (1968) 852–7.

1894. BOYNTON, LINDSAY OLIVER JOHN. The Elizabethan militia, 1558–1638. London: Routledge; Toronto: Toronto U.P., 1967. xvii, 334 pp., illus.

1895. SHELBY, L. R. John Rogers: Tudor military engineer. Clarendon P., 1967. xi, 182 pp., illus.

1896. GLASGOW, TOM, *Jnr*. The Navy in the French wars of Mary and Elizabeth I. *Mariner's Mirror*, LIII (1967) 321–42, LIV (1968) 23–37, 281–96.

1897. HIRSCHFELD, BURT. The Spanish Armada. Macdonald & Co., 1968. 143 pp., illus. [Originally pubd. New York: Messner, 1966.]

1898. MARX, ROBERT FRANK. The battle of the Spanish Armada, 1588. Weidenfeld, 1968. 128 pp., illus. [Originally pubd. Cleveland, Ohio: World Pubg., 1965.]

1899. BOULIND, RICHARD H. The crompster in literature and pictures. *Mariner's Mirror*, LIV (1968) 3–17. [16th cent. naval vessel.]

1900. QUINN, DAVID BEERS. Sebastian Cabot and Bristol exploration. Bristol: Historical Assoc. (Bristol Branch), 1968. 30 pp.

1901. JURICEK, JOHN T. John Cabot's first voyage. *Smithsonian Jour. Hist.*, II no. 4 (1967–8) 1–22.

1902. DAVIES, D. W. Elizabethans errant: the strange fortunes of Sir Thomas Sherley and his three sons, as well in the Dutch wars as in Muscovy, Morocco, Persia, Spain and the Indies. Ithaca, N.Y.: Cornell U.P., 1967. xv, 337 pp.

1903. REED, RICHARD B. Richard Eden: an early English imperialist. *Serif*, IV (1967) 3–16.

1904. ANDREWS, KENNETH RAYMOND. Drake's voyages: a re-assessment of their place in Elizabethan maritime expansion. Weidenfeld, 1967. 190 pp.

1905. HAMSHERE, C. E. Drake's voyage round the world. *History Today*, XVII (1967) 593–601.

1906. ANDREWS, KENNETH RAYMOND. The aims of Drake's expedition of 1577–80. *Amer. Hist. Rev.*, LXXIII no. 3 (1968) 724–41.

1907. BOULIND, RICHARD H. Drake's navigational skills. *Mariner's Mirror*, LIV (1968) 349–71.

1908. CHYNOWETH, JOHN. The wreck of the *St. Anthony*. *Roy. Inst. Cornwall Jour.*, n.s. V (1968) 385–406. [Portuguese goods seized by Cornishmen, 1527–8.]

1909. BOVILL, EDWARD WILLIAM. The *Madre de Dios*. *Mariner's Mirror*, LIV (1968) 129–52. [Portuguese treasure ship captured 1592.]

1910. GLASGOW, TOM, *Jnr*. Sixteenth century English seamen meet a new enemy: the shipworm. *Amer. Neptune*, XXVII (1967) 177–84.

FOREIGN RELATIONS

1911. CLOUGH, CECIL H. The relations between the English and Urbino courts, 1474–1508. *Studies in the Renaissance*, XIV (1967) 202–18.

1912. PARMITER, GEOFFREY DE CLIFTON. The King's 'great matter': a study of Anglo-Papal relations 1527–34. Longmans, 1967. xiii, 322 pp.

1913. ROELOFSEN, C. G. De onderhandelingen over een verdrag van bijstand tussen de Staten-Generaal en Engeland in 1585–6. *Bijd. voor de Gesch. Nederlanden*, XX (1968) 138–48.

WALES

1914. COLE, ERNEST JOHN LESLIE. Brief notes on the early high sheriffs of Radnorshire. *Radnors. Soc. Trans.*, XXXVII (1967) 41–3, XXXVIII (1968) 51–3.

1915. ROBINSON, W. R. B. The litigation of Edward, earl of Worcester concerning Gower, 1590–6. *Board of Celtic Studies Bull.*, XXII pt. 4 (1968) 357–88, XXIII pt. 1 (1968) 60–99.

1916. ROBERTS, ENID. Ymryson y Salsbriaid, 1593. *Denbighs. Hist. Soc. Trans.*, XVII (1968) 108–46. ['Strife and the Salisburys'.]

1917. WILLIAMS, W. OGWEN. The social order in Tudor Wales. *Hon. Soc. Cymmrodorion Trans.* (1967) 167–78.

1918. THOMAS, COLIN. Enclosure and the rural landscape of Merioneth in the 16th century. *Inst. Brit. Geographers Trans.*, XLII (1967) 153–62.

1919. DICKS, T. R. B. Farming in Elizabethan Pembrokeshire, 1588–1603. *Nat. Lib. Wales Jour.*, XV (1967–8) 215–25.

1920. COLE, ERNEST JOHN LESLIE. The dry way over Smatcher. *Radnors. Soc. Trans.*, XXXVII (1967) 36–40. [Sheep stealing.]

1921. GRESHAM, COLIN A. The origin of the Clenennau estate. *Nat. Lib. Wales Jour.*, XV (1967–8) 335–43.

1922. WILLIAMS GLANMOR. Welsh Reformation essays. Cardiff: Wales U.P., 1967. 232 pp.

1923. WILLIAMS, G. Yr esgob Richard Davies, 1501–81. *Caernarvons. Hist. Soc. Trans.*, XXIX (1968) 137–57. [Bishop.]

1924. GRUFFYDD, R. GERAINT. The Welsh Book of Common Prayer, 1567. *Hist. Soc. Church in Wales Jour.*, XVII (1967) 43–55.

1925. THOMAS, ISAAC. Y fersiynau cyntaf o'r Testament Newydd Cymraeg. *Y Traethodydd*, CXXII (1967) 147–59. ['The first Welsh New Testament'.]

1926. JONES, GWILYM H. Y sallwyr Cymraeg: William Salesbury. *Y Traethodydd*, CXXII (1967) 160–72, CXXIII (1968) 29–41. ['The Welsh psalter: William Salesbury'.]

1927. JONES, EVAN J. Salman William Salesbury. *Llên Cymru*, IX nos. 3–4 (1967) 166–76. [Psalms.]

1928. GRUFFYDD, R. GERAINT. 'Carol santaidd i'r Grawys' o waith y tad William Davies. *Caernarvons. Hist. Soc. Trans.*, XXVIII pt. 1 (1967) 37–46.

1929. BOWEN, GERAINT. Apêl at y pab ynghylch dilysrwydd *Historia Regum*, sieffre o fynwy. *Nat. Lib. Wales Jour.*, XV (1967–8) 127–46. [Letter from Robert Owen (*d.* 1629) to Cardinal Sirleto, 1584.]

1930. ROBERTS, ENID. Eisteddfod Caerwys, 1567. *Denbighs. Hist. Soc. Trans.*, XVI (1967) 23–61.

SCOTLAND

1931. ROUGHOL, D. Les régences en Écosse sous les Stuarts. *Rev. Hist. Droit Franç. Étranger*, 4 sér. XLVI (1968) 467–79.

1932. MERRIMAN, MARCUS H. The assured Scots: Scottish collaborators with England during the Rough Wooing. *Scot. Hist. Rev.*, XLVII (1968) 10–34.

1933. THOMSON, GEORGE MALCOLM. The crime of Mary Stuart. Hutchinson, 1967. 176 pp., illus.

1934. FRASER, *Lady* ANTONIA. The murder of Darnley. *History Today*, XVII (1967) 3–12.

1935. BINGHAM, CAROLINE. The making of a king: the early years of James VI and I. Collins, 1968. 224 pp., illus.

1936. MURRAY, ATHOL L. The revenues of the bishopric of Moray in 1538. *Innes Rev.*, XIX (1968) 40–56.

1937. HAWS, CHARLES H. Scottish religious orders at the Reformation. *Scot. Church Hist. Soc. Records*, XVI pt. 3 (1968) 203–24.

1938. DILWORTH, MARK. Two Scottish pilgrims in Germany. *Innes Rev.*, XVIII (1967) 19–24. [William Robertoun and George Donaldson.]

1939. RIDLEY, JASPER. John Knox. Oxford, London: Clarendon P., 1968. vii, 596 pp., illus.

1940. MACKIE, JOHN DUNCAN. John Knox. Rev. edn. (Gen. ser., 20). Historical Assoc., 1968. 24 pp. [Previous edn., 1951.]

1941. MCQUEEN, JOHN. Some aspects of the early Renaissance in Scotland. *Forum for Mod. Lang. Studies*, III (1967) 201–22.

1942. MERRIMAN, MARCUS H. The platte of Castlemilk, 1547. *Dumfries. & Galloway Nat. Hist. & Antiq. Soc. Trans.*, XLIV (1967) 175–81.

IRELAND

Note: Writings on Irish domestic and local history are not included unless they have a direct bearing on English history.

1943. HAYES-MCCOY, G. A. 'The Tudor conquest'. *In* The course of Irish history, *ed.* T. W. Moody *and* F. X. Martin (Cork: Mercier P., 1967) pp. 174–88.

1944. EDWARDS, R. DUDLEY. The Irish Reformation parliament of Henry VIII, 1536–7. *Hist. Studies*, VI (1968) 59–84.

1945. MORTON, R. C. The enterprise of Ulster. *History Today*, XVII (1967) 114–21.

1946. VALKENBURG, AUGUSTINE. Gerald, eleventh earl of Kildare (1525–85): a study in diplomacy. *Kildare Archaeol. Soc. Jour.*, XIV (1968) 293–315.

1948. BUTLER, GEORGE. The battle of Affane. *Irish Sword*, VIII (1967) 33–47. [1565.]

1949. MORTON, R. G. Naval activity on Lough Neagh, 1558–1603. *Irish Sword*, VIII (1968) 288–93.

1950. ANDREWS, J. H. Robert Lythe's petitions, 1571. *Analecta Hibernica*, XXIV (1967) 232–41. [To map Ireland.]

BIOGRAPHY

1951. LLOYD, RACHEL. Dorset Elizabethans at home and abroad. Murray, 1967. xviii, 332 pp., illus.

1952. *Bell.* SMITH, BRIAN STANLEY. Edward Bell of Newland. *Bristol & Glos. Archaeol. Soc. Trans.* for 1966, LXXXV (1967) 147–55.

1953. *Bourne.* CALISTA, *Sister.* Sir John Bourne of Battenhall, Holt and Wick (*d.* 1563). *Worcs. Recusant*, no. 3 (1964) 1–9.

1954. *Dee.* DEACON, RICHARD. John Dee: scientist, geographer, astrologer and secret agent to Elizabeth I. Muller, 1968. x, 309 pp., illus.

1955. *Katharine.* LUKE, MARY M. Catherine the Queen. Muller, 1968. 510 pp., illus. [Originally pubd. New York: Coward-McCann, 1967.]

1956. *Lee.* GRASS, MILTON NATHANIEL, *and* GRASS, ANNA MICHELMAN. Stockings for a queen: the life of the Rev. William Lee, the Elizabethan inventor. Heinemann, 1967. xvi, 188 pp., illus.

1957. *North.* BELLORINI, MARIA GRAZIA. Tracce di cultura italiana nella formazione di Thomas North. *Aevum*, XLI (1967) 333–8.

1958. *Reynold.* MORGAN, P. T. J. Robert Ap Reynold of Oswestry, a friend of Thomas Cromwell. *Shropshire Archaeol. Soc. Trans.* for 1965, LVIII pt. 1 (1967) 77–83.

1959. *Sidney.* HOWELL, ROGER. Sir Philip Sidney: the shepherd knight. Hutchinson, 1968. x, 308 pp.

1960. *Walsingham.* CECIONI, CESARE G. Frances Walsingham ispiratrice dell *Hecatompathia. Riv. di Letterature Mod. e Comparate*, n.s. XX (1967) 27–9. [By Thomas Watson.]

STUART PERIOD, 1603–1714

GENERAL

1961. BRIDENBAUGH, CARL. Vexed and troubled Englishmen, 1590–1642. Oxford: Clarendon P., 1968. xxiii, 487 pp.

1962. IVES, ERIC WILLIAM (*ed.*). The English Revolution, 1600–60: essays. Arnold, 1968. viii, 164 pp. [Contains: 'The English Revolution: an introduction' by A. H. Woolrych, pp. 1–33; 'The central government and the local community' by I. Roots, pp. 34–47; 'The country community' by A. Everitt, pp. 48–63; 'The country community at war' by D. H. Pennington, pp. 64–75; 'The growth of London' by J. H. Fisher, pp. 76–86; 'Puritanism, politics and society' by A. H. Woolrych, pp. 87–100; 'Scientists and society' by H. F. Kearney, pp. 101–14; 'Social change and the law' by E. W. Ives, pp. 115–30; 'Class and social tension: the case of the merchant' by B. Supple, pp. 131–43; 'The Levellers' by B. Manning, pp. 144–58.]

1963. RUBINI, DENNIS. Court and country, 1688–1702. Hart-Davis, 1968. 304 pp.

1964. CRINÒ, ANNA MARIA (*ed.*). Un principe di Toscana in Inghilterra e in Irlanda nel 1669: relazione ufficiale del viaggio di Cosimo de' Medici tratta dal giornale di L. Magalotti. Rome: Ed. Storia e Letteratura, 1968. xxxix, 276 pp., illus.

1965. MAGALOTTI, LORENZO. Relazioni di viaggio in Inghilterra, Francia e Svezia, *ed.* W. Moretti. Bari: G. Laterza, 1968. 468 pp. [1669.]

1966. FORSTER, GORDON C. F. Jacobean Leeds. *Univ. Leeds Rev.*, X (1966–7) 143–7.

1967. AHIER, PHILIP. Col. Legge's 'Accompt of Jersey' (1679). *Soc. Jersiaise Bull. Annuel*, XIX pt. 3 (1967) 238–43.

CONSTITUTIONAL AND POLITICAL HISTORY

1968. AYLMER, GERALD EDWARD. The struggle for the constitution, 1603–89: England in the 17th century. 2nd edn. Blandford P., 1968. viii, 263 pp., illus.

1969. MATHEW, DAVID. James I. Eyre & Spottiswoode, 1967. xiii, 354 pp., illus.

1970. HIBBERT, CHRISTOPHER. Charles I. Weidenfeld, 1968. 295 pp., illus.

1971. TOYNBEE, MARGARET RUTH. King Charles I. Morgan-Grampian Books, 1968. 92 pp., illus.

1972. BRETTLE, R. E. John Marston and the duke of Buckingham, 1627–8. *N. & Q.*, CCXII (1967) 326–30.

1973. TREVALLYN JONES, G. J. Saw-pit Wharton: the political career from 1640 to 1691 of Philip, 4th Lord Wharton. Sydney: Sydney U.P.; London: Methuen, 1967. x, 300 pp.

1974. GRUBER, MICHAEL. The English Revolution: a concise history and interpretation. New York: Ardmore P., 1967. 153 pp.

1975. FALKUS, C. Revolution, reaction and the English Civil War. *Australian Jour. Politics & Hist.*, XIII (1967) 365–81.

1976. PEARL, VALERIE. The 'Royal Independents' in the English Civil War. *Roy. Hist. Soc. Trans.*, 5th ser. XVIII (1968) 69–96.

1977. UNDERDOWN, DAVID. The Independents again. *Jour. Brit. Studies*, VIII no. 1 (1968) 83–93.

1978. YULE, GEORGE. Independents and Revolutionaries. *Jour. Brit. Studies*, VII no. 2 (1968) 11–32.

1979. HOWELL, ROGER. Newcastle-upon-Tyne and the Puritan Revolution: a study of the Civil War in north England. Oxford: Clarendon P., 1967. xiv, 397 pp.

1980. LEVINE, ISRAEL E. Oliver Cromwell. Macdonald & Co., 1967. 150 pp., illus. [Originally pubd. New York: J. Messner, 1966.]

1981. YOUNG, PETER. Oliver Cromwell. Morgan-Grampian Books, 1968. 92 pp., illus.

1982. PINCKNEY, PAUL J. Bradshaw and Cromwell in 1656. *Huntington Lib. Quart.*, XXX (1966–7) 233–40.

1983. UNDERDOWN, DAVID. Cromwell and the officers, February 1658. *E.H.R.*, LXXXIII (1968) 101–7.

1984. BARUCH, FRANKLIN R. Cromwell and the commentary of death. *Jour. Hist. Studies*, II (1968–9) 91–8.

1985. ASHLEY, MAURICE. Oliver Cromwell and the Levellers. *History Today*, XVII (1967) 539–44.

1986. LUTAND, OLIVER (*ed.*). Les niveleurs, Cromwell et la république. Paris: Julliard, 1967. 282 pp.

1987. SHAW, HOWARD. The Levellers. (Seminar Studies in Hist.). Longmans, 1968. vii, 128 pp.

1988. DAVIS, J. C. The Levellers and democracy. *Past & Present*, no. 40 (1968) 174–80.

1989. SALEVOURIS, MICHAEL J. The impact of left-wing Puritanism on Leveller political and social policies. *Rocky Mountain Soc. Sci. Jour.*, IV (1967) 68–77.

1990. AYERS, ROBERT W. Major-General Thomas Harrison: herald of the Fifth Monarchy. *Jour. Hist. Studies*, II (1968–9) 1–11.

1991. HEATH, GEORGE D. Making the Instrument of Government. *Jour. Brit. Studies*, VI no 2 (1967) 15–34.

1992. HABAKKUK, HROTHGAR JOHN. The Parliamentary army and the Crown land. *Welsh. Hist. Rev.*, III (1966–7) 403–26.

1993. SMITH, GEOFFREY RIDSDILL. Royalist secret agents at Dover during the Commonwealth. *Hist. Studies Australia & N.Z.*, XII (1967) 477–90.

1994. AYERS, ROBERT W. Milton's *Letter to a friend* and the anarchy of 1659. *Jour. Hist. Studies*, I (1967–8) 229–39.

1995. MATTHEWS, WILLIAM (*ed.*). Charles II's escape from Worcester: a collection of narratives assembled by Samuel Pepys. Bell, 1967. 178 pp., illus.

1996. TREVALLYN JONES, G. F. The Bristol affair, 1663. *Jour. Religious Hist.*, V (1968) 16–30. [Clarendon accused of treason by earl of Bristol.]

1997. MITCHELL, A. A. Charles II and the Treaty of Dover, 1670. *History Today*, XVII (1967) 674–82.

1998. BECKERLEGGE, JOHN J. Charles II's visits to Plymouth. *Devon Assoc. Repts. & Trans.*, C (1968) 219–25.

1999. HATTON, RAGNHILD MARIE, *and* BROMLEY, J. S. (*eds.*). William III and Louis XIV: essays 1680–1720, by and for Mark A. Thomson. Liverpool: Liverpool U.P., 1968. xi, 332 pp.

2000. JONES, GEORGE HILTON. Charles Middleton: the life and times of a Restoration politician. Chicago, London: Chicago U.P., 1968. 332 pp.

2001. WEBB, STEPHEN SAUNDERS. William Blathwayt, imperial fixer: from Popish Plot to Glorious Revolution. *William & Mary Quart.*, 3rd ser. XXV (1968) 3–21.

2002. BEDDARD, ROBERT A. The Commission for Ecclesiastical Promotions, 1681–4: an instrument of Tory reaction. *Hist. Jour.*, X (1967) 11–40.

2003. BEDDARD, R. A. The loyalist opposition in the Interregnum: a letter of Dr. Francis Turner, bishop of Ely, on the Revolution of 1688. *Inst. Hist. Research Bull.*, XL (1967) 101–9.

2004. BEDDARD, R. A. Observations of a London clergyman on the Revolution of 1688–9: being an excerpt from the autobiography of Dr. William Wake. *Guildhall Misc.*, II no. 9 (1967) 406–17.

2005. BEDDARD, R. A. The Guildhall declaration of 11 December 1688 and the counter-revolution of the loyalists. *Hist. Jour.*, XI (1968) 403–20.

2006. HOLMES, GEOFFREY SHORTER, *and* SPECK, WILLIAM ARTHUR (*eds.*). The divided society: parties and politics in England, 1694–1716. Edward Arnold, 1967. xii, 179 pp.

2007. FRANCIS, ALAN DAVID. The Grand Alliance in 1698. *Hist. Jour.*, X (1967) 352–60.

2008. DE BEER, E. S. John Locke: the appointment offered to him in 1698. *Inst. Hist. Research Bull.*, XL (1967) 213–19.

2009. HOLMES, GEOFFREY SHORTER. British politics in the age of Anne. London: Macmillan; New York: St. Martin's P., 1967. xiv, 546 pp.

2010. SNYDER, HENRY L. The formulation of foreign and domestic policy in the reign of Queen Anne: memoranda by Lord Chancellor Cowper of conversations with Lord Treasurer Godolphin. *Hist. Jour.*, XI (1968) 144–60.

2011. DICKINSON, H. T. The Tory party's attitude to foreigners: a note on party principles in the age of Anne. *Inst. Hist. Research Bull.*, XL (1967) 153–65.

2012. SNYDER, HENRY L. The defeat of the Occasional Conformity Bill and the Tack: a study in the techniques of parliamentary management in the reign of Queen Anne. *Inst. Hist. Research Bull.*, XLI (1968) 172–92.

2013. MCINNES, ANGUS. The appointment of Harley in 1704. *Hist. Jour.*, XI (1968) 255–71.

2014. SNYDER, HENRY L. Godolphin and Harley: a study of their partnership in politics. *Huntington Lib. Quart.*, XXX (1966–7) 241–71.

2015. BENNETT, G. V. Robert Harley, the Godolphin ministry, and the bishopric crises of 1707. *E.H.R.*, LXXXII (1967) 726–46.

2016. DICKINSON, H. T. The poor Palatines and the parties. *E.H.R.*, LXXXII (1967) 464–85.

2017. DICKINSON, H. T. Henry St. John: a reappraisal of the young Bolingbroke. *Jour. Brit. Studies*, VII no. 2 (1968) 33–55.

2018. DICKINSON, H. T. Letters of Bolingbroke to James Grahme. *Cumberland & Westmorland Antiq. & Archaeol. Soc. Trans.*, LXVIII (1968) 117–31.

2019. CARROLL, ROY. Yorkshire parliamentary boroughs in the 17th century. *Northern Hist.*, III (1968) 70–104.

2020. KENNY, ROBERT W. Parliamentary influence of Charles Howard, earl of Nottingham, 1536–1624. *Jour. Mod. Hist.*, XXXIX (1967) 215–32.

2021. ASHTON, ROBERT. The parliamentary agitation for free trade in the opening years of the reign of James I. *Past & Present*, no. 38 (1967) 40–55.

2022. EPSTEIN, JOEL J. Francis Bacon: mediator in the parliament of 1604. *Historian*, XXX (1968) 219–37.

2023. GRUENFELDER, JOHN K. The parliamentary election in Northamptonshire, 1626. *Northants. Past & Present*, IV no. 3 (1968) 159–65.

2024. HILLABY, JOSEPH. The parliamentary borough of Weobley, 1628–1708. *Woolhope Naturalists' F.C. Trans.*, XXXIX (1967) 104–51.

2025. CLARKE, AIDAN, *and* FENLON, DERMOT. Two notes on the parliament of 1634. *Roy. Soc. Antiq. Ireland Jour.*, XCVII (1967) 85–90.

2026. GRUENFELDER, JOHN K. The election for knights of the shire for Essex in the spring, 1640. *Essex Archaeol. Soc. Trans.*, 3rd ser. II pt. 2 (1968) 143–6.

2027. GRUENFELDER, J. K. The spring parliamentary election at Hastings, 1640. *Sussex Archaeol. Coll.*, CV (1967) 49–55.

2028. ANDRIETTE, EUGENE A. Members of parliament for Devon and Exeter, 1640–6. *Devon & Cornwall N. & Q.*, XXXI (1968) 47–52.

2029. RUSSELL, CONRAD S. R. The authorship of the bishop's diary of the House of Lords in 1641. *Inst. Hist. Research Bull.*, XLI (1968) 229–36. [By Bishop John Warner of Rochester.]

2030. UNDERDOWN, DAVID. Party management in the recruiter elections, 1645–8. *E.H.R.*, LXXXIII (1968) 235–64.

2031. FARNELL, JAMES E. The usurpation of honest London householders: Barebone's parliament. *E.H.R.*, LXXXII (1967) 24–46.

2032. HOFFMAN, W. J., *Jnr.* Thurloe and the elections of 1654 and 1656. *Historian*, XXIX (1967) 323–42.

2033. PINCKNEY, PAUL J. The Cheshire election of 1656. *John Rylands Lib. Bull.*, XLIX (1966–7) 387–426.

2034. PINCKNEY, P. J. The Scottish representation in the Cromwellian parliament of 1656. *Scot. Hist. Rev.*, XLVI (1967) 95–114.

2035. SCHOENFELD, MAXWELL P. The restored House of Lords. (Studies in European Hist., 9). The Hague: Mouton, 1967. 244 pp.

2036. BEDDARD, ROBERT A. The Sussex general election of 1695: a contemporary account by Robert Middleton, Vicar of Cuckfield. *Sussex Archaeol. Coll.*, CVI (1968) 145–57.

POLITICAL THOUGHT

2037. VOEGELIN, ERIC (*ed.*). Zwischen Revolution und Restauration: politisches Denken in England im 17. Jahrhundert. Munich: List V., 1968. 180 pp.

2038. FEINBERG, BARBARA SILBERDICK. The political thought of Oliver Cromwell: revolutionary or conservative? *Social Research*, XXXV (1968) 445–65.

2039. AYLMER, GERALD EDWARD. *England's spirit unfoulded, or an incouragement to take the engagement:* a newly discovered pamphlet by Gerrard Winstanley. *Past & Present*, no. 40 (1968) 3–15.

2040. SELIGER, MARTIN. The liberal politics of John Locke. Allen & Unwin, 1968. 387 pp.

2041. STRACURRI, GIUSEPPE. Stato di natura e stato civile nel pensiero di J. Locke. *Historica*, XXI (1968) 63–75.

2042. DUNN, JOHN. Justice and the interpretation of Locke's political theory. *Polit. Studies*, XVI (1968) 68–87.

2043. DUNN, J. Consent in the political theory of John Locke. *Hist. Jour.*, X (1967) 153–82.

2044. GUNN, J. A. W. The *Civil polity* of Peter Paxton. *Past & Present*, no. 40 (1968) 42–57.

2045. DUNN, MARY MAPLES. William Penn: politics and conscience. Princeton, N.J.: Princeton U.P.; London: O.U.P., 1967. x, 206 pp.

ADMINISTRATIVE AND LEGAL HISTORY

2046. TAVERNER, R. L. The administrative work of the Devon justices in the 17th century. *Devon Assoc. Repts. & Trans.*, C (1968) 55–84.

2047. MCGURK, J. J. N. Letter book relating to the Lieutenancy of Kent, 1604–28. *Archaeologia Cantiana* for 1967, LXXXII (1968) 124–42.

2048. YOUINGS, JOYCE. King James's charter to Tiverton, 1615. *Devon Assoc. Repts. & Trans.* XCIX (1967) 147–63.

2049. ANDRIETTE, EUGENE A. Royalist war-time administration of Devon and Exeter, 1643–6. *Devon & Cornwall N. & Q.*, XXXI (1968) 41–6.

2050. SAINTY, JOHN C. A reform in the tenure of offices during the reign of Charles II. *Inst. Hist Research Bull.*, XLI (1968) 150–71.

2051. LEWIS, JOHN UNDERWOOD. Sir Edward Coke (1552–1633): his theory of 'artificial reason' as a context for modern basic legal theory. *Law Quart. Rev.*, LXXXIV (1968) 330–42.

2052. CROWE, MICHAEL BERTRAM. An eccentric 17th century witness to the natural law: John Selden, 1584–1654. *Natural Law Forum*, XII (1967) 184–95.

2053. JONES, GARETH. Francis Moore's reading on the Statute of Charitable Uses. *Cambridge Law Jour.* (1967) 224–38.

2054. SIMON, *Sir* JOCELYN. Dr. Cowell. *Cambridge Law Jour.* (1968) 260–72.

2055. PREVOST, WILLIAM AUGUSTIN JOHN. The death of Christie Armstrong, a border reiver. *Cumberland & Westmorland Antiq. & Archaeol. Soc. Trans.*, LXVIII (1968) 55–71. [1606.]

2056. PREVOST, W. A. J. The death of Christie Armstrong, a border reiver. *Hawick Archaeol. Soc. Trans.* (1968) 25–32.

2057. TYRER, FRANK. A Star Chamber case: Assheton *v.* Blundell, 1624–31. *Hist. Soc. Lancs. & Cheshire Trans.* for 1966, CXVIII (1967) 19–37.

2058. BALL, J. N. 'The impeachment of the duke of Buckingham in the parliament of 1626'. *In* Mélanges Antonio Marongiu: convegno internazionale di studi sulla storia dei parlamenti, Palermo-Agrigento, 1966 (Palermo: Ist. Stor. Mediev. dell'Univ., 1967) pp. 35–48.

2059. SNAPP, HARRY F. The impeachment of Roger Maynwaring. *Huntington Lib. Quart.*, XXX (1966–7) 217–32.

2060. COTTERELL, MARY. Interregnum law reform: the Hale Commission of 1652. *E.H.R.*, LXXXIII (1968) 689–704.

2061. FORBES, ANTHONY H. The English penal laws: persecution or precaution? The case of Middlesex, 1690–1709. *Catholic Hist. Rev.*, LIII no. 4 (1968) 556–72.

2062. QUINLAN, MAURICE J. The prosecution of Swift's *Public spirit of the Whigs. Texas Studies in Lit. & Lang.*, IX (1967–8) 167–84.

ECONOMIC AND SOCIAL HISTORY

General

2063. MALAMENT, BARBARA. The 'economic liberalism' of Sir Edward Coke. *Yale Law Jour.*, LXXVI (1967) 1321–58.

2064. DOCKÈS, PIERRE. Les problèmes du développement au 17ème siècle: deux analyses anglaises: William Temple et Josiah Child. *Rev. d'Hist. Écon. et Sociale*, XLV (1967) 433–58.

2065. CANTARELLI, D. (*ed.*). Il movimento dei prezzi in Inghilterra dal 1650 al 1700. *Giornale degli Economisti e Annali di Economia*, n.s. XXVI (1967) 430–69.

2066. EVANS, G. HEBERTON, *Jnr.* The law of demand: the roles of Gregory King and Charles Davenant. *Quart. Jour. Econ.*, LXXXI (1967) 483–92.

2067. MILLS, PETER, *and* OLIVER, JOHN. The survey of building sites in the City of London after the Great Fire of 1666. Vol. 1, Introduction by P. E. Jones and T. F. Reddaway, and index to vols. 1–5. (London Topographical Soc. Pubns., 103). The Society, 1967. xlii, 166 pp., illus.

2068. EDIE, CAROLYN ANDERVONT. New buildings, new taxes, and old interests: an urban problem of the 1670s. *Jour. Brit. Studies*, VI no. 2 (1967) 35–63.

2069. WILLIS, GEOFFREY. English pottery in 1696: an unpublished document. *Apollo*, LXXXV (1967) 436–43. [Tax assessment on earthenware.]

Trade and commerce

2070. WHITFORD, HAROLD C. Expos'd to sale: the marketing of goods and services in 17th century England as revealed by advertisements in contemporary newspapers and periodicals. *New York Public Lib. Bull.*, LXXI (1967) 496–515, 606–13.

2071. VAISEY, D. G. A Charlbury mercer's shop, 1623. *Oxoniensia* for 1966, XXXII (1968) 107–16.

2072. HAMER, J. H. Trading at Saint White Down Fair, 1637–49. *Somerset Archaeol. & Nat. Hist. Soc. Proc.*, CXII (1968) 61–70.

2073. LAWLER, JOHN. Book auctions in England in the 17th century, with a chronological list of the book auctions of the period. Detroit, Mich.: Gale Research, 1968. 242 pp.

2074. RIES, PAUL. Robert Molesworth's *Account of Denmark*: a study in the art of political publishing and bookselling in England and on the continent before 1700. *Scandinavia*, VII (1968) 108–25.

2075. ÅSTRÖM, SVEN-ERIK. The reliability of the English port books. *Scandinavian Econ. Hist. Rev.*, XVI (1968) 125–36.

2076. TAYLOR, HARLAND. Price revolution or price revision? The English and Spanish trade after 1604. *Renaissance & Mod. Studies*, XII (1968) 5–32.

2077. WALTER, R., *and* TOMS, H. N. W. An Exeter merchant in Spain. *Devon & Cornwall N. & Q.*, XXX (1967) 241–6. [Richard Yeo, 1586–1656.]

2078. GRAVIL, ROGER. Trading to Spain and Portugal, 1670–1700. *Business Hist.*, X (1968) 69–88.

2079. CERNOVODEANU, PAUL. England and the question of free trade in the Black Sea in the 17th century. *Rev. Roumaine Hist.*, VI (1967) 15–22.

2080. CERNOVODEANU, P. The general condition of English trade in the second half of the 17th century and at the beginning of the 18th century. *Rev. Études Sud-Est Européennes*, V (1967) 447–60.

2081. CERNOVODEANU, P. Relaţiile economice ale Angliei cu ţările române în perioda 1660–1714. *Studii R. Inst.*, XXI (1968) 259–72. ['England's economic relations with Romanian territories'.]

2082. BALDERSTON, MARION (*ed.*). James Claypole's letter book: London and Philadelphia, 1681–4. San Marino, Calif.: Huntington Lib., 1967. vii, 256 pp.

2083. PORTER, R. The Crispe family and the African trade in the 17th century. *Jour. African Hist.*, IX (1968) 57–77.

2084. CHAUDHURI, K. N. Treasure and trade balances: the East India Company's export trade, 1660–1720. *Econ. Hist. Rev.*, 2nd ser. XXI (1968) 480–502.

Social history

2085. NEWTON, S. C. The gentry of Derbyshire in the 17th century. *Derbys. Archaeol. Jour.* for 1966, LXXXVI (1967) 1–30.

2086. CORNWALL, JULIAN. Evidence of population mobility in the 17th century. *Inst. Hist. Research Bull.*, XL (1967) 143–52.

2087. EAST LONDON HISTORY GROUP. The population of Stepney in the early 17th century. *East London Papers*, XI (1968) 75–84.

2088. LITTLE, JOHN EGRAM (*transcr.*). The hearth tax for the parishes of Uffington, Baulking, Woolstone, Kingston Lisle and Fawler, 1663. (Berkshire Tracts, 1). Uffington, Berks.: the transcriber, 1968. 11 pp.

2089. URWIN, ALAN CHARLES BELL. Population and housing in 1664: an analysis of the hearth tax return for Ladyday 1664 for Twickenham, Hampton, Teddington, Isleworth, Heston and Hounslow. (Borough of Twickenham Local Hist. Soc. Papers, 8). Twickenham, Middx.: the Society, 1967. 17 pp.

2090. RALPH, ELIZABETH, *and* WILLIAMS, MARY E. (*eds.*). The inhabitants of Bristol in 1696: assessments under the 1694 Marriage Act. (Bristol Record Soc. Pubns., 25). Bristol: the Society, 1968. xxviii, 303 pp.

2091. TURNER, H. D. George, fourth earl of Northampton: estates and stewards, 1686–1714. *Northants. Past & Present*, IV no. 2 (1967) 97–105.

2092. STEVENS, JOAN. War and peace: some documents from St. Ouen's manor. *Soc. Jersiaise Bull. Annuel*, XIX pt. 3 (1967) 212–21.

2093. STEER, FRANCIS WILLIAM. A Cowdray inventory of 1682. *Sussex Archaeol. Coll.*, CV (1967) 84–102.

2094. DOUGLAS, M. Inventory of Eatons, 1687. *Sussex N. & Q.*, XVI no. 9 (1967) 289–93.

2095. DERN, JOHN P. Die deutsche Auswanderung von 1709 in den Londoner Kirchenbüchern. (Schriften zur Wanderungsgesch. der Pfälzer, 26). Kaiserslautern: Heimatstelle Pfalz, 1968. 55 pp.

Miscellaneous

2096. STRACHAN, MICHAEL. The Mermaid Tavern Club: a new discovery. *History Today*, XVII (1967) 533–8. [Manuscript of Thomas Coryate's 'safe-conduct'.]

2097. FRANCIS, DAVID. Count Wratislaw and the Lord Mayor's show, 1702. *Guildhall Misc.*, II no. 10 (1968) 433–7.

2098. GARRATT, JOHN G. The four Indian kings. *History Today*, XVIII (1968) 93–101. [Visit of N. American Indian chiefs, 1710.]

2099. CLARKE, JOSEPH RYLE. The Royal Society and early Grand Lodge Freemasonry. *Ars Quatuor Coronatorum*, LXXX (1967) 110–19.

2100. BUSSE, G. W. The herem of Rabenu Tam in Queen Anne's London. *Jewish Hist. Soc. Eng. Trans.* for 1962–7, XXI (1968) 138–47.

RELIGIOUS HISTORY

General

2101. HARGRAVE, O. T. The Freewillers in the English Reformation. *Church Hist.*, XXXVII (1968) 271–80.

2102. EMERSON, ROGER L. Heresy, the social order, and English deism. *Church Hist.*, XXXVII (1968) 389–403.

2103. COZZI, GAETANO. Sir Edwin Sandys e la 'Relazione sullo stato della religione'. *Riv. Stor. Ital.*, LXXIX (1967) 1092–121. [1605.]

2104. WARNER, D. H. J. Hobbes's interpretation of the doctrine of the Trinity. *Jour. Religious Hist.*, V (1969) 299-313.

Anglicanism

2105. SNAPP, HARRY F. Church and state relations in early Caroline England. *Jour. Church & State*, IX (1967) 332–48.

2106. RITZ, JEAN-GEORGES. St. François de Sales et l'église anglicane au 17e siècle. *Rev. Savoisienne*, CVII (1967) 47–63.

2107. ITTERZON, G. P. VAN. Engelse belangstellung voor de canones van Doordrecht. *Nederland. Arch. Kerkgesch.*, XLVIII (1968) 267–80. ['English interest in the canons of Doordrecht'.]

2108. MACDONALD, W. W. John Pym's religious policies in the parliaments of the 1620s. *Anglican Theol. Rev.*, XLIX (1967) 385–96.

2109. ECHLIN, EDWARD P. Was Laud's liturgy wholly Laud's? *Hist. Mag. Protestant Episcopal Church*, XXXVII (1968) 105–15.

2110. POGGI, VALENTINA. George Herbert. Bologna: Pàtron, 1967. 263 pp.

2111. FOSTER, D. W. George Herbert. *Theology*, LXX (1967) 68–76.

2112. DAVIDSON, ALAN. The conversion of Bishop King: a question of evidence. *Recusant Hist.*, IX (1967–8) 242–54.

2113. WIDE, S. M., *and* MORRIS, J. A. The episcopal licensing of schoolmasters in the diocese of London, 1627–85. *Guildhall Misc.*, II no. 9 (1967) 392–406.

2114. KING, PETER. Bishop Wren and the suppression of the Norwich lecturers. *Hist. Jour.*, XI (1968) 237–54.

2115. KING, P. The episcopate during the Civil Wars, 1642–9. *E.H.R.*, LXXXIII (1968) 523–37.

2116. FISK, WILLIAM L. John Selden: Erastian critic of the English Church. *Jour. Church & State*, IX (1967) 349–63.

2117. MORRISH, P. S. Dr Griffin Higgs, 1589–1659. *Oxoniensia* for 1966, XXXI (1968) 117–38.

2118. BUSSBY, FREDERICK. George Morley: bishop of Winchester, 1662–84. *Church. Quart. Rev.*, CLXVIII (1967) 433–42.

2119. MCADOO, HENRY ROBERT. Jeremy Taylor, 1667–1967. *Hermathena*, CVII (1968) 14–30.

2120. MARKS, CAROL L. Thomas Traherne's early studies. *Bibliog. Soc. America Papers*, LXII (1968) 511–36.

2121. BRETTON, ROWLAND. Bishop John Lake. *Halifax Antiq. Soc. Trans.* (1968) 89–96.

2122. BOYER, RICHARD E. English declarations of indulgence, 1687 and 1688. (Studies in European Hist., 15). The Hague: Mouton, 1968. 178 pp.

2123. GIFFIN, FREDERICK C. John Locke and religious toleration. *Jour. Church & State*, IX (1967) 378–90.

2124. BARNARD, L. W. Joseph Bingham and the early Church. *Church Quart. Rev.*, CLXIX (1968) 192–205.

2125. HIGHAM, FLORENCE MAY GREIR· John Evelyn, Esq.: an Anglican layman of the 17th century. S.C.M. Press, 1968. 128 pp.

Roman Catholicism

2126. CHAUSSY, YVES. Les bénédictins anglais réfugiés en France au 17e siècle (1611–69). Paris: Lethielleux, 1967. xxiv, 256 pp.

2127. ORCIBAL, J. La règle de perfection de Benoît de Canfield a-t-elle été interpolée? *Divinitas*, XI (1967) 845–74.

2128. LOOMIE, ALBERT J. A Jacobean crypto-Catholic: Lord Wotton. *Catholic Hist. Rev.*, LIII no. 3 (1967) 328–45.

2129. CLANCY, THOMAS H. The Beacon Controversy, 1652–7. *Recusant Hist.*, IX (1967–8) 63–74.

2130. LUNN, MARIUS. William Rudesind Barlow, O.S.B., 1585–1656. *Downside Rev.*, LXXXVI (1968) 139–54, 234–49.

2131. QUINLAN, DAVID. The Fr. Postgate story: the Ven. Nicholas Postgate, 1599–1679. Whitby, Yorks.: Horne & Son, 1967. 46 pp., illus.

2132. HAMMERMAYER, LUDWIG. Restauration und 'Revolution von oben' in Grossbritannien, 1685–8. *Hist. Jahrbuch*, LXXXVII (1967) 26–90.

Puritanism and Protestant Nonconformity

2133. SOLT, LEO F. Puritanism, capitalism, democracy, and the new science. *Amer. Hist. Rev.*, LXXIII no. 1 (1967) 18–29.

2134. GRANT, LEONARD T. Puritan catechizing. *Jour. Presbyterian Hist.*, XLVI (1968) 107–27.

2135. EMERSON, EVERETT HARVEY. Thomas Hooker: the Puritan as theologian. *Anglican Theol. Rev.*, XLIX (1967) 190–203.

2136. WILLIAMS, GEORGE HUNSTON. Called by thy name, leave us not: the case of Mrs. Joan Drake, a formative episode in the pastoral career of Thomas Hooker in England. *Harvard Lib. Bull.*, XVI (1968) 111–28, 278–300.

2137. HITCHCOCK, JAMES. George Gifford and Puritan witch beliefs. *Archiv für Reformationsgesch.*, LVIII (1967) 90–9.

2138. WHITE, BARRINGTON RAYMOND. John Traske (1585–1636) and London Puritanism. *Congregational Hist. Soc. Trans.*, XX (1968) 223–33.

2139. WEINSTEIN, MINNA F. Stephen Marshall and the dilemma of the political Puritan. *Jour. Presbyterian Hist.*, XLVI (1968) 1–25.

2140. BURG, B. RICHARD. The ideology of Richard Mather and its relationship to English Puritanism prior to 1660. *Jour. Church & State*, IX (1967) 364–77.

2141. DEWAR, M. W. The Synod of Dort, the Westminster Assembly and the French Reformed Church, 1618–43. *Huguenot Soc. London Proc.*, XXI no. 2 (1967) 119–23.

2142. SELLIN, PAUL R. Puritan and Anglican: a Dutch perspective. *Studies in Philol.*, LXV (1968) 804–15.

2143. SELLIN, P. R. Caesar Calandrini, the London Dutch, and Milton's quarrels in Holland. *Huntington Lib. Quart.*, XXXI (1967–8) 239–49.

2144. SPALDING, JAMES C. Sermons before parliament (1640–9) as a public Puritan diary. *Church Hist.*, XXXVI (1967) 24–35.

2145. CROSS, CLAIRE. Achieving the millennium: the Church in York during the Commonwealth. *Studies in Church Hist.*, IV (1967) 122–42.

2146. GREAVES, RICHARD L. John Bunyan and covenant thought in the 17th century. *Church Hist.*, XXXVI (1967) 151–69.

2147. SPUFFORD, MARGARET. The Dissenting churches in Cambridgeshire from 1660 to 1700. *Cambridge Antiq. Soc. Proc.*, LXI (1968) 67–95.

2148. TIBBUTT, H. GORDON. Early Nonconformity in Huntingdonshire. 1, Kimbolton. *Records of Hunts.*, I pt. 3 (1967) 40–3.

2149. HIGSON, P. J. W. Some leading promoters of Nonconformity and their association with Lancashire chapelries following the Revolution of 1688. *Lancs. & Cheshire Antiq. Soc. Trans.* for 1965–6, LXXV–LXXVI (1968) 123–63.

2150. ROHR, JOHN VON. *Extra ecclesiam nulla salus*: an early congregational version. *Church Hist.*, XXXVI (1967) 107–21.

2151. STEARNS, RAYMOND P. Hugh Peters was a wit. *Amer. Antiq. Soc. Proc.* for 1967, n.s. LXXVII (1968) 13–34.

2152. ALLEN, JUDSON BOYCE. The style and content of Baptist sermons in 17th century England. *Furman Studies*, n.s. XV (1968) 1–21.

2153. WHITE, BARRINGTON RAYMOND. The doctrine of the Church in the particular Baptist confession of 1644. *Jour. Theol. Studies*, n.s. XIX (1968) 570–90.

2154. WHITE, B. R. The Baptists of Reading, 1652–1715. *Baptist Quart.*, XXII no. 5 (1968) 249–70.

2155. MORTIMER, RUSSELL. Early Bristol Quakerism: the Society of Friends in the city, 1654–1700. Bristol: Historical Assoc., (Bristol Branch), 1967. 22 pp., illus.

2156. CADBURY, HENRY J. Friends and the Inquisition at Venice, 1658. *Friends' Hist. Soc. Jour.*, LII no. 1 (1968) 39–45.

2157. BRAITHWAITE, ALFRED W. George Fox's last imprisonment. *Friends' Hist. Soc. Jour.*, LI no. 3 (1967) 159–66.

CULTURAL HISTORY

General

2158. BENSON, DONALD R. Ideas and the problem of knowledge in 17th century English aesthetics. *English Misc.*, XIX (1968) 83–104.

2159. WOOD, DOREEN ANDERSON. The spirit and the candle. *Hist. Mag. Protestant Episcopal Church*, XXXVI (1967) 63–79.

2160. MACKENZIE, NORMAN. Sir Thomas Browne as a man of learning. *Eng. Studies in Africa*, X no. 1 (1967) 67–86.

2161. CROWELL, LAURA. Three 'plain' speakers in Stuart England. *Quart. Jour. Speech*, LIII (1967) 272–8.

2162. OAKESHOTT, WALTER. Sir Walter Raleigh's library. *Library*, 5th ser. XXIII (1968) 285–327.

2163. ROY, IAN. The libraries of Edward, second Viscount Conway, and others: an inventory and valuation of 1643. *Inst. Hist. Research Bull.*, XLI (1968) 35–46.

2164. PACCHI, ARRIGO. Una 'biblioteca ideale' di Thomas Hobbes: il Ms.E.2 dell' archivio di Chatsworth. *Acme*, XXI (1968) 5–42.

2165. LADBOROUGH, R. W. The library of Samuel Pepys. *History Today*, XVII (1967) 476–82.

2166. SEYMOUR, WILLIAM. John Evelyn and his books. *History Today*, XVII (1967) 626–31.

2167. PETERS, ROBERT A. Robert Cawdrey and the first English dictionary. *Jour. Eng. Linguistics*, II (1968) 29–42.

2168. LOADES, D. M. (*ed.*). The papers of George Wyatt, Esq. (Camden 4th ser., 5). Royal Historical Soc., 1968. xi, 261 pp.

2169. STRONG, ROY COLIN. Inigo Jones and the revival of chivalry. *Apollo*, LXXXVI (1967) 102–7.

2170. DANIEL, GLYN. Edward Lhuyd: antiquary and archaeologist. *Welsh Hist. Rev.*, III (1966–7) 345–59.

2171. LISTER, DOUGLAS G. Shorthand as a 17th century Quaker tool: some early shorthand systems and their use by Friends. *Friends' Hist. Soc. Jour.*, LI no. 3 (1967) 154–8.

2172. DAVIS, GAROLD N. Anglo-German cultural relations and the Thirty Years' War. *Rocky Mountain Mod. Lang. Assoc. Bull.*, XXII (1968) 22–9.

Education

2173. MAY, P. R. Richard Baxter on education. *Brit. Jour. Educ. Studies*, XV (1967) 60–73.

2174. JEFFREYS, MONTAGU VAUGHAN CASTELMAN. John Locke: prophet of common sense. Methuen, 1967. viii, 120 pp.

2175. HOWELL, WILBUR SAMUEL. John Locke and the new rhetoric. *Quart. Jour. Speech.*, LIII (1967) 319–33.

2176. QUENNELL, PETER. Alexander Pope: the education of genius, 1688–1728. Weidenfeld, 1968. x, 278 pp., illus.

2177. WALLIS, PETER JOHN. The Newcastle Commonwealth Commissioners and Auckland School. *Durham Research Rev.*, no. 20 (1968) 244–53.

2178. STEPHENS, J. E. Investment and intervention in education during the Interregnum. *Brit. Jour. Educ. Studies*, XV (1967) 253–62.

2179. STEPHENS, J. E. Yorkshire schoolmasters, 1640–60. *Yorks. Archaeol. Jour.*, XLII (1968) 181–6.

2180. POWER, M. J. Sir Balthazar Gerbier's academy at Bethnal Green. *East London Papers*, X (1967) 19–34.

2181. SELLMAN, ROGER RAYMOND. Act of Uniformity, 1662: Devon schoolmasters subscribing from 1662 to 1679. *Devon & Cornwall N. & Q.*, XXXI (1968) 109–12.

2182. WALLIS, PETER JOHN. Westmorland schools about 1676: Christopher

Wase's survey. *Cumberland & Westmorland Antiq. & Archaeol. Soc. Trans.*, LXVII (1967) 168–85.

Literature, drama and music

2183. JACK, RONALD D. S. James VI and renaissance poetic history. *English*, XVI (1967) 208–11.

2184. LEFRANC, PIERRE. Sir Walter Ralegh écrivain: l'œuvre et les idées. Quebec: Presses de l'Univ. Laval, 1968. 733 pp.

2185. LOOMIE, ALBERT J. Bacon and Gondomar: an unknown link in 1618. *Renaissance Quart.*, XXI (1968) 1–10.

2186. JENSON, JOHN R. The author of *Jura cleri. Bibliog. Soc. America Papers*, LXII (1968) 241–5.

2187. NUTTALL, W. L. F. Newspapers and their advertisements in the Commonwealth. *History Today*, XVII (1967) 460–7.

2188. WOODWARD, DANIEL H. Thomas Fuller, William Dugard, and the pseudonymous life of Sydney (1655). *Bibliog. Soc. America Papers*, LXII (1968) 501–10.

2189. BERRY, ELIZABETH K. *The Vale Royal of England. Cheshire Round*, I no. 9 (1968) 304–10. [By Daniel King, 1656.]

2190. KIRK, RUDOLF. A 17th century controversy: extremism *v.* moderation. *Texas Studies in Lit. & Lang.*, IX (1967–8) 5–35. [Joseph Hall and John Milton.]

2191. HYMAN, LAWRENCE W. History of the publication of *Paradise Lost*, 1667–74. *Jour. Hist. Studies*, I (1967–8) 50–64.

2192. FRENCH, A. L. Dryden, Marvell and political poetry. *Studies in Eng. Lit.*, VIII (1968) 397–413.

2193. KING, BRUCE. In search of Andrew Marvell. *Rev. Eng. Lit.*, VIII no. 4 (1967) 31–41.

2194. ROUSSEAU, G. S. Two new Pepys letters. *Rev. Eng. Studies*, XIX (1968) 169–72.

2195. PARKS, STEPHEN. John Dunton and *The works of the learned. Library*, 5th ser. XXIII (1968) 13–24.

2196. MARAMBAUD, PIERRE. Sir William Temple, sa vie, son œuvre. Paris: Minard, 1968. vi, 431 pp.

2197. SNYDER, HENRY L. The circulation of newspapers in the reign of Queen Anne. *Library*, 5th ser. XXIII (1968) 206–35.

2198. SNYDER, H. L. The reports of a press spy for Robert Harley: new bibliographical data for the reign of Queen Anne. *Library*, 5th ser. XXII (1967) 326–45.

2199. STEVENS, J. Prince's *Worthies of Devon*, pt. 2. *Devon & Cornwall N. & Q.*, XXI (1968) 67–77, 96–105. [Includes Prince's biographies of Sir Edward Seymour (1610–88) and John Avery of Plymouth (*b.* 1653).]

2200. BENTLEY, GERALD EADES (*ed.*). The 17th century stage: a collection of critical essays. Chicago, Ill., London: Chicago U.P., 1968. xvi, 287 pp., illus.

2201. BERGERON, DAVID M. The Christmas family: artificers in English pageantry. *ELH*, XXXV (1968) 354–64.

2202. FORKER, CHARLES R. Two notes on John Webster and Anthony Munday: unpublished entries in the records of the Merchant Taylors. *Eng. Lang. Notes*, VI no. 1 (1968) 26–34.

2203. BRACHER, FREDERICK. The letter-books of Sir George Etherege. *Harvard Lib. Bull.*, XV (1967) 238–45.

2204. BRACHER, F. Sir George Etherege and his secretary. *Harvard Lib. Bull.*, XVI (1968) 331–44.

2205. SMITHERS, DON. Seventeenth century English trumpet music. *Music & Letters*, XLVIII (1967) 358–65.

2206. WILLETTS, PAMELA J. Musical connections of Thomas Myriell. *Music & Letters*, XLIX (1968) 36–42.

2207. RILEY, JAMES. The identity of William Gregory. *Music & Letters*, XLVIII (1967) 236–46.

2208. HARLEY, JOHN. Music in Purcell's London: the social background. Dobson, 1968. 189 pp., illus.

2209. ZIMMERMAN, FRANKLIN BERSHER. Henry Purcell, 1659–95: his life and times. London: Macmillan; New York: St. Martin's P., 1967. xvii, 429 pp., illus.

2210. HUFSTADER, ALICE ANDERSON. Samuel Pepys: inquisitive amateur. *Musical Quart.*, LIV (1968) 437–61.

Architecture

2211. WILTON-ELY, JOHN. The architectural model. 1, The English baroque. *Apollo*, LXXXVIII (1968) 250–9.

2212. BAILLIE, HUGH MURRAY. Etiquette and the planning of the state apartments in baroque palaces. *Archaeologia*, CI (1967) 169–99.

2213. BRETTON, ROWLAND. Seventeenth century plaster work. *Halifax Antiq. Soc. Trans.* (1967) 115–22.

2214. COLMAN, SYLVIA. The west Suffolk inventories for 1665: some clues to house types. *Suffolk Rev.*, III (1968) 190–5.

Arts and crafts

2215. TRAPIER, ELIZABETH DU GUÉ. Sir Arthur Hopton and the interchange of paintings between Spain and England in the 17th century. *Connoisseur*, CLXIV (1967) 239–43, CLXV (1967) 60–3.

2216. MILLAR, OLIVER. Van Dyck in London. *Burlington Mag.*, CX (1968) 307–11.

2217. LIGHTBOWN, R. W. Jean Petitot and Jacques Bordier at the English court. *Connoisseur*, CLXVIII (1968) 82–91.

2218. LAVIN, J. A. Three 'owl' blocks, 1590–1640. *Library*, 5th ser. XXII (1967) 143–7.

2219. MORISON, STANLEY. John Fell: the University Press and the 'Fell' types. Oxford: Clarendon P., 1967. xvii, 278 pp.

2220. HEWETT, CECIL A. Some developments in carpentry, illustrated by Essex mill-wrighting. *Art Bull.*, L (1968) 70–4.

2221. NEVINSON, J. L. The embroidery patterns of Thomas Trevelyon. *Walpole Soc. Annual Vol.*, XLI (1968) 1–38.

SCIENCE

2222. KEMSLEY, DOUGLAS S. Religious influences in the rise of modern science: a review and criticism, particularly of the 'Protestant–Puritan ethic' theory. *Annals of Science*, XXIV (1968) 199–226.

2223. SHAPIRO, B. J. Latitudinarianism and science in 17th century England. *Past & Present*, no. 40 (1968) 16–41.

2224. PURVER, MARGERY. The Royal Society: concept and creation. Routledge, 1967. xviii, 246 pp.

2225. RATTANSI, P. M. The intellectual origins of the Royal Society. *Roy. Soc. Notes & Records*, XXIII (1968) 129–43.

2226. HILL, CHRISTOPHER. The intellectual origins of the Royal Society: London or Oxford? *Roy. Soc. Notes & Records*, XXIII (1968) 144–56.

2227. HALL, A. RUPERT, *and* HALL, MARIE BOAS. The intellectual origins of the Royal Society: London and Oxford. *Roy. Soc. Notes & Records*, XXIII (1968) 157–68.

2228. HALL, A. RUPERT, *and* HALL, MARIE BOAS. Further notes on Henry Oldenburg. *Roy. Soc. Notes & Records*, XXIII (1968) 33–42.

2229. SHUGG, WALLACE. Humanitarian attitudes in the early animal experiments of the Royal Society. *Annals of Science*, XXIV (1968) 227–38.

2230. WEBSTER, CHARLES. Henry Power's *Experimental Philosophy*. *Ambix*, XIV (1967) 150–78.

2231. WEBSTER, C. Richard Towneley (1629–1707), the Towneley Group and 17th century science. *Hist. Soc. Lancs. & Cheshire Trans.* for 1966, CXVIII (1967) 51–76.

2232. HENDRY, W. BROWNLIE. John Napier of Merchiston. *History Today*, XVII (1967) 250–6.

2233. TANNER, ROSALIND C. H., *and* PEPPER, JON V. The study of Thomas Harriot's manuscripts. 1, Harriot's will. 2, Harriot's unpublished papers. *Hist. Science*, VI (1967) 1–40.

2234. PEPPER, J. V. A letter from Nathaniel Torporley to Thomas Harriot. *Brit. Jour. Hist. Science*, III (1967) 285–90.

2235. WALLIS, PETER JOHN. An early mathematical manifesto: John Pell's *Idea of Mathematics*. *Durham Research Rev.*, no. 18 (1967) 139–48.

2236. WALLIS, P. J. William Oughtred's *Circles of Proportion* and *Trigonometries*. *Cambridge Bibliog. Soc. Trans.*, IV no. 5 (1968) 372–82.

2237. SCRIBA, CHRISTOPH J. A tentative index of the correspondence of John Wallis, F.R.S. *Roy. Soc. Notes & Records*, XXII (1967) 58–93.

2238. WESTFALL, RICHARD S. Hooke and the law of universal gravitation. *Brit. Jour. Hist. Science*, III pt. 3 (1967) 245–61.

2239. CORSON, DAVID W. Pierre Polinière, Francis Hauksbee, and electro-luminescence: a case of simultaneous discovery. *Isis*, LIX (1968) 402–13.

2240. NORTH, JOHN DAVID. Isaac Newton. O.U.P., 1967. 64 pp., illus.

2241. MANUEL, FRANK EDWARD. A portrait of Isaac Newton. Cambridge, Mass.: Harvard U.P.; London: O.U.P., 1968. xvii, 478 pp., illus.

2242. MANUEL, F. E. Newton as autocrat of science. *Daedalus*, XCVII (1968) 969–1001.

2243. MCGUIRE, J. E. Force, active principles, and Newton's invisible realm. *Ambix*, XV (1968) 154–208.

2244. MCGUIRE, J. E. Transmutation and immutability: Newton's doctrine of physical qualities. *Ambix*, XIV (1967) 69–95.

2245. COHEN, I. BERNARD. Newton's use of 'force', or, Cajori versus Newton: a note on translations of the *Principia*. *Isis*, LVIII (1967) 226–30.

2246. SUCHTING, W. A. Berkeley's criticism of Newton on space and motion. *Isis*, LVIII (1967) 186–97.

2247. RODNEY, JOEL M. Notes on Newton's optical papers: the *experimentum crucis* and the queries of 1672. *Historian*, XXIX (1967) 165–74.

2248. HAWES, JOAN L. Newton and the 'electrical attraction unexcited'. *Annals of Science*, XXIV (1968) 121–30.

2249. WILKINSON, RONALD STERNE. The Hartlib papers and 17th century chemistry. *Ambix*, XV (1968) 54–69.

2250. GOODISON, NICHOLAS. Daniel Quase and the portable barometer. *Annals of Science*, XXIII (1967) 287–93.

2251. LADURIE, EMMANUEL LE ROY. Les comptes fantastiques de Gregory King. *Annales*, XXIII (1968) 1086–1102.

MEDICINE

2252. SILVETTE, HERBERT. The doctor on the stage: medicine and medical men in 17th century England, *ed.* F. Butler. Knoxville, Tenn.: Tennessee U.P., 1967. 291 pp.

2253. WEBSTER, CHARLES. English medical reformers of the Puritan Revolution: a background to the 'Society of Chymical Physitians'. *Ambix*, XIV (1967) 16–41.

2254. WEBSTER, C. The College of Physicians: 'Solomon's House' in Commonwealth England. *Bull. Hist. Medicine*, XLI (1967) 393–412.

2255. BARNET, MARGARET C. The Barber-Surgeons of York. *Medical Hist.*, XII (1968) 19–30.

2256. O'MALLEY, C. D. Helkiah Crooke, M.D., F.R.C.P., 1576–1648. *Bull. Hist. Medicine*, XLII (1968) 1–18.

2257. PAGEL, WALTER, *and* WINDER, MARIANNE. Harvey and the 'modern' concept of disease. *Bull. Hist. Medicine*, XLII (1968) 496–509.

2258. PAGEL, W. Harvey and Glisson on irritability, with a note on van Helmont. *Bull. Hist. Medicine*, XLI (1967) 497–514.

2259. WEBSTER, C. Harvey's *De Generatione*: its origins and relevance to the theory of circulation. *Brit. Jour. Hist. Science*, III pt. 3 (1967) 262–74.

2260. ELKANA, YEHUDA, *and* GOODFIELD, JUNE. Harvey and the problem of the 'capillaries'. *Isis*, LIX (1968) 61–73.

2261. ISLER, HANSRUEDI. Thomas Willis, 1621–75: doctor and scientist. New York, London: Hafner, 1968. xiii, 237 pp., illus. [Originally pubd. Stuttgart: Wissenschaftliche V., 1965, as *Thomas Willis: ein Wegbereiter der moderner Medizin.*]

2262. O'MALLEY, C. D. John Evelyn and medicine. *Medical Hist.*, XII (1968) 219–31.

2263. GORN, JANICE L. The strange 'case' of Edward Clarke, Jnr., attending physician and John Locke, gent. *Educ. Theory*, XVII (1967) 298–316.

MILITARY AND NAVAL HISTORY

2264. ROGERS, HUGH CUTHBERT BASSET. Battles and generals of the Civil Wars, 1642–51. Seeley, 1968. 325 pp., illus.

2265. YOUNG, PETER. Edgehill, 1642: the campaign and the battle. Kineton, Warwicks.: Roundwood P., 1968. xix, 344 pp., illus.

2266. DORE, R. N. Fairfax rides again. *Cheshire Round*, I no. 8 (1967) 270–4. [Battle of Nantwich, 1644.]

2267. DORE, R. N. Beeston Castle in the Great Civil War, 1643–6. *Lancs. & Cheshire Antiq. Soc. Trans.* for 1965–6, LXXV–LXXVI (1968) 103–22.

2268. WANKLYN, M. D. G. The Royalist campaign in Somerset in July 1645 reconsidered. *Soc. Army Hist. Research Jour.*, XLVI (1968) 70–5.

2269. MUNGEAM, GERALD I. Contracts for the supply of equipment to the New Model Army in 1645. *Arms & Armour Soc. Jour.*, VI no. 3 (1968) 53–115.

2270. TUCKER, NORMAN. Lord Byron's final fling. *Anglesey Antiq. Soc. & F.C. Trans.* (1968) 13–19.

2271. BUTCHART, C. B. R. Sir Alexander Hamilton, general of artillery. *Aberdeen Univ. Rev.*, XLII (1967–8) 296–302.

2272. WIENER, FREDERICK BERNAYS. Civilians under military justice: the British practice since 1689, especially in North America. Chicago, Ill.: Chicago U.P., 1967. xxxii, 346 pp.

2273. DICKINSON, H. T. The Richards brothers: exponents of the military arts of Vauban. *Soc. Army Hist. Research Jour.*, XLVI (1968) 76–86.

2274. DICKINSON, H. T. The earl of Peterborough's campaign in Valencia, 1706. *Soc. Army Hist. Research Jour.*, XLV (1967) 35–52.

2275. HATTON, RAGNHILD MARIE. Sir James Jefferyes in the army of William III, Queen Anne and George I. *Soc. Army Hist. Research Jour.*, XLV (1967) 105–16.

2276. SNYDER, HENRY L. The duke of Marlborough's request of his captain-generalcy for life: a re-examination. *Soc. Army Hist. Research Jour.*, XLV (1967) 67–83.

2277. ANDERSON, ROGER CHARLES. List of English naval captains, 1642–60. (Soc. Nautical Research Occas. Pubns., 8). The Society, 1964. 44 pp.

2278. ANDERSON, R. C. Denmark and the first Anglo-Dutch war. *Mariner's Mirror*, LIII (1967) 55–62.

2279. NATIONAL MARITIME MUSEUM. The Second Dutch War: De Tweede Engelse Oorlog, 1665–7. H.M.S.O., 1967. 43 pp., illus.

2280. BOSSCHER, PHILIPPUS MEESSE. The four days' battle: some remarks and reflections. *Roy. United Service Inst. Jour.*, CXII (1967) 56–65. [1666.]

2281. BUISSERET, DAVID. The loss of H.M.S. *Norwich* off Port Royal in June 1682. *Mariner's Mirror*, LIV (1968) 403–7.

2282. HINCHCLIFFE, G. Impressment of seamen during the War of the Spanish Succession. *Mariner's Mirror*, LIII (1967) 137–42.

MARITIME HISTORY AND TRAVEL

2283. LE GUIN, CHARLES A. Sea life in 17th century England. *Amer. Neptune*, XXVII (1967) 111–34.

2284. MACINNES, CHARLES MALCOLM. Captain Thomas James and the North-west passage. Bristol: Historical Assoc. (Bristol Branch), 1967. 28 pp., illus.

2285. BRYDEN, D. J. Two pairs of dividers and *The Mariner's Mirror*. *Mariner's Mirror*, LIV (1968) 77–84.

2286. PREBBLE, JOHN. The Darien disaster. Secker, 1968. ix, 366 pp., illus.

2287. FAIRMAN, PAMELA SHAW. 'Un turista inglés en España a principios del siglo 17'. *In* Homenaje al profesor Alarcos García, vol. 2 (Valladolid: Universidad, 1965–7) pp. 809–27.

2288. WEBER, BERNARD C. An English view of Valletta in 1664: the visit of John Ray, the naturalist. *Annales Ordre Malte*, XXVI (1968) 79–81.

FOREIGN RELATIONS

2289. LEE, MAURICE. The Jacobean diplomatic service. *Amer. Hist. Rev.*, LXXII no. 4 (1967) 1264–82.

2290. BARBICHE, BERNARD. La nonciature de France et les affaires d'Angleterre au début du 17e siècle. *Bibl. École des Chartes*, CXXV (1967) 399–429.

2291. KONOVALOV, S. England and Russia: two missions, 1666–8. *Oxford Slavonic Papers*, XIII (1967) 47–71.

2292. SENNING, CALVIN F. Anglo-Spanish rivalry in the Spitsbergen whale fishery, 1612–16. *Amer. Neptune*, XXVIII (1968) 239–60.

2293. VAN EEROE, KATHERINE S. The Spanish match through an English Protestant's eyes. *Huntington Lib. Quart.*, XXXII (1968–9) 59–75. [Sir Robert Phelips.]

WALES

2294. WILLIAMS, GLANMOR. John Penry: Marprelate and patriot? *Welsh Hist. Rev.*, III (1966–7) 361–80.

2295. PARRY, BRYN R. Hugh Narney Hen (*c.* 1546–1623), squire of Nannau. *Merioneth Hist. & Rec. Soc. Jour.*, V no. 3 (1967) 185–206.

2296. RAMAGE, HELEN. The will of Elizabeth Jones of Llangoed. *Anglesey Antiq. Soc. & F.C. Trans.* (1967) 17–27. [1632.]

2297. DODD, ARTHUR HERBERT. Bishop Lewes Bayly, *c.* 1575–1631. *Caernarvons.*

Hist. Soc. Trans., XXVIII pt. 1 (1967) 13–36.

2298. HOWELL, BENJAMIN. Queen Elizabeth Grammar School in the 17th century. *Carmarthens. Hist.*, III (1966) 36–9.

2299. JENKINS, J. MARSHALL. Ground-rules of Welsh houses: a primary analysis. *Folk Life*, V (1967) 65–91.

SCOTLAND

2300. ROBERTS, F. F. Accounts of losses of the Burgh of Dunbar, 1651. *East Lothian Antiq. Soc. Trans.*, XI (1968) 1–11.

2301. DUNBAR, JOHN G. A siege of Castle Stalker. *Stewarts*, XIII no. 1 (1968) 29–32. [1684.]

2302. FERGUSON, WILLIAM. Religion and the massacre of Glencoe. *Scot. Hist. Rev.*, XLVI (1967) 82–7, XLVII (1968) 203–9.

2303. RILEY, PATRICK WILLIAM JOSEPH. The Scottish parliament of 1703. *Scot. Hist. Rev.*, XLVII (1968) 129–50.

2304. BARCLAY, ROBERT C. (*ed.*). The Court Books of Orkney and Shetland, 1614–15. (Scottish Hist. Soc. Pubns., 4th ser., 4). Edinburgh: the Society, 1967. xxvii, 146 pp., illus.

2305. SNODDY, THOMAS GILLESPIE. Sir John Scot, Lord Scotstarvet: his life and times. St. Andrews, Fife: St. Andrews Univ., 1968. 236 pp., illus.

2306. ARMET, HELEN. Sir John Falconer of Balmakellie, master of the Scottish Mint. *Scot. Geneal.*, XIV (1967) 1–9.

2307. SMOUT, THOMAS CHRISTOPHER. The Glasgow merchant community in the 17th century. *Scot. Hist. Rev.*, XLVII (1968) 53–71.

2308. LOUDEN, R. STUART. Robert Leighton: the bishop. *Scot. Jour. Theol.*, XX (1967) 198–209.

2309. LAMB, JOHN A. (*ed.*). Ecclesiastical rules and constitutions for order and discipline: an unpublished manuscript. *Scot. Church Hist. Soc. Records*, XVI pt. 3 (1968) 151–77.

2310. WHITEFORD, D. H. Jacobitism as a factor in Presbyterian-Episcopalian relationships in Scotland, 1689–90. *Scot. Church Hist. Soc. Records*, XVI pt. 2 (1967) 129–49, XVI pt. 3 (1968) 185–201.

2311. ANDERSON, WILLIAM JAMES. William Thomson of Dundee, friar minor conventual. *Innes Rev.*, XVIII (1967) 99–111.

2312. DILWORTH, MARK. Scottish monks in Würzburg. *Laeta Dies* (1968) 101–6.

2313. DILWORTH, M. The Würzburg Scots and the English congregation. *Downside Rev.*, LXXXV (1967) 39–61.

2314. HORNE, A. SINCLAIR. Torchbearers of the truth: sketches of the Scottish Covenanters. Edinburgh: Scot. Reformation Soc., 1968. 125 pp., illus.

2315. COWAN, IAN BORTHWICK. The Covenanters: a revision article. *Scot. Hist. Rev.*, XLVII (1968) 35–52.

2316. MORGAN, PAUL. Some bibliographical aspects of the Scottish Prayer Book of 1637. *Bibliothek*, V pt. 1 (1967) 1–23.

2317. HOWIE, W. B. Sir Archibald Stevenson, his ancestry and the riot in the College of Physicians at Edinburgh. *Medical Hist.*, XI (1967) 269–84.

IRELAND

Note: Writings on Irish domestic and local history are not included unless they have a direct bearing on English history.

2318. WALSH, MICHELINE. The last years of Hugh O'Neill: Rome, 1608–16. *Irish Sword*, VIII (1967) 120–9, (1968) 230–41, 294–303.

2319. CLARKE, AIDAN. 'The colonisation of Ulster and the rebellion of 1641'. *In* The course of Irish history, *ed.* T. W. Moody *and* F. X. Martin (Cork: Mercier P., 1967) pp. 189–203.

2320. BROOKE-TYRELL, ALMA. Happenings in Dublin, A.D. 1646. *Dublin Hist. Rec.*, XXII (1968) 160–75.

2321. BOTTIGHEIMER, KARL S. English money and Irish land: the 'Adventurers' in the Cromwellian settlement of Ireland. *Jour. Brit. Studies*, VII no. 1 (1967) 12–27.

2322. SIMMS, JOHN GERALD. 'The Restoration and the Jacobite War'. *In* The course of Irish history, *ed.* T. W. Moody *and* F. X. Martin (Cork: Mercier P., 1967) pp. 204–16.

2323. MAYHEW, GEORGE P. Jonathan Swift's 'Preferments of Ireland', 1713–14. *Huntington Lib. Quart.*, XXX (1966–7) 297–305.

2324. KNOX, ROBERT BUICK. James Ussher, archbishop of Armagh. Cardiff: Wales U.P., 1967. 205 pp.

2325. MOODY, T. W., *and* SIMMS, JOHN GERALD. The bishopric of Derry and the Irish Society of London, 1602–1705. Vol. 1, 1602–70. Dublin: Stationery Office, for Irish Mss. Commission, 1968. vi, 430 pp.

2326. MILLETT, BENIGNUS. Survival and reorganisation, 1650–95. (Hist. of Irish Catholicism, vol. 3, fasc. 7). Dublin: Gill, 1968. 63 pp.

2326a. WALKER, BREIFNE. Blessed Oliver Plunket and the Popish Plot in Ireland. *Irish Eccles. Record*, 5th ser. CIX (1968) 313–30.

2327. RYAN, MARTIN. The Franciscan houses of Thomond in 1616. *N. Munster Antiq. Jour.*, X (1967) 112–15.

2328. HUNTER, R. J. (*ed.*). Fragments of the civil survey of counties Kerry, Longford and Armagh. *Analecta Hibernica*, XXIV (1967) 227–31.

2329. MCCOURT, DESMOND, *and* EVANS, E. ESTYN. A late 17th century farmhouse at Shantallow, near Londonderry. *Ulster Folklife*, XIV (1968) 14–23.

2330. GOUHIER, P. Mercenaires irlandais au service de la France, 1635–64. *Rev. Hist. Moderne*, XV (1968) 672–90.

BRITISH EMPIRE

Note: The domestic history of Commonwealth countries is not included unless it has a direct bearing on British history.

2331. RAINBOLDT, JOHN C. A new look at Stuart 'tyranny': the Crown's attack on the Virginia Assembly, 1676–89. *Virginia Mag. Hist. & Biog.*, LXXV (1967) 387–406.

2332. MILLER, GUY HOWARD. Rebellion in Zion: the overthrow of the dominion of New England. *Historian*, XXX (1968) 439–59.

2333. BLANKE, G. H. Die Anfänge des amerikanischen Sendungsbewusstseins. *Archiv für Reformationsgesch.*, LVIII (1967) 171–211.

2334. BENNETT, J. HARRY. The English Caribbees in the period of the Civil War, 1642–6. *William & Mary Quart.*, 3rd ser. XXIV (1967) 359–77.

2335. SARKAR, JAGADISH NARAYAN. A mercantile strike of the 17th century. *Indian Hist. Rec. Comm. Proc.*, XXXVIII (1967) 125–31. [East India Co. at Surat, 1669.]

BIOGRAPHY

2336. *Bayly.* CARROLL, KENNETH L. From bond slave to governor: the strange career of Charles Bayly, 1632?–80. *Friends' Hist. Soc. Jour.*, LII no. 1 (1968) 19–38.

2337. *Brodley.* FACER, PETER. Matthew Brodley (1587–1648). *Halifax Antiq. Soc. Trans.* (1968) 57–62.

2338. *Churchill.* BURTON, IVOR FLOWER. The Captain-General: the career of John Churchill, duke of Marlborough, from 1702–11. Constable, 1968. ix, 230 pp.

2339. *Churchill.* BUTLER, IRIS. Rule of three: Sarah, duchess of Marlborough and her companions in power. Hodder, 1967. 379 pp., illus.

2340. *Cooper.* HALEY, KENNETH HAROLD DOBSON. The first earl of Shaftesbury. Oxford: Clarendon P., 1968. xii, 767 pp.

2341. *Cooper.* HALEY, K. H. D. 'False Achitophel'. *History Today*, XVII (1967) 45–51. [[1st earl of Shaftesbury.]

2342. *Cooper.* ROGERS, GEORGE C., *Jnr.* The first earl of Shaftesbury. *South Carolina Hist. Mag.*, LXVIII (1967) 74–8.

2343. *Constable.* ROEBUCK, PETER. The Constables of Everingham: the fortunes of a Catholic Royalist family during the Civil War and Interregnum. *Recusant Hist.*, IX (1967–8) 75–87.

2344. *Daniel.* CHESTERS, GEOFFREY. John Daniel of Daresbury, 1544–1610. *Hist. Soc. Lancs. & Cheshire Trans.* for 1966, CXVIII (1967) 1–17.

2345. *Fetherston.* FARR, MICHAEL WALTER. The Fetherstons of Packwood in the 17th century. (Dugdale Soc. Occas. Papers, 18). Stratford-upon-Avon, Warwicks.: the Society, 1968. 192 pp.

2346. *Gilbert.* ROBERTS, JOHN. The younger Sir John Gilbert (*c.* 1575–1608). *Devon Assoc. Repts. & Trans.*, C (1968) 205–17.

2347. *Hopton.* EDGAR, FRANK TERRELL RHOADES. Sir Ralph Hopton: the king's man in the West, 1642–52: a study in character and command. Oxford: Clarendon P., 1968. xx, 248 pp.

2348. *Jeffreys.* KEETON, GEORGE WILLIAMS. George Jeffreys: his family and friends. *Hon. Soc. Cymmrodorion Trans.* (1967) 39–56.

2349. *Milton.* PARKER, WILLIAM RILEY. Milton: a biography. Oxford: Clarendon P., 1968. 2 vols.

2350. *Nash.* WHITFIELD, CHRISTOPHER. Anthony and John Nash: Shakespeare's legatees. *N. & Q.*, CCXII (1967) 123–30.

2351. *Pepys.* TAYLOR, IVAN E. Samuel Pepys. New York: Twayne, 1967. 160 pp.

2352. *Popple.* ROBBINS, CAROLINE. Absolute liberty: the life and thought of William Popple, 1638–1708. *William & Mary Quart.*, 3rd ser. XXIV (1967) 190–223.

2353. *Rupert.* KNIGHT, FRANK. Prince of cavaliers: the story of the life and campaigns of Rupert of the Rhine. McDonald & Co., 1967. 184 pp., illus.

2354. *Slingsby.* SMITH, GEOFFREY RIDSDILL. Without touch of dishonour: the life and death of Sir Henry Slingsby, 1602–58. Roundwood P., 1968. 195 pp., illus.

2355. *Stuart.* MCINNES, IAN. Arabella: the life and times of Lady Arabella Seymour, 1575–1615. W. H. Allen, 1968. 190 pp., illus. [Arabella Stuart.]

2356. *Swanley.* BAUMBER, M. L. An East India captain: the early career of Captain Richard Swanley. *Mariner's Mirror*, LIII (1967) 265–79.

2357. *Talbot.* CALISTA, *Sister.* John Talbot, of Grafton Manor, and his son George, the 9th earl of Shrewsbury. *Worcs. Recusant*, no. 8 (1966) 15–23.

2358. VERNEY, *Sir* HARRY (*ed.*). The Verneys of Claydon: a 17th century English family. Maxwell, 1968. xii, 266 pp., illus.

THE EIGHTEENTH CENTURY, 1714–1815

GENERAL

2359. HORN, DAVID BAYNE. Great Britain and Europe in the 18th century. Oxford: Clarendon P., 1967. xi, 411 pp., illus.

2360. CLIFFORD, JAMES LOWRY (*ed.*). Man versus society in 18th century Britain: six points of view. C.U.P., 1968. viii, 175 pp. [By J. H. Plumb, J. Viner, G. R. Cragg, R. Wittkower, P. H. Lang and B. H. Bronson.]

2361. MARSHALL, DOROTHY. Dr. Johnson's London. New York, Chichester: Wiley, 1968. xv, 293 pp.

2362. BECKWITH, IAN S. Georgian Tuxford: a Nottinghamshire township in the early 18th century. *Thoroton Soc. Trans.* for 1967, LXXI (1968) 59–69.

2363. GOODWYN, EDWIN ALVIS. A century of a Suffolk town: Beccles, 1760–1860. Pt. 1, 1760–1815. Ipswich: College Gateway Bookshop, 1968. 156 pp., illus.

2364. ROPER, JOHN STEPHEN. Dudley: the town in the 18th century. Dudley, Worcs.: Public Lib., 1968. 33 pp.

2365. WÜRTTEMBERG, CARL EUGEN, *Herzog von Württemberg*. Tagebucher seiner Rayssen nach . . . den beiden Königreichen Franckreich und Engelland, 1783–91, *ed.* R. Uhland. Tübingen: Wunderlich, 1968. 401 pp.

CONSTITUTIONAL AND POLITICAL HISTORY

2366. BEATTIE, JOHN MAURICE. The English court in the reign of George I. C.U.P., 1967. xii, 306 pp.

2367. LANSBERRY, H. C. F. A Whig inheritance. *Inst. Hist. Research Bull.*, XLI (1968) 47–57.

2368. NAYLOR, JOHN F. (*ed.*). The British aristocracy and the Peerage Bill of 1719. New York, London: O.U.P., 1968. x, 293 pp.

2369. HORWITZ, HENRY. Revolution politicks: the career of Daniel Finch, second earl of Nottingham, 1647–1730. C.U.P., 1968. xii, 306 pp.

2370. BEVAN, BRYAN. King James the Third of England: a study of kingship in exile. Hale, 1967. 192 pp., illus.

2371. JONES, FRANCIS. The Society of Sea Serjeants. *Hon. Soc. Cymmrodorion Trans.* (1967) 57–91.

2372. SPECK, WILLIAM ARTHUR. Swift's politics. *Univ. Rev.*, IV (1967) 53–71.

2373. KENDRICK, T. F. J. Sir Robert Walpole, the Old Whigs and the bishops, 1733–6: a study in 18th century parliamentary politics. *Hist. Jour.*, XI (1968) 421–45.

2374. AVERY, EMMETT L., *and* SCOUTEN, A. H. The opposition to Sir Robert Walpole, 1737–9. *E.H.R.*, LXXXIII (1968) 331–6. [James Lacy, actor, and the Stage Licensing Act.]

2375. KRAMNICK, ISAAC. Bolingbroke and his circle: the politics of nostalgia in the age of Walpole. Cambridge, Mass.: Harvard U.P.; London: O.U.P., 1968. xvi, 321 pp.

2376. SHIPLEY, JOHN B. James Ralph, Prince Titi, and the black box of Frederick, prince of Wales. *New York Public Lib. Bull.*, LXXI (1967) 143–57.

2377. FUCHS, KONRAD. England und Hannover in der Politik William Pitts des Älteren. *Niedersächsisches Jahrb. für Landesgesch.*, XL (1968) 156–65.

2378. KESTEVEN, G. R. The Forty-Five rebellion. (Studies in English Hist.). Chatto, 1968. 94 pp., illus.

2379. The Jacobite occupation of Manchester in 1745: the impressment of horses. *Lancs. & Cheshire Antiq. Soc. Trans.* for 1965–6, LXXV–LXXVI (1968) 164–71.

2380. BROWN, PETER. The Chathamites: a study in the relationship between personalities and ideas in the second half of the 18th century. Macmillan, 1967. xv, 516 pp., illus.

2381. BROWNING, REED. The duke of Newcastle and the imperial election plan, 1749–54. *Jour. Brit. Studies*, VII no. 1 (1967) 28–47.

2382. HIGONNET, PATRICE LOUIS-RENÉ. The origins of the Seven Years' War. *Jour. Mod. Hist.*, XL (1968) 57–90.

2383. VALENTINE, ALAN. Lord North. Norman, Okla.: Oklahoma U.P., 1967. 2 vols.

2384. SMITH, CHARLES DANIEL. Lord North, a reluctant debater: the making of a cabinet minister, 1754–67. *Quart. Jour. Speech*, LIII (1967) 17–27.

2385. MOORE, G. E. The effect of the Act of 1765. *Isle of Man Nat. Hist. & Antiq. Soc. Proc.*, n.s. VII no. 1 (1967) 35–48. [Revestment Act.]

2386. THOMAS, PETER D. G. Charles Townshend and American taxation in 1767. *E.H.R.*, LXXXIII (1968) 33–51.

2387. KESTEVEN, G. R. The loss of the American colonies. (Studies in English Hist.). Chatto, 1968. 95 pp., illus.

2388. SUTHERLAND, LUCY S. Edmund Burke and the relations between members of parliament and their constituents. *Studies in Burke and his Time*, X (1968) 1005–21.

2389. KALLICH, MARTIN. Horace Walpole against Edmund Burke: a study in antagonism. Pt. 1. *Studies in Burke and his Time*, IX (1967–8) 834–63.

2390. LIPSCOMB, PATRICK. William Pitt and the abolition question: a review of an historical controversy. *Leeds Philos. & Lit. Soc. Proc., Lit. & Hist. Section*, XII pt. 4 (1967) 87–128.

2391. MARSHALL, PETER JAMES. The anti-slave trade movement in Bristol. Bristol: Historical Assoc. (Bristol Branch), 1968. 26 pp.

2392. FEARN, EDWARD. Henry Redhead Yorke: radical traitor. *Yorks. Archaeol. Jour.*, XLIII (1968) 187–92.

2393. THOMAS, PETER D. G. La vie politique en Grande-Bretagne vers la fin du 18e siècle. *Rev. Hist.*, CCXXXVIII (1967) 415–32.

2394. SCHILFERT, GERHARD. Deutsches Ständewesen und englischer Parlamentarismus am Vorabend der französischen Revolution. *Wissenschaftliche Zeit. der Univ. Rostock*, XVII (1968) 35–42.

2395. ASPINALL, ARTHUR (*ed.*). The later correspondence of George III. Vol. 3, Jan. 1798–Dec. 1801. Vol. 4, Jan. 1802–Dec. 1807. C.U.P., 1967, 1968. 2 vols.

2396. ASPINALL, A. (*ed.*). The correspondence of George, prince of Wales, 1770–1812. Vol. 4, 1799–1804. Vol. 5, 1804–6. Cassell, 1967, 1968. 2 vols.

2397. ENGEL, CLAIRE-ELIANE. Le Régent et l'Angleterre. *Rev. Française de l'Élite Européenne*, no. 214 (1968) 3–9.

2398. BROOKE, JOHN. The House of Commons, 1754–90: an introductory survey. O.U.P., 1968. viii, 312 pp. [Originally pubd. H.M.S.O., 1964 as *The history of parliament: the House of Commons, 1754–90* vol. 1, by Sir Lewis Namier and J. Brooke.]

2399. BURNE, SAMBROOKE ARTHUR HIGGINS. The Staffordshire county election, 1747. Stafford: the author, 1967. 23 pp.

2400. STUART, D. G. 'Castle' and 'manor': parliamentary patronage in the borough of Tamworth in the mid-18th century. *Lichfield Archaeol. & Hist. Soc. Trans.*, IX (1968) 59–65.

2401. KERR, BARBARA. Thomas Hyde of Arne and the Poole election of 1768. *Dorset Nat. Hist. & Archaeol. Soc. Proc.*, LXXXIX (1968) 282–96.

2402. SMITH, E. ANTHONY. The Yorkshire elections of 1806 and 1807: a study in electoral management. *Northern Hist.*, II (1967) 62–90.

POLITICAL THOUGHT

2403. KRAMNICK, ISAAC. An Augustan reply to Locke: Bolingbroke on natural law and the origin of government. *Political Science Quart.*, LXXXII (1967) 571–94.

2404. FINNIS, J. M. Blackstone's theoretical intentions. *Natural Law Forum*, XII (1967) 163–83.

2405. CHAPMAN, GERALD WESTER. Edmund Burke: the practical imagination. Cambridge, Mass.: Harvard U.P.; London: O.U.P., 1967. xiii, 350 pp.

2406. KIRK, RUSSEL. Edmund Burke: a genius reconsidered. New Rochelle, N.Y.: Arlington House, 1967. 255 pp.

2407. MCLOUGHLIN, T. Edmund Burke's formal training in oratory. *Eng. Studies in Africa*, XI (1968) 161–72.

2408. BOULTON, JAMES T. Edmund Burke's *Letter to a noble lord*: apologia and manifesto. *Burke Newsletter*, VIII (1967) 695–702.

2409. JOY, NEILL R. Burke's *Speech on conciliation with the colonies*: epic prophecy and satire. *Studies in Burke & his Time*, IX (1967–8) 753–72.

2410. GOODWIN, ALBERT. The political genesis of Edmund Burke's *Reflections on the Revolution in France*. *John Rylands Lib. Bull.*, L (1967–8) 336–64.

2411. SALVUCCI, PASQUALE. La filosofia politica di Adam Smith. Urbino: Argalia (S.T.E.U.), 1966. 195 pp.

2412. NURSEY-BRAY, P. F. Thomas Paine and the concept of alienation. *Polit. Studies*, XVI (1968) 223–42.

ADMINISTRATIVE AND LEGAL HISTORY

2413. SHIPKEY, ROBERT. Problems of Irish patronage during the chief secretaryship of Robert Peel, 1812–18. *Hist. Jour.*, X (1967) 41–56.

2414. AVERY, DAVID. Edmonton Workhouse Committee, 1732–7. (Edmonton Hundred Historical Soc. Occas. Papers, n.s. 14). The Society, 1968. 30 pp.

2415. WEBSTER, C. D. Robert Parker, attorney (1732–96), pt. 2. *Halifax Antiq. Soc. Trans.* (1967) 93–113.

2416. MEDD, PATRICK. Romilly: a life of Sir Samuel Romilly, lawyer and reformer. Collins, 1968. 318 pp., illus.

2417. LUCAS, PAUL. On Edmund Burke's doctrine of prescription: or, an appeal from the new to the old lawyers. *Hist. Jour.*, XI (1968) 35–63.

2418. SLOCOMBE, I. M. The Bridgwater Court of Record in the 18th century. *Somerset Archaeol. & Nat. Hist. Soc. Proc.*, CXI (1967) 38–50.

2419. BAKER-JONES, D. L. Notes on the Orielton chancery proceedings. *Nat. Lib. Wales Jour.*, XV (1967–8) 344–61, 405–22.

ECONOMIC AND SOCIAL HISTORY

General

2420. LANTZ, PIERRE. De la richesse des besoins à la richesse des nations: étude sur Adam Smith. *Rev. d'Hist. Écon. et Sociale*, XLVI (1968) 403–22.

2421. HAMOWY, RONALD. Adam Smith, Adam Ferguson, and the division of labour. *Economica*, n.s. XXXV (1968) 249–59.

2422. LUTFALLA, MICHEL. Sur quelques réflexions économiques de Jeremy Bentham. *Rev. d'Hist. Econ. et Sociale*, XLVI (1968) 254–64.

2423. EAGLY, ROBERT V. 'The Swedish and English bullionist controversies: a comparative study of the impact of events on ideas'. *In* Events, ideology and economic theory (Detroit, Mich.: Wayne State U.P., 1968) pp. 13–43.

Finance

2424. CARTER, ALICE CLAIRE. The English public debt in the 18th century. (Helps for Students of History, 74). Historical Assoc., 1968. 25 pp.

2425. CARTER, A. C. A note on numbers of holders of English public debt stocks in the mid-18th century. *Inst. Hist. Research Bull.*, XLI (1968) 99–100.

2426. BOLITHO, HECTOR, *and* PEEL, DEREK. The Drummonds of Charing Cross. Allen & Unwin, 1967. 232 pp., illus.

2427. BOLITHO, H. The house of Drummond. *Three Banks Rev.*, no. 75 (1967) 33–41.

2428. Williams Deacon's and the first Manchester bank. *Three Banks Rev.*, no. 77 (1968) 37–48.

2429. HOLLAND, J. D. An 18th century pioneer, Richard Price, D.D., F.R.S., 1723–91. *Roy. Soc. Notes & Records*, XXIII (1968) 43–64. [Actuary.]

2430. HINDLE, G. B. A venture in charity, 1791–1803. *Wesley Hist. Soc. Proc.*, XXXVI (1967–8) 41–8. [Strangers' Friend Society, Manchester.]

2431. CAPLAN, NIEL. Chailey Friendly Society. *Sussex Archaeol. Coll.*, CV (1967) 31–6.

Industry

2432. HARRIS, JOHN RAYMOND. The employment of steam power in the 18th century. *History*, LII (1967) 133–48.

2433. ALLEN, JOHN S. The 1712 and other Newcomen engines of the earls of Dudley. *Newcomen Soc. Trans.* for 1964–5, XXXVII (1967) 57–84.

2434. UNWIN, GEORGE. Samuel Oldknow and the Arkwrights: the Industrial Revolution at Stockport and Marple. 2nd edn. Manchester: Manchester U.P., 1968. xxii, 260 pp., illus. [Previous edn. 1924.]

2435. MUTTON, NORMAN. Boulton and Watt and the Norfolk marshland. *Norfolk Archaeol.*, XXXIV pt. 2 (1967) 223–38.

2436. HENDERSON, WILLIAM OTTO (*ed.*). Industrial Britain under the Regency: the diaries of Escher, Bodmer, May and de Gallois. Cass, 1968. xi, 188 pp., illus.

2437. RHODES, J. N. The London (Quaker) Lead Company and the Prestatyn mines scandal. *Flints. Hist. Soc. Pubns.*, XXIII (1967–8) 42–53.

2438. KIRKHAM, NELLIE. The ventilation of Hillcarr Sough. *Newcomen Soc. Trans.* for 1964–5, XXXVII (1967) 133–8.

2439. MUTTON, NORMAN. Charlcotte furnace. *Shropshire Archaeol. Soc. Trans.* for 1965, LVIII pt. 1 (1967) 84–8.

2440. CHAPMAN, STANLEY DAVID. The early factory masters: the transition to the factory system in the Midlands textile industry. Newton Abbot, Devon: David & Charles, 1967. 256 pp., illus. [1769–1815.]

2441. HATLEY, VICTOR A. 'Blaze' at Buckby: a note on a forgotten Northamptonshire industry. *Northants. Past & Present*, IV no. 2 (1967) 91–6.

2442. COLLINSON, J. M. Broads and narrows. *Nat. Reg. Archives, W. Riding N. Section Bull.*, XI (1968) 29–35. [Journal of John Brearley.]

2443. CHAPMAN, STANLEY DAVID (*ed.*). Memoirs of two 18th century framework knitters. *Textile Hist.*, I no. 1 (1968) 103–18. [Caleb Herring, 1752–1829 and William Felkin, 1745–1838.]

2444. MEJIDE PARDO, ANTONIO. Los ingleses Lees y su fábrica de tejidos en Pontevedra. *Museo de Pontevedra*, XIX (1965) 55–86.

2445. OTRUBA, GUSTAV. Englische Fabrikanten und Maschinisten zur Zeit Maria Theresias und Joseph II. in Osterreich. *Tradition*, XII (1967) 365–77.

2446. SPIERS, C. H. Sir Humphry Davy and the leather industry. *Annals of Science*, XXIV (1968) 99–113.

2447. HALL, I. V. The Daubenys: the second and third generations of the family at the Halliers Lane Refinery under George II and George III. Pt. 2. *Bristol & Glos. Archaeol. Soc. Trans.* for 1966, LXXXV (1967) 164–201. [Bristol sugar-bakers.]

2448. BELL, R. A. Origins of the canning industry. *Newcomen Soc. Trans.* for 1965–6, XXXVIII (1968) 145–51.

2449. MCCORD, NORMAN, *and* BREWSTER, DAVID E. Some labour troubles of the 1790s in north east England. *Internat. Rev. Soc. Hist.*, XIII (1968) 366–83.

Trade and commerce

2450. The Jersey Chamber of Commerce: the early years. *Soc. Jersiaise Bull. Annuel*, XIX pt. 4 (1968) 299–306.

2451. EDWARDS, MICHAEL M. The growth of the British cotton trade, 1780–1815. Manchester: Manchester U.P., 1967. viii, 276 pp.

2452. WILSON, R. G. The fortunes of a Leeds merchant house, 1780–1820. *Business Hist.*, IX (1967) 70–86. [Rhodes family wool business.]

2453. JONES, GWILYM PEREDUR. The commercial interests of Wilfred Hudlestone. *Cumberland & Westmorland Antiq. & Archaeol. Soc. Trans.*, LXVII (1967) 186–98.

2454. TANN, JENNIFER. Some account books of the Phelps family of Dursley. *Bristol & Glos. Archaeol. Soc. Trans.* for 1967, LXXXVI (1968) 107–17. [Clothiers.]

2455. BOOTH, JENNIFER E. A Wirral account book and notary's register, 1761–90. *Hist. Soc. Lancs. & Cheshire Trans.* for 1966, CXVIII (1967) 77–85.

2456. MUI, HOH-CHEUNG, *and* MUI, LORNA H. Smuggling and the British tea trade before 1784. *Amer. Hist. Rev.*, LXXIV no. 1 (1968) 44–73.

2457. LAMBERT, SHEILA. Printing for the House of Commons in the 18th century. *Library*, 5th ser. XXIII (1968) 25–46.

2458. GILBERTHORPE, ENID C. Book printing at Sheffield in the 18th century. Sheffield, Yorks.: Sheffield City Lib., 1967. 12 pp.

2459. MCKENZIE, DONALD FRANCIS, *and* ROSS, J. C. (*eds.*). A ledger of Charles Ackers, printer of *The London Magazine*. (Oxford Bibliog. Soc. Pubns., n.s. 15). O.U.P., for the Society, 1968. lx, 331 pp., illus.

2460. MOSLEY, JAMES. The early career of William Caslon. *Printing Hist. Soc. Jour.*, III (1967) 66–81.

2461. PAVELKA, HEDWIG. 'Englands Wirtschaftsbeziehungen zu den Habsburgischen Niederlanden im achtzehnten Jahrhundert'. *In* Mélanges offerts à Guillaume Jacquemyns (Brussels: Univ. Libre, 1968) pp. 531–49.

2462. POLAK, ADA. Wolffs and Dorville: et norsk-engelsk handelshus i London under Napoleonskrigene, en kultur-historisk skildring. Oslo: Universitetsforlaget, 1968. xv, 238 pp. ['Wolffs and Dorville: an Anglo-Norwegian commercial firm in London at the time of the Napoleonic Wars, a cultural-historical sketch'.]

2463. MASON, FRANCES NORTON (*ed.*).

John Norton and Sons, merchants of London and Virginia: being the papers from their counting house for the years 1750–95. 2nd edn. Newton Abbot, Devon: David & Charles, 1968. xl, 573 pp. [Previous edn. Richmond, Va.: Dietz P., 1937.]

2464. ROBERTS, WILLIAM I. Ralph Carr: a Newcastle merchant and the American colonial trade. *Business Hist. Rev.*, XLII (1968) 271–87.

2465. MERONEY, GERALDINE. The London entrepôt merchants and the Georgia colony. *William & Mary Quart.*, 3rd ser. XXV (1968) 230–44. [1730–3.]

2466. ROBERTS, WILLIAM I. The losses of a loyalist merchant in Georgia during the revolution. *Georgia Hist. Quart.*, LII (1968) 270–6.

2467. DAVIS, RALPH. Aleppo and Devonshire Square: English traders in the Levant in the 18th century. Macmillan, 1967. xiv, 258 pp., illus.

2468. BAKER, NORMAN. John Durand, stock-splitter: an 18th century Huguenot's activities in the East India Company. *Huguenot Soc. London Proc.*, XXI no. 3 (1968) 280–9.

2469. BAKSHI, S. R. The Napoleonic scare and the East India Company. *Modern Rev.*, CXXI (1967) 142–6.

2470. FITTE, ERNESTO J. Los comerciantes ingleses en vísperas de la Revolución de Mayo. Buenos Aires: Talleres Gráficos Faija, 1967. 75 pp.

Social history

2471. CONE, CARL B. The English Jacobins: reformers in late 18th century England. New York: C. Scribner, 1968. 248 pp.

2472. CASSAIGNE, E. L'anti-esclavagisme de John Woolman. *Études Anglaises*, XXI (1968) 142–51.

2473. CHALKLIN, CHRISTOPHER WILLIAM. Urban housing estates in the 18th century. *Urban Studies*, V (1968) 67–85.

2474. BURTON, ELIZABETH. The Georgians at home: 1714–1830. Longmans, 1967. ix, 422 pp., illus.

2475. WALTERS, JOHN. Splendour and scandal: the reign of Beau Nash. Jarrolds, 1968. 208 pp., illus.

2476. ORIGO, IRIS. The pleasures of Bath in the 18th century. *Horizon*, VII (1965) 4–15.

2477. ADAMS, VICTOR J. Weymouth theatricals. *Dorset Nat. Hist. & Archaeol. Soc. Proc.*, LXXXIX (1968) 302–13.

2478. WILES, ROY MCKEEN. Crowd-pleasing spectacles in 18th century England. *Jour. Popular Culture*, I (1967) 90–105.

2479. WALKER, THOMAS ERNEST CONWAY. The Clives at Claremont. *Surrey Archaeol. Coll.*, LXV (1968) 91–6.

2480. LEWIS, LESLEY. Elizabeth, countess of Home, and her house in Portman Square. *Burlington Mag.*, CIX (1967) 443–53.

2481. WILSON, RICHARD. Ossington and the Denisons. *History Today*, XVIII (1968) 164–72.

2482. HALSBAND, ROBERT. Virtue in danger: the case of Griselda Murray. *History Today*, XVII (1967) 692–700. [Attempted rape by valet, 1721.]

2483. HALSBAND, R. The noble lady and the player. *History Today*, XVIII (1968) 464–72. [Marriage of John Beard, singer, to Lady Harriet Herbert.]

2484. BAGLEY, JOHN JOSEPH (*ed.*). The great diurnal of Nicholas Blundell of Little Crosby, Lancs., *transcr.* F. Tyrer. Vol. 1, 1702–11. Chester: Lancs. & Cheshire Record Soc., 1968. 350 pp., illus.

2485. STEVENS, JOAN. An 18th century diary: Thomas Le Maistre's notebook. *Soc. Jersiaise Bull. Annuel*, XIX pt. 3 (1967) 244–53.

2486. BASTIAN, F. Defoe's *Tour* and the historian. *History Today*, XVII (1967) 845–51.

2487. PILCHER, GEORGE WILLIAM (*ed.*). The Reverend Samuel Davies abroad: the diary of a journey to England and Scotland, 1753–5. Urbana, Ill., London: Illinois U.P., 1968. xv, 176 pp.

2488. RAISTRICK, ARTHUR (*ed.*). The Hatchett diary: a tour through the counties of England and Scotland in 1796 visiting their mines and manufactories. Truro: Barton, 1967. 114 pp., illus.

2489. ROLLINSON, WILLIAM (*ed.*). A tour in the Lakes made in 1797 by William Gell. Newcastle-upon-Tyne: F. Graham, 1968. 53 pp., illus.

2490. MCNAUGHTON, DUNCAN. John MacNaughton and the 'Beggars' Benison'. *Scot. Geneal.*, XIV (1967) 55–8. [Rakes' Club.]

2491. COOPER, COLIN. Sheffield races. *Hunter Archaeol. Soc. Trans.*, IX pt. 3 (1967) 127–31.

2492. STEVENS, JOAN. Further light on the Russians in Jersey. *Soc. Jersiaise Bull. Annuel*, XIX pt. 4 (1968) 327–34.

Agrarian history

2493. GRANGER, C. W. J., *and* ELLIOTT, CHARLES M. A fresh look at wheat prices and markets in the 18th century. *Econ. Hist. Rev.*, 2nd ser. XX (1967) 257–65.

2494. FLINN, MICHAEL WALTER. Agricultural productivity and economic growth in England, 1700–60: a comment. *Jour. Econ. Hist.*, XXVI (1966) 93–8.

2495. TRANTER, N. L. Population and social structure in a Bedfordshire parish: the Cardington listing of inhabitants, 1782. *Population Studies*, XXI (1967) 261–82.

2496. RUSSELL, REX CHARLES. The enclosure of Barton-upon-Humber, 1793–6. Barton-upon-Humber, Lincs.: W.E.A. (Barton Branch), 1968. 46 pp.

2497. RUSSELL, R. C. The enclosures of Searby, 1763–5; Nettleton, 1791–5; Caistor, 1796–8 and Caistor Moors, 1811–14. New edn. Caistor, Lincs.: W.E.A. (Nettleton Branch), 1968. 40 pp. [Previous edn. 1960.]

2498. JONES, R. E. Population and agrarian change in an 18th century Shropshire parish. *Local Population Studies*, no. 1 (1968) 6–29. [Moreton Say.]

2499. MARTIN, J. M. The parliamentary enclosure movement and rural society in Warwickshire. *Agric. Hist. Rev.*, XV (1967) 19–39.

2500. PARTON, ALAN G. The 1801 crop returns for the county of Surrey. *Surrey Archaeol. Coll.*, LXIV (1967) 113–23.

2501. MULLETT, CHARLES F. A village Aristotle and the harmony of interests: James Anderson (1739–1808) of Monks Hill. *Jour. Brit. Studies*, VIII no. 1 (1968) 94–118.

Transport and communications

2502. MOTT, REGINALD ARTHUR. English waggonways of the 18th century. *Newcomen Soc. Trans.* for 1964-5, XXXVII (1967) 1–33.

2503. UNWIN, R. W. The Aire and Calder navigation. Pt. 2, The navigation in the pre-canal age. *Bradford Antiquary*, n.s. pt. XLIII (1967) 151–86.

2504. MARGETSON, STELLA. The mail coach revolution. *History Today*, XVII (1967) 36–44.

Miscellaneous

2505. ROUSSEAU, G. S. The London earthquakes of 1750. *Jour. World Hist.*, XI (1968) 436–51.

2506. FAWCETT, TREVOR. Patriotic transparencies in Norwich, 1798–1814. *Norfolk Archaeol.*, XXXIV pt. 3 (1968) 245–52.

2507. DIAMOND, A. S. Problems of the London Sephardi community, 1720–33: Philip Carteret Webb's notebooks. *Jewish Hist. Soc. Eng. Trans.* for 1962–7, XXI (1968) 39–63.

2508. HEWITT, A. R. The Grand Lodge of England: a history of the first hundred years, 1717–1817. *Ars Quatuor Coronatorum*, LXXX (1967) 210–23.

2509. CLARKE, JOSEPH RYLE. The establishment of the Premier Grand Lodge: why in London and why in 1717? *Ars Quatuor Coronatorum*, LXXXI (1968) 1–8.

2510. FISHER, WILFRED G. The dukes of Atholl and Freemasonry. *Ars Quatuor Coronatorum*, LXXX (1967) 58–69.

RELIGIOUS HISTORY

General and Anglicanism

2511. GREAN, STANLEY. Shaftesbury's philosophy of religion and ethics: a study in enthusiasm. Athens, Ohio: Ohio U.P., 1967. 315 pp.

2512. ROSEN, GEORGE. Enthusiasm, 'a dark lanthorn of the spirit'. *Bull. Hist. Medicine*, XLII (1968) 393–421.

2513. DELTEIL, FRANÇOIS. St. François de Sales et l'église anglicane au 18e siècle. *Prêtres St. François de Sales*, no. 3 (1968) 6–10, no. 5 (1968) 23–7.

2514. WINNETT, ARTHUR ROBERT. Jonathan Swift: churchman. Farnham, Surrey: Moor Park College, 1968. 16 pp., illus.

2515. YOULD, G. M. Archbishop Potter (1674–1747). *Church Quart. Rev.*, CLXVIII (1967) 33–45.

2516. FITCH, J. A. Balthazar Gardeman: a Huguenot squarson and his library. *Huguenot Soc. London Proc.*, XXI no. 3 (1968) 241–72.

2517. CHAPIN, CHESTER F. The religious thought of Samuel Johnson. Ann Arbor, Mich.: Michigan U.P., 1968. viii, 181 pp.

2518. DAVIES, WILLIAM R. John Fletcher's Georgian ordinations and Madeley curacy. *Wesley Hist. Soc. Proc.*, XXXVI (1967–8) 139–43.

2519. MCQUISTON, JULIAN R. Sir Richard Hill: Shropshire evangelist. *Shropshire Archaeol. Soc. Trans.* for 1966, LVIII pt. 2 (1968) 167–77.

2520. RANSOME, MARY (*ed.*). The state of the bishopric of Worcester, 1782–1808. (Worcs. Hist. Soc. Pubns., n.s. 6). Birmingham: the Society, 1968. vii, 252 pp., illus.

2521. NUTTALL, GEOFFREY F. John Ash and the Pershore church: additional notes. *Baptist Quart.*, XXII no. 5 (1968) 271–7. [Adds to article by G. H. Taylor in vol. XX.]

2522. DUNNING, ROBERT WILLIAM. Some Somerset parishes in 1705. *Somerset Archaeol. & Nat. Hist. Soc. Proc.*, CXII (1968) 71–92.

Roman Catholicism

2523. HOLT, GEOFFREY. The English ex-Jesuits and Jesuits and the missions. *Archivum Historicum Societatis Iesu*, XXXVII (1968) 153–65.

2524. WHYTE, JOHN HENRY. The Vicars Apostolics' returns of 1773. *Recusant Hist.*, IX (1967–8) 205–14.

2525. HODGSON, AILEEN M. The mission at Heath Green, near Beoley. *Worcs. Recusant*, no. 7 (1966) 13–19.

Protestant Nonconformity

2526. TIBBUTT, H. GORDON. Pattern of change. *Congregational Hist. Soc. Trans.*, XX (1967) 166–73.

2527. CONE, CARL B. Newington Green: a study of a dissenting community. *Catholic Hist. Rev.*, LIV no. 1 (1968) 1–16.

2528. WHITE, BARRINGTON RAYMOND. John Gill in London, 1719–29. *Baptist Quart.*, XXII no. 2 (1967) 72–91.

2529. STEPHENSON, WILLIAM E. Isaac Watt's education for the dissenting ministry: a new document. *Harvard Theol. Rev.*, LXI (1968) 263–81.

2530. SHORT, H. L. The later history of the English Presbyterians, pts. 5–9. *Hibbert Jour.*, LXV (1967) 117–22, 157–62, LXVI (1967) 31–5, 70–3, LXVI (1968) 131–6.

2531. WILLIAMS, ALBERT HUGHES. The leaders of English and Welsh Methodism, March 1741–May 1750. *Bathafarn*, XXII (1967) 24–36, XXIII (1968) 7–13. [Continuing.]

2532. ROWE, JOHN. Cornish Methodists and emigrants. (Cornish Methodist Hist. Assoc. Occas. Pubns., 11). Redruth: the Association, 1967. 26 pp.

2533. WOOD, ARTHUR SKEVINGTON. The burning heart: John Wesley, evangelist. Exeter: Paternoster P., 1967. 302 pp.

2534. WILSON, D. DUNN. John Wesley and 'mystical prayer'. *London Quart. & Holborn Rev.*, CXCII (Jan. 1968) 61–9.

2535. ROUSSEAU, G. S. John Wesley's *Primitive physic* (1747). *Harvard Lib. Bull.*, XVI (1968) 242–56.

2536. BAKER, FRANK. John Wesley's first marriage. *London Quart. & Holborn Rev.*, CXXII (Oct. 1967) 305–15. [Contract *de praesenti* with Grace Murray.]

2537. NEWTON, JOHN ANTHONY. Susanna Wesley and the Puritan tradition in Methodism. Epworth P., 1968. 216 pp.

2538. BIGGS, BARRY J. The first Methodist of Retford. *Wesley Hist. Soc. Proc.*, XXXVI (1967–8) 149–52. [John Macfarlane.]

2539. DUNSTAN, JOHN. Billy and Alice Brammah: partners in ministry. *Wesley Hist. Soc. Proc.*, XXXVI (1967–8) 169–77.

2540. ROSE, EDWARD ALAN. The first Methodist New Connexion chapels. *Wesley Hist. Soc. Proc.*, XXXVI (1967–8) 7–15.

2541. WELCH, CHARLES EDWIN (*ed.*). Three letters from William Williams, Pantycelyn, to Lady Huntingdon. *Cylchgrawn Cymd. Hanes Meth. Calf.*, LIII (1968) 56–61.

2542. MURDOCH, CATHERINE. A city on a hill. *Nat. Reg. Archives, W. Riding N. Section Bull.*, XI (1968) 1–13. [Moravian settlement at Fulneck.]

2543. CARTER, CHARLES F. Unsettled Friends: church government and the origins of membership. *Friends' Hist. Soc. Jour.*, LI no. 3 (1967) 143–53.

2544. EDWARDS, GEORGE W. Quakers as churchwardens and vestrymen. *Friends' Hist. Soc. Jour.*, LII no. 1 (1968) 48–53.

2545. BUTLER, DAVID M. (*ed.*). Meeting houses built and meetings settled: answers to Yearly Meeting queries, 1688–1791. *Friends' Hist. Soc. Jour.*, LI no. 3 (1967) 174–211.

CULTURAL HISTORY

General

2546. HARRIS, RONALD WALTER. Reason and nature in the 18th century, 1714–80. Blandford P., 1968. 439 pp., illus.

2547. JOHNSON, JAMES WILLIAM. The formation of English neo-classical thought. Princeton, N.J.: Princeton U.P., 1967. xxi, 358 pp.

2548. GREENE, DONALD. Augustinianism and empiricism: a note on 18th century English intellectual history. *Eighteenth Century Studies*, I (1967–8) 33–68.

2549. KRAMNICK, ISAAC. Augustan politics and English historiography: the debate on the English past, 1730–5. *History & Theory*, VI (1967) 33–56.

2550. CELORIA, FRANCIS, *and* SPENCER, B. W. Eighteenth century fieldwork in London and Middlesex: some unpublished drawings by William Stukeley. *London & Middlesex Archaeol. Soc. Trans.*, XXII pt. 1 (1968) 23–31.

2551. JONES, NESTA. 'Mr. Jones' and Francis Tate. *Hon. Soc. Cymmrodorion Trans.* (1968) 99–109.

2552. PULLEN, CHARLES. The Chesterfield myth and 18th century ethics. *Dalhousie Rev.*, XLVII (1967) 369–79.

2553. PARREAUX, ANDRÉ. L'Angleterre de Lady Montagu. *Études Anglaises*, XX (1967) 24–8.

2554. DE BEER, E. S. The Huguenots and the Enlightenment. *Huguenot Soc. London Proc.*, XXI no. 3 (1968) 179–94.

2555. TURCO, LUIGI. La prima *Inquiry* morale di Francis Hutcheson. *Riv. Crit. di Stor. della Filos.*, XXIII (1968) 39–60.

2556. HIELMCRONE, HARALD VON. Berkeley. Copenhagen: Berlingske Filosofi Bibliotek, 1967. 231 pp.

2557. STANLIS, PETER J. (*ed.*). Edmund Burke: the enlightenment and the modern world. Detroit, Mich.: Detroit U.P., 1967. xviii, 129 pp.

2558. MCLOUGHLIN, T. Edmund Burke: the postgraduate years, 1748–50. *Studies in Burke and his Time*, X (1968) 1035–40.

2559. BEVILACQUA, VINCENT M. Adam Smith and some philosophical origins of 18th century rhetorical theory. *Mod. Lang. Rev.*, LXIII (1968) 559–68.

2560. BLAICHER, GUNTHER. England als das 'klassische' Land des Selbstmords im 18. Jahrhundert. *Archiv für Kulturgesch.*, L (1968) 276–88.

2561. KAUFMAN, PAUL. The community library: a chapter in English social history. *Amer. Philos. Soc. Trans.*, n.s. LVII pt. 7 (1967) 5–49.

2562. CAMPBELL, HILBERT. The sale catalogue of Addison's library. *Eng. Lang. Notes*, IV (1967) 269–73.

2563. RUSSELL, A. W. A plan for a public library at Church Langton, Leicestershire, 1760. *Library Hist.*, I (1968) 68–76.

2564. FAWCETT, TREVOR. An 18th century book club at Norwich. *Library*, 5th ser. XXIII (1968) 47–50.

2565. KAUFMAN, PAUL. The loan records of Shrewsbury School library. *Library*, 5th ser. XXII (1967) 252–6.

2566. ENGLISH, JOHN C. The Cambridge Platonists in Wesley's 'Christian Library'. *Wesley Hist. Soc. Proc.*, XXXVI (1967–8) 161–8.

2567. ROCHER, ROSANE. Alexander Hamilton (1762–1824): a chapter in the early history of Sanskrit philology. (Amer. Oriental ser., 51). New Haven, Conn.: Amer. Oriental Soc., 1968. xii, 128 pp.

Education

2568. SALT, JOHN. Early Sheffield Sunday Schools and their educational importance. *Hunter Archaeol. Soc. Trans.*, IX pt. 3 (1967) 179–84.

2569. HANS, NICHOLAS. Educational relations of Geneva and England in the 18th century. *Brit. Jour. Educ. Studies*, XV (1967) 263–74.

2570. BISHOP, GEORGE D. The 'new' approaches to teaching science: how 'new'? *Brit. Jour. Educ. Studies*, XV (1967) 307–13.

2571. BEST, JOHN HARDIN. *The Academy Keeper*: a dimension in the history of English education. *Hist. Educ. Quart.*, VIII (1968) 386–98. [Anonymous hoax, pubd. 1770.]

2572. DANKERT, CLYDE E. Adam Smith, educator. *Dalhousie Rev.*, XLVII (1967) 13–27.

2573. WEST, E. G. Tom Paine's voucher scheme for public education. *Southern Econ. Jour.*, XXXIII (1967) 378–82.

2574. HYMAN, LEONARD. Hyman Hurwitz: the first Anglo-Jewish professor.

Jewish Hist. Soc. Eng. Trans. for 1962–7, XXI (1968) 232–42.

Literature, drama and music

2575. BOUVIER–AJAM, M. Swift et son temps. *Europe*, no. 463 (1967) 33–47.

2576. KORSHIN, PAUL J. The earl of Orrery and Swift's early reputation. *Harvard Lib. Bull.*, XVI (1968) 167–77.

2577. COOK, RICHARD IRVING. Jonathan Swift as a Tory pamphleteer. Seattle, London: Washington U.P., 1968. xxxiv, 157 pp.

2578. THOMPSON, PAUL V. An unpublished letter from Swift. *Library*, 5th ser. XXII (1967) 57–66.

2579. LEEK, HELEN. The Edward Young – Edmund Curll quarrel: a review. *Bibliog. Soc. America Papers*, LXII (1968) 321–35.

2580. BLOOM, EDWARD A., *and* BLOOM, LILLIAN D. Steele in 1719: additions to the canon. *Huntington Lib. Quart.*, XXXI (1967–8) 122–51.

2581. SHIPLEY, JOHN B. The authorship of *The touch-stone* (1728). *Bibliog. Soc. America Papers*, LXII (1968) 189–98.

2582. LIPKING, LAWRENCE. The curiosity of William Oldys: an approach to the development of English literary history. *Philol. Quart.*, XLVI (1967) 385–407.

2583. BOUCE, PAUL-GABRIEL. Smollett and the expedition against Rochefort, 1757. *Mod. Philol.*, LXV (1967) 33–8.

2584. MACLEAN, JAMES N. M. Grant of Blairfindy, *Junius* and Francis. *Inst. Hist. Research Bull.*, XLI (1968) 73–85.

2585. BRINITZER, CARL. Dr. Johnson und Boswell. Mainz: Kupferberg, 1968. 190 pp.

2586. ISLES, DUNCAN. Johnson and Charlotte Lennox. *New Rambler*, CIII (1967) 34–48.

2587. WILES, ROY MCKEEN. The contemporary distribution of Johnson's *Rambler*. *Eighteenth Century Studies*, II (1968–9) 155–71.

2588. WHITELEY, D. PEPYS. A late Pepys encounters Dr. Johnson. *History Today*, XVII (1967) 765–71. [Sir William Weller Pepys (1740–1825).]

2589. SANDERS, JENNINGS B. *The Crisis* of London and American revolutionary propaganda, 1775–6. *Social Studies*, LVIII (1967) 7–12.

2590. ANDERSON, WILLIAM JAMES. Bishop Hay and Patrick Wogan. *Innes Rev.*, XVIII (1967) 61–4. [Bishop George Hay and his Dublin publisher.]

2591. WERKMEISTER, LUCYLE. A newspaper history of England, 1792–3. Lincoln, Nebr.: Nebraska U.P., 1967. 585 pp.

2592. POLLIN, BURTON R. Southey's 'Battle of Blenheim' parodied in the *Morning Chronicle*: a Whig attack on the battle of Copenhagen. *New York Public Lib. Bull.*, LXXII (1968) 507–17.

2593. CUMMINGS, FREDERICK. Boothby, Rousseau, and the romantic malady. *Burlington Mag.*, CX (1968) 659–66.

2594. SHELDON, ESTHER K. Thomas Sheridan of Smock Alley. Princeton, N.J.: Princeton U.P., 1967. 530 pp.

2595. DOTY, GRESDNA. Anne Brunton in Bath and in London. *Theatre Survey*, VIII no. 1 (1967) 53–65.

2596. MULLIN, DONALD C. The Queen's Theatre, Haymarket: Vanbrugh's Opera House. *Theatre Survey*, VIII no. 2 (1967) 84–105.

2597. MULLIN, D. C. The Theatre Royal, Bridges Street: a conjectoral restoration. *Educ. Theatre Jour.*, XIX (1967) 17–29.

2598. HIGHFILL, PHILIP H., *Jnr.* Rich's 1744 inventory of Covent Garden properties. *Restoration and 18th Cent. Theatre Research*, VI (1967) 27–35.

2599. WALLER, A. BRET, *and* CONNELLY, JAMES L. Thomas Rowlandson and the London theatre. *Apollo*, LXXXVI (1967) 130–4.

2600. EDWARDS, OWAIN. Revolution in 18th century music. *History Today*, XVIII (1968) 755–9.

2601. EDWARDS, O. English string concertos before 1800. *Roy. Musical Assoc. Proc.* (1968–9) 1–13.

2602. DAWES, FRANK. The music of Philip Hart (*c.* 1676–1749). *Roy. Musical Assoc. Proc.* (1967–8) 63–75.

2603. BEECHEY, GWILYM. Thomas Linley, Junior, 1756–78. *Musical Quart.*, LIV (1968) 74–82.

2604. ROSCOE, CHRISTOPHER. Haydn and London in the 1790s. *Music & Letters*, XLIX (1968) 203–12.

Architecture

2605. WILTON-ELY, JOHN. The architectural model. *Archit. Rev.*, CXLII (1967) 26–32.

2606. STUTCHBURY, HOWARD EDWARD. The architecture of Colin Campbell. Manchester: Manchester U.P., 1967. xvi, 186 pp., illus.

2607. ADAMS, JOHN. The Bastards of Blandford. *Archit. Rev.*, CXLIII (1968) 445–50.

2608. HARRIS, JOHN. The Dundas empire. *Apollo*, LXXXVI (1967) 170–9.

2609. ROGERS, KENNETH HERBERT. Esau Reynolds of Trowbridge, architect: some account of his family and his work, especially the building of the Heytesbury Hospital, 1766–8. Devizes, Wilts.: Historical Assoc. (West Wilts. Branch), 1967. 20 pp., illus.

2610. HARRIS, JOHN. Pritchard redivivus. *Archit. Hist.*, XI (1968) 17–24.

2611. RICE, TAMARA TALBOT. Charles Cameron: Catherine the Great's British architect. *Connoisseur*, CLXV (1967) 240–5.

2612. HARRIS, JOHN. Georgian country houses. Feltham, Middx.: Country Life Books, 1968. 64 pp., illus.

2613. DOWNES, KERRY. The Kings Weston book of drawings. *Archit. Hist.*, X (1967) 9–88.

2614. BLUTMAN, SANDRA. Books of designs for country houses, 1780–1815. *Archit. Hist.*, XI (1968) 25–33.

2615. THOMPSON, F. H. Norton Priory, near Runcorn, Cheshire. *Archaeol. Jour.* for 1966, CXXIII (1967) 62–8.

2616. MARSDEN, T. L. Foxdenton Hall, Chadderton, Lancashire. *Lancs. & Cheshire Antiq. Soc. Trans.* for 1965–6, LXXV–LXXVI (1968) 172–80.

2617. Uxbridge House. *Three Banks Rev.*, no. 78 (1968) 34–45.

2618. LEES-MILNE, JAMES. Shugborough, Staffs. Pt. 1, The park and its monuments. Pt. 2, The house. *Connoisseur*, CLXIV (1967) 211–15, CLXV (1967) 4–11.

2619. MUSGRAVE, CLIFFORD. Sennicotts, a Regency villa near Chichester. *Connoisseur*, CLXV (1967) 69–73.

2620. WORSLEY, MARCUS. Hovingham Hall. *Ryedale Historian*, no. 3 (1967) 3–10.

2621. COX, CHRISTOPHER. Turnpike houses of the Stroud district. *Bristol & Glos. Archaeol. Soc. Trans.* for 1967, LXXXVI (1968) 118–50.

2622. BRUNSKILL, RONALD WILLIAM. Lowther village and Robert Adam. *Ancient Monuments Soc. Trans.* for 1966–7, n.s. XIV (1968) 57–73.

2623. GREEN, ANGELA. Letters of Sarah Churchill, duchess of Marlborough, on the Column of Victory at Blenheim. *Oxoniensia* for 1966, XXXI (1968) 139–45.

2624. PHYSICK, J. F. Some 18th century designs for monuments in Westminster Abbey. *Victoria & Albert Museum Bull.*, III (1967) 26–38.

Arts and crafts

2625. HAYES, JOHN. British patrons and landscape painting. *Apollo*, LXXXV (1967) 254–9.

2626. SHIPLEY, JOHN B. Ralph, Ellys, Hogarth, and Fielding: the cabal against Jacopo Amigoni. *Eighteenth Century Studies*, I (1967–8) 313–31.

2627. PAULSON, RONALD. The *Harlot's Progress* and the tradition of history painting. *Eighteenth Century Studies*, I (1967–8) 69–92.

2628. KITSON, MICHAEL. Hogarth's 'Apology for painters'. *Walpole Soc. Annual Vol.*, XLI (1968) 46–111.

2629. RAINE, ROBERT. Philip Mercier: a little known 18th century painter. *Huguenot Soc. London Proc.*, XXI no. 2 (1967) 124–37.

2630. THOMPSON, J. R. FAWCETT. The elusive Mr. Shackleton: light on the 'principal painter in ordinary' to Kings George II and George III. *Connoisseur*, CLXV (1967) 232–9.

2631. HAYES, JOHN. Gainsborough and the Bedfords. *Connoisseur*, CLXVII (1968) 217–24.

2632. HERRMANN, LUKE. The drawings of Sir Joshua Reynolds in the Herschel Album. *Burlington Mag.*, CX (1968) 650–8.

2633. WATERHOUSE, ELLIS K. Reynold's 'Sitter book' for 1755. *Walpole Soc. Annual Vol.*, XLI (1968) 112–67.

2634. GOLDSTEIN, HARVEY D. *Ut Poesis Pictura*: Reynolds on imitation and imagination. *Eighteenth Century Studies*, I (1967–8) 213–35.

2635. EDWARDS, RALPH. Thomas Jones, 1742–1803. *Connoisseur*, CLXVIII (1968) 8–14.

2636. MAYNE, JONATHAN. Rowlandson at Vauxhall. *Victoria & Albert Museum Bull.*, IV (1968) 77–81.

2638. HAMMELMANN, H. A. Eighteenth

century English illustrators: John Vanderbank, 1694–1739. *Book Collector*, XVII (1968) 284–99.

2639. HAMMELMANN, H. A. Anthony Walker, a gifted illustrator and engraver. *Connoisseur*, CLXVIII (1968) 167–74.

2640. MAN, FELIX H. Die Anfänge der Kunstlerlithographie in England, 1801–10. *Philobiblon*, XI (1967) 191–227.

2641. HODGKINSON, TERENCE. Joseph Wilton and Dr. Cocchi. *Victoria & Albert Museum Bull.*, III (1967) 73–80.

2642. BEARD, GEOFFREY. The Rose family of plasterers. *Apollo*, LXXXV (1967) 266–77.

2643. MALLET, J. V. G. Hogarth's pug in porcelain. *Victoria & Albert Museum Bull.*, III (1967) 45–54.

2644. DE BELLAIGUE, GEOFFREY. The furnishings of the Chinese Drawing Room, Carlton House. *Burlington Mag.*, CIX (1967) 519–28.

2645. FARMERY, EVA. Craftsmen of Croft. *Lincs. Hist. & Archaeol.*, no. 2 (1967) 21–9. [Beane family, carpenters.]

2646. COLERIDGE, ANTHONY. Georgian cabinet-makers at Uppark, Sussex. *Connoisseur*, CLXVI (1967) 74–9, 157–63.

2647. COLERIDGE, A. Chippendale furniture: the work of Thomas Chippendale and his contemporaries in the rococo taste, *c.* 1745–65. Faber, 1968. 229 pp., illus.

2648. COLERIDGE, A. Sir Lawrence Dundas and Chippendale. *Apollo*, LXXXVI (1967) 190–203.

2649. BOYNTON, LINDSAY OLIVER JOHN. Thomas Chippendale at Mersham-le-Hatch. *Furniture Hist.*, IV (1968) 81–104.

2650. STEPHENSON, ANTHEA. Chippendale furniture at Harewood. *Furniture Hist.*, IV (1968) 62–9.

2651. BEARD, GEOFFREY (*ed.*). The Harewood Chippendale account, 1772–7. *Furniture Hist.*, IV (1968) 70–80.

2652. BOYNTON, LINDSAY OLIVER JOHN, *and* GOODISON, NICHOLAS. Thomas Chippendale at Nostell Priory. *Furniture Hist.*, IV (1968) 10–61.

2653. KIRHAM, PATRICIA ANNE. The careers of William and John Linnell. *Furniture Quart.*, III (1967) 29–44.

2654. DE BELLAIGUE, GEOFFREY. The Vulliamys and France. *Furniture Hist.*, II (1967) 45–53. [1800–15.]

SCIENCE

2655. NICOLSON, MARJORIE, *and* ROUSSEAU, G. S. 'This long disease, my life': Alexander Pope and the sciences. Princeton, N.J.: Princeton U.P., 1968. viii, 315 pp.

2656. COLEY, N. G. The Animal Chemistry Club: assistant society to the Royal Society. *Roy. Soc. Notes & Records*, XXII (1967) 173–85.

2657. ALLIBONE, T. E. The Club of the Royal College of Physicians, the Smeatonian Society of Civil Engineers, and their relationship to the Royal Society Club. *Roy. Soc. Notes & Records*, XXII (1967) 186–92.

2658. ALLAN, D. G. C. William Shipley: founder of the Royal Society of Arts; a biography with documents. Hutchinson, 1968. xvi, 240 pp., illus.

2659. ROBINSON, ERIC. The origins and lifespan of the Lunar Society. *Univ. Birmingham Hist. Jour.*, XI (1967–8) 5–16.

2660. SCHOFIELD, ROBERT E. The Lunar Society and the Industrial Revolution. *Univ. Birmingham Hist. Jour.*, XI (1967–8) 94–111.

2661. ARMYTAGE, WALTER HARRY GREEN. The Lunar Society and its contribution to education. *Univ. Birmingham Hist. Jour.*, XI (1967–8) 65–78.

2662. WISE, M. J. The influence of the Lunar Society in the development of Birmingham. *Univ. Birmingham Hist. Jour.*, XI (1967–8) 79–93.

2663. SMEATON, W. A. The Lunar Society and chemistry: a conspectus. *Univ. Birmingham Hist. Jour.*, XI (1967–8) 51–64.

2664. SMITH, BARBARA M. D., *and* MOILLIET, J. L. James Keir of the Lunar Society. *Roy. Soc. Notes & Records*, XXII (1967) 144–54.

2665. MCCORMMACH, RUSSELL. John Michell and Henry Cavendish: weighing the stars. *Brit. Jour. Hist. Science*, IV pt. 2 (1968) 126–55.

2666. AUSTIN, R. H. Uranus observed. *Brit. Jour. Hist. Science*, III (1967) 275–84.

2667. LOVELL, D. J. Herschel's dilemma in the interpretation of thermal radiation. *Isis*, LIX (1968) 46–60.

2668. ROWBOTTOM, MARGARET E. John Theophilus Desaguliers (1683–1744). *Huguenot Soc. London Proc.*, XXI no. 3 (1968) 196–218.

2669. HANKINS, THOMAS L. The reception of Newton's second Law of Motion in the 18th century. *Archives Internat. d'Hist. des Sciences*, XX (1967) 43–65.

2670. HEATHCOTE, NIELS H. DE V. The early meaning of *electricity*: some *Pseudodoxia Epidemica*, 1. *Annals of Science*, XXIII (1967) 261–75.

2671. THACKRAY, ARNOLD. 'Matter in a nut-shell': Newton's *Opticks* and 18th century chemistry. *Ambix*, XV (1968) 29–53.

2672. MCKIE, DOUGLAS. On some Ms. copies of Black's chemical lectures, 6. *Annals of Science*, XXIII (1967) 1–33.

2673. SCHOFIELD, ROBERT E. Joseph Priestley, natural philosopher. *Ambix*, XIV (1967) 1–15. [Comment by J. G. McEvoy, vol. XV (1968) pp. 115–23.]

2674. DUNCAN, A. M. William Keir's *De Attractione Chemica* (1778) and the concepts of chemical saturation, attraction and repulsion. *Annals of Science*, XXIII (1967) 149–73.

2675. GERSTNER, PATSY A. James Hutton's theory of the earth and his theory of matter. *Isis*, LIX (1968) 26–31.

2676. SWEET, JESSIE M., *and* WATERSTON, CHARLES D. Robert Jameson's approach to the Wernerian theory of the earth, 1796. *Annals of Science*, XXIII (1967) 81–95.

2677. LAWRENCE, DEREK W. The miraculous machine. *History Today*, XVII (1967) 308–16. [James Watt's steam-engine.]

2678. BOUCHER, CYRIL THOMAS GOODMAN. James Brindley, engineer, 1716–72. Norwich: Goose, 1968. 130 pp., illus.

2679. QUILL, HUMPHREY. John Harrison: the man who found longitude. Baker, 1966. xiv, 255 pp., illus.

2680. GOODISON, NICHOLAS. Matthew Boulton's geographical clock. *Connoisseur*, CLXVI (1967) 213–21.

2681. OLIVER, JOHN. William Borlase's weather journal, 1753–72. *Roy. Inst. Cornwall Jour.*, n.s. V (1967) 267–90.

2682. SKINNER, ANDREW. Natural history in the age of Adam Smith. *Polit. Studies*, XV (1967) 32–48.

2683. RAUSCHENBERG, ROY A. Daniel Carl Solander, the naturalist on the *Endeavour* voyage. *Isis*, LVIII (1967) 367–74.

2684. MCMICHAEL, JOHN. William Withering in perspective. *Univ. Birmingham Hist. Jour.*, XI (1967–8) 41–50.

2685. TURNER, G. L'E. The auction sales of the earl of Bute's instruments, 1793. *Annals of Science*, XXIII (1967) 213–42.

MEDICINE

2686. MORGAN, *Sir* CLIFFORD MORGAN. Surgery and surgeons in 18th century London. *Roy. College of Surgeons Eng. Annals*, XLII (1968) 1–37.

2687. HUARD, P. Les échanges médicaux franco-anglais au 18e siècle. *Clio Medica*, III (1968) 41–58.

2688. TOWNSEND, GARY L. Sir John Floyer (1649–1734) and his study of pulse and respiration. *Jour. Hist. Medicine & Allied Sciences*, XXII (1967) 286–316.

2689. BROCKBANK, WILLIAM, *and* KENWORTHY, FRED (*eds.*). The diary of Richard Kay, 1716–51, of Baldingstone near Bury, a Lancashire doctor. (Remains . . . connected with the Palatine counties of Lancaster and Chester, 3rd ser. 16). Manchester: Manchester U.P., for Chetham Soc., 1968. vii, 179 pp., illus.

2690. TILDESLEY, NORMAN W. Dr. Richard Wilkes of Willenhall, Staffs.: an 18th century country doctor. *Lichfield Archaeol. & Hist. Soc. Trans.* for 1965–6, VII (1967) 1–10.

2691. MUSHER, DANIEL M. The medical views of Dr. Tobias Smollett (1721–71). *Bull. Hist. Medicine*, XLI (1967) 455–62.

2692. ILLINGWORTH, *Sir* CHARLES. The story of William Hunter. Edinburgh, London: E. &. S. Livingstone, 1967. viii, 134 pp., illus.

2693. ILLINGWORTH, *Sir* CHARLES. The erudition of William Hunter. *Scot. Medical Jour.*, XI (1967) 421–8.

2694. DOBSON, JESSIE. John Hunter's anatomy. *Roy. College of Surgeons Eng. Annals*, XLI (1967) 493–501.

2695. DOBSON, J. Lost treasures. *Roy. College of Surgeons Eng. Annals*, XLII (1968) 387–93. [From John Hunter's collection.]

2696. DOBSON, J. Some of John Hunter's patients. *Roy. College of Surgeons Eng. Annals*, XLII (1968) 124–33.

2697. PORRITT, *Sir* ARTHUR. John Hunter: distant echoes. *Roy. College of Surgeons Eng. Annals*, XLI (1967) 1–24.

2698. COHEN, HENRY, *Baron Cohen*. Erasmus Darwin. *Univ. Birmingham Hist. Jour.*, XI (1967–8) 17–40.

2699. MCCONAGHEY, R. M. S. Sir George Baker and the Devonshire colic. *Medical Hist.*, XI (1967) 345–60. [Lead poisoning.]

2700. CARTWRIGHT, F. F. The association of Thomas Beddoes, M.D. with James Watt, F.R.S. *Roy. Soc. Notes & Records*, XXII (1967) 131–43. [To treat tuberculosis.]

2701. VISELTEAR, ARTHUR J. The last illness of Sir Robert Walpole, first earl of Orford. *Bull. Hist. Medicine*, XLI (1967) 195–207.

2702. VISELTEAR, A. J. Joanna Stephens and the 18th century lithontriptics: a misplaced chapter in the history of therapeutics. *Bull. Hist. Medicine*, XLII (1968) 199–220.

2703. MCHENRY, LAWRENCE C., *Jnr.* Samuel Johnson's tics and gesticulations. *Jour. Hist. Medicine & Allied Sciences*, XXII (1967) 152–68.

2704. MADDEN, J. S. Samuel Johnson's alcohol problem. *Medical Hist.*, XI (1967) 141–9.

2705. PUGH, PATTERSON DAVID GORDON (*ed.*). Nelson and his surgeons: an account of the illnesses and wounds sustained by Lord Nelson and his relationship with the surgeons of the day. Edinburgh: Livingstone, 1968. 68 pp., illus.

2706. FEIBEL, ROBERT M. What happened at Walcheren: the primary medical sources. *Bull. Hist. Medicine*, XLII (1968) 62–79.

2707. MACALPINE, IDA, *and others*. George III's illness and its impact on psychiatry. *Roy. Soc. Medicine Proc.*, LXI (1968) 1017–26.

2708. MACALPINE, I., *and* HUNTER, RICHARD. A clinical reassessment of the 'insanity' of George III and some of its historical implications. *Inst. Hist. Research Bull.*, XL (1967) 166–85.

2709. MACALPINE, I., *and others*. Porphyria in the royal houses of Stuart, Hanover and Prussia: a follow-up study of George III's illness. *Brit. Medical Jour.* (6 Jan. 1968) 7–18.

MILITARY HISTORY

2710. SCOULLER, RAIBEART ELDER. Marlborough's administration in the field. *Army Quart.*, LXXXXVI no. 1 (1968) 102–13.

2711. LAMONTAGNE, ROLAND, *and others*. Traitement graphique d'une information: les marines royales de France et de Grande-Bretagne, 1697–1747. *Annales*, XXII (1967) 991–1004.

2712. DAWNAY, N. P. The clothing warrant of 1743. *Soc. Army Hist. Research Jour.*, XLVI (1968) 87–90.

2713. GRAHAM, DOMINICK. The planning of the Beauséjour operation and the approaches to war in 1755. *New Eng. Quart.*, XLI (1968) 550–66.

2714. MIDDLETON, RICHARD. A reinforcement for North America, summer 1757. *Inst. Hist. Research Bull.*, XLI (1968) 58–72.

2715. ALI, M. MOHAR. The background of the battle of Plassey. *Asiatic Soc. Pakistan Jour.*, XI no. 3 (1966) 37–70.

2716. FREARSON, C. W. (*ed.*). 'To Mr. Davenport': being letters of Major Richard Davenport (1719–60) to his brother. (Soc. Army Hist. Research Special Pubns., 9). Gale & Polden, for the Society, 1968. 87 pp.

2717. BRADFORD, S. SYDNEY (*ed.*). The common British soldier. *Maryland Hist. Mag.*, LXII (1967) 219–53.

2718. COOK, H. C. B. The 38th Foot: a line regiment in 1769–72. *Soc. Army Hist. Research Jour.*, XLVI (1968) 91–6.

2719. HERBERT, CHARLES. Coxheath camp, 1778–9. *Soc. Army Hist. Research Jour.*, XLV (1967) 129–48.

2720. HARGREAVES, REGINALD. Proud foot of the conqueror. *Roy. United Service Inst. Jour.*, CXII (1967) 165–70. [Invasion of Jersey, 1781.]

2721. ANNAND, A. M. Sir Cecil Bysshopp, Bart., (later 12th Baron Zouche) and the Parham troop of Sussex Yeomanry, *c.* 1798. *Soc. Army Hist. Research Jour.*, XLV (1967) 17–23.

2722. ANNAND, A. M. Lieutenant-General Norman MacLeod of Macleod, 1754–1801. *Soc. Army Hist. Research Jour.*, XLV (1967) 226–30.

2723. HARGREAVES, REGINALD. 'Good-natured Billy', *Army Quart.*, LXXXXIII no. 2 (1967) 177–90. [Sir William Howe.]

2724. WARD, S. GEORGE P. 'Die englische Kriegskunst zur Zeit Napoleons unter besonderer Berücksichtigung Wellingtons'. *In* Napoleon I. und das Militärwesen seiner Zeit, *ed.* W. von Groote *and* K.-J. Müller (Freiburg: Rombach, 1968) pp. 79–100.

2725. GLOVER, MICHAEL. Wellington as military commander. Batsford, 1968. 288 pp., illus.

2726. WARNER, OLIVER MARTIN WILSON. Wellington meets Nelson. *History Today*, XVIII (1968) 125–8.

2727. MCGUFFIE, TOM H. An early field-day exercise. *Soc. Army Hist. Research Jour.*, XLV (1967) 84–90. [*c.* 1805–8.]

2728. ROSSELLI, JOHN. Il progetto italiano di Lord William Bentinck, 1811–15. *Riv. Stor. Ital.*, LXXIX (1967) 355–404. [Expedition against Genoa.]

2729. KIMBALL, JEFFREY. The battle of Chippawa: infantry tactics in the war of 1812. *Military Affairs*, XXXI (1967) 169–86.

2730. OWSLEY, FRANK L., *Jnr.* British and Indian activities in Spanish West Florida during the War of 1812. *Florida Hist. Quart.*, XLVI (1967–8) 111–23.

NAVAL HISTORY

2731. PRIESTLEY, E. J. The voyages of H.M.S. *Eltham. Mariner's Mirror*, LIV (1968) 227–32. [1736–63.]

2732. GIBSON, JOHN SIBBALD. Ships of the '45: the rescue of the Young Pretender. Hutchinson, 1967. xv, 172 pp., illus.

2733. MAY, WILLIAM EDWARD. The *Shark* and the '45. *Mariner's Mirror*, LIII (1967) 281–5.

2734. MONIER, E. Le débarquement des Anglais à Cancale le 5 juin 1758, à travers la correspondance du duc d'Aiguillon. *Annales Soc. Hist. Archéol. St. Malo* (1966) 51–82.

2735. WILLIAMS, GLYNDWR. Commodore Anson and the Acapulco galleon. *History Today*, XVII (1967) 525–32.

2736. CLARK, WILLIAM BELL (*ed.*). Naval documents of the American Revolution. Vol. 3. American theatre, Dec. 1775–Feb. 1776; European theatre, Nov. 1775–Jan. 1776. Washington, D.C.: U.S. Navy Dept., 1968. xxxii, 1486 pp.

2737. VOLTES BOU, PEDRO. El intento hispano-francés de desembarco in Inglaterra del año 1779. *Hispania*, XXVII (1967) 528–607.

2738. SYRETT, DAVID. The West India merchants and the conveyance of the King's troops to the Caribbean, 1779–82. *Soc. Army Hist. Research Jour.*, XLV (1967) 169–76.

2739. MIDDLETON, H. G. The loss of H.M.S. *Cerberus. Bermuda Hist. Quart.*, XIV (1967) 121–8. [1783.]

2740. WARNER, OLIVER MARTIN WILSON. The life and letters of Vice-Admiral Lord Collingwood. O.U.P., 1968. xix, 276 pp., illus.

2741. MARSHALL, M. A. N. John Gibson and his cutter, *Fox. Mariner's Mirror*, LIII (1967) 179–82.

2742. GRENFELL, RUSSELL. Horatio Nelson: a short biography. New edn. Faber, 1968. xv, 247 pp., illus. [Previous edn. pubd. 1952 as *Nelson the Sailor*.]

2743. POCOCK, TOM. Nelson and his world. Thames & Hudson, 1968. 143 pp., illus.

2744. RODRÍGUEZ BATTLORI, F. Nelson, el manco de Tenerife. *Rev. Gen. de Marina*, CLXIII (1967) 361–4.

2745. CAHILL, RICHARD A. The significance of Aboukier Bay. *U.S. Naval Inst. Proc.*, XCIII (1967) 79–89.

2746. CRIMMIN, P. K. Admiralty relations with the Treasury, 1783–1806: the preparation of naval estimates and the beginnings of Treasury control. *Mariner's Mirror*, LIII (1967) 63–72.

2747. PATTERSON, ALFRED TEMPLE. The naval mutiny at Spithead, 1797. (Portsmouth Papers, 5). Portsmouth, Hants.: City Council, 1968. 15 pp.

2748. THOMPSON, EDGAR K. Saga of a mutineer. *Mariner's Mirror*, LIII (1967) 171–8. [Thomas Nash and the *Hermione* mutiny, 1797.]

2749. LLOYD, CHRISTOPHER. The mutiny of the *Nereide. Mariner's Mirror*, LIV (1968) 245–51. [1808–9.]

2750. GLOVER, RICHARD. The French fleet, 1807–14: Britain's problem, and Madison's opportunity. *Jour. Mod. Hist.*, XXXIX (1967) 233–52.

2751. RYAN, A. N. (*ed.*). The Saumarez papers: selection from the Baltic correspondence of Vice-Admiral Sir James Saumarez, 1808–12. (Navy Records Soc. Pubns., 110). The Society, 1968. xxv, 287 pp.

2752. DIETZ, ANTHONY G. The use of cartel vessels during the war of 1812. *Amer. Neptune*, XXVIII (1968) 165–94.

2753. PADFIELD, PETER. The great sea battle. *Amer. Heritage*, XX no. 1 (1968) 29–65. [Between the frigates *Shannon* and *Chesapeake*, 1813.]

2754. PADFIELD, P. Broke and the *Shannon*. Hodder, 1968. x, 246 pp., illus.

2755. KENNEDY, P. A., *and others*. H.M. ships at Plymouth, 1814. *Devon & Cornwall N. & Q.*, XXX (1967) 304–9.

MARITIME HISTORY, TRAVEL AND EXPLORATION

2756. CRAIG, ROBERT, *and* JARVIS, RUPERT C. Liverpool registry of merchant ships. (Remains . . . connected with the Palatine counties of Lancaster and Chester, 3rd ser., 15). Manchester: Manchester U.P. for Chetham Soc., 1967. xli, 238 pp.

2757. JACKSON, GORDON. The foundation of Trinity House School, Kingston-Upon-Hull: an experiment in marine education. *Durham Research Rev.*, no. 21 (1968) 313–23.

2758. POLLARD, FRANK. Smuggler: Captain Harry Carter. *Roy. Inst. Cornwall Jour.*, n.s. V (1968) 324–84.

2759. DICKINS, BRUCE. Merchantmen of war in Nelson's day. *Mariner's Mirror*, LIII (1967) 33–8.

2760. ROWE, D. J. The strikes of the Tyneside keelmen in 1809 and 1819. *Internat. Rev. Soc. Hist.*, XIII (1968) 58–75.

2761. RIDGELY-NEVITT, CEDRIC. The *Steam Boat*, 1807–14. *Amer. Neptune*, XXVII (1967) 5–29.

2762. GREENHILL, BASIL. The schooner *Peggy*. *Manx Museum Jour.*, VII no. 84 (1968) 68–76.

2763. WILLIAMS, GLYNDWR (*ed.*). Documents relating to Anson's voyage round the world, 1740–4. (Navy Records Soc. Pubns, 109). The Society, 1967. xiii, 303 pp., illus.

2764. BEAGLEHOLE, JOHN CAWTE (*ed.*). The journals of Captain James Cook on his voyages of discovery. Vol. 3, The voyage of the *Resolution* and *Discovery*, 1776–80. (Hakluyt Soc. Extra ser., no. 36). Cambridge: C.U.P., for Hakluyt Soc., 1967. 2 vols., illus.

2765. FRY, H. T. Early British interest in the Chagos archipelago and the Maldive Islands. *Mariner's Mirror*, LIII (1967) 343–56. [1772–1810.]

2766. ROE, MICHAEL (*ed.*). The journal and letters of Captain Charles Bishop on the north west coast of America, in the Pacific and in New South Wales, 1794–9. (Hakluyt Soc. Pubns. 2nd ser., no. 131). Cambridge: C.U.P., for Hakluyt Soc., 1967. lvi, 342 pp., illus.

2767. BOVILL, EDWARD WILLIAM. The death of Mungo Park. *Geog. Jour.*, CXXXIII (1967) 1–9.

2768. PLAISANT, MICHELE. La tradition du Grand Tour en Angleterre au 18e siècle. *Les Langues Modernes*, IV (1968) 510–20.

2769. DE BEER, *Sir* GAVIN, *and* ROUSSEAU, ANDRÉ-MICHEL (*eds.*). Voltaire's British visitors. (Studies on Voltaire and the 18th century, 49). Geneva: Inst. et Musée Voltaire, 1967. 201 pp.

2770. REID, JAMES MACARTHUR. Traveller extraordinary: the life of James Bruce of Kinnaird. Eyre & Spottiswoode, 1968. 320 pp., illus.

FOREIGN RELATIONS

2771. HORN, DAVID BAYNE. The machinery for the conduct of British foreign policy in the 18th century. *Soc. Archivists Jour.*, III no. 5 (1967) 229–40.

2772. SETH, RONALD. The spy in silk breeches: the story of Montagu Fox, 18th century Admiralty agent extraordinary. Frewin, 1968. 176 pp.

2773. EDMONDS, WALTER D. The musket and the cross: the struggle of France and England for North America. Boston, Mass.: Little, Brown, 1968. xiii, 514 pp.

2774. CROSS, JACK L. London mission: the first critical years. East Lansing, Mich.: Michigan State U.P., 1968. 165 pp.

2775. MOLONEY, BRIAN. Anglo-Florentine diplomatic relations and the French Revolution. *English Misc.*, XIX (1968) 273–93.

2776. BERTI, AGOSTINO. Un ultimatum britannico al Granduca di Toscana (8–10 ottobre, 1793). *Riv. Maritt.*, C (1967) 65–77.

2777. ANNECOU, ERNESTO C. P. 'Intento hispano-británico de pacificación de América, 1815'. *In* 4o Congreso Internacional de Historia de América, Buenos Aires, 1966. Vol. 6. (Buenos Aires: Acad. Nacional de la Hist., 1967) pp. 323–41.

2778. CONRADY, SIGISBERT. Die Wirksamkeit König Georgs III. für die hannoverschen Kurlande. *Niedersächsisches Jahrb. für Landesgesch.*, XXXIX (1967) 150–91.

2779. MEDIGER, WALTHER. Mecklenburg, Russland und England-Hannover, 1706–21. Hildesheim: Lax, 1967. 2 vols.

2780. ANDERSON, M. S. 'The continental system and Russo-British relations during the Napoleonic wars'. *In* Studies in international history, *ed.* K. Bourne *and* D. C. Watt (Longmans, 1967) pp. 68–80.

2781. CRANMER-BYNG, JOHN LAUNCELOT. Russian and British interests in the Far East, 1791–3. *Canadian Slavonic Papers*, X (1968) 357–75.

2782. BAKSHI, S. R. Francophobia *versus* British diplomacy in Kabul. *Islamic Culture*, XLII (1968) 35–45.

2783. BAKSHI, S. R. Elphinstone's mission to Kabul. *Jour. Indian Hist.*, XLV (1967) 605–13.

2784. YAPP, M. E. The establishment of the East India Company Residency at Baghdad, 1798–1806. *School of Oriental & African Studies Bull.*, XXX (1967) 323–36.

2785. AMIN, A. A. British interests in the Persian Gulf, 1747–78. Leiden: Brill, 1967. 163 pp.

WALES

2786. THOMAS, PETER D. G. Eighteenth century elections in the Cardigan Boroughs constituency. *Ceredigion*, V no. 4 (1967) 402–23.

2787. THOMAS, P. D. G. The Montgomeryshire election of 1774. *Montgomerys.Coll.* for 1965–6, LIX (1968) 116–29.

2788. JACKSON, JOHN. Letters from and relating to North Wales. *Merioneth Hist. & Rec. Soc. Jour.*, V no. 3 (1967) 207–20.

2789. WILLIAM, ELIZABETH (*ed.*). Iolo Morganwg in Denbighshire: extracts from his itinerary in 1799. *Denbighs. Hist. Soc. Trans.*, XVI (1967) 82–99.

2790. WILIAM, DAFYDD WYN. Y Gwyndy. *Anglesey Antiq. Soc. & F.C. Trans.* (1967) 28–40. [Coaching inn, 1758–1822.]

2791. LEWIS, ANTHONY H. T. The early effects of Carmarthenshire's turn-pike trusts, 1760–1800. *Carmarthens. Hist.*, IV (1967) 41–54.

2792. LLOYD, GEORGE. The canalization of the River Dee in 1737. *Flints. Hist. Soc. Pubns.*, XXIII (1967–8) 35–41.

2793. ROBERTS, GOMER M. (*ed.*). Early society reports. *Cylchgrawn Cymd. Hanes Meth. Calf.*, LII (1967) 8–28, 44–61, 84–9, LIII (1968) 19–24, 45–52, 83–8.

2794. JONES, H. G. METCALFE, *and* JONES, GRACE E. Hanes cychwyniad yr achos yn Nhanycelyn. *Denbighs. Hist. Soc. Trans.*, XVII (1968) 177–82. [Methodism in Tanycelyn.]

2795. HOWELLS, ELISEUS. David Jones, Llan-gan a Maernorowen. *Cylchgrawn Cymd. Hanes Meth. Calf.*, LIII (1968) 66–77.

2796. BENNETT, RICHARD. Blaenoriaid cyntaf Eglwys y Bont, Llanbryn-Mair. *Cylchgrawn Cymd. Hanes Meth. Calf.*, LII (1967) 3–8. ['First leaders of Eglwys y Bont, Llanbryn-Mair'.]

2797. NUTTALL, GEOFFREY F. The students of Trevecca College, 1768–91. *Hon. Soc. Cymmrodorion Trans.* (1967) 249–77.

2798. BASSETT, THOMAS MYRFYN. Trobwynt y ddeunawfed ganrif. *Trafodion Cymdeithas Hanes Bedyddwyr Cymru* (1967) 24–37. ['18th century turning-point'.]

2799. WALTERS, G. The 18th century 'Pembroke Society'. *Welsh Hist. Rev.*, III (1966–7) 291–8.

2800. CRIMMIN, P. K. Samuel Pepys Cockerell: his work in west Wales, 1793–1810. *Carmarthens. Hist.*, IV (1967) 7–21.

2801. ROBINSON, A. H. W. Lewis Morris: an early Welsh hydrographer. *Anglesey Antiq. Soc. & F.C. Trans.* (1968) 38–48.

2802. JONES, EMYR GWYNNE (*ed.*). Llythyrau Lewis Morris at William Vaughan, Corsygedol. *Llên Cymru*, X nos. 1–2 (1968) 3–58.

2803. JONES, GLYN PENRHYN. Meddygaeth ym Môn. *Anglesey Antiq. Soc. & F.C. Trans.* (1968) 58–79. ['Medical practice in Anglesey'.]

SCOTLAND

2804. YOUNG, DOUGLAS, *and others.* Edinburgh in the age of reason. Edinburgh: Edinburgh U.P., 1967. 67 pp.

2805. FENWICK, HUBERT. Northern Athenians. *Stewarts*, XIII no. 1 (1968) 33–41. [18th cent. Edinburgh.]

2806. ARMET, HELEN (*ed.*). Extracts from the records of the burgh of Edinburgh, 1701–18. Edinburgh, London: Oliver &

Boyd, for Corporation of City of Edinburgh, 1967. xliii, 413 pp.

2807. PREVOST, WILLIAM AUGUSTIN JOHN. Letters reporting the rising of the Levellers in 1724. *Dumfries. & Galloway Nat. Hist. & Antiq. Soc. Trans.*, XLIV (1967) 196–204.

2808. LYTHE, SAMUEL GEORGE EDGAR. The Tayside meal mobs, 1772–3. *Scot. Hist. Rev.*, XLVI (1967) 26–36.

2809. DUCKHAM, BARON FREDERICK. Life and labour in a Scottish colliery, 1698–1755. *Scot. Hist. Rev.*, XLVII (1968) 109–28.

2810. DUCKHAM, B. F. Some 18th century Scottish coal mining methods: the 'Dissertation' of Sir John Clerk. *Industrial Archaeol.*, V (1968) 217–32.

2811. DONNACHIE, IAN L., *and* BUTT, JOHN. The Wilsons of Wilsontown ironworks, 1779–1813: a study in entrepreneurial failure. *Explorations in Entrepreneurial Hist.*, 2nd ser. IV (1967) 150–68.

2812. CARTWRIGHT, J. NORMAN. The Meikle threshing mill at Beltonford. *East Lothian Antiq. Soc. Trans.*, XI (1968) 71–80.

2813. MEIN, E. M. 'Resurrection men' in Kelso. *Berwicks. Naturalists' Club Hist.* for 1966, XXXVII pt. 2 (1967) 120–3.

2814. GAFFNEY, VICTOR. Shielings of the Drumochter. *Scot. Studies*, XI (1967) 91–9.

2815. DUNLOP, A. IAN. William Carstares and the Kirk by law established. Edinburgh: St. Andrew P., 1967. 189 pp.

2816. STEWART, MARY MARGARET. James Boswell and the National Church in Scotland. *Huntington Lib. Quart.*, XXX (1966–7) 369–87.

2817. ANDERSON, WILLIAM JAMES. The autobiographical notes of Bishop John Geddes. *Innes Rev.*, XVIII (1967) 36–57.

2818. JEFFERIES, ALFRED. John Wesley in Scotland. *Scot. Geog. Mag.*, LXXXIII (1967) 105–12.

2819. SHORT, L. BAKER. William Christie and the first Unitarian church in Scotland. *Unitarian Hist. Soc. Trans.*, XIV no. 1 (1967) 10–27, no. 2 (1968) 78–92.

2820. BEVILACQUA, VINCENT M. Baconian influences in the development of Scottish rhetorical theory. *Amer. Philos. Soc. Proc.*, CXI (1967) 212–18.

2821. MACDONALD, WILLIAM R. Book-auctions and book-sales in the Aberdeen area, 1749–1800. *Aberdeen Univ. Rev.*, XLII (1967–8) 114–32.

2822. DRESCHER, HORST W. Johnson in Scotland, from an unpublished notebook. *Anglia*, LXXXVI (1968) 113–23.

2823. PITCHER, H. J. A Scottish view of Catherine's Russia: William Richardson's *Anecdotes of the Russian Empire* (1784). *Forum for Mod. Lang. Studies*, III (1967) 236–51.

2824. TAIT, A. A. William Adam at Chatelherault. *Burlington Mag.*, CX (1968) 316–25.

2825. The Dundas mansion in the new town of Edinburgh. *Three Banks Rev.*, no. 79 (1968) 28–38.

2826. MACKAY, P. H. R. Torphichen preceptory: a footnote to the published descriptions. *Soc. Antiq. Scotland Proc.* for 1966–7, XCIX (1968) 167–72.

2827. SKELTON, RALEIGH ASHLIN. The military survey of Scotland, 1747–55. *Scot. Geog. Mag.*, LXXXIII (1967) 5–16.

2828. MILLER, RONALD. The road north. *Scot. Geog. Mag.*, LXXXIII (1967) 78–88. [Roads into the Highlands.]

2829. SMOUT, THOMAS CHRISTOPHER. Customhouse letters to the officers at Dunbar, 1765. *East Lothian Antiq. Soc. Trans.*, XI (1968) 17–36.

2830. M'CRACKEN, ALEX. Notes on the militia raised against Napoleon. *Dumfries. & Galloway Nat. Hist. & Antiq. Soc. Trans.*, XLV (1968) 228–35.

2831. CROMACK, ALEXANDER A. Scots in the Swedish East India Company: passports in Drum Castle for 1730–60. *Aberdeen Univ. Rev.*, XLII (1967–8) 38–47.

IRELAND

Note: Writings on Irish domestic and local history are not included unless they have a direct bearing on English history.

2832. WALL, MAUREEN. 'The age of the penal laws'. *In* The course of Irish history, *ed.* T. W. Moody *and* F. X. Martin (Cork: Mercier P., 1967) pp. 217–31. [1691–1778.]

2833. MACDERMOT, FRANK. Theobald Wolfe Tone and his times. Tralee, Co. Kerry: Anvil Books, 1968. xiii, 306 pp., illus.

2834. RIVOALLAN, ANATOLE. Un patriote irlandais: Theobald Wolfe Tone, 1763–98. *Annales de Bretagne*, LXXIV (1967) 279–97.

2835. CRAWFORD, W. H. The market-book of Thomas Greer, a Dungannon linen-draper, 1758–9. *Ulster Folklife*, XIII (1967) 54–60.

2836. SWEET, JESSIE M. Robert Jameson's Irish journal, 1797. *Annals of Science*, XXIII (1967) 97–126.

2837. DALY, MARGIE. Entertainment in 18th century Dublin. *Dublin Hist. Rec.*, XXII (1968) 288–95.

2838. NEU, IRENE D. From Kilkenny to Louisiana: notes on 18th century Irish emigration. *Mid-America*, XLIX (1967) 101–14.

2839. MCDOWELL, R. B. 'The Protestant nation'. *In* The course of Irish history, *ed.* T. W. Moody *and* F. X. Martin (Cork: Mercier P., 1967) pp. 232–47. [1775–1800.]

2840. O'CONNELL, PHILIP. The plot against Fr. Nicholas Sheehy: the historical background. *Irish Eccles. Record*, 5th ser. CVIII (1968) 372–84.

2841. FINEGAN, FRANCIS. Rectors of the Irish College of Salamanca, 1705–67. *Irish Eccles. Record*, 5th ser. CX (1968) 231–49.

2842. FENNING, HUGH. Laurence Richardson, O.P., bishop of Kilmore, 1747–53. *Irish Eccles. Record*, 5th ser. CIX (1968) 137–57.

2843. QUANE, MICHAEL. Aspects of education in Ireland, 1695–1795. *Cork Hist. Soc. Jour.*, LXXIII (1968) 120–36.

2844. NEWHOUSE, NEVILLE H. The founding of Friends' School, Lisburn. *Roy. Soc. Antiq. Ireland Jour.*, XCVIII (1968) 47–55.

2845. MORTON, R. G. The rise of the yeomanry. *Irish Sword*, VIII (1967) 58–64.

2846. PATERSON, T. G. F. The volunteer companies of Ulster, 1778–93. Pts. 5–8. *Irish Sword*, VIII (1967) 23–32, 92–7, (1968) 210–17.

2847. VAN BROCK, FRANÇOIS. Dilemma at Killala. *Irish Sword*, VIII (1968) 261–71. [Naval battle, 1798.]

BRITISH EMPIRE

Note: The domestic history of Commonwealth countries is not included unless it has a direct bearing on British history.

American colonies

2848. VAUGHAN, ALDEN T. America before the Revolution, 1725–75. Englewood Cliffs, N.J.: Prentice-Hall, 1967. vi, 185 pp.

2849. HAVIGHURST, WALTER. Alexander Spotswood: portrait of a governor. Williamsburg, Va.: Rinehart & Winston, for Colonial Williamsburg, 1967. ix, 118 pp.

2850. VÁZQUEZ, RENÉ. Amat and Spotswood: the representative in America. *Atenea* (Puerto Rico), V nos. 3–4 (1968) 131–62. [Comparison of colonial styles.]

2851. WILSON, JUDITH A. My country is my colony: a study in Anglo-American patriotism, 1739–60. *Historian*, XXX (1968) 333–49.

2852. REA, ROBERT R. Military deserters from British West Florida. *Louisiana Hist.*, IX (1968) 123–38.

2853. YAPLE, ROBERT L. Braddock's defeat: the theories and a reconsideration. *Soc. Army Hist. Research Jour.*, XLVI (1968) 194–201.

2854. SOSIN, JACK M. The revolutionary frontier, 1763–83. New York: Holt, Rinehart & Winston, 1967. xiv, 241 pp.

2855. JOHNSON, HERBERT A., *and* SYRETT, DAVID. Some nice sharp quillets of the customs law: the *New York* affair, 1763–7. *William & Mary Quart.*, 3rd ser. XXV (1968) 432–51.

2856. STOUT, NEIL R. Goals and enforcement of British colonial policy, 1763–75. *Amer. Neptune*, XXVII (1967) 211–20.

2857. ERNST, JOSEPH ALBERT. The Currency Act repeal movement: a study of imperial politics and revolutionary crisis, 1764–7. *William & Mary Quart.*, 3rd ser. XXV (1968) 177–211.

2858. CURREY, CECIL B. Road to revolution: Benjamin Franklin in England, 1765–75. Garden City, N.Y.: Doubleday, 1968. xi, 422 pp.

2859. BURLINGAME, WILLIAM ROGER. Benjamin Franklin: envoy extraordinary. New York: Coward-McCann, 1967. 255 pp. [Missions to England.]

2860. HARLAN, ROBERT D. David Hall and the Stamp Act. *Bibliog. Soc. America Papers*, LXI (1967) 13–37.

2861. MARSHALL, PETER JAMES. Sir William Johnson and the treaty of Fort Stanwix, 1768. *Jour. Amer. Studies*, I (1967) 149–79.

2862. GIPSON, LAWRENCE HENRY. The British empire before the American Revolution. Vol. 13, The triumphant empire. New York: Knopf, 1967. xlii, 454 pp.

2863. KAMMEN, MICHAEL G. A rope of sand: the colonial agents, British politics, and the American Revolution. Ithaca, N.Y.: Cornell U.P., 1968. xviii, 349 pp.

2864. WELLS, PETER. The American War of Independence. Univ. of London P., 1967. 232 pp.

2865. MORGAN, EDMUND S. The Puritan ethic and the American Revolution. *William & Mary Quart.*, 3rd ser. XXIV (1967) 3–43.

2866. GREENE, JACK P. The plunge of lemmings: a consideration of recent writings on British politics and the American Revolution. *South Atlantic Quart.*, LXVII (1968) 141–75.

2867. SMITH, PAUL H. The American loyalists: notes on their organization and numerical strength. *William & Mary Quart.*, 3rd ser. XXV (1968) 259–77.

2868. FINGERHUT, EUGENE R. Uses and abuses of the American loyalists' claims: a critique of quantitative analyses. *William & Mary Quart.*, 3rd ser. XXV (1968) 245–58.

2869. BROWN, WALLACE. The American farmer during the Revolution: rebel or loyalist. *Agric. Hist.*, XLII (1968) 327–38.

2870. LUTNICK, SOLOMON. The American Revolution and the British press, 1775–83. Columbia, Mo.: Missouri U.P., 1967. xi, 249 pp.

2871. DORNFEST, WALTER T. British, Hessian, and provincial troops at Paulus Hook, 18th–19th August, 1779. *Soc. Army Hist. Research Jour.*, XLV (1967) 177–83.

2872. SALISBURY, WILLIAM. John Paul Jones and his ships: the need for more research. *Amer. Neptune*, XXVIII (1968) 195–205.

2873. ALEXANDER, JOHN K. Forton prison during the American Revolution: a case study of British prisoner-of-war policy and the American prisoner response to that policy. *Essex Inst. Hist. Coll.*, CIII (1967) 365–89.

2874. MACMASTER, RICHARD K., *and* SKAGGS, DAVID C. (*eds.*). The letterbooks of Alexander Hamilton, Piscatawa factor, 1775–6. *Maryland Hist. Mag.*, LXII (1967) 135–69.

Bermuda

2875. JACKMAN, S. W. (*ed.*). Reports on Bermuda by two 18th century governors. *Bermuda Hist. Quart.*, XV (1968) 35–61. [1749 and 1773.]

2876. JACKMAN, S. W. The governor of Bermuda and the military garrison, 1765–8: a study in conflict. *Soc. Army Hist. Research Jour.*, XLVI (1968) 132–6.

2877. DURNFORD, ANDREW. Letters from Bermuda, 1788–95. *Bermuda Hist. Quart.*, XXV (1968) 111–28.

Jamaica

2878. SHERIDAN, RICHARD B. The wealth of Jamaica in the 18th century: a rejoinder. *Econ. Hist. Rev.*, 2nd ser. XXI (1968) 46–61.

Canada

2879. CHIDSEY, DONALD BARR. The war in the north: an informal history of the American Revolution in and near Canada. New York: Crown, 1967. 214 pp.

2880. LANCTOT, GUSTAVE. Canada and the American Revolution, 1774–83, *transl.* from the French by M. M. Cameron. Harrap, 1967. xiv, 321 pp., illus.

2881. RAWLYK, GEORGE A. Revolution rejected, 1775–6. Scarborough, Ont.: Prentice-Hall, 1968. vi, 128 pp.

2882. COHEN, SHELDON S. Lieutenant John Starke and the defence of Quebec. *Dalhousie Rev.*, XLVII (1967) 57–64.

2883. GRIFFITHS, RALPH A. Governor Richard Philips and the Province of Nova Scotia. *Hon. Soc. Cymmrodorion Trans.* (1968) 265–92.

2884. FINGARD, JUDITH. Charles Inglis and his 'primitive bishoprick' in Nova Scotia. *Canadian Hist. Rev.*, XLIX (1968) 247–66.

2885. FERGUSSON, CHARLES BRUCE (*ed.*). The diary of Simeon Perkins, 1797–1803. (Champlain Soc. Pubns., 43). Toronto: the Society, 1967. lxxii, 550 pp.

2886. VAN STEEN, MARCUS. Governor Simcoe and his lady. Toronto, London: Hodder, 1968. 191 pp., illus.

2887. WALLOT, JEAN-PIERRE. La crise sous Craig (1807–11): nature des conflicts et historiographie. *Canadian Hist. Assoc. Rept.* (1967) 59–74.

Africa

2888. Sir George Yonge and his aide-de-camp, 1800–1. *South African Lib. Quart. Bull.*, XXIII (1968) 2–10.

2889. PORTER, R. An English family at Cape Coast, 1802–4. *Hist. Soc. Ghana Trans.*, IX (1968) 43–64. [The Fountaines.]

India

2890. GUPTA, BRIJEN KISHORE. Sirajuddaullah and the East India Company, 1756–7: background to the foundation of British power in India. Leiden: E. J. Brill, 1966. 172 pp.

2891. JHA, JAGDISH CHANDRA. Some light on the early judicial system of the East India Company. *Bihar Research Soc. Jour.*, LIII (1967) 214–23.

2892. PANDEY, BISHWA NATH. The introduction of English law into India: the career of Elijah Impey in Bengal, 1774–83. Asia Pubg. House, 1967. xv, 248 pp.

2893. HEANEY, G. F. Rennell and the surveyors of India. *Geog. Jour.*, CXXXIV (1968) 318–25.

2894. MARSHALL, PETER JAMES. Private British investment in 18th century Bengal. *Bengal Past & Present*, LXXXVI (1967) 52–67.

2895. SINHA, S. P. Early British penetration in Tamar, 1794–5. *Indian Hist. Rec. Comm. Proc.*, XXXIX (1968) 60–6.

BIOGRAPHY

2896. *Allen.* BOYCE, BENJAMIN. The benevolent man: a life of Ralph Allen of Bath. Cambridge, Mass.: Harvard U.P.; London: O.U.P., 1967. xiv, 304 pp., illus.

2897. *Bowen.* MORGAN, W. ISLWYN. George Bowen, Llwyn-gwair, a'i deulu. *Bathafarn*, XXII (1967) 37–48, XXIII (1968) 14–24. ['George Bowen of Llwyngwair and family.']

2898. *Brummell.* TENENBAUM, SAMUEL. The incredible Beau Brummell. South Brunswick, N.Y.: Barnes; London: Yoseloff, 1967. 285 pp.

2899. *Chubb.* BUSHELL, THOMAS L. The sage of Salisbury: Thomas Chubb, 1679–1747. Vision, 1968. ix, 159 pp. [Orig. pubd. New York: Philosophical Lib., 1967.]

2900. *Churchill.* GREEN, DAVID. Sarah, duchess of Marlborough. Collins, 1967. 351 pp., illus.

2901. *Dashwood.* KEMP, BETTY. Sir Francis Dashwood: an 18th century independent. London: Macmillan; New York: St. Martin's P., 1967. ix, 210 pp., illus.

2902. *Douglas.* BLYTH, HENRY. Old Q., the rake of Piccadilly: a biography of the 4th duke of Queensberry. Weidenfeld, 1967. xiii, 238 pp., illus.

2903. *Gibbon.* DE BEER, *Sir* GAVIN. Gibbon and his world. Thames & Hudson, 1968. 144 pp., illus.

2904. *L'Estrange.* CHERRY, DAVID. Sir Nicholas L'Estrange, non-juror: his politics, fortune and family. *Norfolk Archaeol.*, XXXIV pt. 3 (1968) 314–29.

2905. *Leyden.* GUTHRIE, DOUGLAS. Dr. John Leyden, 1775–1811. *Univ. Edinburgh Jour.*, XXIII no. 2 (1967) 161–6.

2906. *Macdonald.* NICHOLAS, DONALD. Reluctant heroine: a brief life of Flora Macdonald. *Stewarts*, XIII no. 1 (1968) 5–19.

2907. *Metcalf.* HOGG, GARRY. Blind Jack of Knaresborough, road builder extraordinary. Phoenix House, 1967. xii, 145 pp., illus.

2908. *Noel.* ELWIN, MALCOLM (*comp.*). The Noels and the Milbankes: their letters for 25 years, 1767–92. Macdonald & Co., 1967. 471 pp., illus.

2909. *Salvador.* WOOLF, MAURICE. Joseph Salvador, 1716–86. *Jewish Hist. Soc. Eng. Trans.* for 1962–7, XXI (1968) 104–37.

2910. *Sheffield.* MORTIMER, JEAN E. 'Princess Buckingham'. *Univ. Leeds Rev.*, X (1966–7) 148–58. [Katherine Sheffield, duchess of Buckingham.]

2911. *Siddons.* MACKENZIE, KATHLEEN. The great Sarah: the life of Mrs. Siddons. Evans Bros., 1968. 144 pp., illus.

2912. *Smith.* CHECKLAND, SYDNEY GEORGE. Adam Smith and the biographer. *Scot. Jour. Polit. Econ.*, XIV (1967) 70–9.

2913. *Stout.* MARSHALL, JOHN DUNCAN (*ed.*). The autobiography of William Stout of Lancaster, 1665–1752. (Chetham Soc. 3rd ser., 14). Manchester: Manchester U.P. for the Society, 1967. viii, 311 pp.

2914. *Thompson.* BRADLEY, DUANE. Count Rumford. Van Nostrand, 1967. vii, 176 pp., illus.

2915. *Urie.* GILLESPIE, R. A. The parentage of Robert Urie, printer in Glasgow. *Bibliotheck*, V pt. 1 (1967) 38–40.

2916. *Wesley.* HARMON, REBECCA LAMAR. Susanna, mother of the Wesleys. Hodder, 1968. 175 pp., illus. [Originally pubd. Nashville, Tenn.: Abingdon P., 1968.]

2917. *Whitbread.* FULFORD, ROGER. Samuel Whitbread, 1764–1815: a study in opposition. Macmillan, 1967. xiv, 336 pp., illus.

2918. *Whitbread.* FULFORD, R. Samuel Whitbread. *History Today*, XVII (1967) 162–9.

2919. *Woffington.* DUNBAR, JANET. Peg Woffington and her world. Heinemann, 1968. 245 pp., illus.

THE NINETEENTH CENTURY, 1815–1900

GENERAL

2920. TULL, GORDON KEITH, *and* BULWER, PETER MCGENNIS. Britain and the world in the 19th century. New York: Humanities P., 1967. 342 pp.

2921. EVANS, ROBERT JOCELYN. The Victorian age, 1815–1914. 2nd edn. Edward Arnold, 1968. lx, 357 pp. [Previous edn. 1950.]

2922. BRASHER, NORMAN HENRY. Arguments in history: Britain in the 19th century. Macmillan, 1968. viii, 248 pp., illus.

2923. ROBSON, ROBERT (*ed.*). Ideas and institutions of Victorian Britain: essays in honour of George Kitson Clark. Bell, 1967. viii, 343 pp. [Contains: 'Parliamentary parties and the "Independent" member, 1810–60' by D. E. D. Beales, pp. 1–19; 'Social structure, political structure and public opinion in mid-Victorian England' by D. C. Moore, pp. 20–57; 'Coal mines regulation: the first decade, 1842–52' by O. O. G. M. MacDonagh, pp. 58–86; 'Cobden and Bright in politics, 1846–57' by N. McCord, pp. 87–114; 'Popular Protestantism in Victorian Britain' by G. F. A. Best, pp. 115–42; 'Mid-century Scottish nationalism: romantic and radical' by H. J. Hanham, pp. 143–79; 'The uses of philology in Victorian England' by J. W. Burrow, pp. 180–205; 'The atheist mission, 1840–1900' by F. B. Smith, pp. 205–35; 'John Robert Seeley and the idea of a national Church' by R. T. Shannon, pp. 236–67; 'The parliamentary foundations of the Hotel Cecil' by J. P. Cornford, pp. 268–311; 'Trinity College in the age of Peel' by R. Robson, pp. 312–36.]

2924. KITSON CLARK, GEORGE SIDNEY ROBERTS. An expanding society: Britain, 1830–1900. Cambridge: C.U.P.; Melbourne: Melbourne U.P., 1967. xv, 188 pp.

2925. BRIGGS, ASA. Victorian cities. New edn. Harmondsworth, Middx.: Penguin, 1968. 412 pp. [Previous edn. Odhams, 1963.]

2926. BRIGGS, A. The Victorian city: quantity and quality. *Victorian Studies*, XI (1967–8) 711–30.

2927. BELL, ALDON D. London in the age of Dickens. Norman, Okla.: Oklahoma U.P., 1967. 184 pp.

2928. PHILIP, KATHLEEN. Victorian Wantage. Wantage, Berks.: the author, 1968. 125 pp., illus.

2929. HARRIS, ALAN. Denton Holme, Carlisle: Pt. 2, The growth of a suburb. *Cumberland & Westmorland Antiq. & Archaeol. Soc. Trans.*, LXVII (1967) 206–28.

2930. NEWTON, ROBERT. Victorian Exeter, 1837–1914. Leicester: Leicester U.P., 1968. xxi, 415 pp., illus.

2931. WOOD, ROBERT. West Hartlepool: the rise and development of a Victorian new town. Hartlepool, Durham: the Corporation, 1967. xiv, 354 pp., illus.

2932. SIMMONS, JACK. Mid-Victorian Leicester. *Leics. Archaeol. Soc. Trans.* for 1965–6, XLI (1967) 41–56.

2933. BECKWITH, IAN S. Victorian village: Roxby, a Lincolnshire village in the 19th century. Lincoln: the author, 1967. 24 pp., illus.

2934. PACKWOOD, G. F. L., *and* COX, ARCHIBALD HENRY (*eds.*). West Drayton and district during the 19th century. West Drayton, Middx.: West Drayton & District Local Hist. Soc., 1967. 73 pp., illus.

2935. DALE, ANTONY. Fashionable Brighton, 1820–60. 2nd edn. Newcastle-upon-Tyne: Oriel P., 1967. 192 pp., illus. [Previous edn. Country Life, 1948.]

2936. DALE, A. Regency Brighton. *Ancient Monuments Soc. Trans.* for 1966–7, n.s. XIV (1968) 23–38.

2937. DUCKHAM, BARON FREDERICK. York in the 1830s: an ancient city on the threshold of change. *Univ. Leeds Rev.*, X (1966–7) 17–26.

2938. MILLER, EDWIN (*comp.*). Eye-witness: the North East in the early 19th century. Newcastle-upon-Tyne: Hill & Son, for Sunderland College of Education, 1968. 64 pp., illus.

CONSTITUTIONAL AND POLITICAL HISTORY

2939. MORRIS, ANDREW JAMES ANTHONY. Parliamentary democracy in the 19th century. Oxford: Pergamon, 1967. xiv, 188 pp.

2940. BERRINGTON, HUGH. Partisanship and dissidence in the 19th century House of Commons. *Parliamentary Affairs*, XXI (1967–8) 338–74.

2941. MCCORD, NORMAN. Some difficulties of parliamentary reform. *Hist. Jour.*, X (1967) 376–90.

2942. VINCENT, JOHN RUSSELL. Poll-books: how Victorians voted. C.U.P., 1967. xi, 194 pp.

2943. RINTALA, MARVIN. Two compromises: Victorian and Bismarckian. *Government & Opposition*, III (1968) 207–21. [Responses to challenge of industrial middle class.]

2944. POOL, BERNARD (*ed.*). The Croker papers, 1808–57. New edn. Batsford, 1967. vii, 277 pp., illus.

2945. MILLER, NAOMI CHURGIN. John Cartwright and radical parliamentary reform, 1808–19. *E.H.R.*, LXXXIII (1968) 705–28.

2946. MITCHELL, AUSTIN. The Whigs in opposition, 1815–30. Oxford: Clarendon P., 1967. xi, 266 pp.

2947. KESTEVEN, G. R. Peterloo, 1819. Chatto, 1967. 94 pp., illus.

2948. MCCORD, NORMAN. Tyneside discontents and Peterloo. *Northern Hist.*, II (1967) 91–111.

2949. BROCK, WILLIAM RANULF. Lord Liverpool and liberal Toryism, 1820–7. 2nd edn. Cass, 1967. 300 pp. [Previous edn. 1941.]

2950. THOMIS, MALCOLM IAN. The politics of Nottingham enclosure. *Thoroton Soc. Trans.* for 1967, LXXI (1968) 90–6.

2951. FOOT, M. R. D. (*ed.*). The Gladstone diaries. Vol. 1, 1825–32. Vol. 2, 1833–9. Oxford: Clarendon P., 1968. 2 vols.

2952. BRADFIELD, B. T. Sir Richard Vyvyan and the country gentlemen, 1830–4. *E.H.R.*, LXXXIII (1968) 729–43.

2953. RUDÉ, GEORGE E. English rural and urban disturbances on the eve of the first Reform Bill, 1830–1. *Past & Present*, no. 37 (1967) 87–102.

2954. HOBSBAWM, ERIC JOHN. Soziale Bewegung und Kämpfe auf dem Lande in England in der ersten Hälfte des 19. Jahrhunderts. *Jahrb. für Wirtschaftsgesch.*, I (1968) 309–32.

2955. HOBSBAWM, E. J. Le agitazioni rurali in Inghilterra nel primo Ottocento. *Studi Stor.*, VIII (1967) 256–81.

2956. WARD, JOHN TREVOR. A footnote on the First Reform Act. *Scot. Hist. Rev.*, XLVI (1967) 89–94.

2957. HORN, PAMELA. Banbury and the riots of 1830. *Cake & Cockhorse*, III (1967) 176–9.

2958. THURSTON, GAVIN. The Clerkenwell riot: the killing of Constable Culley. Allen & Unwin, 1967. xvi, 188 pp., illus. [1833.]

2959. BRADFIELD, B. T. Sir Richard Vyvyan and the fall of Wellington's government. *Univ. Birmingham Hist. Jour.*, XI (1967–8) 141–56.

2960. HANHAM, HAROLD JOHN. The reformed electoral system in Great Britain, 1832–1914. (Gen. ser., 69). Historical Assoc., 1968. 38 pp.

2961. KRIEGEL, ABRAHAM D. The politics of the Whigs in opposition, 1834–5. *Jour. Brit. Studies*, VII no. 2 (1968) 65–91.

2962. HENRIQUES, URSULA R. Q. The Jewish emancipation controversy in 19th century Britain. *Past & Present*, no. 40 (1968) 126–46.

2963. AYDELOTTE, WILLIAM O. The country gentlemen and the repeal of the corn laws. *E.H.R.*, LXXXII (1967) 47–60.

2964. OSBORNE, JOHN W. William Cobbett and the corn laws. *Historian*, XXIX (1967) 186–99.

2965. FRASER, DEREK. Birmingham and the corn laws. *Birmingham Archaeol. Soc. Trans.* for 1965, LXXXII (1967) 1–20.

2966. FRASER, D. Nottingham and the corn laws. *Thoroton Soc. Trans.* for 1966, LXX (1967) 81–104.

2967. MCCORD, NORMAN. The Anti-Corn Law League, 1838–46. 2nd edn. Allen & Unwin, 1968. 224 pp. [Previous edn. 1958.]

2968. PRENTICE, ARCHIBALD. History of the Anti-Corn Law League. 2nd edn. with new intro. by W. H. Chaloner. Cass, 1968. 2 vols. [Previous edn. Cash, 1853.]

2969. CHALONER, WILLIAM HENRY. The Anti-Corn Law League. *History Today*, XVIII (1968) 196–204.

2970. GOLBY, JOHN M. Public order and private unrest: a study of the 1842 riots in Shropshire. *Univ. Birmingham Hist. Jour.*, XI (1967–8) 157–69.

2971. ROWE, D. J. The failure of London Chartism. *Hist. Jour.*, XI (1968) 472–87.

2972. EDWARDS, J. K. Chartism in Norwich. *Yorks. Bull. Econ. & Soc. Research*, XIX (1967) 85–100.

2973. HORN, PAMELA. The Chartist Land Company. *Cake & Cockhorse*, IV (1968) 19–24.

2974. SEARBY, PETER. Great Dodford and the later history of the Chartist land scheme. *Agric. Hist. Rev.*, XVI (1968) 32–45.

2975. SALT, JOHN. Chartism in south Yorkshire. (Local Hist. Pamphlets, 1). Sheffield, Yorks.: Univ. Inst. Education, 1967. 32 pp.

2976. HARRISON, BRIAN, *and* HOLLIS, PATRICIA. Chartism, Liberalism and the life of Robert Lowery. *E.H.R.*, LXXXII (1967) 503–35.

2977. READ, DONALD. Cobden and Bright: a Victorian political partnership. Edward Arnold, 1967. ix, 275 pp.

2978. HOBSON, JOHN ATKINSON. Richard Cobden: the international man. New edn. Benn, 1968. ix, 421 pp. [Previous edn. Fisher Unwin, 1918.]

2979. THOMPSON, EDWARD PALMER. The political education of Henry Mayhew. *Victorian Studies*, XI (1967–8) 41–62.

2980. DI NOLFO, ENNIO. Il mancato matrimonio di Vittorio Emanuele II con la principessa Mary di Cambridge. *Risorgimento*, XIX (1967) 93–120.

2981. FRASER, MAXWELL. Sir Benjamin Hall in parliament in the 1850s. *Nat. Lib. Wales Jour.*, XV (1967–8) 72–88, 113–26, 310–24, 389–404.

2982. ANDERSON, OLIVE. A liberal state at war: English politics and economics during the Crimean War. London: Macmillan; New York: St. Martin's P., 1967. xi, 306 pp.

2983. BENTLEY, NICOLAS (*ed.*). Russell's despatches from the Crimea, 1854–6. New York: Hill & Wang, 1967. 286 pp.

2984. CONACHER, JAMES BLENNERHASSET. The Aberdeen coalition, 1852–5: a study of mid-19th century party politics. C.U.P., 1968. xiv, 607 pp., illus.

2985. ANDERSON, OLIVE. The political uses of history in mid-19th century England. *Past & Present*, no. 36 (1967) 87–105.

2986. DONOVAN, THERESE A. Difficulties of a diplomat: George Mifflin Dallas in London. *Pennsylvania Mag. Hist. & Biog.*, XCII (1968) 421–40.

2987. STEELE, E. D. Ireland and the Empire in the 1860s: imperial precedents for Gladstone's first Irish Land Act. *Hist. Jour.*, XI (1968) 64–83.

2988. FULFORD, ROGER (*ed.*). Dearest Mama: letters between Queen Victoria and the Crown Princess of Prussia, 1861–4. Evans Bros., 1968. xvi, 372 pp., illus.

2989. ELDRIDGE, C. C. Newcastle and the Ashanti War of 1863–4: a failure of the policy of 'anti-imperialism'. *Renaissance & Mod. Studies*, XII (1968) 68–90.

2990. ROVER, CONSTANCE. Women's suffrage and party politics in Britain, 1866–1914. London: Routledge; Toronto: Toronto U.P., 1967. xv, 240 pp.

2991. HANHAM, HAROLD JOHN. Opposition techniques in British politics, 1867–1914. *Government & Opposition*, II (1966) 35–48.

2992. COLLIEU, ERIC GEORGE. Gladstone. (Clarendon Biographies, 20). O.U.P., 1968. 63 pp., illus.

2993. HOLMES, DEREK. Gladstone and Newman. *Dublin Rev.*, CCXLI (1967) 141–53.

2994. COWLING, MAURICE. 1867: Disraeli, Gladstone and revolution, the passing of the Second Reform Bill. C.U.P., 1967. xi, 451 pp.

2995. ADELMAN, PAUL. The Second Reform Act of 1867. *History Today*, XVII (1967) 317–25.

2996. FEUCHTWANGER, EDGAR JOSEPH. Disraeli, democracy and the Tory party: Conservative leadership and organisation after the Second Reform Bill. Oxford: Clarendon P., 1968. xiv, 268 pp.

2997. VINCENT, JOHN RUSSELL. The effect of the Second Reform Act in Lancashire. *Hist. Jour.*, XI (1968) 84–94.

2998. PELLING, HENRY MATHISON. Popular politics and society in late Victorian Britain. Macmillan, 1968. vii, 188 pp.

2999. LLOYD, TREVOR. The general election of 1880. O.U.P., 1968. 175 pp.

3000. BAYLEN, JOSEPH O., *and* WALTON, GERALD. The Froude-Stead correspondence, 1877–91. *Huntington Lib. Quart.*, XXX (1966–7) 167–83.

3001. WESTON, CORINNE COMSTOCK. The royal mediation in 1884. *E.H.R.*, LXXXII (1967) 296–322.

3002. THOMPSON, PAUL. Socialists, Liberals and Labour: the struggle for London, 1885–1914. London: Routledge; Toronto: Toronto U.P., 1967. viii, 376 pp.

3003. PELLING, HENRY MATHISON. Social geography of British elections, 1885–1910. Macmillan, 1967. xxxi, 455 pp.

3004. MOODY, T. W. *The Times* versus Parnell and Co., 1887–90. *Hist. Studies*, VI (1968) 147–82.

3005. MOODY, T. W. The Irish Home Rule movement and the British Liberal party. *Topic*, XIII (1967) 44–59.

3006. HURST, MICHAEL. Joseph Chamberlain and Liberal reunion: the Round Table Conference of 1887. London: Routledge; Toronto: Toronto U.P., 1967. xv, 407 pp.

3007. KENDLE, JOHN EDWARD. The Round Table Movement and 'Home Rule all Round'. *Hist. Jour.*, XI (1968) 332–53.

3008. MALLET, VICTOR (*ed.*). Life with Queen Victoria: Marie Mallet's letters from court, 1887–1901. J. Murray, 1968. xxiv, 245 pp., illus.

3009. BROWN, JOHN. Charles Booth and Labour colonies, 1889–1905. *Econ. Hist. Rev.*, 2nd ser. XXI (1968) 349–60.

3010. MORGAN, KENNETH OWEN. John Morley and the crisis of Liberalism, 1894. *Nat. Lib. Wales Jour.*, XV (1967–8) 451–65.

3011. KOSS, STEPHEN E. Morley in the middle. *E.H.R.*, LXXXII (1967) 553–61.

3012. BUTLER, JEFFREY. The Liberal party and the Jameson Raid. Oxford: Clarendon P., 1968. xii, 336 pp.

3013. HARDY, S. M. Joseph Chamberlain and some problems of the 'underdeveloped estates'. *Univ. Birmingham Hist. Jour.*, XI (1967–8) 170–90.

POLITICAL THOUGHT

3014. MAZLISH, BRUCE. James Mill and the Utilitarians. *Daedalus*, LXVII (1968) 1036–61.

3015. RESTAINO, FRANCO. J. S. Mill e la cultura filosofica britannica. Florence: Nuova Italia; Bologna: Azzoguidi, 1968. xvi, 477 pp.

3016. RESTAINO, F. J. S. Mill, 'radical philosopher': gli anni della milizia politica benthamiana (1822–8). *Studi Stor.*, VIII (1967) 283–324.

3017. NEGRO PAVÓN, DALMACIO. John Stuart Mill: el liberalismo como ideología. *Rev. de Estudios Políticos*, nos. 159–60 (1968) 121–45. [English summary.]

3018. HUME, L. J. Jeremy Bentham and the 19th century revolution in government. *Hist. Jour.*, X (1967) 361–75.

3019. NICHOLLS, DAVID. The totalitarianism of Thomas Arnold. *Rev. of Politics*, XXIX (1967) 518–25.

ADMINISTRATIVE AND LEGAL HISTORY

3020. TORRANCE, J. R. Sir George Harrison and the growth of bureaucracy in the early 19th century. *E.H.R.*, LXXXIII (1968) 52–88.

3021. PORT, M. H. The Office of Works and building contracts in early 19th century England. *Econ. Hist. Rev.*, 2nd ser. XX (1967) 94–110.

3022. BISHOP, A. S. Ralph Lingen, Secretary to the Education Department, 1849–70. *Brit. Jour. Educ. Studies*, XVI (1968) 138–63.

3023. MACLEOD, ROY M. Government and resource conservation: the Salmon Acts administration, 1860–86. *Jour. Brit. Studies*, VII no. 2 (1968) 114–50.

3024. MACLEOD, ROY M. Treasury control and social administration: a study of establishment growth at the Local Government Board, 1871–1905. (Occasional Papers on Social Admin., 23). Bell, 1968. 62 pp., illus.

3025. MIDWINTER, ERIC CLARE. Central and local government in mid-19th century Lancashire. *Northern Hist.*, III (1968) 155–61.

3026. MIDWINTER, E. C. State intervention at the local level: the new Poor Law in Lancashire. *Hist. Jour.*, X (1967) 106–12.

3027. HUNT, J. R. The Widnes Local Board of Health, 1865–92. *Hist. Soc. Lancs. & Cheshire Trans.* for 1967, CXIX (1968) 213–24.

3028. MCILVEN, ROY. Edmonton Local Board of Health, 1850–60. (Edmonton Hundred Hist. Soc. Occas. Papers, n.s. 10). The Society, 1967. 33 pp.

3029. HEATH, GERALD DUNCAN. The formation of the local boards of Twickenham, Teddington, Hampton and Hampton Wick. (Borough of Twickenham Local

Hist. Soc. Papers, 10). Twickenham, Middx.: the Society, 1967. 22 pp.

3030. BUTTERFIELD, P. H. Aspects of the work of Matthew Arnold for Royal Commissions. *Brit. Jour. Educ. Studies*, XV (1967) 284–91.

3031. BEHRMAN, CYNTHIA FANSLER. The annual blister: a sidelight on Victorian social and parliamentary history. *Victorian Studies*, XI (1967–8) 483–502. [Marriage of Deceased Wife's Sister Bill.]

3032. SWINFEN, D. B. The genesis of the Colonial Laws Validity Act. *Juridical Rev.*, n.s. XII (1967) 29–61.

3033. TURNER, FRANK L. Origins of the Artisans' Dwellings Act of 1875. *Southern Quart.*, VII no. 1 (1968) 1–15.

3034. HANES, DAVID GORDON. The first British Workmen's Compensation Act, 1897. New Haven, Conn., London: Yale U.P., 1968. xi, 124 pp.

3035. NOWELL-SMITH, SIMON. International copyright law and the publisher in the reign of Queen Victoria. Oxford: Clarendon P., 1968. xii, 109 pp.

3036. BLAIR, CLAUDE. Egg *v.* Pauly. *Arms & Armour Soc. Jour.*, VI no. 1 (1968) 9–27. [Chancery case, 1817. Attempt to recoup losses on failed project to build airship.]

3037. FULFORD, ROGER. The trial of Queen Caroline. Batsford, 1967. 255 pp., illus.

3038. QUEN, JACQUES M. An historical view of the M'Naghten trial. *Bull. Hist. Medicine*, XLII (1968) 43–51.

3039. ANDERSON, OLIVE. The Wensleydale peerage case and the position of lords in the mid-19th century. *E.H.R.*, LXXXII (1967) 486–502.

3040. HEUSTON, ROBERT FRANCIS VERE. The Wensleydale peerage case: a further comment. *E.H.R.*, LXXXIII (1968) 777–82.

3041. SMITH, HARRY. From deodand to dependency. *Amer. Jour. Legal Hist.*, XI (1967) 389–403.

3042. KNIGHT, L. A. The Royal Titles Act and India. *Hist. Jour.*, XI (1968) 488–507.

3043. TOBIAS, JOHN JACOB. Crime and industrial society in the 19th century. Batsford, 1967. 288 pp.

3044. MIDWINTER, ERIC CLARE. Law and order in early Victorian Lancashire. (Borthwick Papers, 34). York: St. Anthony's P., 1968. 42 pp.

3045. PRESCOTT, CATHARINE. The Suffolk constabulary in the 19th century. *Suffolk Inst. Archaeol. Proc.* for 1967, XXXI (1968) 1–46.

ECONOMIC AND SOCIAL HISTORY

General and economic theory

3046. CHAMBERS, JONATHAN DAVID. The workshop of the world: British economic history from 1820 to 1880. 2nd edn. O.U.P., 1968. lx, 165 pp. [Previous edn. 1961.]

3047. ROSENBERG, NATHAN. Anglo-American wage difference in the 1820s. *Jour. Econ. Hist.*, XXVII (1967) 221–9.

3048. BLACK, R. D. COLLISON. Economic policy in Ireland and India in the time of J. S. Mill. *Econ. Hist. Rev.*, 2nd ser. XXI (1968) 321–36.

3049. ALDCROFT, DEREK HOWARD. Factor prices and the rate of innovation in Britain, 1875–1914. *Business Hist.*, IX (1967) 126–31.

3050. WEISS, R. W. 'Economic nationalism in Britain in the 19th century'. *In* Economic nationalism in old and new states, *ed.* H. G. Johnson (Chicago: Chicago U.P., 1967) pp. 31–47.

3051. CROUCH, R. L. Laissez-faire in 19th century Britain: myth or reality? *Manchester School Econ. & Soc. Studies*, XXXV (1967) 199–215.

3052. SAYERS, RICHARD SIDNEY. 'A phase in English monetary thought'. *In* Studi in onore di Marco Fanno, *ed.* T. Bagiotti, vol. 2 (Padua: Ed. Cedam, 1966) pp. 585–9.

3053. PLATT, DESMOND CHRISTOPHER ST. MARTIN. The imperialism of free trade: some reservations. *Econ. Hist. Rev.*, 2nd ser. XXI (1968) 296–306.

3054. COATS, ALFRED W. The origins and early development of the Royal Economic Society. *Econ. Jour.*, LXXVIII (1968) 348–71.

3055. MANNING, DAVID JOHN. The mind of Jeremy Bentham. Longmans, 1968. ix, 118 pp.

3056. BRADY, ALEXANDER. William Huskisson and liberal reform: an essay on the charges in economic policy in the twenties of the 19th century. 2nd edn. Cass,

1967. xiii, 177 pp. [Previous edn. O.U.P., 1928.]

3057. BLACK, R. D. COLLISON. Parson Malthus, the general and the captain. *Econ. Jour.*, LXXVII (1967) 59–74. [Maj.-Gen. Sir William Sleeman, and Capt. William Pettman.]

3058. MACCHIORO, AURELIO. Say, Ricardo, Malthus. *Riv. Internaz. Sci. Econ. Comm.*, XIII (1966) 658–75, 881–95, 1071–89.

3059. MEEK, RONALD L. 'The decline of Ricardian economics in England'. *In* Economics and ideology and other essays (Chapman & Hall, 1967) pp. 51–74.

3060. TAVIANI, PAOLO EMILIO. Mazzini, Carlyle, Ruskin, Tolstoi e la scuola democratico-cristiana. (L'affrancamento dell' economia politica dell' utilitarismo benthamiano). *Civitas*, n.s. XVIII (1967) 3–27.

3061. BARUCCI, PIERO. I primordi del pensiero economico di Jevons. *Giornale degli Economisti e Ann. di Econ.*, n.s. XXVI (1967) 16–43.

Finance

3062. HALL, A. R. (*ed.*). The export of capital from Britain, 1870–1914. Methuen, 1968. ix, 190 pp., illus.

3063. PRESSNELL, L. S. 'Gold reserves, banking reserves and the Baring crisis of 1890'. *In* Essays in money and banking in honour of R. S. Sayers, *ed.* C. R. Whittlesey *and* J. S. G. Wilson (O.U.P., 1968) pp. 167–228.

3064. FETTER, FRANK W. A historical confusion in Bagehot's Lombard Street. *Economica*, n.s. XXXIV (1967) 80–3. [1825 panic.]

3065. LAUREYSSENS, J. Het ontstaan van de Banque des Flandres: ouverwacht eindresultaat van het projekt Banque Anglo–Belge. *Studia Hist. Gandensia*, LXXXIX (1968) 1–30.['The origin of the Banque des Flandres: unexpected results of the Anglo-Belgian Bank project'.]

3066. VERITY, WILLIAM. The rise of the Rothschilds. *History Today*, XVIII (1968) 225–33.

3067. Ironmasters and duke's agent: the Sheffield and Rotherham Bank – the early days. *Three Banks Rev.*, no. 73 (1967) 36–50.

3068. A customer from the colonies. *Three Banks Rev.*, no. 80 (1968) 31–43. [J. W. Hulme's dealings with Child & Co., bankers, 1844–59.]

Industry

3069. WARD, JOHN TREVOR. The factory movement in Lancashire, 1830–55. *Lancs. & Cheshire Antiq. Soc. Trans.* for 1965–6, LXXV–LXXVI (1968) 186–210.

3070. James Montgomery on factory management, 1832. *Business Hist. Rev.*, XLII (1968) 219–26.

3071. PRIDE, EMRYS. Work study and Robert Owen. *Hon. Soc. Cymmrodorion Trans.* (1967) 92–9.

3072. ALDCROFT, DEREK HOWARD (*ed.*). The development of British industry and foreign competition, 1875–1914: studies in industrial enterprise. (Univ. Glasgow Social and Economic Studies, n.s. 12). Allen & Unwin, 1968. 384 pp., illus.

3073. LEVINE, AARON LAWRENCE. Industrial retardation in Britain, 1880–1914. Weidenfeld, 1967. ix, 201 pp.

3074. BOOKER, FRANK. The Tamar Valley. *Industrial Archaeol.*, IV (1967) 1–7.

3075. HAIR, P. E. H. Mortality from violence in British coal-mines, 1800–50. *Econ. Hist. Rev.*, 2nd ser. XXI (1968) 545–61.

3076. KIRKHAM, NELLIE. Steam engines in Derbyshire lead mines. *Newcomen Soc. Trans.* for 1965–6, XXXVIII (1968) 69–88.

3077. WARREN, JOHN. Beam pumping engines at Kew Bridge. *Industrial Archaeol.*, V (1968) 327–34.

3078. HARRIS, ALAN, *and* DAVIS, RONALD B. The Hodbarrow iron mines. *Cumberland & Westmorland Antiq. & Archaeol. Soc. Trans.*, LXVIII (1968) 151–68.

3079. LONG, HILARY. The Bowling ironworks. *Industrial Archaeol.*, V (1968) 171–7.

3080. HAYES, R. H., *and* RUTTER, J. G. The Rosedale ironstone industry and railway. *Scarborough & District Archaeol. Soc. Trans.*, II no. 11 (1968) 7–28.

3081. KING, N. E. The Kennet Valley sarsen industry. *Wilts. Archaeol. & Nat. Hist. Mag.*, LXIII (1968) 83–93.

3082. RUCH, JOHN E. Regency Coade: a study of the Coade record books, 1813–21. *Archit. Hist.*, XI (1968) 34–56.

3083. ALFORD, BERNARD WILLIAM ERNEST. The flint and bottle glass industry in the early 19th century: a case study of a

Bristol firm. *Business Hist.*, X (1968) 12–21. [Phoenix Glassworks.]

3084. FALKUS, M. E. The British gas industry before 1850. *Econ. Hist. Rev.*, 2nd ser. XX (1967) 494–508.

3085. BELLISS, J. EDWARD. A history of G. E. Belliss & Company and Belliss & Morcom Ltd. *Newcomen Soc. Trans.* for 1964–5, XXXVII (1967) 87–98.

3086. HARRIS, ELIZABETH M. Experimental graphic processes in England, 1800–59. *Printing Hist. Soc. Jour.*, IV (1968) 33–86.

3087. HARRIS, E. M. Sir William Congreve and his compound-plate printing. *U.S. Nat. Museum Bull.*, no. 252 (1967) 71–87.

3088. BAIN, IAIN. James Moyes and his Temple Printing Office of 1825. *Printing Hist. Soc. Jour.*, IV (1968) 1–10.

3089. ROSE, MICHAEL E. Samuel Crompton (1753–1827), inventor of the spinning mule: a reconsideration. *Lancs. & Cheshire Antiq. Soc. Trans.* for 1965–6, LXXV–LXXVI (1968) 11–32.

3090. TRIPATHI, DWIJENDRA. Opportunism of free trade: Lancashire cotton famine and Indian cotton cultivation. *Indian Econ. & Soc. Hist. Rev.*, IV no. 3 (1967) 255–63.

3091. LEE, C. H. Marketing organization and policy in the cotton trade: M'Connel & Kennedy of Manchester, 1795–1835. *Business Hist.*, X (1968) 89–100.

3092. WALLWORK, K. L. The calico printing industry of Lancastria in the 1840s. *Inst. Brit. Geographers Trans.*, XLV (1968) 143–56.

3093. IREDALE, D. A. Titus Salt's day book, 1834–7. *Textile Hist.*, I no. 1 (1968) 62–72.

3094. VARLEY, D. E. John Heathcoat (1783–1861) founder of the machine-made lace industry. *Textile Hist.*, I no. 1 (1968) 2–45.

3095. BARTLETT, J. N. The mechanisation of the Kidderminster carpet industry. *Business Hist.*, IX (1967) 49–69.

3096. LAW, C. M., *and* HOOSON, D. J. M. The straw-plait and straw-hat industries of the South Midlands. 1, Luton and the hat industry. 2, The straw industry of the Chilterns in the 19th century. *East Midland Geographer*, IV pt. 6 (1968) 329–50.

3097. HOUGHTON, A. W. J. Caughley Porcelain Works near Broseley, Salop. *Industrial Archaeol.*, V (1968) 184–92.

3098. BRADLEY, R. J. The story of Castle Hedingham pottery. *Connoisseur*, CLXVII (1968) 77–83, 152–7, 210–16.

3099. CONNELL, E. J. Hertford breweries. *Industrial Archaeol.*, IV (1967) 26–43.

Trade and commerce

3100. DUCKHAM, BARON FREDERICK. The founding of Goole: an early 19th century canal port. *Industrial Archaeol.*, IV (1967) 19–28.

3101. ORAM, R. B. The birth and death of a dock. *History Today*, XVIII (1968) 570–7. [St. Katharine Dock, London.]

3102. HOWGEGO, JAMES LAURENCE. Docks on the North Bank: a 19th century transformation. *East London Papers*, X (1967) 75–108.

3103. BLACKMAN, JANET. The development of the retail grocery trade in the 19th century. *Business Hist.*, IX (1967) 110–17.

3104. HOLMES, JULIE M. Father of the salt trade. *Cheshire Round*, I no. 7 (1967) 226–31. [Herman Falk, 1820–98.]

3105. IREDALE, D. A. John and Thomas Marshall and the Society for Improving the British Salt Trade: an example of trade regulation. *Econ. Hist. Rev.*, 2nd ser. XX (1967) 79–93.

3106. FAWCETT, TREVOR. Some aspects of the Norfolk book-trade, 1800–24. *Cambridge Bibliog. Soc. Trans.*, IV no. 5 (1968) 383–95.

3107. BARBER, GILES. Treuttel and Würtz: some aspects of the importation of books from France, *c.* 1825. *Library*, 5th ser. XXIII (1968) 118–44.

3108. PERRY, PETER. The Newfoundland trade: the decline and demise of the port of Poole, 1815–94. *Amer. Neptune*, XXVIII (1968) 275–83.

3109. WILLIAMS, DAVID M. Bulk carriers and timber imports: the British North American trade and the shipping boom of 1824–5. *Mariner's Mirror*, LIV (1968) 373–82.

3110. MARRINER, SHEILA, *and* HYDE, FRANCIS E. The senior: John Samuel Swire, 1825–98: management in Far Eastern shipping trades. Liverpool: Liverpool U.P., 1967. xv, 224 pp., illus.

3111. LE FEVOUR, EDWARD. Western enterprise in late Ch'ing China: a selective survey of Jardine, Matheson and Company's operations, 1842–95. (Harvard East Asian monographs, 26). Cambridge, Mass.: Harvard U.P., 1968. vii, 215 pp.

3112. PINO ITURRIETA, ELÍAS A. Antecedentes generales y esbozo del comercio inglés en Angostura, 1817–20. *Latino América*, I (1968) 131–43.

3113. MATHEW, W. M. The imperialism of free trade: Peru, 1820–70. *Econ. Hist. Rev.*, 2nd ser. XXI (1968) 562–79.

Labour and industrial relations

3114. RIMLINGER, GASTON V. 'Die Legitimierung des Protestes: eine vergleichende Untersuchung der Bergarbeiterbewegung in England und Deutschland'. *In* Die soziale Frage, *ed.* W. Fischer *and* G. Bajor (Stuttgart: Koehler, 1967) pp. 284–304.

3115. MCCORD, NORMAN. The seaman's strike of 1815 in north east England. *Econ. Hist. Rev.*, 2nd ser. XXI (1968) 127–43.

3116. BARNSBY, GEORGE JOHN. The Dudley working class movement, 1832–60. Dudley, Worcs.: Dudley Pub. Lib. (Local Hist. & Archives Dept.), 1967. 48 pp.

3117. USHERWOOD, STEPHEN. The Tolpuddle Martyrs, 1834–7: a case of human rights. *History Today*, XVIII (1968) 14–21.

3118. CHALLINOR, RAYMOND, *and* RIPLEY, BRIAN. The Miners' Association: a trade union in the age of the Chartists. Lawrence & Wishart, 1968. 266 pp.

3119. ROWE, D. J. The London Working Men's Association and the 'People's Charter'. *Past & Present*, no. 36 (1967) 73–86.

3120. ROWE, D. J. Chartism and the Spitalfields silk weavers. *Econ. Hist. Rev.*, 2nd ser. XX (1967) 482–93.

3121. HORN, PAMELA. The New Society of Plush-Weavers. *Cake & Cockhorse*, III (1968) 199–202.

3122. HORN, P. The Banbury Weavers' Union of 1834. *Cake & Cockhorse*, III (1968) 203–6.

3123. WILLIAMS, J. ROOSE. Quarryman's champion: the life and activities of William John Parry of Coetmor, pt. 6. *Caernarvons. Hist. Soc. Trans.*, XXIX (1968) 73–120.

3124. DUNBABIN, JOHN P. D. The incidence and organization of agricultural trades unionism in the 1870's. *Agric. Hist. Rev.*, XVI (1968) 114–41.

3125. PORTER, JEFFREY H. Industrial peace in the cotton trade, 1875–1913. *Yorks. Bull. Econ. & Soc. Research*, XIX (1967) 49–61.

3126. PORTER, J. H. An experiment in industrial relations: the Leeds Boot and Shoe Conciliation Board, 1874–81. *Univ. Leeds Rev.*, XI (1968) 51–5.

3127. PORTER, J. H. The Northampton Arbitration Board and the shoe industry dispute of 1887. *Northants. Past & Present*, IV no. 3 (1968) 149–54.

3128. BEST, GEOFFREY FRANCIS ANDREW. Bishop Westcott and the miners. C.U.P., 1967. 40 pp. [1892 strike.]

3129. BAKER, J. A. C. Richard Juggins and Black Country unionism in the late 19th century. *Lichfield Archaeol. & Hist. Soc. Trans.*, IX (1968) 67–72.

3130. RENSHAW, PATRICK. The origins of the Trades Union Congress. *History Today*, XVIII (1968) 456–63.

Social history

3131. NEALE, R. S. Class and class-consciousness in early 19th century England: three classes or five? *Victorian Studies*, XII (1968–9) 5–32.

3132. BÉDARIDA, FRANÇOIS. Londres au milieu du 19e siècle; une analyse de structure sociale. *Annales*, XXIII (1968) 268–95.

3133. FIELDEN, KENNETH. Samuel Smiles and self-help. *Victorian Studies*, XII (1968–9) 155–76.

3134. MIDWINTER, ERIC CLARE. Victorian social reform. (Seminar Studies in History). Longmans, 1968. vii, 112 pp.

3135. SMITH, PAUL. Disraelian Conservatism and social reform. London: Routledge; Toronto: Toronto U.P., 1967. x, 358 pp., illus.

3136. AYDELOTTE, WILLIAM O. The conservative and radical interpretations of early Victorian social legislation. *Victorian Studies*, XI (1967–8) 225–36.

3137. FLINN, MICHAEL WALTER. Public health reform in Britain. Macmillan, 1968. 72 pp., illus.

3138. O'NEILL, JAMES E. The Victorian background to the British Welfare State. *South Atlantic Quart.*, LXVI (1967) 204–17.

3139. HARRISON, BRIAN. Temperance societies. *Local Historian*, VIII (1968) 135–8.

3140. HARRISON, B. Two roads to social

reform: Francis Place and the 'Drunken Committee' of 1834. *Hist. Jour.*, XI (1968) 272–300.

3141. DUFFY, A. E. P. The eight hours day movement in Britain, 1886–93. Pt. 1. *Manchester School Econ. & Soc. Studies*, XXXVI (1968) 203–22.

3142. RAVETZ, ALISON. The Victorian coal kitchen and its reformers. *Victorian Studies*, XI (1967–8) 435–60.

3143. DYOS, HAROLD JAMES. The slums of Victorian London. *Victorian Studies*, XI (1967–8) 5–40.

3144. DYOS, H. J. The speculative builders and developers of Victorian London. *Victorian Studies*, XI (1967–8) 641–90.

3145. VANCE, JAMES E., *Jnr*. Housing the worker: determinative and contingent ties in 19th century Birmingham. *Econ. Geog.*, XLIII (1967) 97–127.

3146. CARRIER, JOHN. The Four Per Cent Industrial Dwellings Co. Ltd.: the social composition of the shareholders of an east London dwellings company at the end of the 19th century. *East London Papers*, XI (1968) 40–6.

3147. TARN, JOHN NELSON. The Improved Industrial Dwellings Company. *London & Middlesex Archaeol. Soc. Trans.*, XXII pt. 1 (1968) 43–59.

3148. TARN, J. N. The housing problem a century ago. *Urban Studies*, V (1968) 290–300.

3149. VICTORIAN SOCIETY. The Victorian poor. The Society, 1967. 57 pp., illus.

3150. VAUGHAN, JOHN EDMUND. Nasty, brutish and short: the life of the Victorian urban poor. *Local Historian*, VIII (1968) 98–106.

3151. WOHL, ANTHONY S. *The bitter cry of outcast London. Internat. Rev. Soc. Hist.*, XIII (1968) 189–245. [Pamphlet, 1883.]

3152. HENRIQUES, URSULA R. Q. How cruel was the Victorian Poor Law? *Hist. Jour.*, XI (1968) 365–71.

3153. HENRIQUES, U. R. Q. Bastardy and the new Poor Law. *Past & Present*, no. 37 (1967) 103–29.

3154. RICHARDSON, STANLEY IVOR. A history of the Edmonton Poor Law Union, 1837–54. (Edmonton Hundred Historical Soc. Occas. Papers, n.s. 12). The Society, 1968. 87 pp.

3155. MOSS, M. S. The building of, and the subsequent running of, the Westbury-on-Trym workhouse, near Bristol. *Bristol & Glos. Archaeol. Soc. Trans.* for 1967, LXXXVI (1968) 151–72.

3156. WILSON, J. HERBERT. The workhouse master. *Ryedale Historian*, no. 3 (1967) 29–32. [John Wilson at Helmsley and York workhouses, 1849–79.]

3157. PURVES, GLADSTONE DOUGAL. Mudlarks and ragged schools: Lord Shaftesbury and the working children. H. A. Humphrey Ltd., 1968. 61 pp., illus.

3158. WARDLE, DAVID. Working class children in Nottingham, from the blue books, 1842–62. *Thoroton Soc. Trans.* for 1966, LXX (1967) 105–14.

3159. LAW, C. M. The growth of urban population in England and Wales, 1801–1911. *Inst. Brit. Geographers Trans.*, XLI (1967) 125–43.

3160. BANKS, J. A. Population change and the Victorian city. *Victorian Studies*, XI (1967–8) 277–89.

3161. BRANSON, WILLIAM H. Social legislation and the birth rate in 19th century Britain. *Western Econ. Jour.*, VI (1968) 134–44. [Reply by E. G. West, pp. 419–24.]

3162. LAWTON, R. Population changes in England and Wales in the later 19th century: an analysis of trends by registration districts. *Inst. Brit. Geographers Trans.*, XLIV (1968) 55–74.

3163. RICHARDSON, C. Irish settlement in mid-19th century Bradford. *Yorks. Bull. Econ. & Soc. Research*, XX (1968) 40–57.

3164. CURTIS, LEWIS PERRY, *Jnr*. Anglo-Saxons and Celts: a study of anti-Irish prejudice in Victorian England. Bridgeport, Conn.: Bridgeport Univ. Conference on British Studies, 1968. 162 pp.

3165. ROLLIN, A. R. Russo-Jewish immigrants in England before 1881. *Jewish Hist. Soc. Eng. Trans.* for 1962–7, XXI (1968) 202–13.

3166. REICH, JEROME. The slave trade at the Congress of Vienna: a study in English public opinion. *Jour. Negro Hist.*, LIII (1968) 129–43.

3167. RICE, C. DUNCAN. The anti-slavery mission of George Thompson to the United States, 1834–5. *Jour. Amer. Studies*, II (1968) 13–31.

3168. BROOK, MICHAEL. Confederate sympathies in north east Lancashire, 1862–4.

Lancs. & Cheshire Antiq. Soc. Trans. for 1965–6, LXXV–LXXVI (1968) 211–17.

3169. HARRISON, BRIAN. Underneath the Victorians. *Victorian Studies*, X (1966–7) 239–62. [Pornography.]

3170. JEREMY, DAVID J. The social decline of Bath. *History Today*, XVII (1967) 242–9.

3171. HULL, FELIX (*ed.*). A Kentish holiday, 1823. *Archaeologia Cantiana* for 1966, LXXXI (1967) 109–17.

3172. FORD, ALICE (*ed.*). The 1826 journal of John James Audubon. Norman, Okla.: Oklahoma U.P., 1967. xii, 409 pp. [Visited England.]

3173. GAL, ISTVAN. The British travel diary of Sándor Bölöni Farkas, 1831. *Hungarian Studies in English*, III (1967) 33–47.

3174. DEARDEN, JAMES S. John Ruskin's tour of the Lake District in 1837. *Connoisseur*, CLXVII (1968) 165–8.

3175. TAYLOR, WILLIAM COOKE. Notes of a tour in the manufacturing districts of Lancashire. 3rd edn. Cass, 1968. viii, 331 pp. [Previous edn. Duncan & Malcolm, 1842.]

3176. MASSEY, REGINALD, *and* MASSEY, JAMILA. Lutfullah in London. *History Today*, XVIII (1968) 473–9.

3177. HOWELL, ROGER. Prescott's visit to England, 1850. *History Today*, XVII (1967) 750–7.

3178. ESPINAL, VALENTÍN. Diario de un desterrado, *ed.* P. Grases. Caracas: Ed. del Cuatricentenario de Caracas, 1966. 393 pp., illus. [Visited England, 1861.]

3179. CREIGHTON, ELLEN R. C. (*ed.*). Ellen Buxton's journal, 1860–4. Bles, 1967. 96 pp.

3180. FRASER, MAXWELL. Lady Llanover and her circle. *Hon. Soc. Cymmrodorion Trans.* (1968) 170–96.

Agrarian history

3181. WARD, JOHN TOWERS. East Yorkshire landed estates in the 19th century. (East Yorks. Local Hist. ser., 23). York: East Yorks. Local Hist. Soc., 1967. 75 pp.

3182. ELLIOTT, STUART. The role of the open fields in the development of 19th century Stamford. *Lincs. Hist. & Archaeol.*, no. 3 (1968) 11–18.

3183. THOMPSON, FRANCIS MICHAEL LONGSTRETH. The second Agricultural Revolution, 1815–80. *Econ. Hist. Rev.*, 2nd ser. XXI (1968) 62–77.

3184. HUNT, E. H. Labour productivity in English agriculture, 1850–1914. *Econ. Hist. Rev.*, 2nd ser. XX (1967) 280–92.

3185. COLLINS, E. J. T., *and* JONES, ERIC LIONEL. Sectoral advance in English agriculture, 1850–80. *Agric. Hist. Rev.*, XV (1967) 65–81.

3186. STURGESS, R. W. The Agricultural Revolution on the English clays: a rejoinder. *Agric. Hist. Rev.*, XV (1967) 82–7.

3187. HORN, PAMELA. Nineteenth century Naseby farm workers. *Northants. Past & Present*, IV no. 3 (1968) 167–73.

Transport and communications

3188. MINNIS, S. E. The highways of Bourn and their surveyors in the early 19th century. Pt. 2. *Cambridgeshire Local Hist. Council Bull.*, XXIII (1968) 3–10.

3189. WILSON, PAUL N. Canal Head, Kendal. *Cumberland & Westmorland Antiq. & Archaeol. Soc. Trans.*, LXVIII (1968) 132–50.

3190. MUNRO, ALASDAIR. Tramway companies in Liverpool, 1859–97. *Hist. Soc. Lancs. & Cheshire Trans.* for 1967, CXIX (1968) 181–212.

3191. PUDNEY, JOHN SLEIGH. The golden age of steam. H. Hamilton, 1967. 189 pp., illus.

3192. SMULLEN, IVOR. Taken for a ride: a distressing account of the misfortunes and misbehaviour of the early British railway traveller. Jenkins, 1968. 192 pp., illus.

3193. LEWIN, HENRY GROTE. The railway mania and its aftermath, 1845–52. Rev. edn. Newton Abbot, Devon: David & Charles, 1968. xxii, 526 pp. [Originally pubd. Railway Gazette, 1936.]

3194. PEARSON, R. E. Railways in relation to resort development in east Lincolnshire. *East Midland Geographer*, IV pt. 5 (1968) 218–94.

3195. ALDCROFT, DEREK HOWARD. The efficiency and enterprise of British railways, 1870–1914. *Explorations in Entrepreneurial Hist.*, 2nd ser. V (1968) 158–74.

3196. PERRY, PETER. The Dorset ports and the coming of the railways. *Mariner's Mirror*, LIII (1967) 243–9.

3197. JOWITT, R. L. P. Early railway days in Hampshire. *Hants. Archaeol. & Local Hist. Newsletter*, I (1967) 70–4.

3198. WILLIAMS, RONALD ALFRED. The London and South Western Railway. Vol. 1, The formative years. Newton Abbot, Devon: David & Charles, 1968. 267 pp., illus.

3199. MAGGS, COLIN GORDON. The Midland and South Western Junction Railway. Newton Abbot, Devon: David & Charles, 1967. 160 pp., illus.

3200. TOMLINSON, WILLIAM WEAVER. North Eastern Railway: its rise and development. New edn. Newton Abbot, Devon: David & Charles, 1967. xx, 820 pp., illus. [Previous edn. Longmans, 1915.]

3201. JENSON, J. H., *and* ROSEGGER, GERHARD. British railway builders along the lower Danube, 1856–69. *Slavonic & E. European Rev.*, XLVI (1968) 105–28.

3202. LOWE, ROBSON. The British postage stamp: being the history of 19th century postage stamps. Nat. Postal Museum, 1968. viii, 272 pp., illus.

3203. BLAIR, C. N. M. The mails to and from India, 1837–80. *Postal Hist.*, no. 154 (1968) 33–5.

RELIGIOUS HISTORY

General and Anglicanism

3204. HARRISON, BRIAN. Religion and recreation in 19th century England. *Past & Present*, no. 38 (1967) 98–125.

3205. WALKER, R. B. Religious changes in Liverpool in the 19th century. *Jour. Eccles. Hist.*, XIX (1968) 195–211.

3206. FLINDALL, R. P. Anglican and Roman attitudes, 1825–75. *Church Quart. Rev.*, CLXIX (1968) 206–15.

3207. BOWEN, DESMOND. The idea of the Victorian Church: a study of the Church of England, 1833–89. Montreal: McGill U.P., 1968. xiii, 421 pp.

3208. ANSON, PETER F. Confusion and lawlessness. *Church Quart. Rev.*, CLXIX (1968) 178–91.

3209. HERKLOTS, HUGH GERARD GIBSON. The origins of the Lambeth Quadrilateral. *Church Quart. Rev.*, CLXIX (1968) 61–8.

3210. HOPPEN, K. THEODORE. The Oxford Movement. *History Today*, XVII (1967) 145–52.

3211. CLEGG, HERBERT. Evangelicals and Tractarians, pt. 8: leaders of the Oxford Movement. *Hist. Mag. Protestant Episcopal Church*, XXXVI (1967) 127–78.

3212. BARMANN, LAWRENCE F. The liturgical dimension of the Oxford tracts, 1833–41. *Jour. Brit. Studies*, VII no. 2 (1968) 92–113.

3213. ALLEN, LOUIS. Tract 90 and Durham University. *N. & Q.*, CCXII (1967) 43–7.

3214. KENT, JOHN. The Victorian resistance: comments on religious life and culture, 1840–80. *Victorian Studies*, XII (1968–9) 145–54.

3215. MEACHAM, STANDISH. The Church in the Victorian city. *Victorian Studies*, XI (1967–8) 359–78.

3216. FLINDALL, R. P. The parish priest in Victorian England. *Church Quart. Rev.*, CLXVIII (1967) 296–306.

3217. CLOGG, RICHARD. The publication and distribution of Karamanli texts by the British and Foreign Bible Society before 1850. *Jour. Eccles. Hist.*, XIX (1968) 57–81, 171–93.

3218. THOMSON, DAVID M. The 1851 religious census: problems and possibilities. *Victorian Studies*, XI (1967–8) 87–97.

3219. PICKERING, W. S. F. The 1851 religious census: a useless experiment? *Brit. Jour. Sociol.*, XVIII no. 4 (1967) 382–407.

3220. JONES, PETER D'A. The Christian Socialist revival, 1877–1914: religion, class, and social conscience in late Victorian England. Princeton, N.J.: Princeton U.P., 1968. xiii, 504 pp.

3221. ALLEN, PETER R. F. D. Maurice and J. M. Ludlow: a reassessment of the leaders of Christian Socialism. *Victorian Studies*, XI (1967–8) 461–82.

3222. STEPHENSON, ALAN M. G. Archbishop Vernon Harcourt. *Studies in Church Hist.*, IV (1967) 143–54.

3223. GLOVER, MICHAEL. 'An excellent young man': the Rev. Samuel Briscall, 1788–1848. *History Today*, XVIII (1968) 578–84.

3224. BURY, J. P. T. (*ed.*). Cambridge diary, 1832–42: selected passages from the diary of the Rev. Joseph Romilly. C.U.P., 1967. xv, 260 pp., illus.

3225. SCHWARTZ, MARC L. The paradox of commitment: John Keble and the establishment, 1833–50. *Hist. Mag. Protestant Episcopal Church*, XXXVII (1968) 299–310.

3226. DICKINS, BRUCE. Green and black:

Joseph Dornford, 1794–1868. *Church Quart. Rev.*, CLXVIII (1967) 480–9.

3227. COOMBS, JOYCE. William Henry Whitworth, Victorian minister, 1834–85. *Church Quart. Rev.*, CLXVIII (1967) 190–203.

3228. WEATHERBY, J. L. The encircling gloom: Newman's departure from the Caroline tradition. *Victorian Studies*, XII (1968–9) 57–82.

3229. PINNINGTON, JOHN E. Bishop Phillpotts and the Rubrics. *Church Quart. Rev.*, CLXIX (1968) 167–78.

3230. PINNINGTON, J. E. Bishop Blomfield and St. Barnabas's, Pimlico: the limits of ecclesiastical authority. *Church Quart. Rev.*, CLXVIII (1967) 289–96.

3231. KNOX, B. A. Filling the Oxford Chair of Ecclesiastical History, 1866: the nomination of H. L. Mansel. *Jour. Religious Hist.*, V (1968) 62–70.

3232. HOPKINSON, D. M. Parson Hawker of Morwenstow. *History Today*, XVIII (1968) 38–44.

3233. NEAVE, DAVID. Letters of Edward Steere. *Lincs. Hist. & Archaeol.*, no. 2 (1967) 63–72.

3234. TRINDER, BARRIE S. The memoir of William Smith. *Shropshire Archaeol. Soc. Trans.* for 1966, LVIII pt. 2 (1968) 178–85.

Roman Catholicism

3235. NORMAN, EDWARD ROBERT. Anti-Catholicism in Victorian England. (Historical Problems: Studies and Documents, 1). Allen & Unwin, 1968. 240 pp.

3236. DESPREAUX, GILLES-VINCENT. 'To the humane and affluent inhabitants of Paisley'. *Innes Rev.*, XVIII (1967) 67–70. [Appeal for funds to establish Catholic school, 1816.]

3237. DESSAIN, CHARLES STEPHEN (*ed.*). The letters and diaries of John Henry Newman. Vol. 17, Opposition in Dublin and London, Oct. 1855 to March 1857. Nelson, 1967. xvii, 602 pp.

3238. HOLMES, J. DEREK. Cardinal Newman and the Affirmation Bill. *Hist. Mag. Protestant Episcopal Church*, XXXVI (1967) 87–97.

3239. MCELRATH, DAMIAN. Richard Simpson and John Henry Newman: the *Rambler*, laymen, and theology. *Catholic Hist. Rev.*, LII no. 4 (1967) 509–33.

3240. WALGRAVE, J. H. La théorie newmanienne du développement dogmatique et la théologie libérale. *Asprenas*, n.s. XV (1968) 255–79.

3241. PAPA, EGIDIO. Il Sillabo di Pio IX e la stampa francese, inglese e italiana. (Collani di Stor. del Movimento Cattolico, 25). Rome: Cinque Lune, 1968. 474 pp.

3242. NOACK, ULRICH. Liberale Ideen auf dem ersten Vatikanischen Konzil: Lord Acton in Rom, 1869–70. *Hist. Zeit.*, CCV (1967) 81–100.

3243. LESLIE, SHANE. Virginia Crawford, Sir Charles Dilke, and Cardinal Manning. *Dublin Rev.*, CCXLI (1967) 177–205.

Protestant Nonconformity

3244. SALTER, FRANK REYNER. Dissenters and public affairs in mid-Victorian England. Dr. Williams's Trust, 1967. 24 pp.

3245. RUSLING, G. W. The Nonconformist conscience. *Baptist Quart.*, XXII no. 3 (1967) 126–42.

3246. RUSTON, ALAN. Radical Nonconformity in Hackney, 1805–45. *Unitarian Hist. Soc. Trans.*, XIV no. 1 (1967) 1–9.

3247. RAM, R. W. Dissent in urban Yorkshire, 1800–50. *Baptist Quart.*, XXII no. 1 (1967) 3–22.

3248. KAUFMAN, PAUL. Zion's Temple, Manchester: an introduction to libraries of dissent. *Bibliog. Soc. America Papers*, LXII (1968) 337–49.

3249. BINFIELD, CLYDE. The thread of disruption: some 19th century churches in eastern England. *Congregational Hist. Soc. Trans.*, XX (1967) 156–65.

3250. BINFIELD, C. Chapels in crisis: men and issues in Victorian eastern England. *Congregational Hist. Soc. Trans.*, XX (1968) 237–54.

3251. PROSSER, G. P. R. Formation of the General Baptist Missionary Society. *Baptist Quart.*, XXII no. 1 (1967) 23–9.

3252. WHITNEY, J. T. Southend Baptists: a study of origins, 1875–85. *Baptist Quart.*, XXII no. 8 (1968) 447–63.

3253. BACON, ERNEST WALLACE. Spurgeon: heir of the Puritans. Allen & Unwin, 1967. 184 pp.

3254. PAYNE, ERNEST ALEXANDER. The diaries of Joseph Ash. *Baptist Quart.*, XXII no. 7 (1968) 352–9.

3255. BOWMER, JOHN C. Daniel Isaac and Jabez Bunting. *Wesley Hist. Soc. Proc.*, XXXVI (1967–8) 2–6.

3256. EDWARDS, MICHAEL S. The resignation of Joseph Rayner Stephens. *Wesley Hist. Soc. Proc.*, XXXVI (1967–8) 16–21.

3257. HARRIS, THOMAS ROBERTS. Dr. George Smith, 1800–68. (Cornish Methodist Hist. Assoc. Occas. Papers, 13). Redruth, Cornwall: the Association, 1968. 27 pp.

3258. GOWLAND, DAVID A. Political opinion in Manchester Wesleyanism, 1832–57. *Wesley Hist. Soc. Proc.*, XXXVI (1967–8) 93–104.

3259. JONES, BERNARD E. Society and church in Wesleyan Methodism, 1878–93. *Wesley Hist. Soc. Proc.*, XXXVI (1967–8) 134–8.

3260. ROTT, LUDWIG. Die englischen Beziehungen der Erweckungsbewegung und die Anfänge des Wesleyanischen Methodismus in Deutschland. Frankfurt-am-Main: Studiengemeinschaft für Geschichte der Methodismus, 1968. viii, 301 pp.

3261. PINNINGTON, JOHN E. The origins of the Free Church of England. *Church Quart.Rev.*, CLXIX (1968) 54–60.

3262. NICHOLSON, FRED J. One of nature's Quakers: William Wordsworth and his Quaker sympathies. *Friends' Quart.*, XVI no. 3 (1968) 138–44.

3263. MARWICK, WILLIAM HUTTON. Carlyle and Quakerism. *Friends' Quart.*, XVI no. 1 (1968) 37–45.

3264. ROWDON, HAROLD HAMLYN. The origins of the Brethren, 1825–50. Pickering & Inglis, 1967. xii, 323 pp.

3265. BILLINGTON, LOUIS. The Millerite Adventists in Great Britain, 1840–50. *Jour. Amer. Studies*, I (1967) 191–212.

3266. WILSON, J. British Israelism. *Sociol. Rev.*, n.s. XVI (1968) 41–57.

Judaism

3267. GOULSTON, MICHAEL. The status of the Anglo-Jewish rabbinate, 1840–1914. *Jewish Jour. Sociol.*, X (1968) 55–82.

3268. COHEN, NORMAN. Non-religious factors in the emergence of the Chief Rabbinate. *Jewish Hist. Soc. Eng. Trans.* for 1962–7, XXI (1968) 304–13.

3269. BARNETT, RICHARD D. Haham Meldola and Hazan de Sola. *Jewish Hist. Soc. Eng. Trans.* for 1962–7, XXI (1968) 1–38.

3270. ABRAHAMS, PHYLLIS. Abraham Sussman: from Berdichew to Bevis Marks. *Jewish Hist. Soc. Eng. Trans.* for 1962–7, XXI (1968) 243–60.

CULTURAL HISTORY

General

3271. HIMMELFARB, GERTRUDE. Victorian minds. Weidenfeld, 1968. xiii, 397 pp. [Originally pubd. New York: Knopf, 1968.]

3272. AMES, WINSLOW. Prince Albert and Victorian taste. Chapman & Hall, 1968. xvii, 238 pp., illus.

3273. AMES, W. Prince Albert's taste. *History Today*, XVIII (1968) 22–9.

3274. ST. CLAIR, WILLIAM LINN. Lord Elgin and the marbles. O.U.P., 1967. x, 309 pp., illus.

3275. MARANDON, S. L'image de la France dans l'Angleterre victorienne. Paris: A. Colin, 1967. 712 pp.

3276. HASSENFORDER, JEAN. Développement comparé des bibliothèques publiques en France, en Grande-Bretagne et aux Etats-Unis dans la seconde moitié du 19e siècle. Paris: Cercle de la Librairie, 1967. 211 pp.

3277. VOGELER, MARTHA SALMON. The Victorians and the hundred best. *Texas Quart.*, XI no. 1 (1968) 184–98. [Choice of books.]

3278. PAKENHAM, ELIZABETH, *countess of Longford.* The duke of Wellington's books. *History Today*, XVII (1967) 22–8.

3279. NEUDOERFFER, NORMA C. The function of a 19th century catalogue belonging to the Cambridge Philosophical Library. *Cambridge Bibliog. Soc. Trans.*, IV no. 4 (1967) 293–301.

3280. KAUFMAN, PAUL. New light from parochial libraries: the loan records of St. George's, Doncaster. *Libri*, XVII (1967) 225–32.

3281. ENGLISH, J. S. Books and libraries in Gainsborough: a short study with reference to the 19th century. *Lib. Assoc. Record*, LXX (1968) 62–5.

3282. FAWCETT, TREVOR. The founding of the Norfolk and Norwich Literary Institution. *Library Hist.*, I (1967) 46–53.

3283. PARSONS, COLEMAN O. 'Pilgrims of research' in the British Museum, 1820–6. *Quart. Rev.*, CCCV (1967) 54–66.

3284. KAUFMAN, PAUL. Rawdon Brown and his adventures in Venetian archives. *English Misc.*, XVIII (1967) 283–302.

3285. MORGAN, PAUL. George Harris of Rugby and the pre-history of the Historical Manuscripts Commission. *Birmingham Archaeol. Soc. Trans.* for 1965, LXXXII (1967) 28–37.

3286. LOEWE, RAPHAEL. Solomon Marcus Schiller-Szinessy, 1820–90: first reader in Talmudic and Rabbinic literature at Cambridge. *Jewish Hist. Soc. Eng. Trans.* for 1962–7, XXI (1968) 148–89.

3287. JOHN, BRIAN. Thomas Arnold as educator of the liberal conscience. *Jour. General Educ.*, XIX (1967) 132–40.

3288. EISEN, SYDNEY. Frederic Harrison and Herbert Spencer: embattled unbelievers. *Victorian Studies*, XII (1968–9) 33–56.

3289. EISEN, S. Herbert Spencer and the spectre of Comte. *Jour. Brit. Studies*, VII no. 1 (1967) 48–67.

3290. FARMER, MARY E. The positivist movement and the development of English sociology. *Sociol. Rev.*, n.s. XV (1967) 5–20.

3291. D'AMICO, MASOLINO. Oscar Wilde between 'Socialism' and aestheticism. *English Misc.*, XVIII (1967) 111–39.

3292. ANDREWS, JAMES R. The rationale of 19th century pacifism: religious and political arguments in the early British peace movement. *Quaker Hist.*, LVII (1968) 17–27.

3293. TUTTLE, WILLIAM M. Forerunners of Frederick Jackson Turner: 19th century British Conservatives and the frontier thesis. *Agric. Hist.*, XLI (1967) 219–27.

3294. JONES, IVA G. Trollope, Carlyle, and Mill on the negro: an episode in the history of ideas. *Jour. Negro Hist.*, LII (1967) 185–99.

Education

3295. HARRISON, JOHN F. C. 'The steam engine of the new moral world': Owenism and education, 1817–29. *Jour. Brit. Studies*, VI no. 2 (1967) 76–98.

3296. CUMMING, IAN. Wordsworth speaks on education. *Paedagogica Historica*, VIII (1968) 319–34.

3297. STURT, MARY. The education of the people: a history of primary education in England and Wales in the 19th century. Routledge, 1967. xii, 432 pp., illus.

3298. SELLMAN, ROGER RAYMOND. Devon village schools in the 19th century. Newton Abbot, Devon: David & Charles, 1968. 171 pp., illus.

3299. ROSS, ALEXANDER M. Kay-Shuttleworth and the training of teachers for pauper schools. *Brit. Jour. Educ. Studies*, XV (1967) 275–83.

3300. PALLISTER, RAY. Workhouse education in County Durham: 1834–70. *Brit. Jour. Educ. Studies*, XVI (1968) 279–91.

3301. PALLISTER, R. Educational investment by industrialists in the early part of the 19th century in County Durham. *Durham Univ. Jour.*, XXX no. 1 (1968) 32–8.

3302. GRANT, A. CAMERON. A note on 'secular' education in the 19th century. *Brit. Jour. Educ. Studies*, XVI (1968) 308–17.

3303. JONES, D. K. Lancashire, the American Common School, and the religious problem in British education in the 19th century. *Brit Jour. Educ. Studies*, XV (1967) 292–306.

3304. DOCKING, JAMES WOODROW. Victorian schools and scholars: Church of England elementary schools in 19th century Coventry. Kenilworth, Warwicks.: Historical Assoc. (Coventry Branch), 1967. 30 pp.

3305. MURPHY, JAMES. The rise of public elementary education in Liverpool. Pt. 2, 1819–35. *Hist. Soc. Lancs. & Cheshire Trans.* for 1966, LXVIII (1967) 105–38.

3306. RUSSELL, REX CHARLES. A history of schools and education in Lindsey, Lincolnshire, 1800–1902. Pt. 4. Lincoln: Lindsey C.C. Education Committee, 1967. 83 pp.

3307. Some aspects of education in Jersey one hundred years ago. *Soc. Jersiaise Bull. Annuel*, XIX pt. 4 (1968) 346–56.

3308. BALLS, F. E. The Endowed Schools Act, 1869, and the development of the English grammar schools in the 19th century. *Durham Research Rev.*, no. 19 (1967) 207–18, no. 20 (1968) 219–29.

3309. HARWOOD, H. W. Wanley Grammar School. *Halifax Antiq. Soc. Trans.* (1967) 1–11.

3310. EVANS, LESLIE WYNNE. School boards and the works schools system after the Education Act of 1870. *Nat. Lib. Wales Jour.*, XV (1967–8) 89–100.

3311. EVERETT, B. G. The Tynemouth

School Board and the Elementary Education Amendment Act of 1873. *Durham Research Rev.*, no. 19 (1967) 193–6.

3312. PUGH, D. R. The 1902 Education Act: the search for a compromise. *Brit. Jour. Educ. Studies*, XVI (1968) 164–78.

3313. HOLWELL, E. W. The teaching of history in public and endowed schools in the middle of the 19th century. *Durham Research Rev.*, no. 19 (1967) 179–88.

3314. TRACEY, G. W. The origin and growth of scientific instruction in science classes under the Science and Art Department, 1859–70. *Durham Research Rev.*, no. 21 (1968) 305–8.

3315. SEABORNE, MALCOLM, *and* ISHAM, *Sir* GYLES. A Victorian schoolmaster: John James Graves (1832–1903). Pt. 2. *Northants. Past & Present*, IV no. 2 (1967) 107–19. [Contd. from vol. IV no. 1 (1966).]

3316. LEA, JOHN THOMAS. The history and development of the Mechanics' Institutions. (Research in Librarianship, 2). Oldham, Lancs.: Research in Librarianship, 1968. 16 pp.

3317. ASHBY, *Sir* ERIC. Die Zukunft der Universitätsidee des 19. Jahrhunderts in Grossbritannien und in Deutschland. Berlin: Colloquium-V., 1967. 28 pp.

3318. ROTHBLATT, SHELDON. The revolution of the dons: Cambridge and society in Victorian England. Faber, 1968. 319 pp.

3319. COATS, ALFRED W. Alfred Marshall and the early development of the London School of Economics: some unpublished letters. *Economica*, n.s. XXXIV (1967) 408–17.

Literature, drama and music

3320. CHAPMAN, RAYMOND. The Victorian debate: English literature and society, 1832–1909. Weidenfeld, 1968. 377 pp.

3321. BUXTON, JOHN. Byron and Shelley: the history of a friendship. Macmillan, 1968. xii, 289 pp., illus.

3322. RICHARDSON, JOANNA. Creevey and Greville. (Writers and their work, 200). Longmans, for British Council and Nat. Book League, 1967. 36 pp.

3323. PARSONS, COLEMAN O. Scott's sixpenny public. *Columbia Lib. Columns*, XVI (1967) 13–21.

3324. BRIGHTFIELD, MYRON F. Victorian England in its novels. Los Angeles, Calif.: California U.P., 1968. 4 vols.

3325. NOWELL-SMITH, SIMON. The 'cheap edition' of Dickens's works (first series), 1847–52. *Library*, 5th ser. XXII (1967) 245–51.

3326. LEVINE, GEORGE. The boundaries of fiction: Carlyle, Macaulay, Newman. Princeton, N.J.: Princeton U.P., 1968. 278 pp.

3327. CLARKE, I. F. Forecasts of warfare in fiction 1803–1914. *Comparative Studies in Society & Hist.*, X (1967–8) 1–25.

3328. SHERRY, NORMAN. The Greenwich bomb outrage and *The Secret Agent*. *Rev. Eng. Studies*, n.s. XVIII (1967) 412–28. [By Conrad.]

3329. JORDAN, GERALD H. S. Popular literature and imperial sentiment: changing attitudes, 1870–90. *Canadian Hist. Assoc. Rept.* (1967) 149–55.

3330. FRASER, DEREK. The press in Leicester, *c.* 1790–1850. *Leics. Archaeol. Soc. Trans.* for 1966–7, XLII (1968) 53–75.

3331. O'BOYLE, LENORE. The image of the journalist in France, Germany and England, 1815–48. *Comparative Studies in Soc. & Hist.*, X (1968) 290–317.

3332. SHAFTESLEY, JOHN M. Dr. Abraham Benesch as newspaper editor. *Jewish Hist. Soc. Eng. Trans.* for 1962–7, XXI (1968) 214–31.

3333. LLORENS, VICENTE. 'El fracaso de *The London Review* en 1829'. *In* Liber Amicorum: Salvador de Madariaga (Bruges: De Tempel, 1966) pp. 253–61.

3334. MURRAY, BRIAN M. The authorship of some unidentified or disputed articles in *Blackwood's Magazine*. *Studies in Scot. Lit.*, IV (1966–7) 144–54.

3335. BOOTH, MICHAEL R. Queen Victoria and the theatre. *Univ. Toronto Quart.*, XXXVI no. 3 (1967) 249–58.

3336. TREWIN, JOHN COURTENAY (*ed.*). The journal of William Charles Macready, 1832–52. Longmans, 1967. xxxiii, 315 pp., illus.

3337. BOXELL, PAUL J. P. T. Barnum's lectures for Londoners. *Quart. Jour. Speech*, LIV (1968) 140–6.

3338. RAINBOW, BERNARR. The land without music: musical education in England 1800–60, and its continental antecedents. Novello, 1967. 208 pp., illus.

Architecture

3339. WATKIN, DAVID. Thomas Hope, 1769–1831 and the neo-classical idea. Murray, 1968. xxi, 316 pp., illus.

3340. CRALLAN, HUGH. Beckford in Bath. *Archit. Rev.*, CXLIII (1968) 204–8.

3341. GEMMETT, ROBERT J. The critical reception of William Beckford's Fonthill. *English Misc.*, XIX (1968) 133–51.

3342. PORT, M. H. (*ed.*). An architect's progress in the 1850s and '60s: the autobiography of Thomas Wayland Fletcher. *East London Papers*, XI (1968) 20–39.

3343. TAYLOR, JEREMY. Charles Fowler (1792–1867): a centenary memoir. *Archit. Hist.*, XI (1968) 57–74.

3344. CROOK, J. MORDAUNT. Sir Robert Smirke: a pioneer of concrete construction. *Newcomen Soc. Trans.* for 1965–6, XXXVIII (1968) 5–22.

3345. HOWELL, PETER. Victorian churches. Feltham, Middx.: Country Life Books, 1968. 64 pp., illus.

3346. GLYNNE, *Sir* STEPHEN. Sir Stephen Glynne's notes on churches. *Sussex N. & Q.*, XVI no. 10 (1967) 339–49, XVII no. 2 (1968) 41–5.

3347. COOPER, NICHOLAS. Four Banburyshire churches. *Cake & Cockhorse*, III (1967) 151–60. [Barford St. John, Oxon.; Edgcot, Northants.; Tysoe, Warwicks.; Warmington, Warwicks.]

3348. WOOD, E. A. Three Georgian houses: the rebuilding of Thorpe Hall, Thorpe Vicarage and Kirby Vicarage, 1822–8. *Essex Archaeol. Soc. Trans.*, 3rd ser. II pt. 2 (1968) 123–36.

3349. STEVENSON, G. S. Portland Row, Kirkby-in-Ashfield. *Thoroton Soc. Trans.* for 1966, LXX (1967) 63–70.

3350. TAYLOR, NICHOLAS. Monuments of commerce. Feltham, Middx.: Country Life Books, 1968. 64 pp., illus. [Business premises, 1800–75.]

3351. JENKINS, FRANK. John Foulston and his public buildings in Plymouth, Stonehouse and Devonport. *Jour. Soc. Archit. Hist.*, XXVII (1968) 124–35.

3352. COWIE, LEONARD W. Exeter Hall. *History Today*, XVIII (1968) 390–7. [London, 1831–1907.]

3353. PORT, M. H. The new Law Courts competition, 1866–7. *Archit. Hist.*, XI (1968) 75–93.

3354. KEELING, DENIS F. British public library buildings, 1850–70. *Library Hist.*, I (1968) 100–26.

3355. TAYLOR, NICHOLAS. A duke's library. *Archit. Rev.*, CXLII (1967) 287–91. [At Arundel Castle.]

3356. LLOYD, DAVID, *and* INSALL, DONALD. Railway station architecture. *Industrial Archaeol.*, IV (1967) 185–225, 293–310.

3357. SIMMONS, JACK. St. Pancras station. Allen & Unwin, 1968. 120 pp., illus.

3358. COSSEY, F. Cast-iron railway bridge at Peterborough. *Industrial Archaeol.*, IV (1967) 138–47.

3359. PACEY, A. J. Technical innovation in some late 19th century railway warehouses. *Industrial Archaeol.*, V (1968) 364–72.

3360. CURL, JAMES. Highgate: a great Victorian cemetery. *R.I.B.A. Jour.*, LXXV (1968) 179–83.

3361. TRINDER, BARRIE S. The re-building of Banbury cross. *Cake & Cockhorse*, III (1967) 192–6.

Arts and crafts

3362. ASLIN, ELIZABETH. The rise and progress of the Art Union of London. *Apollo*, LXXXV (1967) 12–16.

3363. BELL, QUENTIN. Victorian artists. Routledge, 1967. xiv, 111 pp., illus.

3364. ISHAM, *Sir* GYLES. Francis William Wilkin, *c.* 1791–1842. *Connoisseur*, CLXVII (1968) 144–51.

3365. ORMOND, RICHARD. George Chinnery's image of himself. *Connoisseur*, CLXVII (1968) 89–93, 160–4.

3365a. ORMOND, R. John Partridge and the Fine Arts Commissioners. *Burlington Mag.*, CIX (1967) 397–402.

3366. GAGE, JOHN. Turner's academic friendships: C. L. Eastlake. *Burlington Mag.*, CX (1968) 677–85.

3367. WHALLEY, J. IRENE. Illustrations for Isaac Watt's *Divine and Moral Songs*. *Victoria & Albert Museum Bull.*, IV (1968) 149–57. [1780–1866.]

3368. HUNT, JOHN DIXON. The Pre-Raphaelite imagination, 1848–1900. Routledge, 1968. xv, 262 pp., illus.

3369. FLEMING, GORDON HOWARD. Rossetti and the Pre-Raphaelite Brotherhood. Hart-Davies, 1967. xv, 233 pp., illus.

3370. SMITH, JACK. William Morris and his theory of art: its bases and its meaning. *Southern Quart.*, VII no. 1 (1968) 59–71.

3371. MUNDAY, JOHN. E. W. Cooke, marine painter. *Mariner's Mirror*, LIII (1967) 99–113.

3372. HOFER, PHILIP. Edward Lear, one of the ablest topographical draughtsmen of his day. *Connoisseur*, CLXIV (1967) 31–5.

3373. LAMBOURNE, LIONEL. Abraham Solomon, painter of fashion, and Simeon Solomon, decadent artist. *Jewish Hist. Soc. Eng. Trans.* for 1962–7, XXI (1968) 274–86.

3374. FILDES, LUKE VAL. Luke Fildes, R.A.: a Victorian painter. Joseph, 1968. xiv, 241 pp., illus.

3375. TAYLOR, NICHOLAS, *and* SYMONDSON, ANTHONY. Burges and Morris at Bingley: a discovery. *Archit. Rev.*, CXLIV (1968) 34–8.

3376. JERVIS, SIMON. Victorian furniture. Ward Lock, 1968. 96 pp., illus.

3377. BOYNTON, LINDSAY OLIVER JOHN. High Victorian furniture: the example of Marsh and Jones of Leeds. *Furniture Hist.*, III (1967) 54–91.

3378. ASLIN, ELIZABETH. The furniture designs of E. W. Godwin. *Victoria & Albert Museum Bull.*, III (1967) 145–54.

3379. GOODMAN, JOCELYNE BATY (*ed.*). Victorian cabinet maker: the memoirs of James Hopkinson, 1819–94. Routledge, 1968. xiii, 138 pp., illus.

3380. JAGGER, CEDRIC. Paul Philip Barraud: a study of a fine chronometer maker. Antiquarian Horological Soc., 1968. x, 177 pp., illus.

3381. BURY, SHIRLEY. In search of Pugin's church plate. *Connoisseur*, CLXV (1967) 29–35.

SCIENCE

3382. BROCK, WILLIAM H. The London Chemical Society, 1824. *Ambix*, XIV (1967) 133–9.

3383. REINGOLD, NATHAN. Babbage and Moll on the state of science in Great Britain: a note on a document. *Brit. Jour. Hist. Science*, IV pt. 1 (1968) 58–64.

3384. LAYTON, DAVID. Lord Wrottesley, F.R.S., pioneer statesman of science. *Roy. Soc. Notes & Records*, XXIII (1968) 230–46.

3385. KNIGHT, DAVID MARCUS. Atoms and elements: a study of theories of matter in England in the 19th century. Hutchinson, 1967. 167 pp.

3386. DAUB, EDWARD E. Atomism and thermodynamics. *Isis*, LVIII (1967) 293–303.

3387. WILLIAMS, L. PEARCE. Michael Faraday and the ether: a study in heresy. *Roy. Inst. Great Britain Proc.*, XLI pt. 6 (1967) 666–80.

3388. BROCK, WILLIAM H. William Bollaert, Faraday and the Royal Institution. *Roy. Inst. Great Britain Proc.*, XLII pt. 2 (1968) 75–86.

3389. LEVERE, T. H. Faraday, matter and natural theology: reflections on an unpublished manuscript. *Brit. Jour. Hist. Science*, IV pt. 2 (1968) 95–107.

3390. STALLYBRASS, OLIVER. How Faraday 'produced living animalculae': Andrew Crosse and the story of a myth. *Roy. Inst. Great Britain Proc.*, XLI pt. 5 (1967) 597–619.

3391. GILL, ARTHUR T. Faraday and photography. *Roy. Inst. Great Britain Proc.*, XLII pt. 1 (1968) 54–67.

3392. MILLIGAN, H. 1852–6: significant years in the history of photography in Manchester. *Industrial Archaeol.*, V (1968) 340–63.

3393. BORK, ALFRED M. Maxwell and the vector potential. *Isis*, LVIII (1967) 210–22.

3394. EYLES, JOAN M. William Smith: the sale of his geological collection to the British Museum. *Annals of Science*, XXIII (1967) 175–212.

3395. FARRAR, W. V. Thomas Allan, mineralogist: an autobiographical fragment. *Annals of Science*, XXIV (1968) 115–20.

3396. EDWARDS, W. N. The early history of palaeontology. British Museum (Nat. Hist), 1967. viii, 58 pp., illus.

3397. WALKER, HILDA H., *and* SUTCLIFFE, ANTHONY J. James Lyon Widger, 1823–92, and the Torbryan caves. *Devon Assoc. Repts. & Trans.*, XCIX (1967) 49–110.

3398. PARSONS, LAURENCE MICHAEL HARVEY, *6th earl of Rosse.* William Parsons, third earl of Rosse. *Hermathena*, CVII (1968) 5–13.

3399. RANDALL, H. A. Some mid-Gloucestershire engineers and inventors. *Newcomen Soc. Trans.* for 1965–6, XXXVIII (1968) 89–96.

3400. EGERTON, M. C. William Strutt and the application of convection to the heating of buildings. *Annals of Science*, XXIV (1968) 73–87.

3401. GREGOR, ARTHUR STEPHEN. Charles Darwin. Angus & Robertson, 1967. 189 pp., illus. [Originally pubd. New York: Dutton, 1966.]

3402. OLBY, ROBERT CECIL. Charles Darwin. O.U.P., 1967. 64 pp., illus.

3403. BARLOW, NORA (*ed.*). Darwin and Henslow: the growth of an idea. Letters, 1831–60. Murray, 1967. xii, 251 pp., illus.

3404. FREEMAN, RICHARD BROKE. *On the origin of species*, 1859. *Book Collector*, XVI (1967) 340–4.

3405. SWISHER, CHARLES N. Charles Darwin on the origin of behaviour. *Bull. Hist. Medicine*, XLI (1967) 24–43.

3406. DE BEER, *Sir* GAVIN (*ed.*). The Darwin letters at Shrewsbury School. *Roy. Soc. Notes & Records*, XXIII (1968) 68–85.

3407. VORZIMMER, PETER J. Darwin and Mendel: the historical connection. *Isis*, LIX (1968) 77–82.

3408. HULL, DAVID L. The metaphysics of evolution. *Brit. Jour. Hist. Science*, III (1967) 309–37.

3409. DAVIES, GORDON L. The tour of the British Isles made by Louis Agassiz in 1840. *Annals of Science*, XXIV (1968) 131–46.

3410. GARDENER, WILLIAM. Six cinchona trees. *History Today*, XVII (1967) 52–7.

MEDICINE

3411. GIBSON, WILLIAM CARLETON. The scientific contribution of medical undergraduates in London. *Medical Hist.*, XII (1968) 359–70.

3412. YOUNG, ROBERT M. The functions of the brain: Gall to Ferrier, 1808–86. *Isis*, LIX (1968) 251–68.

3413. LIPSCHUTZ, DANIEL E. The water question in London, 1827–31. *Bull. Hist. Medicine*, XLII (1968) 510–26.

3414. ROSS, DALE L. Leicester and the anti-vaccination movement, 1853–89. *Leics. Archaeol. Soc. Trans.* for 1967–8, XLIII (1968) 35–44.

3415. MACLEOD, ROY M. The edge of hope: social policy and chronic alcoholism, 1870–1900. *Jour. Hist. Medicine & Allied Sciences*, XXII (1967) 215–45.

3416. MACLEOD, R. M. The frustration of state medicine, 1880–99. *Medical Hist.*, XI (1967) 15–40.

3417. COLEY, N. G. Alexander Marcet (1770–1822), physician and animal chemist. *Medical Hist.*, XII (1968) 394–402.

3418. ROMAGNOLI, GIOVANNI. Un grande chirurgo inglese: Sir Astley Cooper. *Pagine Stor. Medicina*, XII (1968) 61–71.

3419. THORNTON, JOHN L. Charles Hunnings Wilkinson (1763 or 64–1850). *Annals of Science*, XXIII (1967) 272–86.

3420. CROSSE, VICTORIA MARY. A surgeon in the early 19th century: the life and times of John Green Crosse, 1790–1850. Edinburgh, London: Livingstone, 1968. xii, 210 pp., illus.

3421. BONHAM-CARTER, VICTOR (*ed.*). Surgeon in the Crimea: the experiences of George Lawson recorded in letters to his family, 1854–6. Constable, 1968. xiv, 209 pp., illus.

3422. BAYLEN, JOSEPH O., *and* CONWAY, ALAN. Soldier-surgeon: the Crimean War letters of Dr. Douglas A. Reid, 1855–6. Knoxville, Tenn.: Tennessee U.P., 1968. v, 158 pp.

3423. SHANKS, R. A. Granville Pattison and the uses of history. *Scot. Medical Jour.*, XI (1967) 267–76. [Anatomist.]

3424. LEIBOWITZ, JOSHUA O. Thomas Hodgkin, 1798–1866. *Clio Medica*, II (1967) 97–101.

3425. BRYAN, CHARLES S. Dr. Samuel Dickson and the spirit of chrono-thermalism. *Bull. Hist. Medicine*, XLII (1968) 24–42

3426. CHAPMAN, CARLETON B. Edward Smith (1818?–74): physiologist, human ecologist, reformer. *Jour. Hist. Medicine & Allied Sciences*, XXII (1967) 1–26.

3427. FRANK, JUSIN A. Non-restraint and Robert Gardiner Hill. *Bull. Hist. Medicine*, XLI (1967) 140–60.

3428. CRELLIN, JOHN K. The growth of professionalism in 19th century British pharmacy. *Medical Hist.*, XI (1967) 215–27.

3429. GUEST-GORNALL, R. The Warrington Dispensary Library. *Medical Hist.*, XI (1967) 285–96.

3430. RICHARDS, N. DAVIDS. Dentistry in England in the 1840s: the first indications of a movement towards professionalization. *Medical Hist.*, XII (1968) 137–52.

MILITARY HISTORY

3431. ENTRACT, J. P. The Tramore and Kinsdale tragedies, 30th January, 1816 (His Majesty's 59th, 62nd & 82nd Regiments). *Soc. Army Hist. Research Jour.*, XLVI (1968) 225–34. [Troopships wrecked.]

3432. COLLINS, R. M. Colonel the Hon. Frederick Cavendish Ponsonby, 12th Light Dragoons. *Soc. Army Hist. Research Jour.*, XLVI (1968) 1–5.

3433. BOND, BRIAN (*ed.*). Victorian military campaigns. Hutchinson, 1967. xii, 328 pp., illus.

3434. BLANCO, RICHARD L. The attempted control of venereal disease in the army of mid-Victorian England. *Soc. Army Hist. Research Jour.*, XLV (1967) 234–41.

3435. BLANCO, R. L. Attempts to abolish branding and flogging in the army of Victorian England before 1881. *Soc. Army Hist. Research Jour.*, XLVI (1968) 137–45.

3436. FEATHERSTONE, DONALD FREDERICK. At them with the bayonet! The First Sikh War. Jarrolds, 1968. x, 197 pp., illus.

3437. NORRIS, JAMES ALFRED. The first Afghan War, 1838–42. Cambridge: C.U.P., 1967. xvi, 500 pp.

3438. ENTRACT, J. P. 'Cumming of the 9th'. *Soc. Army Hist. Research Jour.*, XLV (1967) 214–25.

3439. AMES, EDWARD, *and* ROSENBERG, NATHAN. The Enfield Arsenal in theory and history. *Econ. Jour.*, LXXVIII (1968) 827–42.

3440. P., A. (*ed.*). Contemporary notes from the Crimea, 1854. *Soc. Army Hist. Research Jour.*, XLVI (1968) 116–20.

3441. BRADY, T. J. Fenton and the Crimean War. *History Today*, XVIII (1968) 75–83.

3442. COLLINS, R. M. 12th Lancers at Leeds, 1860. *Soc. Army Hist. Research Jour.*, XLV (1967) 248–51.

3443. PATTERSON, ALFRED TEMPLE. 'Palmerston's folly': the Portsdown and Spithead forts. (Portsmouth Papers, 3). Portsmouth, Hants.: City Council, 1967. 18 pp., illus.

3444. IRVING, W. J. Tregantle Fort, Plymouth. *Soc. Army Hist. Research Jour.*, XLV (1967) 117–21. [Completed 1865.]

3445. HARFIELD, A. G. The great volunteer review at Salisbury on 29th May, 1867. *Soc. Army Hist. Research Jour.*, XLV (1967) 149–68.

3446. BLANCO, RICHARD L. Army recruiting reforms, 1861–7. *Soc. Army Hist. Research Jour.*, XLVI (1968) 217–24.

3447. GIBSON, D. C. General Garrett, 1791–1869. *Archaeologia Cantiana* for 1966, LXXXI (1967) 126–35.

3448. PRESTON, ADRIAN W. The Russian crisis and the British army: origins of professionalism in Canada, 1874–80. *Army Quart.*, LXXXXVI no. 1 (1968) 88–97, no. 2 (1968) 241–51.

3449. PRESTON, A. W. Sir Garnet Wolseley and the Cyprus expedition, 1878. *Soc. Army Hist. Research Jour.*, XLV (1967) 4–16.

3450. PRESTON, A. W. (*ed.*). In relief of Gordon: Lord Wolseley's campaign journal of the Khartoum relief expedition, 1884–5. Hutchinson, 1967. xliv, 267 pp., illus.

3451. PEARN, BERTIE REGINALD (*ed.*). Military operations in Burma, 1890–2: letters from Lieut. J. K. Watson, K.R.R.C. Ithaca, N.Y.: Cornell Univ. Dept. Asian Studies, 1967. 72 pp.

3452. GLASS, STAFFORD. The Matabele War. Harlow, Essex: Longmans, 1968. xvii, 308 pp., illus.

3453. KIRK-GREENE, A. H. M. The Niger Sudan expeditionary force, 1897. *Soc. Army Hist. Research Jour.*, XLVI (1968) 49–56.

3454. BEACHEY, R. W. Macdonald's expedition and the Uganda mutiny, 1897–8. *Hist. Jour.*, X (1967) 237–54.

NAVAL HISTORY

3455. BONNETT, STANLEY HUBERT. The price of Admiralty: an indictment of the Royal Navy, 1805–66. Hale, 1968. 272 pp., illus.

3456. MCCORD, NORMAN. The Impress Service in north east England during the Napoleonic War. *Mariner's Mirror*, LIV (1968) 163–80.

3457. POOL, BERNARD. Navy contracts after 1832. *Mariner's Mirror*, LIV (1968) 209–26.

3458. The Woodhead Prize Account ledger, 1842–65. *Three Banks Rev.*, no. 76 (1967) 36–47. [Woodhead & Co., naval agents', distribution of bounties to naval vessels.]

3459. BACH, JOHN. The Royal Navy in the Pacific islands. *Jour. Pacific Hist.*, III (1968) 3–20.

3460. LEWIS, A. F. P. Captain of the Fleet: the career of Admiral Sir William Domett, G.C.B., 1751–1828. Richmond, Surrey: Keepsake P., 1967. 18 pp.

3461. LUBBOCK, ADELAIDE. Owen Stanley, R.N., 1811–50, captain of the *Rattlesnake*. Melbourne, London: Heinemann, 1968. xiii, 298 pp., illus.

3462. KNIGHT, FRANK. Rebel admiral: the life and exploits of Admiral Lord Cochrane, tenth earl of Dundonald. Macdonald, 1968. 172 pp., illus.

3463. COURTEMANCHE, REGIS A. The Royal Navy and the end of William Walker. *Historian*, XXX (1968) 350–65.

3464. MELLERSH, HAROLD EDWARD LESLIE. Fitzroy of the *Beagle*. Hart-Davis, 1968. 307 pp., illus.

3465. WILLOCK, ROGER. Gunboat diplomacy: operations of the North America and West Indies squadron, 1875–1915. *Amer. Neptune*, XXVIII (1968) 5–30, 85–112.

3466. LLOYD, HENRY T. R. Diary of a young Marine. *Bermuda Hist. Quart.*, XXIV (1967) 8–52. [Service in Bermuda, 1898.]

MARITIME HISTORY

3467. TEUTEBERG, HANS-JÜRGEN. Die englischen Binnen- und Küstenschiffahrt während der Frühindustrialisierung im Spiegel zeitgenössischer deutscher Reiseberichte. *Technikgesch.*, XXXIV (1967) 115–45, 226–64.

3468. GRAHAM, GERALD SANDFORD. Great Britain in the Indian Ocean: a study of maritime enterprise, 1810–50. Clarendon P., 1967. xiii, 479 pp.

3469. CAPPER, Y. M. Captain Cowan's sails. *Mariner's Mirror*, LIV (1968) 181–6.

3470. HATHEWAY, G. G. The great North Atlantic steamship race. *History Today*, XVII (1967) 89–97.

3471. READER, WILLIAM JOSEPH. The voyage of the *Great Tasmania*. *History Today*, XVII (1967) 153–61.

3472. SMITH, EDWIN GREEN. The fishing log of Edwin Green Smith, 1884–8. Grimsby, Lincs.: Grimsby Pub. Lib., 1967. 49 pp.

3473. HORNBY, W. M. PHIPPS. Grace Horsley Darling, 1815–42: Northumbrian heroine. *Mariner's Mirror*, LIV (1968) 55–68.

3474. SHARP, ERIC W. Wrecks in the Bailiwick of Guernsey. *Soc. Guernesiaise Rept. & Trans.* for 1967, XVIII (1968) 206–25.

3475. CLEAVES, FREEMAN. All souls saved. *Amer. Neptune*, XXVII (1967) 61–5. [*Unicorn*, wrecked off Newfoundland, 1851.]

TRAVEL AND EXPLORATION

3476. ROBBINS, RICHARD MICHAEL. Some English guide books of the 19th century. *London & Middlesex Historian*, no. 4 (1967) 1–8.

3477. PAKENHAM, SIMONA. Sixty miles from England: the English at Dieppe, 1814–1914. Macmillan, 1967. xii, 236 pp., illus.

3478. BOYER, FERDINAND. 'Refugiés italiens et anglaises libérales à Paris sous la Restauration'. *In* Mélanges offerts a G. Jacquemyns (Brussels: Univ. Libre, Ed. de l'Inst. de Sociol., 1968) pp. 88–92.

3479. TREASE, GEOFFREY (*ed.*). Matthew Todd's journal: a gentleman's gentleman in Europe, 1814–20. Heinemann, 1968. x, 165 pp., illus.

3480. MELCHIORI, BARBARA. A light-fingered English visitor to Italy. *English Misc.*, XVIII (1967) 257–82. [Robert Gray, 1821.]

3481. SUNDER, JOHN E. British Army officers on the Santa Fe trail. *Missouri Hist. Soc. Bull.*, XXIII (1966–7) 147–57. [1840s.]

3482. WINTHER, OSCAR OSBURN. The English in Nebraska, 1857–80. *Nebraska Hist.*, XLVIII (1967) 209–23.

3483. WINTHER, O. O. The British in Oregon country: a triptych view. *Pacific Northwest Quart.*, LVIII no. 4 (1967) 179–87.

3484. GRANT, A. R. C., *and* COMBE, CAROLINE (*eds.*). Lord Rosebery's North American journal, 1873. Sidgwick & Jackson, 1967. 191 pp., illus.

3485. JONES, A. G. E. Captain Peter Kemp and Kemp land. *Mariner's Mirror*, LIV (1968) 233–43.

3486. LUBBOCK, ADELAIDE. Owen Stanley in the Pacific. *Jour. Pacific Hist.*, III (1968) 47–63.

3487. CLEMENT, A. J. Chapman Khama: the story of James Chapman. *Africana Notes & News*, XVII (1967) 195–215. [Crossed South Africa.]

3488. CHOJNACKI, STANISLAW. William Simpson and his journey to Ethiopia,1868. *Jour. Ethiopian Studies*, VI no. 2 (1968) 7–38.

3489. BRIDGES, ROY C. The sponsorship and financing of Livingstone's last journey. *African Hist. Studies*, I (1968) 79–104.

3490. BENNETT, NORMAN R. Livingstone's letters to William F. Stearns. *African Hist. Studies*, I (1968) 243–54.

3491. IKLÉ, FRANK W. Sir Aurel Stein: a Victorian geographer in the tracks of Alexander. *Isis*, LIX (1968) 144–55.

FOREIGN RELATIONS

General

3492. PLATT, DESMOND CHRISTOPHER ST. MARTIN. Finance, trade and politics in British foreign policy, 1815–1914. Oxford, London: Clarendon P., 1968. xl, 454 pp.

3493. PRESTON, ANTHONY, *and* MAJOR, JOHN. Send a gunboat! A study of the gunboat and its role in British policy, 1854–1904. Longmans, 1967. xi, 266 pp., illus.

3494. LOWE, CEDRIC JAMES. The reluctant imperialists: British foreign policy, 1878–1902. Routledge, 1967. 2 vols.

3495. HOWARD, CHRISTOPHER HENRY DURHAM. Splendid isolation: a study of ideas concerning Britain's international position and foreign policy during the later years of the 3rd marquess of Salisbury. London: Macmillan; New York: St. Martin's P., 1967. xv, 120 pp.

3496. HOWARD, C. H. D. The policy of isolation. *Hist. Jour.*, X (1967) 77–88.

Europe

3497. THORNTON, MICHAEL JOHN. Napoleon after Waterloo: England and the St. Helena decision. Stanford, Calif.: Stanford U.P., 1968. ix, 241 pp.

3498. LINTINGRE, PIERRE. Note sur la rivalité franco-britannique au sujet de Madagascar: l'entrée en scène de la Congregation du Saint Esprit (1820). *Bull. Madagascar*, XVII (1967) 767–92.

3499. LEFÈVRE, ANDRÉ. La reconnaissance de la Seconde République par l'Angleterre. *Rev. d'Hist. Diplomatique*, LXXXII (1968) 213–31.

3500. SCHERER, PAUL. British reaction to French annexation of Nice and Savoy. *Internat. Rev. Hist. & Polit. Science*, II (1965) 31–40.

3501. SCHERER, P. British neutrality during the Franco-Prussian War. *Internat. Rev. Hist. & Polit. Science*, I (1964) 107–17.

3502. VALSECCHI, FRANCO. L'Inghilterra e la questione italiana nel 1859: la missione Cowley (27 febbraio – 10 marzo 1859). *Arch. Stor. Ital.*, CXXVI (1968) 479–94.

3503. BLAKISTON, NOEL. 'L'opinione pubblica inglese e la questione italiana dal 1859 al 1866'. *In* La questione veneta e la crisi italiana del 1866. (Atti del 43o Congresso di storia del Risorgimento italiano, Venice, 1966. Rome: Ist. per la storia del Risorgimento italiano, 1968) pp. 189–207.

3503a. Inghilterra e Toscana nell' Ottocento. Atti del Congresso di Bagni di Lucca per il cinquantenario del British Institute of Florence, 1967. Florence: Nuova Italia; Bologna: Azzoguidi, 1968. 230 pp., illus.

3504. ISTITUTO STORICO ITALIANO PER L'ETA MODERNA E CONTEMPORANEA. Le relazioni diplomatiche fra la Gran Bretagna e il Regno di Sardegna. 3 serie: 1848–60 . . . a cura di F. Curato. Vol. 4, 27 gennaio 1852–10 gennaio 1855. Vol. 5, 11 gennaio 1855–30 diciembre 1856. Rome: the Instituto, 1968. 2 vols.

3505. MENNA, PIETRO. Un episodio della lotta diplomatica tra l'Inghilterra e il Regno delle Due Sicilie. *Samnium*, XLI (1968) 78–89.

3506. MARSDEN, ARTHUR. Salisbury and the Italians in 1896. *Jour. Mod. Hist.*, XL (1968) 91–117.

3508. BÓBR-TYLINGO, STANISLAW. Lord Clarendon's mission to Germany in 1863. *Antemurale*, XI (1967) 185–9.

3509. PAVELKA, HEDWIG. Englisch- österreichische Wirtschaftsbeziehungen in der ersten Hälfte des 19. Jahrhunderts. (Wiener Forschungen zur Wirtschafts-und Sozialgesch., 2). Graz, Vienna: Böhlau, 1968. 192 pp.

3510. HJELHOLT, HOLGER. Breve fra den engelske gesandt i København, Wynn, til hans kolleger Bloomfield i St. Petersborg og Cowley i Frankfurt fra aret 1848. *Danske Mag.*, 8th ser. III (1967) 44–70. ['Letters from the English ambassador in Copenhagen, Wynn, to his colleagues Bloomfield in St. Petersburg and Cowley in Frankfurt in 1848'.]

3511. DUTKIEWICZ, JÓZEF. Anglia a sprawa polska w latach 1830–1. Łódź: Zakl. Narod. im. Ossolińskich. Wydawn. Pan, 1967. 88 pp. ['England and the Polish situation'.]

3512. WEISSER, HENRY G. Polonophilism and the British working class, 1830–45. *Polish Rev.*, XII (1967) 78–96.

3513. WEISSER, H. G. The British working class and the Cracow uprising of 1846. *Polish Rev.*, XIII (1968) 3–19.

3514. WALKER, FRANKLIN A. The rejection of Stratford Canning by Nicholas I. *Inst. Hist. Research Bull.*, XL (1967) 50–64.

3515. STRONG, JOHN W. A Russian effort to rescue British agents, 1841–2. *Canadian Jour. Hist.*, II pt. 1 (1967) 1–12.

3516. LUXENBURG, NORMAN. England and the Caucasus during the Crimean war. *Jahrb. für Gesch. Östeuropa*, XVI (1968) 499–504.

3517. SALT, JOHN. Local manifestations of the Urquhartite movement. *Internat. Rev. Soc.Hist.*, XIII (1968) 350–9.

3518. TAPPE, ERIC DITMAR. Rumania and the Bible Society until the Crimean War. *Slavonic & E. European Rev.*, XLVI (1968) 91–104.

3519. PANTEV, ANDREJ. 'The Macedonian question in Britain's policy during the first years of Stefan Stambolov's régime, 1887–92'. *In* Études historiques vol. 4, 6e Congrès internat. des études slaves, Prague, 1968, *ed.* D. Angelov *and others* (Sofia: Izd. Bălgarsk Akad. Nauk., 1968) pp. 357–73.

Asia

3520. ISEMINGER, GORDON L. The old Turkish hands: the British Levantine consuls, 1856–76. *Middle East Jour.*, XXII (1968) 297–316.

3521. FRIEDMAN, ISAIAH. Lord Palmerston and the protection of Jews in Palestine, 1839–51. *Jewish Soc. Studies*, XXX (1968) 23–41.

3522. KELLY, JOHN BARRETT. Britain and the Persian Gulf, 1795–1880. Oxford: Clarendon P., 1968. xvi, 911 pp.

3523. KAZEMZADEH, FIRUZ. Russia and Britain in Persia, 1864–1914: a study in imperialism. New Haven, Conn., London: Yale U.P., 1968. xii, 711 pp.

3524. KEDDIE, NIKKI R. British policy and Iranian opposition 1901–7. *Jour. Mod. Hist.*, XXXIX (1967) 266–82.

3525. BUSCH, BRITON COOPER. Britain and the status of Kuwayt, 1896–9. *Middle East Jour.*, XXI (1967) 187–98.

3526. MAJUMDAR, KANCHANMOY. A note on Anglo-Nepalese relations in 1838. *Bengal Past & Present*, LXXXVI (1967) 1–9.

3527. KLEIN, IRA. Salisbury, Rosebery, and survival of Siam. *Jour. Brit. Studies*, VIII no. 1 (1968) 117–39.

3528. HIRSHFIELD, CLAIRE. The struggle for the Mekong banks, 1892–6. *Jour. S.E. Asian Hist.*, IX (1968) 25–52.

3529. DANIELS, GORDON. The British role in the Meiji restoration: a re-interpretative note. *Modern Asian Studies*, II (1968) 291–313.

3530. MCMASTER, JOHN. Alcock and Harris: foreign diplomacy in Bakumatsu, Japan. *Monumenta Nipponica*, XXII (1967) 305–67.

3531. DEAN, BRITTEN. Evolving Sino-British relations in the 1860s. *Chinese Culture*, VIII (1967) 63–98.

3532. QUO, F. Q. British diplomacy and the cession of Formosa, 1894–5. *Modern Asian Studies*, II (1968) 10–15.

United States of America

3533. BOURNE, KENNETH. Britain and the balance of power in North America, 1815–1908. Longmans, 1967. xii, 439 pp., illus.

3534. LAURENT, PIERRE-HENRI. Anglo-American diplomacy and the Belgian indemnities controversy. *Hist. Jour.*, X (1967) 197–217.

3535. HERNON, JOSEPH M., *Jnr*. British sympathies in the American Civil War: a reconsideration. *Jour. Southern Hist.*, XXXIII (1967) 356–67.

3536. MACCHESNEY, BRUNSON. The *Alabama* and the Queen's advocate: a mystery of history. *Northwestern Univ. Law Rev.*, LXII (1967–8) 568–85.

3537. GRESSLEY, GENE M. Broker to the British: Francis Smith and Company. *Southwestern Hist. Quart.*, LXXI no. 1 (1967–8) 7–26.

3538. TATE, MERZE. Twisting the lion's tail over Hawaii. *Pacific Hist. Rev.*, XXXVI (1967) 27–46.

Latin America

3539. WINN, WILKINS B. Reports of British diplomats concerning the status of Protestantism in Latin America in 1851. *Jour. of Church & State*, X (1968) 437–44.

3540. HUMPHREYS, ROBIN ARTHUR. Anglo-American rivalries in Central America. *Roy. Hist. Soc. Trans.*, 5th ser. XVIII (1968) 174–208.

3541. FRAZIER, CHARLES E., *Jnr.* An 18th [sic] century intervention: the London Convention and the Preliminares de la Soledad. *Jour. of the West*, VI (1967) 262–77. [Mexico, 1861.]

3542. GUZMÁN, JOSÉ R. Una sociedad secreta en Londres al servicio de la independencia Hispanoamericano. *Bol. Archivo General de la Nación* [Mexico], 2nd ser. VIII (1967) 109–28.

3543. HUMPHREYS, ROBIN ARTHUR. Anglo-American rivalries and the Venezuela crisis of 1895. *Roy. Hist. Soc. Trans.*, 5th ser. XVII (1967) 131–64.

3544. ROSS, GARY M. Mosquito Indians and Anglo-American diplomacy. *Washington State Univ. Research Studies*, XXXV (1967) 220–33.

3545. ROSS, G. M. Britain at Corinto: her 'forwardness' examined. *Washington State Univ. Research Studies*, XXXVI no. 3 (1968) 196–213.

3546. MOLINA, RAÚL A. Lord Strangford y el Río de la Plata: su correspondencia secreta. *Historia* (Buenos Aires), XIII (1967) 78–9, XIV (1967) 3–45, 75–93.

3547. GANDÍA, ENRIQUE DE. 'El Río de la Plata y lord Strangford'. *In* 4o Congreso Internacional de Historia de América, Buenos Aires, 1966. Vol. 6. (Buenos Aires: Acad. Nacional de la Hist., 1967) pp. 365–403.

WALES

3548. JONES, DAVID J. V. The South Wales strike of 1816. *Morgannwg*, XI (1967) 27–45.

3549. JONES, D. J. V. The Carmarthen riots of 1831. *Welsh Hist. Rev.*, IV (1968–9) 129–42.

3550. BEAZLEY, ELISABETH. Madocks and the wonder of Wales: the life of W. A. Madocks, M.P., 1773–1828 . . . with some account of his agent, John Williams. Faber, 1967. 276 pp., illus.

3551. HUGHES, D. G. LLOYD. David Williams of Castell Deudraeth, 1799–1869. *Caernarvons. Hist. Soc. Trans.*, XXIX (1968) 25–72.

3552. HUGHES, D. G. L. David Williams, Castell Deudraeth and the Merioneth elections of 1859, 1865 and 1868. *Merioneth Hist. & Rec. Soc. Jour.*, V no. 4 (1968) 335–51.

3553. JONES, IEUAN GWYNEDD. Merioneth politics in the mid-19th century. *Merioneth Hist. & Rec. Soc. Jour.*, V no. 4 (1968) 273–334.

3554. EDWARDS, IFOR. History of the Monsanto Chemical Works site, Cefn Mawr, Wrexham: a study in industrial archaeology. *Denbighs. Hist. Soc. Trans.*, XVI (1967) 128–48.

3555. ROGERS, EMLYN, *and* ROBERTS, R. O. The history of trade unionism in the coal mining industry of North Wales to 1914. *Denbighs. Hist. Soc. Trans.*, XVI (1967) 100–27, XVII (1968) 147–76.

3556. POWELL, J. M. Parish registers and industrial structure: the Montgomeryshire baptismal registers. *Nat. Lib. Wales Jour.*, XV (1967–8) 325–34.

3557. DEWAR, IAN. George Clive and the establishment of the new Poor Law in south Glamorgan, 1836–8. *Morgannwg*, XI (1967) 46–70.

3558. ASHTON, GLYN MILLS. Dirwest ynteu llwyrymwrthod? *Y Traethodydd*, CXXIII (1968) 128–35. ['Temperance or total abstinence?']

3559. CULE, JOHN. Wreath on the crown: the story of Sarah Jacob, the Welsh fasting girl. Llandysul, Cardigs.: Gomerian P., 1967. 143 pp.

3560. BAKER-JONES, D. L. Sir Lawrence Hugh Jenkins of Cilbronnan, Cardiganshire: his family background and career. *Hon. Soc. Cymmrodorion Trans.* (1968) 122–32.

3561. GRIFFITHS, D. N. Robert Griffiths and his relations: the migration of a Denbighshire family. *Hon. Soc. Cymmrodorion Trans.* (1967) 278–301.

3562. MORRIS, E. RONALD. G. R. Wythen Baxter, Upper Bryn, Newtown, 1814–54. *Montgomerys. Coll.* for 1965–6, LIX (1968) 82–101.

3563. JONES-EVANS, PERIS. Evan Pan Jones: land reformer. *Welsh Hist. Rev.*, IV (1968–9) 143–59.

3564. PHILLIPS, RICHARD. The last of the drovers: Dafydd Isaac. *Hon. Soc. Cymmrodorion Trans.* (1968) 110–21.

3565. JONES, J. LLYWELYN. Owen Glynne Jones (1867–99). *Hon. Soc. Cymmrodorion Trans.* (1967) 302–12.

3566. WILLIAMS, W. OGWEN. Datgysylltiad yr eglwys a gwleidyddiaeth Cymru yn y ganrif ddiwethaf. *Efrydiau Athronyddol*, XXX (1967) 56–64. ['Disestablishment of the Church and Welsh politics in the last century'.]

3567. JONES, OWAIN W. The mind of Robert Raikes. *Hist. Soc. Church in Wales Jour.*, XVIII (1968) 57–64. [Oxford Movement in diocese of St. Davids.]

3568. EVANS, TREBOR LLOYD. Lewis Edwards: ei fywyd a'i waith. Swansea: Gwasg John Penry, 1967. xvi, 280 pp., illus. [Methodist.]

3569. KNOX, ROBERT BUICK. Edwards *v.* Edwards: a 19th century controversy. *Cylchgrawn Cymd. Hanes Meth. Calf.*, LIII (1968) 8–19.

3570. JONES, IEUAN GWYNEDD. Denominationalism in Swansea and district: a study of the ecclesiastical census of 1851. *Morgannwg*, XII (1968) 67–96.

3571. EVANS, EIFION. When He is come: an account of the 1858–60 revival in Wales. 2nd edn. Evangelical P., 1967. 124 pp. [Previous edn. Bala, Merioneth: Evangelical Movement of Wales, 1959.]

3572. ROBERTS, RHIANNON FRED. Plan Cylchdaith Dinbych a Llanrwst, 1819. *Bathafarn*, XXII (1967) 52–5. ['Plan of the Dinbych and Llanrwst circuit'.]

3573. ROBERTS, R. F. Llyfr cofnodau Cyfarfod Misol Meirionnydd, 1830–9. *Cylchgrawn Cymd. Hanes Meth. Calf.*, LII (1967) 33–9. ['Minute books of the Merioneth monthly meeting'.]

3574. GRIFFITHS, G. LLEWELYN. John Elias's Ms. letters and associated Ms. correspondence. *Cylchgrawn Cymd. Hanes Meth. Calf.*, LIII (1968) 52–5.

3575. DAVIES, K. MONICA. Mary Jones, 1784–1864. *Cylchgrawn Cymd. Hanes Meth. Calf.*, LII (1967) 74–80.

3576. EDWARDS, ERIC. Llyfrfa'r Methodistiaid Wesleaidd Cymraeg, 1809–1909. *Bathafarn*, XXII (1967) 8–23. ['The Welsh Wesleyan Methodist library'.]

3577. WILLIAMS, ROGER JONES. Hanes cyhoeddi *Y Gwyddoniadur Cymreig*. *Llên Cymru*, IX nos. 3–4 (1967) 133–65. ['History of the publication of *Y Gwyddoniadur Cymreig*' (Welsh encyclopaedia).]

3578. CYNAN. Jac Glan-y-gors, 1766–1821: darlith deucanmlwyddiant. *Denbighs. Hist. Soc. Trans.*, XVI (1967) 62–81. ['Jac Glan-y-gors, bicentenary lecture'.]

3579. JONES, G. J. John Williams Ab Ithel. *Y Traethodydd*, CXXIII (1968) 49–61, 113–61, 213–27.

3580. MILLWARD, E. G. Siôn Wyn o Eifion, 1785–1859. *Caernarvons. Hist. Soc. Trans.*, XXVIII pt. 1 (1967) 60–6.

3581. ASHTON, GLYN MILLS. Islwyn a thorri cyhoeddiadau. *Cylchgrawn Cymd. Hanes Meth. Calf.*, LII (1967) 81–4. ['Islwyn and his published writings'.]

3582. ELLIS, TECWYN. Bardd y Brenin, Iolo Morganwg a derwyddiaeth. Pt. 7. *Nat. Lib. Wales Jour.*, XV (1967–8) 177–96. [Influence of Edward Williams ('Iolo Morganwg') on Edward Jones ('Bardd y Brenin').]

3583. OWENS, BENJAMIN GEORGE. Benjamin Williams ('Gwynionydd'), 1821–91. *Ceredigion*, V no. 4 (1967) 347–401. [In Welsh.]

3584. THOMAS, R. MALDWYN, *and* PARRY, CYRIL. John Owen Jones, 'Ap Ffarmwr', 1861–99. *Anglesey Antiq. Soc. & F.C. Trans.* (1967) 72–107.

3585. BARTHOLOMEW, MARY. John Edmunds: pioneer educationalist. *Caernarvons. Hist. Soc. Trans.*, XXVIII pt. 1 (1967) 47–59.

3586. THOMAS, DEWI W. Addysg yng Ngheredigion, 1800–50, yn ôl y cofiannau. *Ceredigion*, VI no. 1 (1968) 45–89. ['Education in Cardiganshire, 1800–50, according to memoirs'.]

3587. GIBBARD, NOEL. Llanelli schools, 1800–70. *Carmarthens. Hist.*, V (1968) 67–82.

3588. ELLIS, E. L. Some aspects of the early history of the University College of Wales. *Hon. Soc. Cymmrodorion Trans.* (1967) 203–19.

3589. JONES, BEDWYR LEWIS. Wilham Roos yr artist, 1808–73. *Anglesey Antiq. Soc. & F.C. Trans.* (1967) 109–19. ['William Roos the artist'.]

SCOTLAND

3590. DAICHES, DAVID. Edinburgh in 1816. *Univ. Edinburgh Jour.*, XXIII no. 2 (1967) 167–72.

3591. BEST, GEOFFREY. The Scottish Victorian city. *Victorian Studies*, XI (1967–8) 329–58.

3592. GASKELL, PHILIP. Morvern transformed: a Highland parish in the 19th century. C.U.P., 1968. xix, 273 pp., illus.

3593. TAYLOR, WILLIAM. Glen Fincastle, 1841–1901: a study of a Perthshire glen. Edinburgh, London: Oliver & Boyd, for Dundee College of Education, 1967. xi, 53 pp.

3594. SHERRY, FRANK ANDREW. The rising of 1820. Glasgow: Maclellan, 1968. 59 pp.

3595. BRASH, J. I. The Conservatives in the Haddington district of Burghs, 1832–52. *East Lothian Antiq. Soc. Trans.*, XI (1968) 37–70.

3596. MILLER, J. BENNETT. The trial of Malcolm Gillespie, or the life and hard times of an exciseman. *Juridical Rev.*, n.s. XII (1967) 225–44.

3597. JACKSON, WILLIAM TURRENTINE. The enterprising Scot: investors in the American West after 1873. (History, Philosophy and Economics, 22). Edinburgh: Edinburgh U.P., 1968. xv, 415 pp., illus.

3598. BUTT, JOHN. The Scottish iron and steel industry before the hot-blast. *W. Scotland Iron & Steel Indust. Jour.*, LXXIII (1967) 195–220.

3599. GULVIN, C. Wages and conditions in the border woollen industry about 1890. *Hawick Archaeol. Soc. Trans.* (1967) 36–48.

3600. MUI, HOH-CHEUNG, *and* MUI, LORNA H. Andrew Melrose, tea dealer and grocer of Edinburgh, 1812–33. *Business Hist.*, IX (1967) 30–48.

3601. COULL, JAMES R. Crofters' common grazings in Scotland. *Agric. Hist. Rev.*, XVI (1968) 142–54.

3602. Early Scottish railways. *Three Banks Rev.*, no. 74 (1967) 29–39.

3603. FOSKETT, REGINALD. The Drummond controversy, 1842. *Scot. Church Hist. Soc. Records*, XVI pt. 2 (1967) 99–109.

3604. WALSH, JAMES. Archbishop Manning's visitation of the western district of Scotland. *Innes Rev.*, XVIII (1967) 3–18. [1867.]

3605. MACLAREN, A. ALLAN. Presbyterianism and the working class in a mid-19th century city. *Scot. Hist. Rev.*, XLVI (1967) 115–39. [Aberdeen.]

3606. BUCHANAN, FREDERICK S. Scots among the Mormons. *Utah Hist. Quart.*, XXXVI (1968) 328–52.

3607. FINLAYSON, C. P. David Laing and his friends. *Univ. Edinburgh Jour.*, XXIII no. 2 (1967) 145–56.

3608. KAUFMAN, PAUL. Leadhills: library of Diggers. *Libri*, XVII (1967) 13–20.

3609. DOUGHTY, DENNIS WILLIAM. The Tullis Press, Cupar, 1803–49. (Abertay Hist. Soc. Pubns., 12). Dundee: the Society, 1967. vi, 74 pp., illus.

3610. CRUICKSHANK, MARJORIE. The Argyll Commission Report, 1865–8: a landmark in Scottish education. *Brit. Jour. Educ. Studies*, XV (1967) 133–47.

3611. WATSON, WILLIAM N. BOOG. The first eight ladies. *Univ. Edinburgh Jour.*, XXIII no. 3 (1968) 227–34. [Edinburgh University graduates, 1893.]

3612. JONES, MARY JEANNE A., *and* GEMMILL, CHALMERS L. The notebook of Robley Dunglison, student of clinical medicine in Edinburgh, 1815–16. *Jour. Hist. Medicine & Allied Sciences*, XXII (1967) 261–73.

3613. LARDER, DAVID F. Alexander Crum Brown and his doctoral thesis of 1861. *Ambix*, XIV (1967) 112–32. [Chemical pharmacy.]

3614. UNDERWOOD, E. ASHWORTH. Dumfries and the early history of surgical anaesthesia. *Annals of Science*, XXIII (1967) 35–75.

IRELAND

Note: Writings on Irish domestic and local history are not included unless they have a direct bearing on English history.

3615. JUPP, P. J. Irish parliamentary elections and the influence of the Catholic vote, 1801–20. *Hist. Jour.*, X (1967) 183–96.

3616. CURRAN, CHARLES. The spy behind the Speaker's chair. *History Today*, XVIII (1968) 745–54.

3617. WHYTE, JOHN HENRY. 'The age of Daniel O'Connell'. *In* The course of Irish history, *ed.* T. W. Moody *and* F. X. Martin (Cork: Mercier P., 1967) pp. 248–62.

3618. BODKIN, MATHIAS. Thomas Francis Meagher, 1822–67. *Studies*, LVII (1968) 49–53.

3619. GREEN, EDWARD RODNEY RICHARD. 'The Great Famine'. *In* The course of Irish history, *ed.* T. W. Moody *and* F. X. Martin (Cork: Mercier P., 1967) pp. 263–74.

3620. WHYTE, JOHN HENRY. Political problems, 1850–60. (Hist. of Irish Catholicism, vol. 5, fasc. 2). Dublin: Gill, 1967. 39 pp.

3621. HERNON, JOSEPH M., *Jnr.* Celts, Catholics and copperheads: Ireland views the American Civil War. Columbus, Ohio: Ohio State U.P., 1968. viii, 150 pp.

3622. MCCORD, NORMAN. The Fenians and public opinion in Great Britain. *Univ. Rev.*, IV (1967) 227–40.

3623. MOODY, T. W. (*ed.*). The Fenian movement. Cork: Mercier P., 1968. 126 pp.

3624. MOODY, T. W. 'Fenianism, Home Rule and the land war'. *In* The course of Irish history, *ed.* T. W. Moody *and* F. X. Martin (Cork: Mercier P., 1967) pp. 275–93. [1850–91.]

3625. MCGRATH, WALTER. The Fenian rising in Cork. *Irish Sword*, VIII (1968) 245–54. [1867.]

3626. GWYNN, DENIS R. James Stephens and the Fenian rising. *Old Kilkenny Rev.*, XX (1968) 27–44.

3627. IRELAND, JOHN DE COURCY. A preliminary study on the Fenians and the sea. *Eire*, II (1967) 36–54.

3628. IRELAND, J. DE C. Fenianism and naval affairs. *Irish Sword*, VIII (1967) 10–22.

3629. O'FIAICH, TOMÁS. The clergy and Fenianism, 1860–70. *Irish Eccles. Record*, 5th ser. CIX (1968) 81–103.

3630. BATEMAN, ROBERT J. Captain Timothy Deasy, Fenian. *Irish Sword*, VIII (1967) 130–7.

3631. SAVAGE, DONALD C. The Irish unionists, 1867–86. *Eire*, II (1967) 86–101.

3632. CORFE, THOMAS HOWELL. The Phoenix Park murders: conflict, compromise and tragedy in Ireland, 1879–82. Hodder, 1968. 286 pp., illus.

3633. EDWARDS, OWEN DUDLEY. American diplomats and Irish coercion, 1880–3. *Jour. Amer. Studies*, I (1967) 213–32.

3634. COOKE, A. B., *and* VINCENT, JOHN RUSSELL. Ireland and party politics, 1885–7: an unpublished Conservative memoir. *Irish Hist. Studies*, XVI (1968–9) 154–72.

3635. GILLGANNON, MARY MCAULEY. Charles Stewart Parnell: political paradox. New York: Vantage P., 1967. vii, 117 pp.

3636. TIERNEY, MARK. Dr. Croke, the Irish bishops and the Parnell crisis, 18 November 1890–21 April 1891. *Collectanea Hibernica*, XI (1968) 111–48.

3637. HURST, MICHAEL. Parnell and Irish nationalism. Routledge, 1968. ix, 117 pp.

3638. JOHNSON, JAMES H. Harvest migration from 19th century Ireland. *Inst. Brit. Geographers Trans.*, XLI (1967) 97–112.

3639. ROBINS, JOSEPH A. Irish orphan emigration to Australia, 1848–50. *Studies*, LVII (1968) 372–87.

3640. GILLESPIE, GEORGE. Notes on social life and craftwork in Ballygawley. *Ulster Folklife*, XIV (1968) 39–43. [Poor Law Dispensary minute book, 1850s.]

3641. LEE, JOSEPH. The construction costs of Irish railways, 1830–53. *Business Hist.*, IX (1967) 95–109.

3642. MCCLELLAND, AIKEN. The origin of the Imperial Grand Black Chapter of the British Commonwealth. *Roy. Soc. Antiq. Ireland Jour.*, XCVIII (1968) 191–5.

3643. PINNINGTON, JOHN E. The Church of Ireland's apologetic position in the years before disestablishment. *Irish Eccles. Record*, 5th ser. CVIII (1967) 303–25.

3644. ROBINS, JOSEPH A. Religious issues in the early workhouse. *Studies*, LVII (1968) 54–66.

3645. NORMAN, EDWARD ROBERT. The Maynooth question of 1845. *Irish Hist. Studies*, XV (1966–7) 407–37. *Studies*, XV (1966–7) 407–37.

3646. MACHIN, G. I. T. The Maynooth grant, the dissenters and disestablishment, 1845–7. *E.H.R.*, LXXXII (1967) 61–85.

3647. MCCLELLAND, VINCENT ALAN. The Irish clergy and Archbishop Manning's apostolic visitation of the western district of Scotland, 1867. *Catholic Hist. Rev.*, LIII no. 1 (1967) 1–27, no. 2 (1967) 229–50.

3648. RUSLING, G. W. The schools of the Baptist Irish Society. *Baptist Quart.*, XXII no. 8 (1968) 429–42.

3649. MCCARTNEY, DONAL. Lecky and the Irish university question. *Irish Eccles. Record*, 5th ser. CVIII (1967) 102–12.

3650. KERR, DONAL. Dr. Quinn's school and the Catholic University, 1850–67. *Irish Eccles. Record*, 5th ser. CVIII (1967) 89–101.

3651. O'DANACHAIR, CAOIMHIN. A timber-framed house near Slane, Co. Meath. *Ulster Folklife*, XIV (1968) 24–7.

3652. MEENAN, F. O. C. The Victorian doctors of Dublin: a social and political portrait. *Irish Jour. Medical Science*, 7th ser. I (1968) 311–20.

BRITISH EMPIRE

Note: The domestic history of Commonwealth countries is not included unless it has a direct bearing on British history.

General

3653. MORRIS, JAMES. Pax Britannica: the climax of an empire. Faber, 1968. 544 pp., illus.

3654. PLATT, DESMOND CHRISTOPHER ST. MARTIN. Economic factors in British policy during the 'new imperialism'. *Past & Present*, no. 39 (1968) 120–38.

3655. MOMMSEN, WOLFGANG J. Nationale und ökonomische Faktoren im britischen Imperialismus vor 1914. *Hist. Zeit.*, CCVI (1968) 618–64.

3656. MCINTYRE, WILLIAM DAVID. The Imperial frontier in the tropics, 1865–75: a study of British colonial policy in West Africa, Malaya and the South Pacific in the age of Gladstone and Disraeli. London: Macmillan; New York: St. Martin's P., 1967. x, 421 pp.

West Indies

3657. HIGMAN, B. W. The West India 'interest' in parliament, 1807–33. *Hist. Studies Australia & N.Z.*, XIII (1967) 1–19.

3658. RECKORD, MARY. The Jamaica slave rebellion of 1831. *Past & Present*, no. 40 (1968) 108–25.

3659. WELLER, JUDITH ANN. The East Indian indenture in Trinidad. (Caribbean monograph ser., 4). Río Piedras: Puerto Rico Univ. Inst. of Caribbean Studies, 1968. xxii, 172 pp.

Bermuda

3660. ZUILL, WILLIAM E. S. Emigrants to Bermuda, 1850. *Bermuda Hist. Quart.*, XV (1968) 77–85. [Pauper children from London.]

Central America

3661. NAYLOR, ROBERT A. The mahogany trade as a factor in the British return to the Mosquito Shore in the second quarter of the 19th century. *Jamaican Hist. Rev.*, VII (1967) 40–67.

3662. PENDERGAST, DAVID M. (*ed.*). Palenque: the Walker-Caddy expedition to the ancient Maya city, 1839–40. Norman, Okla.: Oklahoma U.P., 1967. xvi, 213 pp.

3663. CLEGERN, WAYNE M. British Honduras: colonial dead end 1859–1900. Baton Rouge, La.: Louisiana U.P., 1967. vii, 214 pp.

Falkland Islands

3664. DESTEFANI, LAURIO H. La evacuación española de las islas Malvinas. *Investigaciones y Ensayos*, no. 4 (1968) 269–91.

Canada

3665. BURROUGHS, PETER. Parliamentary radicals and the reduction of imperial expenditure in British North America, 1827–34. *Hist. Jour.*, XI (1968) 446–61.

3666. GREENHILL, BASIL, *and* GIFFARD, ANN. Westcountrymen in Prince Edward's Isle: a fragment of the great migration. Newton Abbot, Devon: David & Charles; Toronto: Toronto U.P., 1967. 248 pp., illus.

3667. REAMAN, G. ELMORE. The trail of the Iroquois Indians: how the Iroquois nation saved Canada for the British Empire. New York: Barnes & Noble, 1967. xix, 138 pp.

3668. JOHNSON, J. K. (*ed.*). The letters of Sir John A. Macdonald, 1836–57. (Papers of the Prime Ministers, 1). Ottawa: Pub. Archives of Canada, 1968. xxiii, 600 pp.

3669. ARNELL, J. C. Samuel Cunard and the Nova Scotia government vessels *Earl Bathurst* and *Chebucto*. *Mariner's Mirror*, LIV (1968) 337–47.

3670. ARNELL, J. C. Trooping to the Canadas. *Mariner's Mirror*, LIII (1967) 143–60. [1838.]

3671. SMITH, WILFRED I. Confederation and the British connection. *Rev. de Hist. de América*, LXV–LXVI (1968) 15–24.

3672. PRESTON, RICHARD A. Canada and 'imperial defense': a study of the origins of the British Commonwealth's defense organization, 1867–1919. Durham, N.C.: Duke U.P., 1967. xxi, 576 pp.

3673. SHIELDS, R. A. The Canadian treaty negotiations with France: a study in imperial relations, 1878–83. *Inst. Hist. Research Bull.*, XL (1967) 186–202.

Africa

3674. MAGID, ALVIN. British rule and indigenous organisation in Nigeria: a case-study in normative-institutional change. *Jour. African Hist.*, IX (1968) 299–313.

3675. HOPKINS, A. G. Economic imperialism in West Africa: Lagos, 1880–92. *Econ. Hist. Rev.*, 2nd ser. XXI (1968) 580–606.

3676. TORDOFF, WILLIAM. The dismemberment and revival of the Ashanti Confederacy. *Jour. Brit. Studies*, VII no. 2 (1968) 151–68.

3677. AMENUMEY, D. E. K. The extension of British rule to Anlo (Southeast Ghana), 1850–90. *Jour. African Hist.*, IX (1968) 99–117.

3678. HARTWIG, GERALD W. Bukerebe, the Church Missionary Society and East African politics, 1877–8. *African Hist. Studies*, I (1968) 211–32.

3679. PACHAI, BRIDGLAL. In the wake of Livingstone and the British administration: some considerations of commerce and Christianity in Malawi. *Soc. Malawi Jour.*, XX (1967) 40–70.

3680. WINGATE, RONALD. Sir Samuel Baker's papers, 1875–93. *Quart. Rev.*, CCCV (1967) 295–308.

3681. LUFTI AL-SAYYID, AFAF. Egypt and Cromer: a study in Anglo-Egyptian relations. Murray, 1968. xiii, 236 pp., illus.

3682. OYEDEJI, E. B. L. Cromer in Egypt: an assessment. *African Historian*, II no. 4 (1968) 21–4.

3683. DANIEL, N. A. Bishop Gwynne and General Gordon. *Sudan Notes*, XLVIII (1967) 62–70.

South Africa

3684. FISCHER, GEORGES. Les conflits entre états et compagnies privées: La Zambie et la British South Africa Company. *Rev. Française de Science Politique*, XVII pt. 2 (1967) 329–38.

3685. HUTTENBACK, ROBERT A. Some fruits of Victorian imperialism: Gandhi and the Indian question in Natal, 1893–9. *Victorian Studies*, XI (1967–8) 153–80.

India

3686. BRAUN, PETER C. Die Verteidigung Indiens, 1800–1907: Das Problem der Vorwärtsstrategie. (Kölner historische Abhandlungen, 15). Cologne, Graz: Böhlau, 1968. xvi, 280 pp.

3687. BRUCE, GEORGE. The stranglers: the cult of Thuggee and its overthrow in British India. Longmans, 1968. ix, 234 pp., illus.

3688. PANIKKAR, K. N. British diplomacy in north India: a study of the Delhi residency, 1803–57. New Delhi: Assoc. Pub. House, 1968. 200 pp.

3689. LUNT, JAMES. Simla: the British in India. *History Today*, XVIII (1968) 599–605.

3690. PANIGRAHI, D. N. Charles Metcalfe in India: ideas and administration, 1806–35. Delhi: M. Manoharlal, 1968. 254 pp.

3691. THEODORIDÈS, JEAN. La mission de Victor Jacquemont dans l'Inde anglaise, 1828–32: documents inédits. *Rev. d'Hist. Diplomatique*, LXXXI (1967) 125–42.

3692. 'A STUDENT OF HISTORY'. The Darjeeling grant. *Quart. Rev. Hist. Studies*, VII (1967–8) 175–9.

3693. JHA, JAGDISH CHANDRA. The British occupation of Kolhan (Singhbhum), 1836–7. *Jour. Indian Hist.*, XLV (1967) 799–806.

3694. MEHROTRA, S. R. The British India Society and its Bengal branch, 1839–46. *Indian Econ. & Soc. Hist. Rev.*, IV no. 2 (1967) 131–54.

3695. MOLESWORTH, G. N. The defence of Jallalabad, 1841–3. *Soc. Army Hist. Research Jour.*, XLVI (1968) 146–53.

3696. GHOSE, DILIP KUMAR. The Kashmir Residency question, 1846–85. Pt. 1. *Quart. Rev. Hist. Studies*, VII (1967–8) 269–75.

3697. BOSE, NEMAI SADHAN. James Silk Buckingham and Indian affairs. *Quart. Rev. Hist. Studies*, VI (1966–7) 90–4.

3698. CHATTERJEE, PRASHANTO KUMAR. The secret committee of the East India Company, 1853–8. *Bengal Past & Present*, LXXXVII (1968) 165–80.

3699. COMPTON, J. M. Indians and the Indian Civil Service, 1853–79: a study in national agitation and imperial embarrassment. *Roy. Asiatic Soc. Jour.* (1967) 99–113.

3700. COMPTON, J. M. Open competition and the Indian Civil Service 1854–76. *E.H.R.*, LXXXIII (1968) 265–84.

3701. DATTA, KALIKINKAR. Reflections on the 'Mutiny'. Calcutta: Calcutta U.P., 1967. iv, 82 pp.

3702. BAKSHI, S. R. The Madras mutiny. *Modern Rev.*, CXXII (1967) 117–22.

3703. BISHOP, ANTHONY. John Nicholson in the Indian mutiny. *Irish Sword*, VIII (1968) 277–87.

3704. ALLEN, A. R. Disarmed but not dishonoured: the 63rd Bengal Native Infantry in 1857. *Soc. Army Hist. Research Jour.*, XLVI (1968) 57–60.

3705. SINHA, D. P. The British government and the Indian states, 1857–62. *Univ. Ceylon Rev.*, XXII (1964) 105–34.

3706. QANUNGO, BHUPEN. A study of British relations with the native states of India, 1858–62. *Jour. Asian Studies*, XXVI (1967) 251–65.

3707. QANUNGO, B. The modernisation of British Indian finance, 1859–62. *Jour. Indian Hist.*, XLV (1967) 439–64.

3708. RAO, K. BHASKARA. Rudyard Kipling's India. Norman, Okla.: Oklahoma U.P., 1967. ix, 190 pp.

3709. NAIDIS, MARK. Herbert Edwardes: man on the spot. *Bengal Past & Present*, LXXXVII (1968) 137–49.

3710. WILLIAMS, DONOVAN. Clements Robert Markham and the Geographical Department of the India Office, 1867–77. *Geog. Jour.*, CXXXIV (1968) 343–52.

3711. MOULTON, EDWARD CALVIN. India and British party politics in the 1870s: conflicting attitudes of empire. *Canadian Hist. Assoc. Rept.* (1968) 164–79.

3712. MOULTON, E. C. Lord Northbrook's Indian administration, 1872–6. Asia Pubg. House, 1968. vii, 313 pp., illus.

3713. MOULTON, E. C. British India and the Baroda crisis, 1874–5: a problem in a princely state. *Canadian Jour. Hist.*, III (1968) 58–94.

3714. BARRIER, N. GERALD. The Punjab government and communal politics, 1870–1908. *Jour. Asian Studies*, XXVII (1968) 523–39.

3715. CHAUDHARY, VIJAY CHANDRA PRASAD. Imperial policy of the British in India, 1876–80: the birth of Indian nationalism. Calcutta: Punthi Pustak, 1968. 398 pp.

3716. GROVER, B. L. A documentary study of British policy towards Indian nationalism, 1885–1909. Delhi: National Pubns., 1967. xxv, 295 pp.

3717. MARTIN, BRITON. Lord Dufferin and the Indian National Congress, 1885–8. *Jour. Brit. Studies*, VII no. 1 (1967) 68–96.

3718. BISHUI, KALPANA. The nationalistic Indian press *vis-à-vis* the conservative Anglo-Indian press on nascent Indian nationalism. *Quart. Rev. Hist. Studies*, VII (1967–8) 29–35.

3719. KLEIN, IRA. Politics and public opinion in Lytton's tariff policy. *Jour. Indian Hist.*, XLV (1967) 465–80.

3720. MOORE, R. J. The twilight of the Whigs and the reform of the Indian councils, 1886-92. *Hist. Jour.*, X (1967) 400–14.

3721. ANNAND, A. M. Captain Henry Thurburn (1826–97), 42nd Madras Native Infantry. *Soc. Army Hist. Research Jour.*, XLV (1967) 24–30.

3722. KANAMORI, AKIHIRO. The siege of Chitral as an imperial factor. *Jour. Indian Hist.*, XLVI (1968) 387–404.

3723. KAUSHIK, D. British India: relations with Sinkiang. *Research Jour.* (Kurukshetra Univ.), II (1968) 173–89.

Ceylon

3724. DE SILVA, K. M. The third Earl Grey and the maintenance of an imperial policy on the sale of crown lands in Ceylon, *c.* 1832–52: some influences of Edward Gibbon Wakefield's doctrines in a tropical colony. *Jour. Asian Studies*, XXVII (1967) 5–20.

3725. BASTIAMPILLAI, B. The Colonial Office and Sir William Gregory, governor of Ceylon 1872–7: a study in British imperial administration. *Ceylon Jour. Hist. Soc. Studies*, IX (1966) 20–43.

Far East

3726. KLEIN, IRA. British expansion in Malaya, 1897–1902. *Jour. S.E. Asian Hist.*, IX (1968) 53–68.

3727. HURD, DOUGLAS. Sir John Bowring: the radical governor. *History Today*, XVII (1967) 651–9.

Australasia

3728. BURROUGHS, PETER. Britain and Australia, 1831–55: a study in imperial relations and crown lands administration. O.U.P., 1967. xi, 419 pp.

3729. NEALE, R. S. John Stuart Mill on Australia: a note. *Hist. Studies Australia & N.Z.*, XIII (1968) 239–45.

3730. WARDS, IAN. The shadow of the land: a study of British policy and racial conflict in New Zealand, 1832–52. Wellington, N.Z.: A. R. Shearer, for Hist. Pubns. Branch, Dept. of Internal Affairs, 1968. xix, 422 pp.

3731. DAVIS, R. P. Sir George Grey and Irish nationalism. *New Zealand Jour. Hist.*, I (1967) 185–98.

BIOGRAPHY

3732. *Acton.* MATHEW, DAVID. Lord Acton and his times. Eyre & Spottiswoode, 1968. 397 pp.

3733. *Beardsley.* WEINTRAUB, STANLEY. Beardsley: a biography. W. H. Allen, 1967. xvii, 285 pp., illus.

3734. *Browning.* WARD, MAISIE. Robert Browning and his world. Vol. 1, The private face, 1812–61. Cassell, 1968. xix, 331 pp., illus. [Originally pubd. New York: Holt, 1967.]

3735. *Burton.* BRODIE, FAWN MCKAY. The devil drives: a life of Sir Richard Burton. Eyre & Spottiswoode, 1967. 390 pp., illus.

3736. *Byron.* PARKER, DEREK. Byron and his world. Thames & Hudson, 1968. 143 pp., illus.

3737. *Caroline.* RUSSELL, EDWARD FREDERICK LANGLEY, *Baron Russell.* Caroline, the unhappy queen. Hale, 1967. 173 pp., illus.

3738. *Cobbett.* BRIGGS, ASA. William Cobbett. O.U.P., 1967. 63 pp., illus.

3739. *Dallaway.* STEER, FRANCIS WILLIAM. Memoir and letters of James Dallaway, 1763–1834: a postscript. *Sussex Archaeol. Coll.*, CV (1967) 62–9. [To article in vol. CIII (1965) 1–48.]

3740. *Davison.* ISAAC, PETER CHARLES GERALD. William Davison of Alnwick: pharmacist and printer, 1781–1858. Oxford: Clarendon P., 1968. ix, 40 pp.

3741. *Dibdin.* O'DWYER, EDWARD JOHN. Thomas Frognall Dibdin: bibliographer and bibliomaniac extraordinary, 1776–1847. Pinner, Middx.: Private Libraries Assoc., 1967. 45 pp.

3742. *Edwards.* WILD, J. Sir Henry Edwards, Bt., C.B. *Halifax Antiq. Soc. Trans.* (1967) 13–35, (1968) 97–116.

3743. *Evans.* HAIGHT, GORDON SHERMAN. George Eliot: a biography. Clarendon P., 1968. xvi, 616 pp., illus.

3744. *Evans.* SPRAGUE, ROSEMARY. George Eliot: a biography. Philadelphia, Pa., London: Chilton Book Co., 1968. xiii, 337 pp., illus.

3745. *Flower.* BENNETT, JOHN DAVID. John Flower, 1793–1861. *Leics. Archaeol. Soc. Trans.* for 1966–7, XLII (1968) 76–81.

3746. *Gascoyne-Cecil.* OMAN, CAROLA. The Gascoyne heiress: the life and diaries of Frances Mary Gascoyne-Cecil, 1802–39. Hodder, 1968. 320 pp., illus.

3747. *Gilbert.* TODD, ARTHUR CECIL. Beyond the blaze: a biography of Davies Gilbert. Truro, Cornwall: D. Bradford Barton, 1967. 293 pp., illus.

3748. *Graham.* WARD, JOHN TREVOR. Sir James Graham. London: Macmillan; New York: St. Martin's P., 1967. xx, 356 pp., illus.

3749. *Graves-Perceval.* BÄCKER-RANKE, GISBERT. Rankes Ehefrau Clarissa geboren Graves-Perceval. (Studien zum Geschichtsbilde, 21). Göttingen: Musterschmidt, 1967. 23 pp.

3750. *Grosvenor.* HUXLEY, GERVAS. Victorian duke: the life of Hugh Lupus Grosvenor, 1st duke of Westminster. O.U.P., 1967. xiii, 214 pp., illus.

3751. *Harding.* HAIGH, ALICE H. Edward Harding of no. 2 Quay Street, Scarborough. *Scarborough & District Archaeol. Soc. Trans.*, II no. 10 (1967) 3–7.

3752. *Huxley.* CLARK, RONALD WILLIAM. The Huxleys. Heinemann, 1968. xvi, 398 pp., illus.

3753. *Jameson.* THOMAS, CLARA. Love and work enough: the life of Anna Jameson. Macdonald & Co., 1967. xiii, 252 pp., illus.

3754. *Kane.* CLARKE, DESMOND. Sir Robert Kane. *Administration*, XVI (1968) 155–9.

3755. *Keats.* HILL, DOUGLAS. John Keats. Morgan-Grampian Books, 1968. 92 pp., illus.

3756. *Lear.* NOAKES, VIVIEN. Edward Lear: the life of a wanderer. Collins, 1968. 359 pp., illus.

3757. *Leigh.* GUNN, PETER. My dearest Augusta: a biography of the Hon. Augusta Leigh, Lord Byron's half-sister. Bodley Head, 1968. 272 pp., illus.

3758. LOUSLEY, JOB EDWARD. Job Lousley (1790–1855) of Blewbury and

Hampstead Norris. *Berks. Archaeol. Jour.*, LXIII (1967–8) 57–65.

3759. *Marx.* TSUZUKI, CHUSHICHI. The life of Eleanor Marx, 1855–98: a socialist tragedy. Oxford: Clarendon P., 1967. xi, 354 pp., illus.

3760. *Montefiore.* LIPMAN, SONIA L. Judith Montefiore: first lady of Anglo-Jewry. *Jewish Hist. Soc. Eng. Trans.* for 1962–7, XXI (1968) 287–303.

3761. *Munro.* BEAGLEHOLE, TIMOTHY HOLMES. Sir Thomas Munro. *Indo-British Rev.*, I (1968) 19–30.

3762. *Owen.* JONES, DAVID GWYN. Robert Owen, 1771–1858. Cardiff: Gwasg Prifysgol Cymru, 1968. 66 pp., illus. [In Welsh.]

3763. *Panizzi.* MILLER, EDWARD. Prince of librarians: the life and times of Antonio Panizzi of the British Museum. Deutsch, 1967. 356 pp., illus.

3764. *Pankhurst.* MITCHELL, DAVID. The fighting Pankhursts: a study in tenacity. Cape, 1967. 352 pp., illus.

3765. *Petrie.* DILLON, MYLES. George Petrie (1789–1866). *Studies*, LVI (1967) 266–76.

3766. *Phillipps.* MUNBY, ALAN NOEL LATIMER. Portrait of an obsession: the life of Sir Thomas Phillipps, the world's greatest book collector. Constable, 1967. 278 pp., illus.

3767. *Pringle.* BUIST, A. A. Thomas Pringle: poet and pioneer. *Berwicks. Naturalists' Club Hist.* for 1966, XXXVII pt. 2 (1966) 87–100.

3768. *Rae.* COOKE, ALAN. The autobiography of Dr. John Rae: a preliminary note. *Polar Record*, XIV (1968) 173–7.

3769. *Robinson.* JONES, WILBUR DEVEREUX. 'Prosperity' Robinson: the life of Viscount Goderich, 1782–1859. London: Macmillan; New York: St. Martin's P., 1967. x, 324 pp., illus.

3770. *Shelley.* FULLER, JEAN OVERTON. Shelley: a biography. Cape, 1968. 336 pp., illus.

3771. *Smith.* FITZSIMONS, RAYMUND. The Baron of Piccadilly: the travels and entertainments of Albert Smith, 1816–60. Bles, 1967. 192 pp., illus.

3772. *Southey.* RAIMOND, J. Robert Southey: l'homme et son temps, l'oeuvre, le rôle. Paris: Didier, 1968. 680 pp.

3773. *Stanhope.* HUGHES, JEAN GORDON. Queen of the desert: the story of Lady Hester Stanhope. Macmillan, 1967. 160 pp.

3774. *Stanhope.* SMITH, DOROTHY J. Queen Hester. *Huntington Lib. Quart.*, XXXI (1967–8) 153–78. [Hester Stanhope.]

3775. *Swinburne.* FULLER, JEAN OVERTON. Swinburne: a critical biography. Chatto, 1968. 319 pp., illus.

3776. *Turnly.* KENNEDY, DAVID. Francis Turnly, 1766–1845: a prophet of the United Nations. *Irish Eccles. Record*, 5th ser. CX (1968) 40–51.

3777. *Wellesley.* HARDING, JAMES. The duke of Wellington. Morgan-Grampian Books, 1968. 90 pp., illus.

3778. *Wilberforce.* KENT, JOHN. William Wilberforce, 1759–1833. *London Quart. & Holborn Rev.*, CXCII (Jan. 1967) 64–8.

3779. *Wilde.* LAMBERT, ERIC. Mad with much heart: a life of the parents of Oscar Wilde. Muller, 1967. x, 165 pp., illus.

3780. *Wilde.* WHITE, TERENCE DE VERE. The parents of Oscar Wilde: Sir William and Lady Wilde. Hodder, 1967. 303 pp., illus.

THE TWENTIETH CENTURY, 1900–1939

GENERAL

3781. MONTGOMERY, JOHN. 1900: the end of an era. Allen & Unwin, 1968. 248 pp., illus.

3782. MARWICK, ARTHUR. Britain in the century of total war: war, peace and social change, 1900–67. Bodley Head, 1968. 511 pp.

3783. JULLIAN, PHILIPPE. Edward and the Edwardians, *transl.* P. Dawnay. Sidgwick & Jackson, 1967. viii, 312 pp., illus. [Originally pubd. Paris: Hachette, 1962 as *Édouard VII.*]

3784. HAWSON, HERBERT KEEBLE. Sheffield: the growth of a city, 1893–1926. Sheffield: J. W. Northend, 1968. xxii, 348 pp., illus.

3785. MEDLICOTT, WILLIAM NORTON. Contemporary England, 1914–64. Longmans, 1967. 614 pp.

3786. CASATI, MARC. Le Royaume-Uni de 1914 à nos jours. Paris: Soc. d'Edn. d'Enseignement Supérieur, 1967. 349 pp.

3787. GILBERT, BENTLEY BRINKERHOFF. Britain since 1918. Batsford, 1967. 206 pp.

POLITICAL CONSTITUTIONAL AND LEGAL HISTORY

3788. BUTLER, DAVID EDGEWORTH, *and* FREEMAN, JENNIE. British political facts, 1900–67. 2nd edn. Macmillan, 1968. xix, 314 pp. [Previous edn. 1963.]

3789. MARWICK, ARTHUR. The Labour party and the Welfare State in Britain, 1900–48. *Amer. Hist. Rev.*, LXXIII no. 2 (1967) 380–403.

3790. LOEWENSTEIN, KARL. Staatsrecht und Staatspraxis von Grossbritannien. Berlin: Springer V., 1967. 2 vols.

3791. CROSS, J. A. Withdrawal of the Conservative party whip. *Parliamentary Affairs*, XXI (1967–8) 166–75.

3792. BROWN, JOHN. Scottish and English land legislation, 1905–11. *Scot. Hist. Rev.*, XLVII (1968) 72–85.

3793. SPINNER, THOMAS S. George Joachim Goschen: the man Lord Randolph Churchill 'forgot'. *Jour. Mod. Hist.*, XXXIX (1967) 405–24.

3794. MORGAN, KENNETH OWEN. Keir Hardie. O.U.P., 1967. 64 pp., illus.

3795. BARDENS, DENNIS. Churchill in parliament. Hale, 1967. 381 pp., illus.

3796. HALLADAY, E. The debate on the Congo, 1900 to 1908. *Parliamentary Affairs*, XXI (1967–8) 277–84.

3797. MCCREADY, HERBERT WILLIAM. Sir Alfred Milner, the Liberal party and the Boer War. *Canadian Jour. Hist.*, II pt. 1 (1967) 13–44.

3798. NIMOCKS, WALTER. Milner's young men: the 'Kindergarten' in Edwardian imperial affairs. Durham, N.C.: Duke U.P., 1968. xi, 234 pp.

3799. ZEBEL, SYDNEY H. Joseph Chamberlain and the genesis of tariff reform. *Jour. Brit. Studies*, VII no. 1 (1967) 131–57.

3800. CRATON, MICHAEL, *and* MCCREADY, HERBERT WILLIAM. The great Liberal revival, 1903–6. Hansard Soc. for Parliamentary Govt., 1967. 47 pp.

3801. REMPEL, R. A. Tariff reform and the resurgence of the Liberal party: May 1903–Feb. 1904. *Canadian Hist. Assoc. Rept.* (1967) 156–66.

3802. ROWLAND, PETER. The last Liberal governments: the promised land, 1905–10. Barrie & Rockliff, 1968. xviii, 404 pp.

3803. HYAM, RONALD. Elgin and Churchill at the Colonial Office, 1905–8: the watershed of the Empire-Commonwealth. Macmillan, 1968. xvi, 574 pp., illus.

3804. BLEWETT, NEAL. Free Fooders, Balfourites, Whole Hoggers: factionalism within the Unionist party, 1906–10. *Hist. Jour.*, XI (1968) 95–124.

3805. NICHOLLS, DAVID. Few are chosen: some reflections on the politics of A. J. Balfour. *Rev. of Politics*, XXX (1968) 33–42.

3806. STEINER, ZARA. Grey, Hardinge and the Foreign Office, 1906–10. *Hist. Jour.*, X (1967) 415–39.

3807. JENKINS, ROY. Mr. Balfour's poodle: an account of the struggle between the House of Lords and the government of Mr. Asquith. New edn. Collins, 1968. 320 pp., illus. [Previous edn. Heinemann, 1954.]

3808. WESTON, CORINNE COMSTOCK. The Liberal leadership and the Lords' veto, 1907–10. *Hist. Jour.*, XI (1968) 508–37.

3809. KOSS, STEPHEN E. The destruction of Britain's last Liberal government. *Jour. Mod. Hist.*, XL (1968) 257–77.

3810. VERITY, WILLIAM. Haldane and Asquith. *History Today*, XVIII (1968) 447–55.

3811. MAGILL, BARRY. Asquith's predicament, 1914–18. *Jour. Mod. Hist.*, XXXIX (1967) 283–303.

3812. WOODWARD, *Sir* ERNEST LLEWELLYN. Great Britain and the war of 1914–18. London: Methuen; New York: Barnes & Noble, 1967. xxxiii, 610 pp.

3813. WOODWARD, *Sir* ERNEST LLEWELLYN. Impressions in retrospect: the Great War of 1914–18. *Jour. Hist. Studies*, I (1967–8) 207–28.

3814. ROBBINS, KEITH G. Lord Bryce and the First World War. *Hist. Jour.*, X (1967) 255–77.

3815. BÜNGER, SIEGFRIED. Die sozialistische Antikriegsbewegung in Grossbriannien, 1914–17. Berlin: Deutscher V. Wissenschaften, 1967. 212 pp.

3816. KURTZ, HAROLD. The Lansdowne letter. *History Today*, XVIII (1968) 84–92.

3817. CREGIER, DON M. The Lloyd George political fund. *Washington State Univ. Research Studies*, XXV no. 3 (1967) 198–219.

3818. JOHNSON, PAUL BARTON. Land fit for heroes: the planning of British reconstruction, 1916–19. Chicago, Ill., London: Chicago U.P., 1968. viii, 540 pp., illus.

3819. RODMAN, BARBEE-SUE. Britain debates justice: an analysis of the reparations issue of 1918. *Jour. Brit. Studies*, VIII no. 1 (1968) 140–54.

3820. WARD, STEPHEN R. The British veterans' ticket of 1918. *Jour. Brit. Studies*, VIII no. 1 (1968) 155–69.

3821. BROOKES, PAMELA. Women at Westminster: an account of women in the British parliament, 1918–66. P. Davies, 1967. xv, 287 pp.

3822. GILBERT, MARTIN (*ed.*). Lloyd George. Englewood Cliffs, N.J.: Prentice-Hall, 1968. ix, 182 pp.

3823. ARNOT, ROBERT PAGE. The impact of the Russian Revolution in Britain. Lawrence & Wishart, 1967. 191 pp.

3824. MACFARLANE, LESLIE JOHN. Hands off Russia: British Labour and the Russo-Polish war, 1920. *Past & Present*, no. 38 (1967) 126–52.

3825. KLUGMANN, JAMES. History of the Communist party of Great Britain. Vol. 1, 1919–24. Lawrence & Wishart, 1968. 381 pp., illus.

3826. CLINE, CATHERINE ANN. E. D. Morel and the crusade against the Foreign Office. *Jour. Mod. Hist.*, XXXIX (1967) 126–37.

3827. REINDERS, ROBERT C. Racialism on the left: E. D. Morel and the 'black horror on the Rhine'. *Internat. Rev. Soc. Hist.*, XIII (1968) 1–28. [1920–1.]

3828. WILDING, PAUL R. The genesis of the Ministry of Health. *Public Admin.*, XLV (1967) 149–68.

3829. HONIGSBAUM, FRANK. Unity in British public health administration: the failure of reform, 1926–9. *Medical Hist.*, XII (1968) 109–21.

3830. SMITH, BURTON M. Harold Nicolson and the promise of the New party. *Washington State Univ. Studies*, XXXVI no. 1 (1968) 15–25.

3831. SKIDELSKY, ROBERT. Politicians and the slump: the Labour government of 1929–31. Macmillan, 1967. xiv, 431 pp., illus.

3832. ROWE, E. A. Broadcasting and the 1929 general election. *Renaissance & Mod. Studies*, XII (1968) 108–19.

3833. GILBERT, MARTIN, *and* GOTT, RICHARD. The appeasers. 2nd edn. Weidenfeld, 1967. xviii, 444 pp., illus. [Previous edn. 1963.]

3834. THOMPSON, J. N. The failure of Conservative opposition to appeasement in the 1930s. *Canadian Jour. Hist.*, III no. 2 (1968) 25–52.

3835. SCOTT, WILLIAM E. 'Neville Chamberlain and Munich: two aspects of power'. *In* The responsibility of power, *ed.* L. Krieger *and* F. Stern (New York: Doubleday, 1967) pp. 353–69.

3836. PATRICK, KATHERINE. The mass pursuit of peace: England, 1934–40. *Melbourne Hist. Jour.*, VII (1968) 11–23. [Peace Pledge Union.]

3837. THOMPSON, J. N. Prophet without honour: Winston Churchill and the gathering storm. *Queen's Quart.*, LXXV (1968) 229–46.

3838. SLAVIN, ARTHUR J. Churchill's 'Bolshevism on the brain': intervention and hypocrisy. *Bucknell Rev.*, XV (1967) 71–98.

ECONOMIC AND SOCIAL HISTORY

3839. JOHNSON, WALFORD, *and others.* A short economic and social history of 20th century Britain. Allen & Unwin, 1967. xii, 208 pp.

3840. YOUNGSON, ALEXANDER JOHN. Britain's economic growth, 1920–66. Allen & Unwin, 1967. 306 pp.

3841. BUXTON, NEIL K. Economic progress in Britain in the 1920s: a reappraisal. *Scot. Jour. Polit. Econ.*, XIV (1967) 175–86. [With rejoinder by D. H. Aldcroft, pp. 187–91.]

3842. ALDCROFT, DEREK HOWARD. Economic growth in Britain in the inter-war years: a reassessment. *Econ. Hist. Rev.*, 2nd ser. XX (1967) 311–26.

3843. DOWIE, J. A. Growth in the inter-war period: some more arithmetic. *Econ. Hist. Rev.*, 2nd ser. XXI (1968) 93–112.

3844. RICHARDSON, H. W. Economic recovery in Britain, 1932–9. Weidenfeld, 1967. ix, 337 pp.

3845. CALZA, GIANNI. Il radicalismo di J. M. Keynes. *Rassegna di Polit. e Storia*, XIII (1967) 267–74.

3846. REVELL, J. 'Changes in the social distribution of property in Britain during the 20th century'. *In* Proc. 3rd International Conference of Economic History, Munich, 1965 (Paris, Hague: Mouton & Co., 1968) pp. 367–84.

3847. DAVIS, L. E. Capital immobilities, institutional adaptation and financial development: the United States and England, an international comparison. *Zeit. Gesamte Staatswissenschaft*, CXXIV (1968) 14–34.

3848. JACK, MARIAN. The purchase of the British government's shares in the British Petroleum company, 1912–14. *Past & Present*, no. 39 (1968) 139–68.

3849. RICHARDSON, H. W., *and* ALDCROFT, DEREK. Building in the British economy between the wars. (Univ. Glasgow Social and Economic Studies, n.s. 14). Allen & Unwin, 1968. 355 pp., illus.

3850. MARSHALL, J. L. The pattern of housebuilding in the inter-war period in England and Wales. *Scot. Jour. Polit. Econ.*, XV (1968) 184–205.

3851. TROUNSON, JOHN H. Cornish engines and the men who handled them. *Roy. Inst. Cornwall Jour.*, n.s. V (1967) 213–49.

3852. HIGHAM, ROBIN. Quantity *vs.* quality: the impact of changing demand on the British aircraft industry, 1900–60. *Business Hist. Rev.*, XLII (1968) 443–66.

3853. HARROP, J. The growth of the rayon industry in the inter-war years. *Yorks. Bull. Econ. & Soc. Research*, XX (1968) 71–84.

3854. MOUNFIELD, P. R. The footwear industry of the East Midlands. 5, The modern phase: Northamptonshire and Leicestershire since 1911. *East Midland Geographer*, IV pt. 3 (1967) 154–75.

3855. LOVELL, JOHN, *and* ROBERTS, B. C. A short history of the T.U.C. Macmillan, 1968. 200 pp.

3856. Avec ou sans l'État? Le mouvement ouvrier français et anglais au tournant du siècle. Colloque de Londres, 1966. *Mouvement Social*, no. 65 (1968) 1–167.

3857. GREGORY, ROY. The miners and British politics, 1906–14. O.U.P., 1968. xi, 207 pp.

3858. JUDGE, ANTHONY. The first fifty years: the story of the Police Federation. The Federation, 1968. 140 pp.

3859. MOREAU, REGINALD ERNEST. The departed village: Berrick Salome at the turn of the century. O.U.P., 1968. 178 pp., illus.

3860. HEAUME, DORIS OLIVE. Life in Guernsey, 1904–14. St. Peter Port: Toucan P., 1967. 8 pp.

3861. HEATH, GERALD DUNCAN. The women's suffrage movement in and around Richmond and Twickenham. (Twickenham Local Hist. Soc. Papers, 13). Twickenham, Middx.: the Society, 1968. 40 pp.

3862. LEAFE, R. V. The port of Immingham. *East Midland Geographer*, IV pt. 3 (1967) 127–42.

3863. DUCKHAM, BARON FREDERICK. Railway steamship enterprise; the Lancashire and Yorkshire Railway's east coast fleet, 1904–14. *Business Hist.*, X (1968) 44–57.

3864. ALDCROFT, DEREK HOWARD. British railways in transition: the economic problems of Britain's railways since 1914. Macmillan, 1968. xvi, 252 pp.

3865. HAMILTON, JAMES ALAN BOUSFIELD. Britain's railways in World War I. Allen & Unwin, 1967. 220 pp., illus.

3866. DAVIES, WILLIAM JAMES KEITH. Light railways of the First World War: a history of tactical rail communications on the British fronts, 1914–18. Newton Abbot, Devon: David & Charles, 1967. 196 pp.

3867. MCDERMOTT, EDWARD TERENCE (*ed.*). History of the Great Western Railway. Vol. 3, 1923–47, by O. S. Nock. Allan, 1967. xii, 268 pp., illus.

3868. BROWN, DAVID BYRON. The history of the Guild of Air Pilots and Navigators, 1929–64. Vol. 1. The Guild, 1967. x, 105 pp., illus.

RELIGIOUS HISTORY

3869. OLIVER, JOHN. The Church and social order: social thought in the Church of England, 1918–39. Mowbray, 1968. ix, 228 pp., illus.

3870. CHADWICK, OWEN. Edward King, bishop of Lincoln, 1885–1910. Lincoln: Friends of Lincoln Cathedral, 1968. 31 pp.

3871. REID, R. D. Dean Robinson in Somerset. *Downside Rev.*, LXXXVI (1968) 266–75.

3872. NUTTALL, GEOFFREY F. Charles Gore and the solidarity of faith. *Church Quart.*, I no. 1 (1968) 52–64.

3873. BURNINGHAM, GEORGE W. Christian Socialism in the Church of England: Charles Gore. *Univ. Leeds Rev.*, X (1966–7) 36–46.

3874. HEASMAN, KATHLEEN. Army of the Church. Lutterworth P., 1968. 180 pp.

3875. GOODALL, NORMAN. Some Congregational pathfinders in the ecumenical movement. *Congregational Hist. Soc. Trans.*, XX (1967) 184–99.

3876. CLIPSHAM, ERNEST F. The Baptist Historical Society: sixty years' achievement. *Baptist Quart.*, XXII no. 7 (1968) 339–51.

3877. The history of the Salvation Army. Vol. 5, 1904–14, by A. R. Wiggins. Nelson, 1968. xv, 319 pp., illus.

CULTURAL HISTORY

3878. HYNES, SAMUEL. The Edwardian turn of mind. Princeton, N.J.: Princeton U.P.; London: O.U.P., 1968. xiv, 427 pp., illus.

3879. DUBOIS, PIERRE. Le problème dans la philosophie anglaise de 1900 à 1950. Paris: Vrin, 1967. 254 pp.

3880. NAAMANI, I. T. The theism of Lord Balfour. *History Today*, XVII (1967) 660–6.

3881. MUNFORD, WILLIAM ARTHUR. James Duff Brown, 1862–1914: portrait of a library pioneer. Library Assoc., 1968. ix, 101 pp., illus.

3882. GILLAM, STANLEY. Hagberg Wright and the London Library. *Library Hist.*, I (1967) 24–7.

3883. MÜLLENBROCK, HEINZ-JOACHIM. Literatur und Zeitgeschichte in England zwischen dem Ende des 19. Jahrhunderts und dem Ausbruch des Ersten Weltkrieges. (Britannica et Americana, 16). Hamburg, Cram: de Gruyter, 1967. 235 pp.

3884. TOLLEY, A. T. The thirties poets at Oxford. *Univ. Toronto Quart.*, XXXVII no. 4 (1968) 338–58.

3885. BAYLEN, JOSEPH O. W. T. Stead and the Russian Revolution of 1905. *Canadian Jour. Hist.*, II pt. 1 (1967) 45–66.

3886. MORRIS, ANDREW JAMES ANTHONY. The *Birmingham Post* and Anglo-German relations, 1933–5. *Univ. Birmingham Hist. Jour.*, XI (1967–8) 191–201.

3887. JOHNSON, JAMES WILLIAM. Horace Walpole and W. S. Lewis. *Jour. Brit. Studies*, VI no. 2 (1967) 64–75.

3888. BROWN, REGINALD F. Fifty years of university Spanish. *Univ. Leeds Rev.*, XI (1968) 26–41. [At Leeds.]

3889. HALLIDAY, R. J. The sociological movement, the Sociological Society and the genesis of academic sociology in Britain. *Sociol. Rev.*, n.s. XVI (1968) 377–98.

3890. COHEN, SOL. Sir Michael E. Sadler and the sociopolitical analysis of education. *Hist. Educ. Quart.*, VII (1967) 281–94.

3891. MACLEOD, ROBERT. Charles Rennie Mackintosh. Feltham, Middx.: Country Life, 1968. 160 pp., illus.

3892. WALKER, DAVID M. Charles Rennie Mackintosh. *Archit. Rev.*, CXLIV (1968) 355–63.

3893. COOPER, HENRY. The royal chapel of St. Katharine in Ratcliffe. *East London Papers*, X (1967) 125–32.

3894. BACKHOUSE, JANET. Pioneers of modern calligraphy and illumination. *Brit. Museum Quart.*, XXXIII (1968–9) 71–9.

3895. KENNEDY, MICHAEL. Portrait of Elgar. O.U.P., 1968. xi, 324 pp., illus.

3896. REID, CHARLES. Malcolm Sargent: a biography. Hamilton, 1968. xiv, 491 pp., illus.

SCIENCE AND MEDICINE

3897. BULLEID, HENRY ANTHONY VAUGHAN. The Aspinall era. Allan, 1967. viii, 270 pp., illus.

3898. BENSON, RONALD C. Baker Bessemer's historic axle-forging plant. *Newcomen Soc. Trans.* for 1965–6, XXXVIII (1968) 97–105.

3899. HEIMANN, P. M. Moseley and celtium: the search for a missing element. *Annals of Science*, XXIII (1967) 249–60.

3900. MCCORMMACH, RUSSELL. J. J. Thomson and the structure of light. *Brit. Jour. Hist. Science*, III (1967) 362–87.

3901. POCOCK, ROWLAND F. Marconi and the Isle of Wight. *Industrial Archaeol.*, V (1968) 43–53.

3902. DOUGLAS, D. Joseph Lister. *Scot. Medical Jour.*, X (1967) 346–55.

3903. Surgery and Lister. *Roy. College of Surgeons Eng. Annals*, XL (1967) 355–72.

MILITARY AND NAVAL HISTORY

3904. JERUSSALIMSKI, A. S. 'Der deutsche Imperialismus und der Ausbruch des Burenkrieges'. *In* Der deutsche Imperialismus, by A. S. Jerussalimski (Berlin: Dietz, 1968) pp. 90–161.

3905. RANSFORD, OLIVER. The battle of Majuba Hill: the First Boer War. Murray, 1967. ix, 154 pp., illus. [1881.]

3906. DUBREY, NEAL. Stereograms of the South African war, 1899–1902. *South African Lib. Quart. Bull.*, XXIII (1968) 28–31.

3907. POE, BRYCE. British army reforms, 1902–14. *Military Affairs*, XXXI (1967) 131–8.

3908. WELLS, SAMUEL F., *Jnr.* British strategic withdrawal from the western hemisphere, 1904–6. *Canadian Hist. Rev.*, XLIX (1968) 335–56.

3909. TEAGARDEN, ERNEST M. Lord Haldane and the origins of Officer Training Corps. *Soc. Army Hist. Research Jour.*, XLV (1967) 91–6.

3910. GREEN, HOWARD. The British Army in the First World War. Clowes, 1968, lx, 116 pp., illus.

3911. ASHWORTH, A. E. The sociology of trench warfare, 1914–18. *Brit. Jour. Sociol.*, XIX no. 4 (1968) 407–23.

3912. TERRAINE, JOHN A. Mortality and morale. *Roy. United Service Inst. Jour.*, CXII (1967) 364–9. [In First and Second World Wars.]

3913. FARRAR-HOCKLEY, ANTHONY. Death of an army. New York: Morrow, 1968. xi, 195 pp. [British Expeditionary Force, Oct.–Nov. 1914.]

3914. BAYNES, JOHN. Morale: a study of men and courage: the 2nd Scottish Rifles at the battle of Neuve Chapelle, 1915. Cassell, 1967. xiv, 286 pp., illus.

3915. MOOREHEAD, ALAN. Gallipoli. New edn. H. Hamilton, 1967. 384 pp., illus. [Previous edn. 1956.]

3916. BOND, BRIAN. Soldiers and statesmen: British civil-military relations in 1917. *Military Affairs*, XXXII (1968) 62–75.

3917. TERRAINE, JOHN A. Haig in 1918: a strategic survey. *Army Quart.*, XCVII no. 1 (1968) 38–52.

3918. GLENDOWER (*pseud.*). Haig and tanks. *Army Quart.*, LXXXXVI no. 2 (1968) 197–202.

3919. TERRAINE, JOHN A. The March offensive, 1918. *History Today*, XVIII (1968) 147–55, 234–43.

3920. SCHOFIELD, BRIAN BETHAM. British sea power: naval policy in the 20th century. Batsford, 1967. 271 pp., illus.

3921. JELLICOE, JOHN RUSHWORTH, *1st Earl Jellicoe*. The Jellicoe papers. Vol. 1, 1893–1916, *ed.* A. T. Patterson. (Navy Records Soc. Pubns., 108). Shortlands, Kent: the Society, 1966. xi, 322 pp.

3922. NISH, IAN HILL. The Royal Navy and the taking of Weihaiwei, 1898–1905. *Mariner's Mirror*, LIV (1968) 39–54.

3923. FISCHER, WALTHER. Der letzte Grossangriff deutscher Marine-Luftschiffe auf England in der Nacht vom. 19.–20. Oktober 1917. *Marine-Rundschau*, LXV (1968) 46–52.

3924. FIORAVANZO, GIUSEPPE. Le due battaglie dello Atlantico: 1914–18 e 1939–45. *Riv. Marittima*, CI (1968) 5–28.

3925. ROSKILL, STEPHEN. Naval policy between the wars. Vol. 1, The period of Anglo-American antagonism, 1919–29. Collins, 1968. 639 pp., illus.

3926. WILLIAMSON, THOMAS. The finding of Scott's South Pole party, 12 November 1912. *Polar Record*, XIV (1968) 33–9. [Diary of a member of search-party.]

FOREIGN RELATIONS

3927. NIEDHART, GOTTFRIED. Weltmacht-Anspruch und Wirklichkeit: zur britischen Aussenpolitik im 20. Jahrhundert. *Neue Politische Litetatur*, XIII (1968) 233–41.

3928. MEDLICOTT, WILLIAM NORTON. British foreign policy since Versailles, 1919–63. 2nd edn. rev. Methuen, 1968. xxi, 362 pp. [Previous edn. 1940.]

3929. MILLER, K. E. Socialism and foreign policy: theory and practice in Britain to 1931. The Hague: Nijhoff, 1967. 304 pp.

3930. FOREIGN OFFICE. Documents on British foreign policy, 1919–39. 1st ser. Vol. 15, International conferences and conversations, 1921, *ed.* R. Butler *and others*. H.M.S.O., 1967. xxxi, 835 pp.

3931. FOREIGN OFFICE. Documents on British foreign policy, 1919–39. 1st ser. Vol. 16, Upper Silesia, 1921–2; Germany, 1921, *ed.* W. N. Medlicott *and others*. H.M.S.O., 1968. cxi, 1003 pp.

3932. FOREIGN OFFICE. Documents on British foreign policy, 1919–39. Ser. 1a. Vol. 2, The termination of military control in Germany; Middle Eastern and American questions, 1926–7, *ed.* W. N. Medlicott *and others*. H.M.S.O., 1968. lix, 958 pp.

3933. URBANITSCH, PETER. Grossbritannien und die Verträge von Locarno. Wien: Notring, 1968. 329 pp.

3934. CARLTON, DAVID. Great Britain and the League Council crisis of 1926. *Hist. Jour.*, XI (1968) 354–64.

3935. BRAMSTED, ERNEST. Apostles of collective security: the L.N.U. and its functions. *Australian Jour. Politics & Hist.*, XIII (1967) 347–64. [League of Nations Union.]

3936. GEORGE, MARGARET. The hollow men: an examination of British foreign policy between the years 1933 and 1939. Frewin, 1967. 256 pp. [Originally pubd. as *The warped vision: British foreign policy 1933–9*. Pittsburgh, Pa.: Pittsburgh U.P., 1965.]

3937. ANDREW, CHRISTOPHER. France and the making of the Entente Cordiale. *Hist. Jour.*, X (1967) 89–105.

3938. GUILLEN, PIERRE. Les accords coloniaux franco-anglais de 1904 et la naissance de l'Entente Cordiale. *Rev. d'Hist. Diplomatique*, LXXXII (1968) 315–57.

3939. KHAN, RASHEEDUDDIN. The peace settlement, Arab diplomacy and Anglo-French power politics, 1919–20. *Islamic Culture*, XLII (1968) 57–73, 133–50.

3940. JERUSSALIMSKI, A. S. 'Die britische Diplomatie und das deutsche Problem'. *In* Der deutsche Imperialismus, by A. S. Jerussalimski (Berlin: Dietz, 1968) pp. 712–35.

3941. HAUSER, OSWALD. Deutsch-englische Missverständnisse. *Gesch. in Wissenschaft u. Unterricht*, XVIII (1967) 275–88.

3942. BODENSIECK, HEINRICH. Ansätze zur Teilung Deutschlands in anglo-amerikanischen Sicherheitskonzeptionen. *Gesch. in Wissenschaft und Unterricht*, XIX (1968) 585–95.

3943. SCHENK, WILLY. Die deutsch-englische Rivalität vor dem Ersten Weltkrieg in der Sicht deutscher Historiker: Missverstehen oder Machtstreben? Aarau: Keller, 1967. vi, 173 pp.

3944. HATTON, P. H. S. Britain and Germany in 1914: the July crisis and war aims. *Past & Present*, no. 36 (1967) 138–43.

3945. LOUIS, WILLIAM ROGER. Great Britain and Germany's lost colonies, 1914–19. Oxford: Clarendon P., 1967. xiii, 167 pp.

3946. ROTHFELS, HANS (*ed.*). Akten zur deutschen auswärtigen Politik, 1918–45. Serie B, 1925–33. Vol. 1, pt. 2: Aug.–Dez. 1926: Deutschlands Beziehungen zu Frankreich, Grossbritannien.... Göttingen: Vandenhoek & Ruprecht, 1968. xlvi, 712 pp.

3947. SPENCE, JOHN H. The Anglo-German naval agreement of 1935: an interpretation. *Rocky Mountain Soc. Sci. Jour.*, V (1968) 76–85.

3948. ROBBINS, KEITH G. Munich 1938. Cassell, 1968. 398 pp., illus.

3949. FERGUSSON, GILBERT. Munich: the French and British roles. *International Affairs*, XLIV (1968) 649–65.

3950. WOERDEN, A. V. N. VAN. Hitler faces England: theories, images and policies. *Acta Hist. Neerlandica*, III (1968) 141–59.

3951. JERUSSALIMSKI, A. S. 'England und die 'Achse Berlin-Rom-Tokio'.' *In* Der deutsche Imperialismus, by A. S. Jerussalimski (Berlin: Dietz, 1968) pp. 560–76.

3952. COLLINS, ROBERT OAKLEY. King Leopold, England and the Upper Nile, 1899–1909. New Haven, Conn., London: Yale U.P., 1968. xvi, 346 pp.

3953. FORSBERG, STURE. Den brittiska garantin till Polen den 31 Mars 1939: en utrikespolitiskt beslut. *Statsverenkaplig Tids.*, LXXI (1968) 147–73. ['The British guarantee to Poland, a foreign policy decision'.]

3954. GREAVES, ROSE LOUISE. Some aspects of the Anglo-Russian convention and its working in Persia, 1907–14. *School of Oriental & African Studies Bull.*, XXXI (1968) 69–91, 290–308.

3955. FRY, MICHAEL G. Britain, the Allies and the problem of Russia, 1918–19. *Canadian Jour. Hist.*, II pt. 2 (1967) 62–84.

3956. ULLMAN, RICHARD HENRY. Anglo-Soviet relations, 1917–21. Vol. 2, Britain and the Russian Civil War, Nov. 1918–Feb. 1920. Princeton, N.J.: Princeton U.P.; London: O.U.P., 1968. xix, 395 pp., illus.

3957. GALTON, DOROTHY, *and* KEEP, JOHN (*eds.*). Letters from Vladivostok, 1918–23. *Slavonic & E. European Rev.*, XLV (1967) 497–530.

3958. GARAMVÖLGYI, JUDIT. Aus den Anfängen sowjetischer Aussenpolitik: das britischesowjetrussische Handelsabkommen vom 1921. Cologne: V. Wissenschaft und Politik, 1967. 131 pp.

3959. LAMMERS, DONALD N. Britain, Russia, and the revival of 'Entente Diplomacy': 1934. *Jour. Brit. Studies*, VI no. 2 (1967) 99–123.

3960. TOSCANO, MARIO. Il negoziato di Londra del 1915. *Nuova Antologia*, no. 501 (1967) 313–26.

3961. TOSCANO, M. Imperiali e il negoziato per il Patto di Londra. *Storia e Politica*, VII (1968) 177–205. ['Dal diario inedito del nostro ambasciatore in Gran Bretagna'.]

3962. BUSCH, BRITON COOPER. Britain and the Persian Gulf, 1894–1914. Berkeley, Calif.: California U.P.; London: C.U.P., 1968. xv, 432 pp.

3963. PLASS, JENS, *and* GEHRKE, ULRICH. Die Aden-Grenze in der Südarabienfrage, 1900–67: Die Adener Grenzkommission, 1901–7; Überblick über die englisch-jemenitischen Beziehungen unter dem Geschichtspunkt des Süd-Jemenanspruchs, 1900–67. (Schriften des Deutschen Orient-Institute, Materialien und Dokumente). Opladen: C. W. Leske, 1967. x, 345 pp.

3964. CATALUCCIO, FRANCESCO. La questione araba dopo la prima guerra mondiale: i mandati britannici in Iraq e Palestina. *Archivio Stor. Italiano*, CXXV (1967) 291–351.

3965. CLIFFORD, NICHOLAS ROWLAND. Retreat from China: British policy in the Far East, 1937–41. Longmans, 1967. x, 222 pp.

3966. FRY, MICHAEL G. The North Atlantic triangle and the abrogation of the Anglo-Japanese alliance. *Jour. Mod. Hist.*, XXXIX (1967) 46–64.

3967. MEHRA, PARSHOTAM. The Younghusband expedition: an interpretation. Asia Pubg. House, 1968. xxi, 408 pp., illus.

3968. MEHRA, P. Beginnings of the Lhasa expedition: Younghusband's own words. *Bull. Tibetology*, IV no. 4 (1967) 9–17.

3969. ALLEN, J. DE VERE. The elephant and the mousedeer: a new version: Anglo-Kedah relations, 1905–15. *Roy. Asiatic Soc. Malaysian Branch Jour.*, XLI pt. 1 (1968) 54–94.

3970. ULLENDORFF, EDWARD. The Anglo-Ethiopian treaty of 1902. *School of Oriental & African Studies Bull.*, XXX (1967) 641–54.

3971. LEBOW, RICHARD NED. Woodrow Wilson and the Balfour Declaration. *Jour. Mod. Hist.*, XL (1968) 501–23.

3972. CARLTON, DAVID. Great Britain and the Coolidge Naval Disarmament Conference of 1927. *Political Science Quart.*, LXXXIII (1968) 573–98.

3973. KOTTMAN, RICHARD N. Reciprocity and the North Atlantic triangle, 1932–8. Ithaca, N.Y.: Cornell U.P., 1968. ix, 294 pp.

3974. COKER, WILLIAM S. Mediación británica en el conflicto Wilson-Huerta. *Hist. Mexicana*, XVIII (1968) 244–57.

3975. SCHOLES, WALTER V., *and* SCHOLES, MARIE V. Wilson, Grey and Huerta. *Pacific Hist. Rev.*, XXXVII (1968) 151–8.

WALES

3976. PARRY, CYRIL. Fabianism and Gwynedd politics, 1890–1918. *Caernarvons. Hist. Soc. Trans.*, XXIX (1968) 121–36.

3977. PARRY, C. The Independent Labour Party and Gwynedd politics, 1900–20. *Welsh Hist. Rev.*, IV (1968–9) 47–66.

3978. MORGAN, KENNETH O. Cardiganshire politics: the Liberal ascendancy, 1885–1923. *Ceredigion*, V no. 4 (1967) 311–46.

3979. MORGAN, K. O. Twilight of Welsh Liberalism: Lloyd George and the 'Wee Frees', 1918–35. *Board of Celtic Studies Bull.*, XXII pt. 4 (1968) 389–405.

3980. ARNOT, ROBERT PAGE. South Wales miners: Glowyr de Cymru: a history of the South Wales Miners' Federation, 1898–1914. Allen & Unwin, 1967. 390 pp.

3981. LLOYD, D. TECWYN. Hanes masnachol rhai o gyhoeddiadau Syr O. M. Edwards. *Nat. Lib. Wales Jour.*, XV (1967–8) 55–71. ['Some publishing ventures of Sir Owen M. Edwards'.]

SCOTLAND

3982. BUXTON, NEIL K. The Scottish shipbuilding industry between the wars: a comparative study. *Business Hist.*, X (1968) 101–20.

3983. RICHARDS, PETER S. Viscose rayon manufacture on Deeside. *Flints. Hist. Soc. Pubns.*, XXIII (1967–8) 75–81.

3984. MARWICK, WILLIAM H. The Glasgow Study Circle. *Friends' Hist. Soc. Jour.*, LI no. 3 (1967) 167–73.

3985. KENNETH, *Brother*. The Education (Scotland) Act, 1918, in the making. *Innes Rev.*, XIX (1968) 91–128.

3986. CRAIG, W. S. John Thomson: pioneer and father of Scottish paediatrics, 1856–1926. Edinburgh, London: Livingstone, 1967. viii, 96 pp., illus.

IRELAND

Note: Writings on Irish domestic and local history are not included unless they have a direct bearing on English history.

3987. O'BROIN, LEON. Charles Gavan Duffy, patriot and statesman. Dublin: Duffy & Co., 1967. vii, 164 pp.

3988. VAN VORIS, JACQUELINE. Constance de Markievicz in the cause of Ireland. Amherst, Mass.: Massachusetts U.P., 1967. 384 pp.

3989. BUCKLAND, P. J. The southern Irish Unionists, the Irish question, and British politics 1906–14. *Irish Hist. Studies*, XV (1966–7) 228–55.

3990. WARD, ALAN J. America and the Irish problem, 1899–1921. *Irish Hist. Studies*, XVI (1968–9) 64–90.

3991. WARD, A. J. Frewen's Anglo-American campaign for federalism, 1910–21. *Irish Hist. Studies*, XV (1966–7) 256–75.

3992. TUCKER, DAVID M. Some American responses to the Easter Rebellion, 1916. *Historian*, XXIX (1967) 605–18.

3993. EDWARDS, OWEN DUDLEY, *and* PYLE, FERGUS (*eds.*). 1916: the Easter Rising. MacGibbon & Kee, 1968. 189 pp., illus.

3994. BOURKE, MARCUS. Thomas MacDonagh's role in the plans for the 1916 rising. *Irish Sword*, VIII (1968) 178–85.

3995. SAVAGE, DAVID W. The attempted Home Rule settlement of 1916. *Eire*, II (1967) 132–45.

3996. COSTIGAN, GIOVANNI. The Anglo-Irish conflict, 1919–22: a war of independence or systematised murder? *Univ. Rev.*, V (1968) 64–89.

3997. NEESON, EOIN. The life and death of Michael Collins. Cork: Mercier P., 1968. 163 pp., illus.

3998. HACHEY, THOMAS E. The Irish question: the British Foreign Office and the American political conventions of 1920. *Eire*, III (1968) 92–106.

3999. STEWART, ANTHONY TERENCE QUINCEY. The Ulster crisis. Faber, 1967. 284 pp., illus. [Ulster Volunteer Force, 1911–14.]

4000. MCCRACKEN, J. L. 'Northern Ireland, 1921–66'. *In* The course of Irish history, *ed.* T. W. Moody *and* F. X. Martin (Cork: Mercier P., 1967) pp. 313–23.

4001. COUSENS, S. R. Population trends in Ireland at the beginning of the 20th century. *Irish Geog.*, V no. 5 (1968) 387–401.

4002. MILLER, DAVID W. The Roman Catholic Church in Ireland, 1898–1918. *Eire*, III (1968) 75–91.

4003. O'FIAICH, TOMÁS. The Irish bishops and the conscription issue, 1918. *Capuchin Annual*, XXXV (1968) 396–403.

4004. HARRIS, HENRY E. D. The Irish regiments in the First World War. Cork: Mercier P., 1968. xii, 230 pp., illus.

4005. PHILLIPS, W. Kitchener's army: a company of the Royal Dublin Fusiliers.

An Cosantoir, XXVIII (1968) 101–4, 169–70.

4006. HALLY, PATRICK J. The Easter 1916 rising in Dublin: the military aspects. Pt. 2. *Irish Sword*, VIII (1967) 48–57.

BRITISH EMPIRE AND COMMONWEALTH

Note: The domestic history of Commonwealth countries is not included unless it has a direct bearing on British history.

4007. CROSS, JOHN ARTHUR. Whitehall and the Commonwealth: British departmental organisation for Commonwealth relations, 1900–66. London: Routledge; New York: Humanities P., 1967. ix, 93 pp.

4008. CROSS, COLIN. The fall of the British Empire: 1918–68. Hodder, 1968. 368 pp., illus.

4009. HAUSER, OSWALD. Das britische Commonwealth zwischen nationale Souveränität und imperialer Integration, 1917–31. *Vierteljahr. für Zeitgesch.*, XVI (1968) 230–46.

4010. LOUIS, WILLIAM ROGER. Sir John Harris and 'colonial trusteeship'. *Acad. Roy. des Sciences d'Outre-mer Bull.*, n.s. XIV (1968) 832–56.

4011. MORRISON, DAVID R. The politics of the Yukon territory, 1898–1909. (Canadian Studies in Hist. & Govt., 12). Toronto: Toronto U.P., 1968. vi, 136 pp.

4012. NEARY, PETER. Grey, Bryce, and the settlement of Canadian-American differences, 1905–11. *Canadian Hist. Rev.*, XLIX (1968) 357–80.

4013. FITZHARDINGE, L. F. Hughes, Borden, and Dominion representation at the Paris Peace Conference. *Canadian Hist. Rev.*, XLIX (1968) 160–9.

4014. PORTER, BERNARD. Critics of empire: British radical attitudes to colonialism in Africa, 1895–1914. Macmillan, 1968. xvi, 369 pp., illus.

4015. CROWDER, MICHAEL. West Africa under colonial rule. Hutchinson, 1968. xv, 540 pp.

4016. DUMETT, RAYMOND E. The campaign against malaria and the expansion of scientific, medical and sanitary services in British West Africa, 1898–1910. *African Hist. Studies*, I (1968) 153–97.

4017. WEISBORD, ROBERT G. African Zion: the attempt to establish a Jewish colony in the East African protectorate, 1903–5. Philadelphia, Pa.: Jewish Publ. Soc. of America, 1968. viii, 347 pp.

4018. WALT, H. R. VAN DER. The pan-Boer movement and the South African war. *Tijds. voor Geschiedenis*, LXXX (1967) 52–62.

4019. SACKS, BENJAMIN. South Africa, an imperial dilemma: non-Europeans and the British nation, 1902–14. Alberquerque, N. Mex.: New Mexico U.P., 1967. xii, 356 pp.

4020. WATT, DONALD CAMERON. 'South African attempts to mediate between Britain and Germany, 1935–8'. *In* Studies in international history, *ed.* K. Bourne *and* D. C. Watt (Hamden, Conn.: Archon Books, 1967) pp. 402–22.

4021. TERRY, JANICE J. Official British reaction to Egyptian nationalism after World War I. *Al-Abhāth*, XXI (1968) 15–29.

4022. BHATTACHARYA, SUKUMAR. Lord Curzon and Simla. *Bengal Past & Present*, LXXXVII (1968) 150–6.

4023. COHEN, STEPHEN P. Issue, rule, and personality: the Kitchener-Curzon dispute. *Comparative Studies in Society & Hist.*, X (1967–8) 337–55.

4024. JAECKEL, HORST. Die Nordwestgrenze in der Verteidigung Indiens 1900–8 und der Weg Englands zum russisch-britischen Abkommen von 1907. Cologne, Opladen: Westdeutscher V., 1968. 296 pp.

4025. WOLPERT, STANLEY A. Morley and India, 1906–10. Berkeley, Calif.: California U.P.; London: C.U.P., 1967. xi, 299 pp.

4026. MOORE, R. J. John Morley's acid test: India, 1906–10. *Pacific Affairs*, XL (1967) 333–40.

4027. BARRIER, N. GERALD. The Punjab disturbances of 1907: the response of the British government in India to agrarian unrest. *Modern Asian Studies*, I (1967) 353–83.

4028. YARWOOD, A. T. The overseas Indians as a problem in Indian and imperial politics at the end of World War I. *Australian Jour. Politics & Hist.*, XIV (1968) 294–18.

4029. VERMA, D. N. India and the League of Nations. Patna: Bharati Bhawan, 1968. xii, 350 pp.

4030. LEIFER, MICHAEL. Astride the Straits of Johore: the British presence and

Commonwealth rivalry in South East Asia. *Modern Asian Studies*, I (1967) 283–96.

4031. TREGONNING, KENNEDY GORDON. A history of modern Malaya. New York: D. McKay, 1967. 339 pp.

4032. CHAI, HON-CHAN. The development of British Malaysia, 1896–1909. 2nd edn. Kuala Lumpur, London: O.U.P., 1968. xvii, 366 pp., illus. [Previous edn. 1964.]

4033. CHEW, ERNEST. Sir Frank Swettenham and the Federation of the Malay States. *Modern Asian Studies*, II (1968) 51–69.

4034. BROWN, D. E. (*ed.*). Two Colonial Office memoranda on the history of Brunei, by Sir Reginald Edward Stubbs. *Roy. Asiatic Soc. Malaysian Branch Jour.*, XL pt. 2 (1968) 83–116. [1905, 1911.]

4035. ALLEN, J. DE VERE. The Kelantan rising of 1915: some thoughts on the concept of resistance in British Malayan history. *Jour. S.E. Asian Hist.*, IX (1968) 241–57.

4036. DRABBLE, J. H. The plantation rubber industry in Malaya up to 1922. *Roy. Asiatic Soc. Malaysian Branch Jour.*, XL pt. 1 (1967) 52–77.

BIOGRAPHY

4037. *Beecham*. FRANCIS, ANNE. A guinea a box: a biography. Hale, 1968. 199 pp., illus. [Thomas Beecham, 1820–1907.]

4038. *Butler*. MCCOURT, EDWARD. Remember Butler: the story of Sir William Butler. Routledge, 1967. xii, 276 pp., illus.

4039. *Chotzner*. CARLEBACH, ALEXANDER. The Rev. Dr. Joseph Chotzner. *Jewish Hist. Soc. Eng. Trans.* for 1962–7, XXI (1968) 261–73.

4040. *Cunningham*. WARNER, OLIVER MARTIN WILSON. Cunningham of Hyndhope, Admiral of the Fleet: a memoir. Murray 1967. ix, 301 pp., illus.

4041. *Cunninghame-Graham*. LOTT, ROBERT E. Un hispanófilo escocés que quería a Colombia: Robert Bontine Cunninghame-Graham. *Bol. Hist. Antigüedades* (Bogotá), LV (1968) 707–13.

4042. *Dillon*. LYONS, F. S. L. John Dillon: a biography. Chicago: Chicago U.P., 1968. xi, 516 pp.

4043. *Greville*. BLUNDEN, MARGARET. The countess of Warwick: a biography. Cassell, 1967. xiii, 356 pp., illus.

4044. *Isaacs*. HYDE, HARFORD MONTGOMERY. Lord Reading: the life of Rufus Isaacs, 1st marquess of Reading. Heinemann, 1967. 454 pp., illus.

4045. *Jebb*. WILSON, FRANCESCA MARY. Rebel daughter of a country house: the life of Eglantyne Jebb. Allen & Unwin, 1967. 228 pp., illus.

4046. *Keppel*. STUART, VIVIAN. The beloved little admiral: the life and times of Admiral of the Fleet the Hon. Sir Henry Keppel, G.C.B., O.M., D.C.L., 1809–1904. Hale, 1967. 272 pp., illus.

4047. *Maude*. FALLS, CYRIL. Lieutenant General Sir Stanley Maude. *History Today*, XVII (1967) 1–7.

4048. *Morley*. HAMER, DAVID ALAN. John Morley: liberal intellectual in politics. Oxford: Clarendon P., 1968. xvi, 412 pp.

4049. MOSLEY, *Sir* OSWALD. My life. Nelson, 1968. 521 pp., illus.

4050. *Murray*. WATSON, WILLIAM N. BOOG. Sir John Murray: a chronic student. *Univ. Edinburgh Jour.*, XXIII no. 2 (1967) 123–38.

4051. *Nicolson*. HUDSON, DEREK. Harold Nicolson. *Quart. Rev.*, CCCV (1967) 163–71.

4052. *Norman*. BOYLE, ANDREW. Montague Norman: a biography. Cassell, 1967. xi, 349 pp.

4053. *Pugh*. ANDREWS, ALLEN. The prosecutor: the life of M. P. Pugh, prosecuting solicitor and agent for the Director of Public Prosecutions. Harrap, 1968. 232 pp., illus.

4054. *Sassoon*. JACKSON, STANLEY. The Sassoons. Heinemann, 1968. 304 pp., illus.

4055. *Scott*. BETJEMAN, JOHN. Mackay Hugh Baillie Scott. *Manx Museum Jour.*, VII no. 84 (1968) 77–80.

4056. *Stephens*. RYAN, DESMOND. The Fenian chief: a biography of James Stephens. Dublin: Gill, 1967. xxv, 390 pp.

4057. *Terry*. MANVELL, ROGER. Ellen Terry. Heinemann, 1968. x, 390 pp., illus.

4058. *Thompson*. WALSH, JOHN. Strange harp, strange sympathy: the life of Francis Thompson. W. H. Allen, 1968. xix, 298 pp., illus.

4059. *Townshend*. BARKER, ARTHUR J. Townshend of Kut: a biography of Major-General Sir Charles Townshend. Cassell, 1967. xiv, 265 pp., illus.

4060. *Webb.* MUGGERIDGE, KITTY, *and* ADAM, RUTH. Beatrice Webb: a life, 1858–1943. Secker, 1967. 272 pp., illus.

4061. *Wilson.* MARLOWE, JOHN. Late Victorian: the life of Sir Arnold Talbot Wilson. Cresset P., 1967. xii, 418 pp., illus.

4062. *Wilson.* ASH, BERNARD. The lost dictator: a biography of Field-Marshal Sir Henry Wilson, Bart., G.C.B., D.S.O., M.P. Cassell, 1968. xi, 308 pp., illus.

APPENDIX

SELECT LIST OF WORKS PUBLISHED IN THE YEARS 1967–1968 ON BRITISH HISTORY SINCE 1939.

4063. HILLGRUBER, ANDREAS (*ed.*). Probleme des zweiten Weltkrieges. (Neue Wissenschaftliche Bibliothek, 20). Köln, Berlin: Kiepenheuer & Witsch, 1967. 455 pp. [Contents include: 'Hitlers Konzept des Blitzkrieges' by A. S. Milward, pp. 19–40; 'Grundlagen der Strategie Grossbritanniens und Frankreichs, 1939' by J. R. M. Butler, pp. 41–51; 'Die Schlacht im Atlantik in der deutschen Strategie' by K. Dönitz, pp. 159–70; 'Strategische Kontroversen der Alliierten' by F. von Senger und Etterlin, pp. 277–91; 'Grosse und Versagen im Sieg der Alliierten, 1944–5' by J. L. Snell, pp. 312–41.]

4064. GUIERRE, MAURICE. Bataille de l'Atlantique: la victoire des convois. Paris: Flammarion, 1967. 320 pp.

4065. MCLACHLAN, DONALD. Naval intelligence in the Second World War. *Roy. United Service Inst. Jour.*, CXII (1967) 221–6.

4066. ANRYS, HENRI. Le jour de juillet 1940 où la France et l'Angleterre s'affrontèrent a Mers-el-Kébir. *Rev. Générale Belge* (1968) 17–33.

4067. BEAUX, JEAN. Dunkerque 1940. Paris: Presses de la Cité, 1967. 346 pp.

4068. PLEHWE, FRIEDRICH-KARL VON. Die geplante Landung in England: Unternehmen 'Seelöwe', 1940. *Wehrwissenschaftliche Rundschau*, XVII (1967) 385–404.

4069. TAYLOR, TELFORD. The breaking wave: the German defeat in the summer of 1940. Weidenfeld, 1967. xi, 381 pp., illus. [Originally pubd. New York: Simon & Schuster, 1967.]

4070. PEMBERTON, R. F. The Royal Air Force in the Second World War. Pts. 2–3. *Army Quart.*, XCIV (1967) 111–14, 240–3.

4071. JULLIAN, MARCEL. The battle of Britain, July–Sept. 1940, *transl.* A.-Y. and A. Stewart. Cape, 1967. 295 pp., illus. [Originally pubd. Paris: Presses de la Cité, 1965 as *La Bataille d'Angleterre*.]

4072. GROEHLER, OLAF. Der 'strategische' Luftkrieg Grossbritanniens gegen Hitlerdeutschland (Februar 1942–März 1944). *Zeit. für Militärgesch.*, VII (1968) 439–53.

4073. GROEHLER, O. Krieg in Westen: die Haltung der herrschenden Kreise der U.S.A. und Grossbritanniens zur politischen und militärischen Vorbereitung der zweiten Front, 1942–4. Berlin: Deutscher Militärverlag, 1968. 278 pp.

4074. SCHLAUCH, WOLFGANG. Rüstunghilfe der U.S.A. an die Verbündeten im zweiten Weltkrieg. (Beitr. zur Wehrforschung, 13). Darmstadt: Wehr und Wissen, 1967. 163 pp.

4075. KINGHORN, ALAN. The dynamic war: a study in military leadership in the British-German campaigns in North Africa, February 1941–January 1943. New York: Exposition P., 1967. 121 pp.

4076. FRANZOLIN, UGO. I giorni di El Alamein. Rome: Trevi Ed. (Aldina), 1967. 236 pp.

4077. ZIEGER, GOTTFRIED. Die Teheran-Konferenz, 1943. Hanover: Niedersächsische Landeszentrale für Politische Bildung, 1967. 190 pp.

4078. FISCHER, ALEXANDER (*ed.*). Teheran, Jalta, Potsdam: die sowjetische Protokolle von den Kriegskonferenzen der 'Grossen Drei'. (Dokumente zur Aussenpolitik, 1). Cologne: V. Wissenschaft und Politik, 1968. 414 pp.

4079. LORENZ, HERMANN. Operation 'Jubilee': der Raid gegen Dieppe. *Marine-Rundschau*, LXIV (1967) 228–37, 300–3.

4080. GRIMM, GERHARD. Churchills *The Second World War* als Quelle für die Politik und Strategie der Westalliierten in Südosteuropa. *Südost-Forschungen*, XXVI (1967) 276–313.

4081. BENTWICH, NORMAN. The Paris Peace Conference, July–October 1946. *History Today*, XVII (1967) 727–34, 799–804.

4082. WILLIAMS, GEOFFREY, *and* FRANKEL, JOSEPH. A political scientist's look at the Cold War as history. *Polit. Studies*, XVI (1968) 285–92.

4083. GARDNER, BRIAN. Churchill in his time: a study in a reputation, 1939–45. Methuen, 1968. xvi, 349 pp., illus.

4084. SAMPSON, ANTHONY. Macmillan: a study in ambiguity. Allen Lane, the Penguin P., 1967. 272 pp., illus.

4085. SCHNEIDER, HERBERT. Grossbritanniens Weg nach Europa. Freiburg: Rombach, 1968. 253 pp.

4086. MARCHAND, JEAN. La Grande-Bretagne et l'Afrique Noire. *Rev. Défense Nat.*, XXIV (1968) 240–55.

4087. MURTI, V. V. RAMANA. Satyagraha as an Indo-British dialogue. *Jour. World Hist.*, X (1967) 872–90. [Gandhi's non-violent protest.]

4088. FISCHER, GEORGES. Le parti travailliste et la doctrine de la porte ouverte. *Polit. Étr.*, XXXIII (1968) 361–95.

4089. GREGG, PAULINE. The Welfare State: an economic and social history of Great Britain from 1945 to the present day. Harrap, 1967. xii, 388 pp.

4090. DEVONS, ELY, *and others*. Wage rate indexes by industry, 1948–65. *Economica*, n.s. XXXV (1968) 392–423.

4091. BEST, ROBIN H. Extent of urban growth and agricultural displacement in post-war Britain. *Urban Studies*, V (1968) 1–23.

4092. KRAUS, JEROME. The British electron-tube and semiconductor industry, 1935–62. *Technology & Culture*, XI (1968) 544–61.

4093. BEDOUELLE, GUY. L'église d'Angleterre et la société politique contemporaine. Paris: Libr. Gén. de Droit et de Jurisprudence, 1968. iv, 299 pp.

INDEX

Numbers refer to items not to pages. Names of authors are in SMALL CAPITALS. Subject headings such as abbeys, castles, schools etc., refer to general works and groupings in the classification. Particular examples are indexed separately.